Faith and
Understanding

FORTRESS TEXTS IN MODERN THEOLOGY

Faith and Understanding

Rudolf Bultmann

**Edited with an introduction by
Robert W. Funk**

Translated by Louise Pettibone Smith

Fortress Press   **Philadelphia**

Translated from the German *Glauben und Verstehen*, I, sixth edition, 1966, J. C. B. Mohr (Paul Siebeck), Tübingen

Reprinted by arrangement with Harper & Row

FIRST FORTRESS PRESS EDITION 1987

Library of Congress Cataloging-in-Publication Data

Bultmann, Rudolf Karl, 1884–1976.
   Faith and understanding.

   (Fortress texts in modern theology)
   Translation of: Glauben und Verstehen.
   Includes bibliographical references and indexes.
   1. Theology. 2. Bible. N.T.—Theology. I. Title
II. Series.
BT80.B7813   1987   230   86–45901
ISBN 0-8006-3202-8

2648B87   Printed in the United States of America   1–3202

CONTENTS

ABBREVIATIONS

CW	*Die christliche Welt*
DT	*Deutsche Theologie*
EA	Martin Luther, Werke, Erlangen Ausgabe, eds. J. G. Plochmann and J. K. Irmischer, 67 vols., Erlangen, 1826–57
FRLANT	*Forschungen zur Religion und Literatur des Alten und Neuen Testaments*
RGG	*Die Religion in Geschichte und Gegenwart*
TB	*Theologische Blätter*
TR	*Theologische Rundschau*
ZNW	*Zeitschrift für die neutestamentliche Wissenschaft*
ZST	*Zeitschrift für systematische Theologie*
ZThK	*Zeitschrift für Theologie und Kirche*
ZZ	*Zwischen den Zeiten*

INTRODUCTION

THE essays of Rudolf Bultmann collected and published under the title, *Glauben und Verstehen I* (first edition, 1933), are of signal importance in understanding not only the development of Bultmann's work but the course of New Testament scholarship as well, from the First World War down to the present time. And, one might add, they are essential also to a grasp of the unfolding of theology in the twentieth century. In view of their importance, it is the more remarkable that they are only now being presented as a group in English translation.[1]

The dated (previously published) essays in the collection appeared between 1924 and 1930. To these were added five previously unpublished essays, all of seminal significance for Bultmann's programme.

Faith and Understanding, volume I, is dedicated to Martin Heidegger. It may be recalled that Heidegger's *Sein und Zeit* (*Being and Time*) first appeared in 1927, and it was during the period 1923–27 that Bultmann and Heidegger were closely associated as colleagues at Marburg. To the extent that Bultmann can be said to have shaped his theological programme in dialogue with Heidegger, these essays may be taken as indicative of the groundwork Bultmann was laying for all his future work. The remarkable consistency with which Bultmann has developed his initial fundamental insights suggests that he made most of his germinal decisions during the crucial period

---

[1] The German text has gone through six editions (1933–66). Individual essays have appeared in English: 'Welchen Sinn hat es, von Gott zu reden?' was translated by F. H. Littell under the title, 'What Sense is there to Speak of God?' (*The Christian Scholar* 43 [1960], pp. 213–22); 'Das christliche Gebot der Nächstenliebe' appeared in the *Scottish Periodical*, I (1947), pp. 42–56, as 'To Love Your Neighbour'; 'Das Bedeutung des Alten Testaments für den christlichen Glauben' was translated by B. W. Anderson as 'The Significance of the Old Testament for the Christian Faith' and appeared in *The Old Testament and Christian Faith*, ed. B. W. Anderson (New York: Harper and Row; London: SCM Press, 1963), pp. 8–35. The first has been re-translated for this English edition; the last two have been omitted since they are already available in English elsewhere.

represented by this collection and his intimate association with Heidegger.

These essays introduce most of the major theological themes which were to occupy Bultmann's attention in subsequent years. In them he frames the basic questions, sketches out the lines of his answers, and so charts his future course. In retrospect it can be seen that nothing appeared later, including the demythologizing proposal, the preparation for which had not already been made during these formative years.

I

It is not much of an exaggeration to say that Bultmann burst on the English language scene as a theologian with two putative papers in his portfolio, one insisting that the Gospels provide us with very little hard information about Jesus of Nazareth, the other calling for the elimination of all myth in the New Testament. He appeared, as it were, virtually out of the night, so far as English readers were concerned. No one seemed to know where he had come from or what made him tick.

Very little of Bultmann's work had been translated into English at the time the second war broke out.[2] Among the few, in the interval between the world wars, who read German theological literature in general and Bultmann in particular were a handful of New Testament scholars. These scholars knew Bultmann as a form critic who allegedly held radically sceptical views about the historical reliability of the gospel material. At the time when someone was called upon to identify the author of the demythologizing proposal, first presented in 1941 but not widely known until after the second war, the characterization of a few New Testament scholars, notably British, was recalled. Typical is the judgment of Vincent

---

[2] One notable exception is Louise Pettibone Smith's translation (with E. H. Lantero) of *Jesus* (Berlin: Deutsche Bibliothek, 1926; [2]1929) as *Jesus and the Word* (New York: Scribner, 1934; paperback edition, 1958). Unlike the vast majority of such cases, the alteration of the title in this instance was an illuminating advance over the German form. Professor Smith remarked in her preface to the paperback edition that Bultmann was little known in the U.S. in 1934. It is altogether fitting that she, who led the way in presenting Bultmann originally to English readers, should return after so many years to the unfinished task of providing the wider context for *Jesus and the Word*.

Taylor, advanced as early as 1932, in which he echoes the opinion of E. Fascher:[3]

> Bultmann is radical to the point of scepticism, and it is not strange that he has been looked upon as *Strauss Redivivus*. If Bultmann is right, we have not only lost the Synoptic framework but also much the greater part of the material. The narratives are mainly legends and ideal constructions, and most of the sayings, while Palestinian in origin, are products of primitive Christianity which puts back its own ideas and beliefs into the lips of Jesus.[4]

Bultmann thus stepped out of the shadows as a radical New Testament critic in the tradition of H. S. Reimarus, D. F. Strauss and F. C. Baur.

The original image doubtless did much to shape the demythologizing debate in the years following the second war – at least west of the English Channel. The gross ignorance of Bultmann's theological ancestry and history that characterized the onset of the debate has been modified only modestly. Bultmann's work has gradually appeared in English dress, to be sure. And a few competent studies of his work have been produced. Yet acquaintance with Bultmann's earlier writings, where he attaches himself to dialectical theology, re-evaluates his own liberal heritage, and lays the foundations for his life work, *Theology of the New Testament*, remains the exception rather than the rule. The appearance in English of this key collection of early essays should contribute materially to the formation of a proper perspective from which to view Bultmann's theological programme.

What is the significance of Rudolf Bultmann for contemporary theology? It is probably too early to say definitively, yet nearly all parties to the controversies with which his name is connected would probably concede that he has played a major

[3] *Die formgeschichtliche Methode* (Giessen: Töpelmann, 1924).

[4] *The Formation of the Gospel Tradition* (London: Macmillan, 1933), p. 14; cf. pp. 14f. On might compare the no less flat judgment of E. Basil Redlich (*Form Criticism* [London: Duckworth, 1939], pp. 181f.): 'The whole argument [of Bultmann's treatment of Legends in his *Die Geschichte der synoptischen Tradition* (Göttingen: Vandenhoeck and Ruprecht, 1921; FRLANT, 29)] is so subjective and so influenced not by the imagination of the community but by that of the author that he loses the sympathy of any who desire to find a substratum of truth in it. When it is recalled that he found the narrative portions of his Apothegms unreliable in the main and held that the Miracle-Stories were unhistorical, and classes nearly all the rest of the narrative in the same category, it is not surprising that to him the figure and Personality of Jesus are very faint and unsubstantial.'

role in the unfolding drama of theological history, on both sides of the Atlantic, during the half-century that follows World War I.

At least this much can be said with confidence: Bultmann, together with Karl Barth, has reshaped the questions which inform theological inquiry, in relation both to Protestant orthodoxy and to liberalism. And it was the reformulation of the questions which put Bultmann on the path that led to the famous demythologizing essay of 1941. Even for those who refused to follow Bultmann's lead, it became impossible any longer to ask questions in the older forms without a deliberate, and sometimes violent, consideration of the challenge Bultmann laid down. And the cogency of a theological thinker is correlative with the degree to which other thinkers feel compelled, positively or negatively, to meet his challenge.

In the transition from liberalism to dialectical theology, Bultmann chose to link his name with that of Karl Barth. Karl Barth subsequently pursued a path that led to his *Church Dogmatics*, which was intended to be the answer to the questions he originally posed in the *Römerbrief*.[5] Bultmann found it impossible to follow the course set by Barth and so charted his own. It led him in a different direction, to be sure, but over against Anglo-Saxon theology, Barth and Bultmann had and have a good deal in common. What they have in common is often overlooked across the English Channel, mainly because Bultmann is taken to be merely a radical New Testament critic, and Barth is taken to be a repristination of Protestant orthodoxy. The double distortion is the result of the fact that English-language theology has rarely grasped dialectical theology in relation to its history. Another way of putting it is that Barth and Bultmann were read with liberal and/or orthodox eyes, as though twentieth-century theology were merely an extension of nineteenth. If it had been understood that Barth and Bultmann were jointly turning a corner in the history of theology, it might have been possible for Anglo-Saxon theology to comprehend the real import of their work earlier.

As evidence that Barth and Bultmann were negotiating a significant turn in the history of the tradition, it might be

[5] *Der Römerbrief* (München: Chr. Kaiser, 1919; ²1921); *The Epistle to the Romans*, tr. E. C. Hoskyns (Oxford, 1933), from the 6th German edition.

observed that many of the newer theological modes, which appear to forecast the shape of the second half of the century, are traceable, directly or indirectly, to one or the other of them. It is astonishing, for example, that so many of the new 'radical' theologians are of Barthian parentage. Is it possible that Barth seized the gravity of the issue already in 1919? And Bultmann has also spawned a variety of new theological movements, some of which, at least, are also in the theological vanguard.

It is not our aim here to indulge in prediction. It is our purpose, rather, to invite the reader to a more perceptive perusal of the essays included in the collection, with the reservation, of course, that the essays may prove to be more perspicuous than the introduction. In any case, we might look back along the road Bultmann has come, and inquire, in relation to the two putative papers in his portfolio, mentioned earlier, just how he has marshalled his troops on a variety of fronts in an effort to win through to fresh and higher ground. In so doing we may notice how popular critical attributions sometimes merely expose a raw nerve in their propounders.

II

The direction Bultmann's theological programme has taken is to be understood within a complex network of relationships, most of which are a mixture of positive and negative factors. In associating himself with Barth and Friedrich Gogarten, Bultmann joins in the attack on the so-called liberal theology (i.e. on the Ritschlian theology, broadly speaking), but he takes care to observe that dialectical theology is the immediate and grateful progeny of liberal theology.[6] He similarly pays homage to the history of religions school, in which he was trained, and to its interpretation of the Christ cult, while at the same time pointing to the limitations imposed upon theology where thinking is split off from living.[7] In these two respects Bultmann is identifying himself with dialectical theology under the leadership of Barth and Gogarten, but he is later to diverge from Barth as well. Behind the intra-party warfare on the part of those who stem from the liberal tradition, Bultmann, along with

---

[6] Cf. his essay, 'Liberal Theology and the Latest Theological Movement', pp. 28–52.
[7] Cf. e.g. 'The Christology of the New Testament', pp. 262 ff.

his liberal colleagues of various persuasions, is prosecuting the case against old Protestant orthodoxy, which continues to persist, albeit in increasingly modified form. In all these instances Bultmann returns to Luther and invokes what he takes to be the genius of the Reformation. Bultmann is thus to be read in positive and negative relation to Protestant orthodoxy in its older and newer forms, to liberalism, to the history of religions school, and finally even to dialectical theology.

It should not need emphasizing that, while many of the components in this nexus of relationships strike familiar notes in the history of the American tradition, the situation in and against which Bultmann worked took fundamentally different shape in Germany in the 'twenties and 'thirties from the corresponding situation in America.

The multiple relations of Bultmann, as complex as they are, nevertheless head up in a crisp theological programme of his own. Reduced to a catch-phrase, his programme may be said to aim at the radicalization of Luther's doctrine of justification by faith.[8] This phrase indicates Bultmann's positive relation to the Reformation and yet his negative stance *vis-à-vis* the latter-day version of orthodoxy and the liberal life-of-Jesus theology. And it is in this connection that the first of the items in Bultmann's popular portfolio can best be seen in perspective. We may first allow him to give credence to the popular conception in very strong language of his own before going on to inquire after its basis in his theological history:

> I have never yet felt uncomfortable with my critical radicalism; on the contrary, I have been entirely comfortable. But I often have the impression that my conservative New Testament colleagues feel very uncomfortable, for I see them perpetually engaged in salvage operations. I calmly let the fire burn, for I see that what is consumed is only the fanciful portraits of Life-of-Jesus theology, and that means nothing other than the Χριστὸς κατὰ σάρκα.[9]

The fundamental question for Bultmann concerns the proper ground of faith, without which faith would no longer be faith, as the statement just quoted shows. He approaches the question from two sides, corresponding, respectively, to his liberal and his Reformation heritages. On the one side, faith cannot have

[8] The characterization is Bultmann's own: *Kerygma and Myth*, ed. H. W. Bartsch, tr. R. H. Fuller (London: SPCK, 1957), pp. 210f.
[9] See below, p. 132.

an objective, demonstrable basis, otherwise it would no longer be faith. This means above all that faith cannot refer itself to 'Christ after the flesh'. On the other hand, historical criticism produces results, in accordance with all historical investigation, that are only relative.[10] Historical criticism could not, therefore, provide faith with an objective basis even if it tried – and to try would be to misunderstand the nature of historical criticism. And faith must not aspire to an objective basis in dogma or in history on pain of losing its character as faith. Bultmann is free, consequently, to pursue his study of Christian origins ruthlessly, since only false conceptions of the ground of faith are at stake. His stance as a Christian theologian does not require him to blunt the critical edge of historical investigation; indeed it requires him to be as erosive as the nature of the data allows. It might be said that Bultmann aspires to join historical criticism and faith so that, as a result of the union, each is permitted to come into its own. The immediate impetus to move in this direction arises from opposition to his own predecessors in liberalism, but it is surcharged by the increasing realignment of orthodox theologians with life-of-Jesus research.

It is necessary to pause momentarily, however, and consider the more remote background of this move. The cardinal error of Protestant orthodoxy was that it made the 'faith by which one believes' (*fides qua creditur*) derived and dependent upon the 'faith which is believed' (*fides quae creditur*), that is, it gave to the former the dependent role of merely acceding to the latter, understood as right doctrine. Theology since Schleiermacher has rejected this confusion of faith with theology – and rightly so, according to Bultmann. The theological truths that are to be believed never lose their rational character, even when regarded as 'supernatural truths'. That implies, of course, that such 'truths' must submit to rational criticism and judgment, or they must be accepted as 'true' by virtue of a resolve that holds them to be 'true' though they contradict reason. In either case, faith becomes detached from its proper ground.[11]

In the wake of Schleiermacher, however, theology moved to the other extreme: It reversed the orthodox position by holding that 'believing faith' precedes theology and in fact produces it; theology as *fides quae creditur* ('faith which is believed') is made

[10] Cf. below, pp. 30ff.   [11] See below, pp. 117f.

derivative in relation to 'believing faith' as *fides qua creditur*. The result – in retrospect, at least – was as absurd in its own way as the orthodox position. Theology has now lost its reason for being – except as a matter of intellectual curiosity. 'It [theology] is now included in the social sciences (Troeltsch) and has gained "universal validity" at the cost of no longer mattering to anyone.'[12]

If, in the struggle against the older Protestant orthodoxy, dogmatic propositions were abandoned as the object and content of faith, what was put in their place? Two substitutions were proposed, as Bultmann read the situation at the time he entered formally upon his theological career. These might be characterized broadly as the historical and the experimental ground of faith, respectively. It is the first option that Emmanuel Hirsch has chosen, whose views Bultmann submits to critical analyses in his essay, 'On the Question of Christology'.[13] Hirsch and other liberal and conservative theologians view the biblical faith as a historical phenomenon and assume that historical knowledge of this phenomenon provides faith with its object. This is essentially the route taken by the life-of-Jesus theologians. On the other hand, the history of religions school views faith as anchored in cultic or mystical piety (Bousset, Troeltsch),[14] or in the experience of the numinous (Otto).[15] In either case Christ is the *symbol* of the divine power that invades the world of darkness in the form of divine light.[16]

Crucial advocates of the historical position were two of Bultmann's own teachers at Marburg, Johannes Weiss and Wilhelm Herrmann.[17] Weiss and Herrmann endeavoured to ground faith in the powerful and inspiring personality of Jesus, which was the predominant influence in producing naïve and unreflective faith in God on the part of the first disciples, including Paul.[18] The only legitimate relation to Jesus is therefore imitative (Weiss)[19] or one of trust (Herrmann).[20] Aside from

---

[12] See below, p. 118.   [13] See below, pp. 116–44, especially p. 122
[14] See below, pp. 269–73.   [15] See below, p. 49.
[16] See below, p. 273.
[17] The work of Weiss is discussed in some detail, see below, pp. 263–69; that of Herrmann, pp. 132–43.
[18] Herrmann, see below, pp. 135f.; Weiss, p. 265.
[19] See below, p. 267.
[20] See below, pp. 136f; the characterization applies also to Hirsch.

whether this view reflects anything like the New Testament view of Jesus, Bultmann points out that 'Jesus could have this meaning only for those who had been personally associated with him'.[21] Those who came later would have to 'catch' their faith from those who had 'caught' their faith from Jesus. What is wrong with this view ultimately is that faith in someone else's faith cannot be faith in God, even when that someone else is Jesus. The connection with the person of Jesus is broken, moreover, when Jesus dies; thereafter he is no longer a Thou to whom an I can have a personal relation.[22] But even if the preceding assumptions are granted, the New Testament does not preserve a picture of Jesus' personality, not even in the Gospels, so that it is difficult to see how the 'powerful personality of Jesus' could be transmitted in history. Weiss endeavoured to maintain some connection between Paul and the earthly Jesus in the interest of his general thesis, but Bultmann argues that Paul's relation is to the risen and exalted Christ, not to Jesus of Nazareth.[23] Minimally it has to be said that Weiss' view falls to the ground on the basis of historical evidence, quite apart from theological considerations.

Over against every effort to establish a historical basis for faith Bultmann was quite willing, even eager, to let the critical fires burn. If such efforts came to grief on the shoals of historical criticism, Bultmann's positive theological task could be the more easily executed.

Bultmann did not feel himself so strongly constrained to oppose the views of the history of religions school, as represented, for example, by the work of H. Gunkel, W. Wrede, W. Bousset and E. Troeltsch.[24] He readily agrees that the history of religions school came much closer to the real state of affairs in the Hellenistic church than did scholars working under the older liberal, i.e. idealistic, viewpoint. The virtue of the school lay in the fact that religion is conceived not as a compendium of doctrines, a body of timeless truths, whether medi-

---

[21] See below, p. 267; pp. 136f.   [22] See below, pp. 136f.
[23] Cf. below, pp. 239ff. for a discussion of what Jesus is and is not for Paul.
[24] 'The Christology of the New Testament', below, pp. 262–85, is especially relevant here. Cf. his 'Epilogue' to *Theology of the New Testament*, II, tr. K. Grobel (New York: Scribner; London: SCM Press, 1955), pp. 245–7, 248f.; and *Kerygma and Myth*, pp. 14f.

ated by supranatural revelation or discovered by rational thought, but rather as an independent force, a 'feeling' or a piety, which can assume various forms. And it was representatives of this school who first discovered how extensively the New Testament is permeated with mythology. Ethical idealism, which had come to dominate liberal theology, was dealt a decisive blow by this movement as it rediscovered the formative power of primitive Christianity, in contrast to the alleged ethical religion of Jesus, then in such great favour. Historic Christianity, as represented by the Hellenistic church and Paul, was permitted to re-emerge as a decisive factor – if not *the* decisive factor – in the shaping of the Christian tradition. Wrede went so far as to designate Paul the second founder of Christianity.

As much as the work of this school threw light on the affinities of the Hellenistic church with the Greek mysteries and gnosticism, and as much as it opened up a new understanding of the locus of religion in the primary affective life of man – one could even say, in the existential bearing of man[25] – it fell prey to an error of an opposite sort, in Bultmann's judgment. Wrede, Bousset and others held, as a consequence of their definition of religion, that theological thoughts are the result of secondary reflection on the experiences of faith and therefore not an integral part of the life of faith. This means, of course, that the content of the Christian proclamation is split off from faith as experience, that the act of thinking and the act of living are sundered, as Adolf Schlatter emphasized.[26] The end result is that the history of religions school eliminates the decisive event of Christ.[27]

The error was twofold.[28] In the first place, the school overlooked the fact that in the New Testament the Christ event is understood eschatologically rather than mystically. Jesus Christ brought an end to the old age and inaugurated a new one, precisely within historical existence; he does not lure man into the heavenly world of mystical union. In the second place, scripture is denied its unique position in that the proclamation is no longer viewed as the sole ground of faith. Bultmann holds,

---

[25] *Theology of the New Testament*, II, p. 247.
[26] *Ibid.*, p. 246.   [27] *Kerygma and Myth*, p. 27.
[28] See below, pp. 138f.

as we shall observe, that the Christian proclamation, the kerygma, belongs to the Christ event as its consummation. 'Faith is response to the Word; the new self-understanding is the response to the proclamation.'[29] Far from being an accessory after the fact of a cultic or mystical experience, the theological thoughts of the proclamation are integral to the possibility and character of faith.

This error reaches beyond the sentences of the primitive credo. It also affects, for example, one's understanding of the sacraments. On the analogy of the Greek mysteries, the sacraments might be understood as the medium of divine power, as the cultic act where mystic contact and union with the deity is achieved. But, insists Bultmann, this is to fail to see that the sacraments as Paul understands them are the means by which 'the saving event, the death and resurrection of Christ, becomes an event in the present as something which happens objectively to the believer'.[30]

The history of religions school taught Bultmann that the historic form of Christianity (i.e. the form in which it survived) originated in the primitive church. He also learned that the kerygma, which he takes to be the primary bearer of the tradition, was thoroughly mythological. The former appealed to his latent neo-orthodox instincts, and he was prepared to rest his case for Christianity on the post-Easter confession of the primitive church: Jesus is Lord. There is no Christianity where there is no faith in Christ! But the confession of the primitive church was mythological, and he was as stoutly *un*prepared to allow the mythical Christ to stand as a cult symbol. The proclamation of the church, with all its mythology, had to refer to what God had done in Jesus Christ, and that means, at a certain point in human history. The question thus arose: How could he affirm that fact of past history and still account for the ongoing salvific effectiveness of the Christ event, particularly in the face of modern man's proclivity to misunderstand the mythological character of the kerygma?

If the mythological kerygma is not to be allowed to disintegrate into a symbolic representation of religious piety, and if it refers to a historical event, albeit not one that can be laid bare by historical criticism and thus 'established', it is clear

[29] See below, p. 278.   [30] See below, p. 274.

that Bultmann has to walk a fine line between the Scylla of the historical ground of faith and the Charybdis of the experiential ground of faith. The catchword Bultmann was later to take up as his guide to this narrow path was *Entmythologisierung* (demythologizing).

We are thus brought to the second of the putative items in his portfolio, demythologizing. From what has been said it should be clear that Bultmann has not the slightest intention of *eliminating* myth from the New Testament faith. On the contrary, he chooses, like F. C. Baur and others before him, to take his stand precisely on the mythological kerygma and nowhere else. But because he wants to avoid the pitfall of the history of religions understanding of myth, and because he does not want to fall into the trap of the objectifying tendencies of the life-of-Jesus theology either, he charts out a narrow channel through the dangerous waters of his own theological history, a channel designed to bring him onto the course of *living Christian* tradition. Just how he sounds out this particular demythologizing channel we shall endeavour to indicate in what follows.

III

That God acted in Jesus Christ to redeem man is a theological axiom for Bultmann. His sole concern has been so to understand that act and its correlative, the act of faith, that the two are commensurate with each other, and understandable to modern man. The commensurability of the two means, of course, that the first must be conceived in such a way as to allow it to impinge redemptively upon man's history, then and now, while preserving the Godhood of God, and that the second must be so understood as to permit man his full humanity while bowing in radical obedience to God. It might be said that Bultmann is driven to affirm the radical transcendence but effective immanence of God, together with the radical humanity but redeemability of man.

Bultmann insists, as has been made amply clear, that the fact of God's redemptive act in Jesus Christ cannot be demonstrated by historical science. How then is it to be known? It is characteristic of the biblical view that God is present to man in the word and only in the word.[31] God is present in every

[31] See below, p. 297, with reference to the Old Testament.

time and every place, but he makes his presence known only through his word.[32] It follows that God makes his act in Jesus Christ known to man also through the word. And if the existence of man is qualified ultimately by a particular historical event, that fact can be made known to man only by means of a word which comes from beyond,[33] i.e. by means of a word that transcends the limits of history.

The act of faith that acknowledges Jesus Christ as Lord must be correlative with the word that invokes it. Since God's act in Christ is established through the word and the word only, faith must 'abandon absolutely the search for proof', either in external or in internal form (experience). And faith must seek no other basis for itself, no other authentication, than that offered by the word.[34]

The exclusive correlation of word and faith is what leads Bultmann to affirm: 'Jesus *Christ* confronts men in the kerygma and nowhere else'.[35] The form of this affirmation is to be noted: he does not say that Jesus of Nazareth is known only in the proclamation, but that Jesus as the *Christ* confronts man only there. The difference can be made clear by reference to the twin events of crucifixion and resurrection. The death of Jesus, like his life, is a historical phenomenon that is open to public verification. Nevertheless, in all its ambiguity it corresponds to God's judgment on every human enterprise. It stands, moreover, as a source of embarrassment to all those who wish to confess Jesus as Messiah. On the other hand, the resurrection is visible only to the eyes of faith; the unbeliever is met with only the *assertion* of the resurrection. The significance of Jesus' death is seized in the moment one is able to 'see' the resurrection, and one can 'see' the resurrection in the moment one can acknowledge and accept the 'stumbling block' and the 'folly' of the crucifixion. The two go together and form a paradox, the character of which makes faith what it is. But notice that the paradox does not arise logically out of the event of Jesus' death, but presents itself solely in the form of the Christian proclamation. Jesus *Christ* therefore confronts man nowhere except in the proclamation.

Bultmann is then able to continue: the proclamation an-

---

[32] *Kerygma and Myth*, pp. 206f.
[33] See below, p. 138.
[34] See below, pp. 138, 143, 291, 300, 302.
[35] See below, p. 312.

nounces a fact, but the proclamation is a part of the fact it announces, namely the Christ event.[36] The proclamation is the 'that' of the Christ event; it is the Christ's 'here and now'. It is thus quite easily understood why Bultmann is willing to say that Jesus has risen in the kerygma. As shocking as it sounds to those who wish to lay an objective basis for faith in the resurrection, it goes together with Bultmann's understanding of word and faith. Bultmann sums it up quite vividly:

> It is often said, most of the time in criticism, that according to my interpretation of the kerygma Jesus has risen in the kerygma. I accept this proposition. It is entirely correct, assuming that it is properly understood. It presupposes that the kerygma itself is an eschatological event, and it expresses the fact that Jesus is really present in the kerygma, that it is *his* word which involves the hearer in the kerygma. . . . To believe in the Christ present in the kerygma is the meaning of the Easter faith.[37]

This way of putting the matter also answers a question necessarily raised by those who hold that the Christ event is an event of the past: how can the Christ event continue to be eventful? Bultmann answers: God's act in Christ was consummated in the proclamation and so it continues to be consummated.

With the assertion that Jesus has risen in the kerygma, we are brought to a juncture where it is possible to understand more precisely Bultmann's view of the relation of the historical Jesus to faith. This point may serve as an oblique means of approaching a more explicit consideration of the character of the proclamation.

Over against his own learned mentors, e.g. W. Wrede,[38] Bultmann takes the position that Jesus and Paul depict the situation of man before God in fundamentally the same terms, although Jesus does not employ the same discursive theological language as Paul.[39] But if Jesus and Paul say the same thing

---

[36] See below, pp. 241, 278, 308.

[37] 'The Primitive Christian Kerygma and the Historical Jesus', *The Historical Jesus and the Kerygmatic Christ*, tr. and ed. C. E. Braaten and R. A. Harrisville (New York and Nashville: Abingdon, 1964), p. 42.

[38] Cf. Wrede's book, *Paulus* (Tübingen: J. C. B. Mohr, 1905); *Paul*, tr. E. Lummis (London: P. Green, 1907).

[39] Bultmann presents this view in his essay of 1929, 'The Significance of the Historical Jesus in the Theology of Paul' (see below, pp. 220–46), and confirms and develops it in an essay of 1936, 'Jesus and Paul', *Existence and Faith: Shorter Writings of Rudolf Bultmann*, tr. Schubert Ogden (New York: Meridian, 1960), pp. 183–201.

essentially, if they proclaim the same message, including an eschatological component, is the kerygma then not already present in the proclamation of Jesus? To this question Bultmann responds negatively. There is the ostensible difference that Jesus calls men to repentance in anticipation of the coming wrath, while Paul and the primitive church proclaim Jesus as the Messiah. This difference Bultmann epitomizes thus: 'the proclaimer became the proclaimed'.[40] Yet this difference only suggests the real difference.

We have to ask: What lies between the end of Jesus' public ministry and the proclamation of the proclaimer as the proclaimed? The answer obviously is: the crucifixion, the resurrection and Pentecost (all of which are conjoined in Bultmann's view). When it is recalled that the resurrection represents the consummation of God's act in Christ in the form of his redemptive word and that Pentecost represents the descent of the Spirit, it becomes immediately apparent that for Bultmann, and orthodoxy generally, the turn of the ages comes with Easter–Pentecost. For this very fundamental reason he assigns Jesus of Nazareth as a historical person to the history of Judaism,[41] and draws an indelible line between Jesus and Paul:

> Paul is waiting for the fulfilment, but in a sense different from that of Jesus. Jesus looks to the future, to the *coming* kingdom of God – which is coming or dawning now. But Paul looks back; *the turning point of the ages has already come*.[42]

For the same reason Bultmann holds a very high doctrine of the church and gives a central position to the Holy Spirit:

> If it is true that the kerygma proclaims Jesus as the Christ, as the eschatological event, if it claims that Christ is present in it, then it has put itself in the place of the historical Jesus; it represents him. Then there is no faith in Christ which would not also be faith in the church as the bearer of the kerygma; that is using the terminology of dogmatics, faith in the Holy Ghost. But faith in the church is at the same time faith in Jesus Christ, a faith which the historical Jesus did not demand.[43]

So far from being the radical theologian Bultmann is often accused of being, Bultmann actually opts for the kerygma of

[40] *Theology of the New Testament*, I, tr. K. Grobel (New York: Scribner; London: SCM Press, 1951), p. 33.

[41] *Ibid.*, p. 3.   [42] See below, p. 233.

[43] 'The Primitive Christian Kerygma and the Historical Jesus', *The Historical Jesus and the Kerygmatic Christ*, p. 41.

the primitive church as the basis of faith, over against his own liberal mentors, who sought to refer faith to moralizing and/or psychologizing interpretations of Jesus. If Anglo-Saxon theologians had taken more care to read Bultmann against his theological history, many of them would have exposed their own liberal proclivities, often covered over with a façade of biblicism, less blatantly.

It has been shown how, according to Bultmann, God's redemptive act in Christ is bound up with the proclamation, how it occurs, in fact, by virtue of God's word. On our way to the question of demythologizing, it is appropriate and necessary to clarify the intentionality of word of God. By intentionality is meant what word of God aims at, what it seeks to effect.[44]

Word of God does not effect a magical change in man's life nor does it consist of dogmas which demand blind decision.[45] It does not represent theories about existence, nor does it advocate a particular world view.[46] Furthermore, God's word does not communicate new information in the sense of facts I could ascertain for myself if I made certain observations or travelled to certain places, or in the sense of reports about something which transpired in the past.[47] What, then, does word of God intend?

Unlike the language of the natural sciences, for example, or the language of objective historiography, the proclamation as word of God has the character of *address*. That means it appertains not to objects and temporal events within the world, but to the world itself, which is neither an object nor an event, or to my own existence, my life and my death.[48] Furthermore, as address or summons, word of God is itself a temporal event in a specific situation, in a specific history.[49] In other words, the word as address concerns how I understand myself in the total nexus of relations that forms my world, and it addresses my self-understanding in such a way that my response, my 'hearing', here and now, determines whether or not I accept the self-understanding, the 'world', to which the word calls me.

[44] The following passages are relevant: see below, 155–59, 184–93, 301–12; cf. 204–19.
[45] See below, pp. 140, 301.   [46] See below, p. 302.
[47] See below, pp. 306; cf. pp. 157–9, 204.
[48] See below, p. 156.   [49] Cf. below, pp. 296f.

The word itself is therefore eventful, assuming that I 'hear' it;
it belongs inherently to the event which is the transformation
of my self-understanding, my 'world'.

This is evidently the understanding of word that is operative
in the New Testament. Paul, for example, does not view the
cross and resurrection as 'mere facts of the past',[50] but as event
addressing the present: the cross as inviting me to be crucified
with Christ (Gal. 2.20), the resurrection as calling me to par-
ticipate in a new humanity (Rom. 6.4). The kerygma, consequently, aims at my self-understanding, at the 'world' in which
I dwell and from which I take my ultimate bearings. To understand myself in the way for which the kerygma calls, to live in
the 'world' invoked by the kerygma, means to confess that
Jesus Christ is Lord, i.e. to dwell where Jesus Christ has
dominion.

Bultmann sums up his view in a remarkably lucid para-
graph,[51] which may be encapsulated here: God's word sets
man simultaneously in darkness and in light: in darkness,
because the world is no longer at his disposal; in light, because
this fact illuminates the character of his existence. The power
that has this effect is called God's word: *God's* word because
it is the word of the dark power that looms over him; God's
word because it 'says' something to him, illuminates his existence.

Only a consistent misreading of Bultmann could have led to
the sort of 'subjectivistic' interpretation of Bultmann's term
'self-understanding' found in many of Bultmann's critics. It is
clear, to be sure, that self-understanding corresponds to faith
on the manward side, and 'word' corresponds to redemption
on the Godward side. Yet Bultmann is equally clear that faith
is not the work of man, but the conjunction of God's redeeming
work with man's resolve:

> Could faith then be the Archimedean point from which the world is
> moved off its axis and is transformed from the world of sin into the world
> of God? Yes![52]

Surely no one cares to accuse Bultmann of holding that the
transformation of 'world' which accompanies faith is a mere

---

[50] See below, pp. 306f.   [51] See below, p. 153.
[52] See below, pp. 64f.

illusion induced by 'self-understanding'. Nevertheless, in order
to correct the misunderstanding precipitated by the term 'self-
understanding', it may prove necessary to replace that term by
the term 'world'.[53]

It has been observed that Bultmann understands the redemptive act of God in Christ as consummated in the kerygma
of the primitive church and made effective by the Holy Spirit.
To be 'in Christ' means to be 'led by the Spirit' (Rom. 8.14).
Nevertheless, the act of faith does not cease to be man's. The
conjunction of the Spirit and man's will defines the problem of
faith but does not solve it.[54] It does not solve it because the
Spirit may be conceived as some mysterious entity operating
behind man's resolves. That would result, as Wilhelm Herrmann said, 'in thinking according to Augustine and living
according to Pelagius'.[55] The task of theology is to make this
redemptive act understandable.

It is a legitimate task since the word of God, if it aims at my
self-understanding, at my 'world', must be understandable.[56]
Its understandability is one respect, at least, in which word of
God in the Judeo-Christian tradition differs from the magical
word of paganism.[57] God's word must 'speak' to man, 'say'
something to him.

The stage is now fully set for the demythologizing proposal
which was to follow, formally, about ten years later. The setting
consists of two planks in Bultmann's platform, which when
taken together and framed by his understanding of God's redemptive act in Christ, make demythologizing inevitable.
Those planks are, first, his conviction that God's redemptive
act is consummated and re-consummated in the proclamation
of the church, which, as is generally agreed, is thoroughly
mythological. The second plank is that the proclamation, if it
is to function as word of God, i.e. redemptively, must be understandable to the man to whom it is addressed, and that means

---

[53] Cf. my book, *Language, Hermeneutic and Word of God* (New York:
Harper and Row, 1966) *passim* (Index), where this shift is made, and the
programmatic essay of James M. Robinson, 'World in Modern Theology
and in New Testament Theology', *Soli Deo Gloria: New Testament Studies in
Honor of William Childs Robinson* (Richmond: John Knox Press, 1968),
pp. 88–110, 149–51.
[54] See below, p. 133.   [55] *Ibid.*
[56] See below, pp. 209, 301; cf. p. 133.   [57] See below, p. 301.

in Bultmann's case, to modern man. The pieces of the puzzle fit nicely together once it is known where they go! Modern man cannot understand the kerygma, the proclamation, as it is necessary to understand it if he is to come to faith by it; in fact, his literal-mindedness, made all pervasive by virtue of the modern world view, prohibits him from understanding the traditional proclamation, makes it impossible for that proclamation to *address* him. But salvation is nowhere available other than in the proclamation of the gospel, reasons Bultmann, so that it is necessary to *interpret* that *given* proclamation in such a way that its intention cannot be missed. 'Demythologizing' is nothing other than Bultmann's effort to aim the proclamation, as an intelligible challenge, at modern man's self-understanding, at his 'world'.

The sketch here presented is scarcely an adequate defence of 'demythologizing' in detail. Our aim has not been to defend, but to illuminate the trajectory of Bultmann's thought in relation to his theological history. If that trajectory can be traced in the early essays which constitute the first volume of *Faith and Understanding*, it may prove worthwhile to follow it out in subsequent volumes of *Glauben und Verstehen*,[58] in his *Theology of the New Testament*, in other monographs and essays, and in the series, *Kerygma and Myth*.[59] The reward of pursuit is an encounter with a rich and powerful theological mind, which is at once astonishingly orthodox and breathtakingly modern.

Nashville, Tennessee   ROBERT W. FUNK

---

[58] Vol. II (Tübingen: J. C. B. Mohr, 1952, ²1958, ³1961, ⁴1965), translated as: *Essays Philosophical and Theological*, tr. J. C. Greig (London: SCM Press, 1955; Vol. III (Tübingen: J. C. B. Mohr, 1960, ²1962, ³1965), part of which was translated in *Existence and Faith* (n. 39); Vol. IV (Tübingen: J. C. B. Mohr, 1965, ²1967).

[59] Available in English: *Kerygma and Myth*, I (n. 8); *Kerygma and Myth*, II, ed. H. W. Bartsch, tr. R. H. Fuller (London: SPCK, 1962). The series in German has now grown to six volumes.

I

LIBERAL THEOLOGY AND THE LATEST
THEOLOGICAL MOVEMENT[1]
[1924]

IN THE polemic of the latest theological movement – a movement which is particularly associated with the names of Barth
and Gogarten – the attack against the so-called liberal theology
is not to be understood as a repudiation of its own past, but as
a discussion with that past. The new movement is not a revival
of orthodoxy, but rather a carefully reasoned consideration of
the consequences which have resulted from the situation
brought about by liberal theology.

It is no accident that the latest movement originated not
from within orthodoxy but out of liberal theology. Barth was
a student at Marburg, Gogarten at Heidelberg, Thurneysen
at both.[2]

It is essential to understand also that the issue raised by the
new movement is not a debate with individual theologians but
a protest against a specific theological trend. That trend is, of
course, supported by individual theologians, but it is not to be
identified with all their incidental pronouncements. Liberal
theology therefore cannot evade criticism by showing that this
or that liberal theologian has now and then said something
quite different and is not responsible for what some other
theologian has said. Moreover, it can be readily granted that

---

[1] *TB* III (1924), pp. 73–86.

[2] In this article (based on a previous lecture), I have confined myself to a
discussion of the movement as represented by Barth and Gogarten only.
My reason for so limiting myself in a treatment of the 'latest theological
movement' is that I find that both the recognition of our present theological
situation and the efforts to overcome the difficulties it presents have been
most fruitful in their work. I do not overlook the fact that similar incentives
are operative elsewhere and that important statements are being made by
others.

themes can be seen in the work of some liberal theologians which would lead to the defeat of their own position. As examples, I would mention W. Herrmann and the great proponent of liberal theology, E. Troeltsch.

The subject of theology is *God*, and the chief charge to be brought against liberal theology is that it has dealt not with God but with man. God represents the radical negation and sublimation of man. Theology whose subject is God can therefore have as its content only the 'word of the cross' (λόγος τοῦ σταυροῦ). But that word is a 'stumbling-block' (σκάνδαλον) to men. Hence the charge against liberal theology is that it has sought to remove this stumbling-block or to minimize it.

I shall try to make clear how criticism of liberal theology develops out of this charge by a discussion of the liberal idea of history and of the actual situation of men in this world. I have chosen these two aspects because in them the position of liberal theology reveals itself most clearly. I cannot, of course, give an exhaustive presentation. We are still only at the beginning of our work of analysis and discussion. I should also emphasize that I am not presenting a criticism formulated on the basis of a fully-developed system of theology. We are in the midst of the process of self-examination. For this reason I have not dealt specifically with the question of christology, although the direction in which such inquiry should proceed will soon become clear. Nor have I specifically considered the matter of Scripture and Canon. I hope to deal with these questions elsewhere.

Here I shall seek to demonstrate conclusively what kind of conception of God and man serves as the basis of liberal theology and to make clear the objections raised against it.

I

Liberal theology owed its distinctive character chiefly to the primacy of *historical interest*, and in that field it made its greatest contributions. These contributions were not limited to the clarification of the historical picture. They were especially important for the development *of the critical sense*, that is, for freedom and veracity. We who have come from a background of liberal theology could never have become theologians nor remained such had we not encountered in that liberal theology

the earnest search for radical truth. We felt in the work of
orthodox university theology of all shades an urge towards
compromise within which our intellectual and spiritual life
would necessarily be fragmented. We can never forget our
debt of gratitude to G. Krüger for that often cited article of his
on 'unchurchly theology'. For he saw the task of theology to be
to imperil souls, to lead men into doubt, to shatter all naïve
credulity.[3] Here, we felt, was the atmosphere of truth in which
alone we could breathe.

But to what result has the course of historical criticism actually led? If it was at first directed by a confidence that such
critical research would free men from the burden of dogmatics
and lead to a comprehension of the real figure of Jesus on which
faith could be based, this confidence soon proved to be delusion. Historical research can never lead to any result which
could serve as a basis for faith, for *all its results have only relative
validity.* How widely the pictures of Jesus presented by liberal
theologians differ from one another! How uncertain is all
knowledge of 'the historical Jesus'! Is he really within the scope
of our knowledge? Here research ends with a large question
mark – and here it *ought* to end.

The error is not that men did this historical work and obtained results which are more or less radical; rather, it is that they
did not understand the significance of such work nor the meaning of the inquiry. The real question was evaded even when it
was put as precisely as Troeltsch stated it in his work, *Die
Bedeutung der Geschichtlichkeit Jesu für den Glauben,* (1911). No
matter in what sense, for Troeltsch a picture of the historical
Jesus is necessary for the faith of the church, and, 'Accordingly
there remains an actual dependence (if one likes to put it that
way) on scholars and professors, or – better expressed – on the
general sense of historical reliability which results from the
impact of scientific research' (pp. 34f.). Nicely put – but
'better'?

The very character which is the special 'gift' ($\chi\acute{\alpha}\varrho\iota\sigma\mu\alpha$) of
liberal theology is denied if at the end of the road stands a
sign: The situation is not yet really very bad; the results of
historico-critical theology are still usable for faith. The position
of liberal theology becomes frighteningly clear in the four-

[3] *CW,* 14 (1900), pp. 804–7.

teenth question which von Harnack addressed to Barth. 'If the *person of Jesus Christ* stands at the centre of the Gospel, how can the foundation for a reliable and generally accepted know-ledge of that person be gained except through *historico-critical research?* Is not such research essential to prevent the substitu-tion of an *imagined* Christ for the real Christ? And who can carry on this research unless he pursues it as scientific theology?[4] Barth answers rightly: 'Historico-critical research represents the deserved and necessary end of *the* "foundations" of this understanding (i.e. the understanding of *faith*). Such founda-tions do not exist except when they are laid by God himself. Anyone who does not yet know (and in truth all of us do not know *yet*) that we *cannot* any longer know Christ after the flesh should let himself be taught by critico-biblical research that the more radically he is horrified, the better it is for him and for the cause. This may well be the service which "historical science" can perform in the real task of theology.'[5]

Thus there can be no question of discarding historical criti-cism. But we must understand its true significance. It is needed to train us for freedom and veracity – not only by freeing us from a specific traditional conception of history, but because it frees us from bondage to every historical construction which is within the scope of historical science, and brings us to the realization that the world which faith wills to grasp is abso-lutely unattainable by means of scientific research.

This truth becomes even clearer when a second error in the historical understanding of liberal theology is recognized. It forgets not only that all the results it presents within its overall picture of reality have merely a relative validity, but also that all historical phenomena which are subject to this kind of historical investigation are only relative entities, *entities which exist only within an immense inter-related complex.* Nothing which stands within this inter-relationship can claim absolute value. Even the historical Jesus is a phenomenon among other phenomena, not an absolute entity. Liberal theology has in-deed recognized this conclusion up to a certain point. It speaks of the historical Jesus with great assurance, but in terms which do not ascribe an absolute value to him. Again it is Troeltsch who speaks most unambiguously. On page 14 of the work

[4] *CW*, 37 (1923), p. 8.   [5] *Ibid.*, p. 91.

already cited, we read the plain statement that there cannot be
a *necessary* binding of the Christian faith to the person of Jesus.
Faith in God leads to acknowledgment of the person of Jesus,
not vice versa.

But here again the final result is compromise. We are told
that, almost as by a law of social psychology, the Christian
church, like every religious organization, requires a cult with
a concrete centre. The figure of Christ is such a centre. 'The
linking of the Christian *idea* to the central position of Jesus in
cult and teaching is not a conceptual necessity derived logically
from the idea of salvation. But in terms of social psychology it
is indispensable for the cult, for action, for proselytizing. That
indispensability is sufficient justification for the assertion of
the link' (p. 30).

A statement of that kind makes it entirely clear that *Christianity* is understood as *a phenomenon of this world, subject to the laws
of social psychology*. It is equally clear that such a conception
runs exactly counter to the Christian view. Although Troeltsch's view may to some extent be justified – only orthodoxy
would dispute that – certainly it is not *theology*, not if *God* is the
subject of theology and the theologian is speaking as a *Christian*.

That such a conception could be offered and accepted as
theology was possible partly because no objection was made
to the inclusion of the person of Jesus in the complex of general
historical inter-relations. Indeed, it was acceptable as theology
because of the belief that *the revelation of God in history could be
perceived precisely within this nexus of relations*. Therefore it is possible to speak of a 'pantheism of *history*' in liberal theology,
analogous to a pantheism of nature. This pantheism depends
on the assumption of a similarity between nature and history;
that is, the concepts which are valid for nature are accepted as
equally valid for history. And man, in so far as he acts in this
history, is similarly regarded, as it were from outside, as an
object, rather than under the categories which are drawn from
man himself.

I shall try to make the nature of this pantheism of history
clear by a comparison. In the religion of primitive peoples,
deity is perceived in single objects, in a particular phenomenon
of nature, in stone or tree, river or cloud, sky or constellation,
storm or the burgeoning life of spring. This particularizing

view of nature gradually yields to the tendency to conceive the objects and phenomena of nature as inter-related. The connectives, the cosmic powers, the laws of nature become divine for men. The farther the view of inter-relation develops towards the concept of nature as a whole, of the whole cosmos as a unity, the more completely is the naïve polydemonistic or polytheistic worship of the powers of nature transformed into a pantheism of *nature*. Such pantheism has of course lost most, if not all, truly religious motivation, as its attitude towards miracle shows. For in such pantheism the naïve view of a miraculous act of God, an act in which there is nothing natural at all, has been discarded in favour of the assertion that God acts within natural laws, that these laws are themselves forms of his activity, that they are 'miracles'.

There is actually no reason to ascribe divinity to the laws of nature; such pantheism of nature really merges into a deification of man. For it divinizes the concept of conformity to law and precisely that concept is the human element in the picture of the cosmos. Furthermore, it disregards precisely what is the basis of religion in the naïve conception of nature – the natural event which leaves man at a loss, bewilders him, reveals him to himself as nothing, 'calls him in question'.

Obviously, the idea of nature's conformity to law also *can* result in men's being at a loss. Consider, for example, Strindberg or Spitteler. But in that case pantheism is abandoned; and nature, the cosmos, is seen as a riddle which overwhelms man with terror and horror. By the kind of reaction which such modern figures as Strindberg and Spitteler exemplify, it becomes clear that no *direct* knowledge of God can be derived from nature and that the error of pantheism of nature lies really in its will to win direct knowledge of God. In other words, it tries to view God as a given entity, as an object of the kind to which the relationship of direct knowledge is possible for us.

W. Herrmann was always pointing out that 'the laws of nature hide God as much as they reveal him'. And although different terms are used, that statement is the equivalent of the constantly repeated assertion of Barth and Gogarten: 'There is no direct knowledge of God. God is not a given entity.'

The same objection holds against *the view of history held in liberal theology*. Indubitably, in primitive or ancient religions man saw the act of deity in historical events; but he saw it in particular events: in the misery or the prosperity of a people, in a battle, in a war, in servitude or liberation (for example, the Exodus from Egypt!), or in individual historical persons: Moses, the prophets, men of God of every kind. But here also occurs the shift to a recognition of inter-connection, to the concept of historical forces and laws, to the understanding of history as a unity. The views of individual adherents of liberal theology differ in detail, but on the whole a vague, idealistic, psychological concept of history prevails. Historical forces are viewed as spiritual powers which are none the less conceived entirely on the analogy of the forces of nature. Through the action of such forces, it appears, mankind develops from a state of nature to civilization and culture. History is a struggle in which the powers of the true, the good and the beautiful are victorious, and it is a struggle in which man participates, in that he is supported by these powers and thus emerges from his bondage to nature to become a free personality with all its riches.

In these powers of truth, goodness and beauty lies the meaning of history, its divine character. God reveals himself in human personalities who are the bearers of these powers. And Jesus, so far as he is also in this sense a personality, is the bearer of revelation. Such a doctrine is certainly a pantheism of history. The old 'history of salvation' is wholly divested of its character. By the demonstration of the inter-relatedness of historical phenomena, man thinks he has attained to the comprehension of divine powers. Proof of the historical necessity of the phenomenon of Christendom serves as its best apologetic.[6]

The same concept serves for the interpretation of the 'fullness of the time' (Gal. 4.4) and replaces the recognition of the truth that history has come to a dead end, that its meaninglessness has become plain. At the very least, the liberal view of history is assumed to serve Christian faith by demonstrating that such powers as are manifested in Christianity, the powers of love, of self-sacrifice and the like, are the forces actually operative in history. The essence of Christianity seems so easily understood when it is viewed in its place along with other

---

[6] Cf. O. Pfleiderer, *Das Urchristentum*, 2nd ed., I, Berlin, 1902, p. vii; ET, *Primitive Christianity* I, London, 1906, pp. vii–viii.

forces and ideas which appear in principle in other spiritual movements.[7]

Along with such statements often appears – with a certain inconsistency of viewpoint – the attempt to prove that some ideas or impulses entered history for the first time in Christianity. Apart from the doubtful nature of the proof in specific instances, *newness* is not a category which is determinative for the divine. That category is eternity. Newness can be claimed equally for this or that imbecility. Newness is never a guarantee of the *value* of what claims to be new.

Neither by one road nor by the other can a way be found out of the *unending inter-relatedness* in which no single epoch and no single person can claim absolute significance. It is no more possible to see divine forces or the revelation of the divine in the inter-related complex of history and in historical forces than it is in the inter-relatedness of nature and natural forces. Truly, here, too, it is only man that is deified; for the human powers are alleged to be divine. Here again is to be seen merely the attempt to win direct knowledge of God. Here, too, is the concept of God as a given object.

And here, too, appears the reaction – especially among the young. There is the realization that such inter-relatedness connotes fatalism, that the 'riches' which the personality wins are a curse, because the distinctively human characteristic, the creative in man, has been destroyed or imprisoned. They feel that history so understood 'puts man in question', leaves him at a loss and makes him a ghost. At every point – against both pantheism of nature and pantheism of history – the polemic of Barth and Gogarten is valid. For that polemic is aimed directly against the temptation to deify man; it is a protest against every kind of direct knowledge of God.

In so far as the Word of God is judgment upon the whole nature and condition of man, it is the 'stumbling block' for every kind of pantheism of history. But *only* in so far! It is not so easy to deal with the stumbling block as it seemed to be in

---

[7] This idea finds naïve expression on page 398 of *Morgenandachten*, published in 1909 by the Friends of the Christian World. After a polemic against the idea of 'the splendid sins' (*splendida vitia*) of the heathen, we read, 'It cannot be denied that the spirit of the noblest nations of antiquity, which also is a spirit given by God, built the road for the ideas of the Christian world and helped the progress upward towards freedom.'

the view of history commonly accepted by orthodox theology; that is, by asserting the occurrence of supernatural phenomena and powers within history. We are not required to make *that* sacrifice of reason (*sacrificium intellectus*), which would involve the repudiation of all effort to gain a rational view of history. The meaning of history can be found only by relating visible history to an invisible origin – not by setting up a second, alien history alongside the other (Barth, *Der Römerbrief*, 3rd ed., München, 1923, p. 90; ET, *The Epistle to the Romans*, London and New York, 1933, p. 140). 'The judgment of God is the *end* of history, not the beginning of a new, a second, epoch' (*ibid.*, p. 51; *ibid.*, p. 77).

I am convinced that any one must be appalled if he really perceives the *specific consequences* which follow from the conception of history accepted by liberal theology. (The true nature of these consequences, of course, remains unrecognized by most of its adherents.) I will try to justify this verdict by illustration from the *problem of the Christ*. Ritschlian theology is persuaded of its ability to prove that history as known through scientific research has a positive value for faith. But it mistakenly places the origin of faith in God in man, in man's sense of value. Man has not only a yearning for God; he has also a vision of God as the supreme power and the moral will. And precisely this concept is accepted as 'value'. 'But value itself cannot prove reality to us. An external object is required, a bearer of this value, confronting our sense of value in such a way that out of the sense of value develops inevitably the conviction of the existence of a reality corresponding to that value.'[8] Such an object can only be a personality, which we encounter in Jesus. This statement can be interpreted to mean that the individual becomes conscious of the powers working in himself as real and meaningful powers because he sees them effective in history – or rather, since these are the powers of the spiritual life, in historical personalities. The reality to which I am referred in my search for the meaning of my existence is an historical reality.

How this idea works in the concrete is shown in Reischle's article entitled 'Do We Know the Depths of God?'[9] I shall

[8] R. Paulus, *Das Christusproblem der Gegenwart*, Tübingen, 1922, p. 67.
[9] *ZThK*, I (1891) pp. 287–366.

quote an excerpt from it in full since it gives a characteristic exposition of the significance of the historical person, Jesus. The passage should make clear how wholly impossible that whole way of thinking has become for us today.

In the first place, through Jesus Christ, the more unreservedly we submit ourselves to the influence of his person, the more our conscience is awakened. As the first disciples were made ashamed, sometimes by the word of Jesus, sometimes by his act, sometimes by his silent look, so also our hearts smite us if we open our hearts to Jesus' words, actions, and suffering. Furthermore, anyone who supposes that he has already attained to a religious and ethical character will, through the person Jesus, first come to understand what personality is and how incomplete and inwardly divided we really are in contrast to him. We know ourselves to be double-minded in our assurance of faith, vacillating also in our pursuit of our highest moral ideals, fettered by a grosser or a more refined sensuality, influenced even in noble deeds or heroic suffering by many secondary motives, never free from that self-dramatization (ὑπόκρισις) which enjoys playing a role for the applause of the gallery.

In no other way can the confusion of our ethical concepts be more plainly revealed nor our moral self-deceit be more radically destroyed than by the inexorable clarity with which Jesus Christ displays before us in word and act the will of his heavenly Father. But if we let these harsh truths speak directly to us in the person Jesus, provision has been made that no hatred of moral truth will arise out of the experience. For in him the supreme good meets us directly as true value. Only by this impression is self-judgment awakened in the conscience.

Opposition to that incorruptible moral judge is still less possible for us, since the person Jesus shows not the slightest trace of the pride in virtue which fears association with the pollution of sinners. The worst charge his enemies could bring against him was 'Behold, a glutton and a drunkard, a friend of tax collectors and sinners' (Matt. 11.19). The reproach of the Pharisees (Luke 15.2), 'He receives sinners', has become in all Christendom a ringing, jubilant witness to the second great influence which emanates from him – his love for sinners. That love breaks down for us all shrinking mistrust of him who is better than ourselves; it awakes in us courage for the joyful certainty that we exist for him and therefore for the kingdom of righteousness in which he himself lives and towards which all his work is directed. The conviction that we, in spite of everything, still belong to Christ and to the pure world in which he lives and moves is the conscience's comfort in face of the guilt by which we feel ourselves separated from the kingdom of the good – and this is the forgiveness of sin.

Anyone who clings to Jesus with all his heart in trust and conjoins his life to the person and the purpose of Jesus, already *has* forgiveness of sins. Jesus, in his dealing with the sinful woman who clung to him, the Saviour of sinners, bore witness to the forgiveness of her sins as a completed fact. From her actions it was manifest that her sins were forgiven. This is the mightiest influence which the person Jesus exerts on men's hearts. Sinners, in spite of their sins, feel themselves taken into fellowship with him and called to eternal life – that is, they find forgiveness.

Obviously, a figure of Jesus which modern criticism long ago made dubious is here accepted as historical. But quite apart from that difficulty, are there any of the experiences described which could not equally well result from intimate contact with other personalities of the past and present? The experience of the awakening and sharpening of conscience and the second experience of overcoming the shrinking distrust of someone who is better than I and the realization that even I myself am called to the kingdom of righteousness – these are experiences which have continually occurred in the past and will continue to recur in human society in the future. However, the most cogent objection to Reischle's statement is the fact that in every such experience, the final criterion of validity is man's own moral consciousness. Therefore it is wholly unjustifiable to equate that second experience with the forgiveness of sin, for that forgiveness could then be obtained by contemplating an historical person.

Actually, the forgiveness of sin can never be won through the contemplation of history. Only a *belief* in forgiveness, *acts* of love and forgiveness, *consciousness* of love and forgiveness can be demonstrated in knowable history. I cannot prove from history that more is present than phenomena of this world; I cannot prove that love and forgiveness are here revealed objectively as acts of God and as acts which affect me. The man who is seeking love and forgiveness for himself is not helped by evidence that someone else is confident of having received love and forgiveness. That confidence could be illusion. Jesus' love of sinners may destroy my shrinking distrust of one who is better than I. But my sins are not forgiven by that experience; in my sins I stand immediately before God. The evidence of the actuality of such phenomena in history can certainly disturb and upset us; but no immediate knowledge of God's love and forgiveness can be derived from them. Furthermore, with what right could we assume that consciousness of the forgiveness of sins is not equally reliable when it is based on asceticism or on sacrifice? In history I certainly cannot find love and forgiveness as a force directed towards me, as the Word of God.

I can find only consciousness of love and forgiveness, i.e. subjective activities and conditions.[10]

The same objection holds against similar formulations, for example, that found in Heitmüller's *Jesus* (Tübingen, 1913).[11] He affirms (p. 158) that we have religious experiences even without Jesus. But those experiences 'acquire content and convincing force and certainty, they become revelation, *only* and *first* when they are conjoined with a powerful experience of the divine *outside ourselves*, only through contact with the streams of religious life which flow around us and encompass us'. Further (pp. 174f.), 'For the individual, the road to the Father does not necessarily lead by way of Jesus Christ. But the more sure and independent we wish to become in our faith, so much the less can we refuse to go by that way. . . . No faith escapes periods of uncertainty, of wavering, of trepidation – chiefly as consequence of our own sins. In such times we find a basis and support for our faith in the historical fact, Jesus of Nazareth, in whom we encounter a faith full of power and strength, independent of our desires, as a sure victorious reality.' A reality? What if Jesus' faith were also illusion? Are not illusions which were characterized by convictions of power and victory found elsewhere in history? What is the criterion by which we can determine that we are not allowing our illusions to be strengthened by the stream of life which encompasses us?

The pantheism of history which marks such statements appears especially clear in this excerpt (p. 162): 'The consideration of this figure, bringing him vividly before us, provides us with a means of edification, exaltation and inspiration. All of the religious forces, experiences, moods, impulses, and demands which are active in Christianity are visible, embodied in the figure of Jesus. His figure is the symbol and the bearer of all religious and ethical goods and verities. It becomes ever

[10] Cf. Barth, *Der Römerbrief*, 3rd ed. p. 61 (cf. ET, *The Epistle to the Romans*, p. 86): 'The fear of God as such is neither visible nor tangible nor in any immediate sense "real" in the world. It is not demonstrable historically or intellectually.'

[11] I am concerned – especially because of the voices raised in certain circles since Heitmüller's call to Tübingen – to emphasize once more that this whole discussion is directed against a theological trend and not against individual theologians. The statements I cite are characteristic of that position, not of Heitmüller individually. It would be very unfair to label his work as a whole 'liberal theology'.

richer, ever fuller of content. For into this figure are woven all
that later Christians have experienced. . . .' But what if all that
were illusion? Also, could the statement not apply equally to
the Roman Catholic cult of the Virgin Mary?

Similarly, according to J. Weiss:[12] 'On the whole, for the
majority of Christians today, the figure of the "Lord" has only
this significance. It accompanies us on our way through life as
a reverently honoured travelling companion, warning us and
rousing our conscience, comforting us and encouraging us, a
living, personal, contemporary manifestation of the holy and
gracious will of God.' In similar fashion, the credal confession
'Jesus lives' is understood solely in an earthly sense. 'The figure
of Jesus and his kind of life with God and for God is felt as a
moral power over our life – a power from which we cannot
draw ourselves away.' Likewise the Christmas meditations
which come from this circle have nothing higher to celebrate
than the belief that Jesus was a 'personality'. 'I no longer see
only the Christ-child. I see Christ; I gaze at him avidly, the
man, the strong, noble man . . . a person with a living pulse-
beat, tempted like us but victorious. . . . Before us we see his
form, his personality.'[13] And in an Easter meditation we may
read: 'Because the Lord gained the victory morally, even
though outwardly he succumbed, therefore his cause cannot
fail.'[14]

In all these varied formulations the 'stumbling block' (σκάνδαλον) has been removed from Christianity. All of them totally
lack the insight that God is other than the world, he is beyond
the world, and that this means the complete abrogation of the
whole man, of his whole history. Their common aim is to give
faith the kind of basis which destroys the very essence of faith,
because what they seek is a basis here in this world.

II

Deeply rooted in modern Protestantism, including Protestant
liberal theology, is the view based on Luther that our *secular
daily work* in the place assigned to us in history is service to God.
A man is not required to do some specific kind of work in order

[12] *ZNW,* XIX (1919/20), p. 139.
[13] *Morgenandachten* (see above, note 7), pp. 404, 405, 406.
[14] *Ibid.,* p. 119.

to serve God. Whatever work the labourer and artisan, the farmer and the merchant, the scholar and the official, perform in their own calling can be and ought to be performed as service to God. So far the view really is Luther's. But it becomes un-Lutheran when it is assumed that labour in every kind of occupation is in itself direct service to God; when it is forgotten that my activity in my own occupation can separate me from God and can become service to idols. My secular work, since it serves the purposes and forces which determine and promote human cultural life, can be the service of God only indirectly – never directly. Only when I recognize that the work *in itself* does not serve God, only if I undertake it in *obedience* and maintain an inner detachment from it, only if I do it as if I did not, can it be the service of God.

Here, also, God's Word can act only as a 'stumbling block'. 'My kingdom is not of this world' holds true here, too. However conscientiously we do the work of our calling, that work as such can never make it possible for us to know ourselves as co-workers in the service of God. God is wholly 'Beyond'. He calls in question both ourselves and our faithfulness in our calling. The idea that our regular work is a service of God can, if it is carried consistently to its conclusion, confront us again with the precariousness of our whole self. We are forced to admit honestly that if we *are seeking* God we do not find him in our daily occupation, that we cannot of ourselves prove a right to call our work the service of God.

Here again youth's criticism is indicative of the true situation. The young are searching for some cult in which the meaning of the service of God finds its expression, distinct from all service to the objectively given, distinct from all career-work motivated by the goals of this world. Here again Barth's answer to Harnack's question 13 is valid. 'What kind of theological tradition is it which, having started from the deification of "feeling", now seems to have made a successful landing in the slough of the psychology of the unconscious? . . . What kind of theology is it, if it notoriously stands in constant danger of losing its most gifted adherents to Dr Steiner?'[15]

Such a theology is clearly a theology which has not yet become aware that no activity *within the world* can be service to

---

[15] *CW*, 37 (1923), p. 91.

God, that worldly activity means that man has surrendered to the arbitrary rule of the forces of practical life in this world. The one essential is to understand the question, to listen to the 'stumbling block' of God's Word, the Word which declares that the world exists in sin and that man in the world can do nothing which can sustain the character of service to God.

But the identification of daily labour with the service of God is perhaps not an especially significant facet of liberal theology. Its attitude towards practical life may be more revealing in another aspect. Liberal theology betrays its true character in so far as it commits itself to the view that specific ideals for the activity of life in the world are to be derived from faith. That is to say, that Christian concepts of the kingdom of God, of love, *et al.*, can determine man's life within the world, that they can provide the norm, setting the goal and showing the road to it. The consequences of this view are clear in such slogans as 'the work of God's kingdom', 'the vineyard of God on earth',[16] 'Christian Socialism', 'Christianity and Pacifism'.

If anyone supposes that social work – i.e. work concerned with the creation of proper social conditions which are suitable for human beings, whether the work is officially 'welfare work' or not – is as such the work of God's kingdom, that it is 'Christian action', then he is unaware of the 'stumbling block' of the Word of God. The 'stumbling block' is very much bigger, very much more obvious when that Word speaks the stern judgment, 'That is not a Christian act', against actions which in themselves are a duty, worthy of honour, and terribly necessary.

No act exists which can relate itself directly to God and his kingdom. All forms of community life, the worst and the most ideal alike, stand equally under the judgment of God. We except ourselves from that judgment, we refuse to take it seriously, when we suppose that in social work or in total abstinence from alcohol or the like (just because the duty to perform such acts is recognized) it is possible to produce in this world some sort of situation which is more pleasing to God. Therefore, for example, the *general* question of whether a *Christian* must be a pacifist is to be rejected. *Each man* must answer the question for himself in his specific historical situa-

[16] A. von Harnack, *Das Wesen des Christentums*, Leipzig, 1900, p. 78; ET, *What is Christianity?*, New York and London, 1901, p. 132.

tion. If pacifism is an ideal of human society, then even if its realization lies in the infinite future, in which lie the realizations of all ideals, pacifism would be a *human* possibility. But God's Word demands the impossible from man, impossible in every sense. It demands that man live a sinless life. And we fail to recognize the 'stumbling block' when we ignore the sinfulness of our whole life and activity, when we think we can fulfil God's demands in the historical course of human life.

Harnack fails to recognize this 'stumbling block' when he asks (in question 5); 'If God and the world (life in God and life in the world) are in absolute contradiction, how are we to understand the close conjunction, in fact the equation on one level of *the love of God and love of one's neighbour*, which forms the core of the Gospel? And how is this equation possible without giving *supreme* value to ethics?'[17] Barth answers: 'Precisely the Gospel's combination of love of God and love of neighbour is the strongest proof that the relation between our "life in the world" and our "life in God" is a relation of "absolute contradiction" which can be overcome only by a miracle of the eternal God himself. For what fact in the world is more alien, more incomprehensible than just a "neighbour"? Is there any fact on which we are more in need of God's revelation? The "supreme value of ethics" – yes! But in accepting that value, do we *love* our neighbour? Can we love him? And if we do *not love him*, what about our love of God? Could anything show more clearly than this "core" – not of the Gospel but of the Law – that God does not make alive until he has first put to death?'[18]

The problem of Christianity and Government finds a characteristic answer in Harnack's *Wesen des Christentums* (*What is Christianity?*).[19] When Jesus says: 'Give to Caesar what is Caesar's and to God what is God's'; when he says: 'You know that those who are supposed to rule over the Gentiles lord it over them and their great men exercise authority over them. But it shall not be so among you . . .' one ought not to think at once of our contemporary governments. 'Law and legal requirements which depend only [!] on force, on actual force and its use, have no moral worth.' 'It is a mockery of the

[17] *CW*, 37 (1923), p. 7.   [18] *Ibid.*, pp. 89ff.
[19] Pp. 67f.; ET, pp. 113–16.

Gospel to say that it defends and sanctifies every authority which presents itself as law and government at a given moment.' Of course! But it is an absurdity to suppose that there can ever be any law and government which is apart from a given historical moment, that is apart from force, apart from sin. There can be *no legal authority* which as such is sanctioned by the Gospel. All authority stands always under the judgment of God.

The Sermon on the Mount demands the impossible; therefore to make it the norm of activity within the world is not only entirely futile but also involves the refusal to recognize its character as a 'stumbling block'. This character is ignored when Harnack asks: 'And is the demand which they [the words of Jesus] impose really so out-of-this-world, so impossible?' And he ignores it equally when he speaks of 'the ideal which should hover before our historical development as goal and guiding star'. And what is our reaction today when we read: 'In contrast to two or three hundred years ago, we today already feel a moral obligation to move in this direction. The more sensitive and therefore more prophetic among us no longer view the kingdom of love and peace as a mere Utopia'?[20]

All attempts to derive ideals of possible human conduct from the Christian faith deny the 'stumbling block'. *In Christian faith,* man is without sin and the fellowship of Christian believers is a fellowship without sin. Both, therefore, are impossibilities on earth. On earth there is no direct service of God. 'We cannot be blind to the warning which is raised against the whole, to the final all-encompassing provision which applies not only to forbidden actions, but with especial force to all permitted, even to all commanded actions.'[21]

There is service of God only when man surrenders himself to God's judgment and then obediently under God takes up the work in the world to which God has set him, when he never averts his eyes from the sin of the world – especially not from his own sins – and never dreams that any sort of approximation to God's world can be realized in this world. 'A system of ethics for this world, based on the Gospel, would have this singular

[20] *Ibid.*, pp. 70, 72; ET, pp. 120, 122f. Cf. also *Morgenandachten* (see above, note 7), p. 395: 'Now you are not obligated to do the impossible – only the possible.'

[21] Barth, *Der Römerbrief*, 3rd ed., p. 276; (cf. ET, *The Epistle to the Romans*, p. 293).

character: its action would be without any immediate relation to God and the Eternal.'[22] Certainly the behaviour of the man of faith (if the existence of men of faith may be assumed) will appear different from that of the unbeliever. But in what respects it will differ cannot be deduced from his faith. He will learn the difference through his obedience when he takes upon himself service in this world with the responsibilities and the duties which are realities in this world and for this world.

The Word of God is a 'stumbling block' for this world and primarily a 'stumbling block' for an earnest mind, for the moral consciousness. Here again Barth and Gogarten state the conclusions which are actually inherent in liberal theology. For who has emphasized more forcibly than W. Herrmann that there is no specifically Christian ethic? And who has shown more convincingly than Troeltsch[23] the problematic character of the relation of the Christian to the world?

III

What conception of *God and man* forms the basis for this criticism of liberal theology?

God is not a given entity. The question with which Reischle was concerned, the question of the adequacy of our knowledge of God, must be rejected completely. For that question conceives of God as a given entity of which direct knowledge is possible, as an object which we can recognize in more or less the same way as other objects. Such knowledge could be a possession and could produce effects within our life. It could progress and grow like other segments of knowledge. But it could still not take us to God, who can never be something given, something which is, so to speak, crystallized in knowledge. God, on the contrary, is known only when he reveals himself. His revelation comes only contingently; it is *act*, act directed towards *men*. God's revelation does not make him something known in the sense of intellectual knowledge.

God is not a given entity. This truth is equally valid against a religion of experience, which supposes it possible to achieve

<hr/>

[22] Gogarten, *ZZ* 2, (1923), p. 21.
[23] *Die Soziallehren der christlichen Kirchen und Gruppen*, Tübingen, 1912; ET, *The Social Teaching of the Christian Churches*, London and New York, 1931.

contact with the divine object by substituting spiritual states for intellectual knowledge. God becomes equally a directly accessible object, whether he is conceived as creative life forces, or as the irrational, or as anything else of the sort.

Nor, however, is God 'self-actualizing' or 'unactualized' in the sense of idealistic philosophy, so that God may actualize himself to man's intellect by the process of revelation or may be actualized in the Logos, which lies at the roots of rational human life. That would involve the deification of man. *God represents the total annulment of man, his negation, calling him in question, indeed judging him.* Whether God is known adequately or inadequately, whether or not God is to be spoken of in anthropomorphic terms is irrelevant.[24] The one essential question is: What does God represent for men? And wherever the idea of God is really grasped, the result is the radical calling of man in question.

Now this result – this 'minus sign before the bracket' – does not mean *scepticism*. No doubt of man's intellectual capacity is involved, no degradation of his reason, no passive resignation. On the contrary, it becomes impossible to speak of God so cheaply as to call him 'the irrational'. Indeed it is impossible to think highly enough of reason. Precisely when reason has followed its road to the end, the point of crisis is reached and man is brought to the great question mark over his own existence.

'Calling in question' is *not pessimism*; it is not despair of the world under the impact of its evil or its suffering. All pessimism makes man its criterion – man's moral judgment or his claim to happiness. And for exactly that reason, such pessimism is sin before God, because it implies both man's claim to happiness and his claim to his own righteousness.

Man as such, the whole man, is called in question by God. Man stands under that question mark, whether he knows it or not. His moral transgressions are not his fundamental sin. 'It is not a matter of a few steps more or less on this road.'[25] *Man's fundamental sin is his will to justify himself as man,* for thereby he makes himself God. When man becomes aware of this, the

[24] Cf. Luther, *Genesisvorlesungen* 1535–45 on Gen. 1.2, Weimar ed., vol. 42, p. 12; for English edition see J. Pelikan, ed., *Luther's Works*, vol. 1: *Lectures on Genesis*, St Louis, 1958.
[25] Eduard Thurneysen, *Dostojewski*, München, 1921, p. 53.

whole world is taken off its hinges; for man then puts himself under the judgment of God. The whole world – which was *man's* world – is annihilated; nothing in it any longer has meaning and value, for everything had received this from man. But to know this judgment is also to know it as grace, since it is really liberation. Man becomes free from himself. And for man to become free from himself is redemption. Man then knows that the question is also the answer; for it is only God who can *so* question him. And he knows that the answer is primary. A question so radical cannot originate from man, from the world. But if the question is asked by God, then it originates from the claim of *God* on man. Man is called.

The knowledge of this truth is called faith. *Faith* cannot generate itself in man; it can only arise as man's answer to the Word of God in which God's judgment and God's grace are preached to him. Indeed, faith can be in man only as God's creation. So far as faith is real in man, it manifests itself in him as obedience to God's Word. The man who has faith is therefore the man whom God has transformed, the man whom God has put to death and made alive again; he is never the natural man. Faith is never self-evident, natural; it is always miraculous. The belief that God is the Father and man is the child of God is not an insight which can be gained directly – it is not an insight at all. On the contrary, it must be believed, ever and again, as the miraculous act of God. But it must be *believed*, truly, in faith.

Evidence of the extent to which liberal theology has bypassed this 'stumbling block' is all too plentiful. For example, we are told that man's sonship to God 'appears in Paul as a definite, specific act of adoption of men who before were not sons of God. But *our* sonship *we* feel in Jesus' sense, like the sunshine which always surrounds us, which we thank for life and happiness, which is always there so that our task is only to make use of it.'[26]

The Word of the cross is often distorted. In orthodox theology it was reduced to the sacrifice of reason (*sacrificium intellectus*). In liberal theology it appears as the demand for sacrifice in a moral sense, as the demand for a self denial which will serve the growth of personality. In the meditation for the Wed-

[26] J. Weiss, *ZNW*, XIX (1919/20), p. 131.

nesday before Easter there is a section describing the school of suffering in which the disciples of Jesus were trained. 'First under the impact of the suffering and death of Jesus and then through their own experience as disciples, the process of separation between the human and the divine continued spontaneously (!). They learned to understand the law of sacrifice, without which the kingdom of God cannot come, and the law of self-denial, without which personality cannot be fully shaped – all in the light of the cross of Christ.'[27]

The meditation for Good Friday reads: 'But how can I believe in the love of God if I do not feel it in my heart? How can I accept as blessing that which is clothed in the trappings of ill (namely, suffering)? There is only one way. You must make something good out of it for yourself. You must lift the stones, lay hold of them and fit them into your building. You may bruise your fingers on them; yet if you consider how the hidden man within your heart grows thereby and becomes strong, then in the apparent evil you will discover the eternal love, the hidden blessing.' Christ is the prototype for this experience. 'He knows the truth: I hold my life in my hands and make out of it what I will, not what they will. Thus he bore patiently the external conditions of his life; but he made something out of it. He moulded his life into something, into the great blessing by which we live and with which we nourish ourselves unto this hour.'[28]

The Easter message reads: 'My work, my struggle, my life is not in vain. The whole has a future. . . . Beyond humanity, yes far beyond and above humanity, grow the men of God. He who sanctifies and purifies himself for a higher life, begins to grow here among men, begins to grow into that "other world", the world of eternity. The meaning of the Easter message is this: there has been One who purified and sanctified his life for a higher life; and when he had fully matured into the complete, divine man, then he discarded this human existence and entered the fullness of the world of spirit, the eternal world of God. Jesus Christ is the first who grew into this world of eternity. He was the first, but he will not be the only one.'[29]

In a meditation for New Year's Eve we find: 'Man is a crea-

[27] *Morgenandachten* (see above, note 7), p. 115.
[28] *Ibid.*, pp. 117f.   [29] *Ibid.*, p. 120.

tion of intelligence; and as he is the latest and newest such creation, his duty is to follow along the trail of that creativity. He must inquire into and ponder over the wonderful designs which are under his feet and visible to his eyes, from the tiny worm in the ground to the idea which like a star at midnight is fixed in the infinite. . . . Keep in mind, you creation of Intelligence, how you have followed the trail of creation and by your observation and wonderment have glimpsed a whole behind the multiplicity as behind a veil. . . . Yes, there is plan and meaning and order and intelligence in all and over all; it is called light.'[30]

It is hard to know whether to be more astonished at the absence of any trace of the message of the New Testament or at the ignorance which does not dream that all the ideas here expressed are a part of the homiletics of the Cynics and Stoics. Anyone acquainted with Epictetus, for example, will at once notice the similarity, which extends to partial verbal identity. The evaluation of Jesus accords with this view of the world and man. He is accepted as the pattern, as was Heracles or Diogenes among the Cynics and Stoics, as one who bore the burden of his labours and 'made something' out of his life. Of course, the passages I have quoted are extreme examples, but they are not exceptional. In their crassness they are symptomatic and they give proof that something significant has been forgotten in liberal theology.

It is not surprising that such disregard of what is essentially Christian has not remained unopposed within liberal theology. It is not only research into the history of religion with its attention focused on what is characteristic in historical phenomena which has registered opposition to the unrestrained rationalization and moralization of Christian ideas. Rudolf Otto's book, *The Idea of the Holy*, in particular, resulted from the theological situation very much as did the protest of Barth, Gogarten and their circle. Otto's designation of God as the 'Wholly Other' and his emphasis on 'creature feeling' as the essential element of religious piety are characteristic of that protest. Just as the purpose underlying his concept of 'the Holy' was to define the nature of the divine as beyond the sphere of the rational and

[30] *Ibid.*, p. 410.

ethical, so equally his emphasis on the inner relatedness of the moments of dread (*tremendum*) and fascination (*fascinans*) in the numinous has an analogy, which is more basic than the obvious parallelism, to the assertion of the inner conjunction of the knowledge of judgment and of grace. But certainly the theological solution which Otto proposed for this paradoxical situation leads in the opposite direction.

Barth's divergence is shown most plainly in his consistent emphasis on the truth that *faith is not a state of consciousness.* No doubt, along with faith there is also a state of consciousness – at least there can be. But as long as it is a state of consciousness it cannot be faith. To speak of the faith of men is to accept the full paradox of asserting something which cannot be affirmed of any visible man, something which is completely unverifiable as a spiritual situation and which must never be identified with any such situation. From this concept of faith arises the polemic against all 'religion of experience', against piety, sense of sin, and inspiration. Hence comes the utter scepticism of religion as such, since religion claims to be a particular area of human spiritual life in which inheres the relation of man to God. On the contrary, the real truth is that what is confessed in faith is the calling in question of the *whole* man by God. The justified man, the new man, is believed in faith.

Whatever belongs to religion is something present with man and in man. It can be, indeed it must be, doubted time and again. I can never so relate myself to my experience that I can put my trust in it. I can trust only the promises of God. Even if the revelation of God is understood as the revelation of judgment and grace, the meaning is not that the two are successive experiences. The despair is not conceived as a sort of overwhelming preliminary stage which must be surmounted so that it may be followed by the consciousness of redemption. The despair, radically conceived, is the realization that the natural man is trying to flee from before God and that he cannot flee because he was trying to flee before *God*. That despair, therefore, comes only when there is awareness of God. But when there is awareness of God as God, flight has ended and a turning to God has begun. There are not two acts. *Faith is not an act which can be performed once for all*, an act by which justification is achieved. Nor is it an act which is repeatable, so that judgment and grace, sin and forgiveness alternate in human life. Only the man who knows *himself* to be a sinner can know what grace is. He knows himself as a sinner only in so far as he stands before *God;* therefore he can only know of sin when he also knows of grace. The sight of God's judgment and God's grace *together* belongs to the nature of faith. There is no grace except grace for sinners, no grace except grace in judgment. And as man can only speak of sin with real meaning if he sees himself before God, so also he can speak of grace only as grace for sinners. There is no possible standing ground on some achieved insight; there is no position which can be permanently won. For man *always* remains a sinner and he is always under condemnation and justified. Here it is truly necessary to speak of 'walking on a knife edge'. Even that metaphor is a very inadequate expression of the paradoxical character of faith. The grace of God is never a general truth; it is always real only in the act of God directed to a specific man. The judgment of God is never universal. Anyone who thinks it can be so conceived does not yet stand under that judgment.

Justification is not a qualitative change in men of this world; it is never present except in the 'Beyond', in God's judgment. The 'new man' is always the man of the 'Beyond', whose identity with the man of this world can only be believed in faith. So Barth can repeat Luther's paradoxical dictum: 'We only believe that we believe.'

Faith so comprehended is distinct from every kind of *mysticism*. Mysticism, too, wills to seek God beyond the given, not only beyond the natural world but also beyond intellectual and spiritual life. Mysticism follows its path methodically, calling upon us to silence everything in us, even all intellectual and spiritual activity. In pure passivity, in the emptying of the self, the mystic is prepared for the revelation of God. God enters the soul so prepared and fills it with joy unutterable.

The first objection to such mysticism is the necessity of rejecting the possibility of any method of reaching God. Even silence as a method is human activity. In this falsity ($\psi\varepsilon\tilde{\upsilon}\delta\sigma\varsigma$) is revealed the primary falsity ($\pi\varrho\tilde{\omega}\tau\sigma\nu\ \psi\varepsilon\tilde{\upsilon}\delta\sigma\varsigma$), the delusion that an escape from the given is possible – as if man could escape from himself, as if he were not obliged to put up with himself just as he is.[31] We cannot suppose that the annulment of men and world is an act within the power of man to perform by abstraction, by averting his eyes or closing them – while all the time it is *I* myself who am practising the annulment.

No! The annulment can come from God alone and it is always dialectical – that is, this world is always sublimated by a 'Beyond' and never replaced by it. In the latter case, the Beyond would always itself become this world, just as it does become a very real this world in that 'joy unutterable'. Since the Beyond can never become this world, just as my justification can always be only justification in the Beyond in which I have faith, clearly this justification is not any kind of supernatural quality in me. Yet *I* am the justified person. This means that man does not need to escape from himself, as the mystic assumes. Only the *sinner* is justified. Hence the justified person is an individual man who accepts the whole burden of his past, present and future. With that burden he stands under God's judgment. To desire to escape that burden means to desire to flee from God's judgment and to know nothing of grace.

In view of the whole situation presented here, we can understand why Barth refuses to assume a definite theological position.[32] Naturally when he is engaged in a theological argument, he cannot avoid adopting a position. Yet there are good grounds for his refusal. One reason is that the refusal is an expression of the truth that faith, the exposition of which is theology, is not an actual position which a man, even if he is a theologian, *can* take. In practice faith always happens as an act of God; and seen from the human point of view it is the abandonment of every position. Faith is the supremely paradoxical cry: 'I believe, Lord help my unbelief'. But then it follows that because theology can be nothing other than the exposition of faith, no concepts of knowledge which have meaning can be gained from it apart from the miraculous actualization of faith. The subject of theology is God. Theology speaks of God because it speaks of man as he stands before God. That is, theology speaks out of faith.

[31] Cf. W. Herrmann, *Realencyc.*, I[3], p. 498, lines 29ff. 'Where we ourselves are, there is the world. The man who seeks to reach God beyond this world is therefore attempting the impossible. When he thinks he has found God, he has got hold of nothing more than a fragment of the world or a world conceived as abstractly as possible, divested of its perceptual concreteness.'
[32] *ZZ*, I (1923), pp. 3f.

2

WHAT DOES IT MEAN TO SPEAK OF GOD?[1]

[1925]

I

I<small>F</small> 'speaking of God' is understood as *'speaking about God'*, then such speaking has no meaning whatever, for its subject, God, is lost in the very moment it takes place. Whenever the idea, God, comes to mind, it connotes that God is the Almighty; in other words, God is the reality determining all else. But this idea is not recognized at all when I speak *about* God, i.e. when I regard God as an object of thought, about which I can inform myself if I take a standpoint where I can be neutral on the question of God and can formulate propositions dealing with the reality and nature of God, which I can reject or, if they are enlightening, accept.

Anyone who is persuaded by arguments to believe the *reality* of God can be certain that he has no comprehension whatever of the reality of *God*. And anyone who supposes that he can offer evidence for God's reality by proofs of the existence of God is arguing over a phantom. For every 'speaking *about*' presupposes a standpoint external to that which is being talked about. But there cannot be any standpoint which is external to God. Therefore it is not legitimate to speak about God in general statements, in universal truths which are valid without references to the concrete, existential position of the speaker.

It is as impossible to speak meaningfully about God as it is about *love*. Actually, one cannot speak *about* love at all unless the speaking about it is itself an act of love. Any other talk about love does not speak about *love*, for it stands outside love.

Therefore a psychology of love would in every case treat of

[1] *TB*, IV (1925), pp. 129–35.

something other than love. Love is not something external in respect of which it is possible either to act and speak or to refrain from acting and speaking. Love exists only as a determining element of life itself. Love *is* there only when I love or am loved; it has no existence alongside me or behind me.

The same is true of the relation of fatherhood and sonship. When that relation is viewed as a natural phenomenon – so that it can be spoken about – the essential character of the relation is not discoverable, for the relation then appears as a special case of a natural process which operates between individuals of the same species. Where the relationship really exists, it cannot be viewed from outside. That is, it is not something in respect of which, for example, the son can claim for himself or permit to himself this or that, or feel himself obligated to this or that because of it. The essential relation is destroyed when any thought of this 'in respect of which' enters. It *is* there only where in his life the father *lives* truly as father and the son as son.

If the preceding statements are correct, then, for example, the *atheistic position* taken by any particular science would not consist in a denial of the reality of God. It would be equally atheistic if, as science, it affirmed that reality. For speaking of God in scientific propositions, that is, in general truths, means speaking in propositions the significance of which is their universal validity – a validity which is not related to the concrete situation of the speaker. But just because the speaker speaks in this manner, he puts himself outside the actual reality of his own existence, and therefore at the same time outside God. He therefore can speak only of what is not God.

To speak of God in this sense is not only error and without meaning – it is *sin*. In his interpretation of Genesis, Luther made it very clear that Adam's sin was not really the act of eating the forbidden fruit by which he disobeyed the command. His sin was that he raised the question, 'Ought God to have said?' He began to 'argue about God' (*disputare de deo*) and so set himself outside God and made God's claim upon men a debatable question.

If we try to evade this condemnation by saying: such discussion may not have intended any ill; it could on the contrary arise from intellectual honesty, from the longing for God, then

we should merely have demonstrated once more that we have
not comprehended the concept of God. We should have fallen
into the old error and should again have represented the
omnipotence of God and the determination of ourselves by it
as a fact to be accepted as a universal truth, like the dependence
of every earthly object on the law of causality. But then we
should have wholly failed to comprehend what the determination of our existence by God means. For that determination
also involves the *claim* of God on us. Consequently, every setting of ourselves outside God would be a denial of God's claim
on us; it would therefore be atheism and would be sin.

A different conclusion would be possible only if neutrality
in relation to God were a possibility. But to assume such a
position of neutrality is to abandon the idea of God. Adam
thought he could flee from before God; but God's claim is not
annulled by flight. Consequently, speaking about God becomes
sin. And *sin* it remains – even when it arises from a sincere
quest for God.

It is therefore evident that if we are in a situation which
requires that we honestly argue about God, we are sinners and
of ourselves can do nothing to escape from sin. It would not
help us at all if, because of a correct understanding of the idea
of God, we determined to stop 'argument about God' (*disputare
de deo*). For to speak otherwise of God – and that would mean
to speak 'from God' – is obviously nothing we can undertake
of ourselves. As *our* undertaking, that would again be sin, because it would be merely an undertaking *of ours* in which the
thought of *God's* omnipotent rule would be abandoned. Speaking of God as *from* God can evidently be only the gift of God
himself.

II

It is therefore clear that if a man will speak of God, he must
evidently *speak of himself.* But how? For if I speak of myself am
I not speaking of man? And is it not essential to the concept
of God that God is the 'Wholly Other', the annulment of man?
Are we not then confronted by two negatives which make no
position possible for us except resignation to silence? On the
one side is the specific certainty: no speaking in which we
detach ourselves from our own concrete existence is a speaking

of God. It can only be a speaking about our own existence. On the other side is the equally specific certainty: no speaking of ourselves can ever be a speaking of God, because it speaks only of man.

Actually, every confession of faith, all talk of experience and of the inner life would be a man's speech. And however enthusiastic the confession of faith which another man makes to me, his confession would be of no help to me in my situation of doubt unless I were willing to deceive myself. Indeed, even my own experiences, if I tried to put my trust in them or to depend on them for support in the situation of doubt, would dissolve in my hands. For who can assure me that the experience was not an illusion? That it is not something I should leave behind? That I do not now see reality more clearly?

Or ought the claim none the less to be made that we are speaking directly *from* God when we confess our faith, when our inner life speaks, when our experience finds expression? That unquestionably can happen. But *at the very moment* when we set before ourselves *our* creed, *our* inner life, *our* experience *on the basis of which* we trust in God, or when we recommend them to others as something *on the basis of which* they can be certain of God – in that moment we are speaking *about* our existence and have detached ourselves from it.

The situation is the same when we go looking for experiences and coveting them for ourselves. We are seeking after ourselves, not after God. If, looking backward or forward, I rely on myself, then I split my personality. The relying self is my existential self; the other self on which I rely, taking it as something objective, is a phantom without existential reality. And the existential self, who looks around, who questions, is proved by this very questioning, this looking around, to be godless. So if we wish to speak of God, evidently we cannot begin by speaking of our experiences and our inner life, for both of these lose their existential character as soon as we objectify them. It is in opposition to this human nature seen as something objectively given that the statement that '*God is the Wholly Other*' is valid.

But that statement has meaning only in such a context. That is, its meaning is understood only in relation to the primary statement that God is the reality that determines our existence. Detached from the first statement, the second can only mean that God is *something* wholly different from man, a metaphysical being, a kind of an immaterial world, perhaps of a complex of mysterious forces, a creative source (at this point any assertion that the terms are used figuratively is itself misunderstanding, because God here is really being thought of in purely naturalistic terms), or finally, *the Irrational.*

A piety which desired to base itself upon this conception of God would be flight from before God, because man would be trying to flee from the very reality in which he exists. What he desires to escape is precisely his own concrete existence; yet only in that existence can he grasp the reality of God. This kind of modern piety strikingly demonstrates how right Luther was in saying that the natural man flees from before God and hates God. For man in seeking to escape from the reality of his own existence is endeavouring to escape from that wherein alone he can find God.

It is quite understandable that the pseudo-god of 'the Creative' or 'the Irrational' can bewitch and seduce the human hunger for God, for this pseudo-god promises man freedom from himself. But this promise is a misconception and a fraud. When man tries in this fashion to be freed from himself, he runs away from God – since God is the power determining his concrete existence – and runs into his own arms, since such concepts as the creative force and the irrational are human abstractions, and the experiences on which man relies in such relations are the most human of transactions. The idea of the 'Wholly Other' can never be utilized in any such way. Moreover, a man does not really escape from God. For since his relation to God is that of hatred (*aversio*), his existence deter· mined by God is the existence of a sinner.

When speaking of God the Almighty, therefore, the concept of God as the 'Wholly Other' cannot mean that God is something apart from me for which I must search, and that in order to find God I must first escape from myself. The statement that the God who determines my existence is nevertheless the 'Wholly Other' can only have the meaning that as *the* 'Wholly Other' he confronts me who am a sinner. Furthermore, in so far as I am *world*, he confronts me as *the* 'Wholly Other'. To speak of God as the 'Wholly Other' has meaning, then, only if I have understood that the actual situation of man is the situation of the sinner who wants to speak of God and cannot; who wants to speak of his own existence and cannot do that either. He must speak of it as an existence determined by God; but he can only speak of it as sinful, as an existence such that *he* cannot see God in it, an existence in which God confronts him as the 'Wholly Other'.

III

We thus find ourselves in the same astonishing predicament in relation to our existence as in relation to God. We cannot really talk about either; we have no power over either. What is involved here?

Reality, as we commonly use the term, reflects a view of the world which has dominated our thinking since the Renaissance and the Enlightenment, both of which were under the influence of the world-view of Greek philosophy. We consider something to be *real* if we can understand it in relation to the unified complex of this world. The relation may be thought of as determined causally or teleologically, its components and forces may be conceived as material or spiritual. The antithesis between idealism and materialism is irrelevant for the question with which we are concerned.

In both views, the picture of the world is conceived without reference to our own existence. We ourselves are observed as an object among other objects and are put in our proper place in the structure of this picture of the world which has been fabricated without reference to the question of our own existence. When this picture of the world is completed by the inclusion of man, it is customary to call it a world-view (*Weltanschauung*). We strive to acquire such a world-view or, if it supposedly has been attained, to propagate it.

It is not surprising that such world-views are very highly valued even though they present an estimate of man which is not very flattering, describing him as the accidental result of a combination of atoms, as the highest vertebrate, related to the apes, or as an interesting phenomenon of psychological complexes. Such explanations do man the great service of freeing him from himself. They relieve him of the problem of his concrete existence, of anxiety about it and responsibility for it.

That is, of course, the reason why man desires a so-called world-view. He can turn to it when he is confronted by the riddle of destiny and death. He can dismiss the problem of his existence from his mind when his existence becomes shattered and precarious. He need not take the moment of crisis seriously, for he can understand it simply as a special case of a general class, fit it into a context, objectify it, and so find a way out of it.

But that very view is the primary falsity (πρῶτον ψεῦδος) and it leads necessarily to mistaking the truth of our own existence, since we are viewing ourselves from outside as an object of scientific investigation. Nor is there any gain if we label ourselves 'subject' in distinction to the other objects with which we see ourselves in interaction. For man is seen from outside even when he is designated 'subject'. Therefore the distinction between subject and object must be kept separate from the question of our own existence.

Nor will there be any improvement if we take a theistic or a Christian 'world-view', accepting some idea of the dependence of our existence upon God, and then assume that the incorporation of such assertions in our world-view will satisfy all claims and comprehend our existence. For here again God is seen from outside as an object, just as men are.

Anyone who holds the modern view of the world as a world governed by law, has a godless conception of the world, even though he may think of the laws governing the world as forces and forms of divine activity, or look upon God as the origin of this rule of law. The work of God cannot be seen as a universal process, as an activity which we can observe (as we observe the workings of the laws of nature), apart from our own existence. Nor can it be conceived as a process into which we can subsequently insert our own existence in order to make it comprehensible to ourselves. In that case, we should have abandoned the primary concept of God as the reality determining our existence. This we admit unintentionally and unconsciously whenever we clearly differentiate ourselves in our essential being from the working of the laws governing the world. Nobody considers the living relationships by which he is bound to others in love, gratitude, and reverence to be functions of law – at least not when he is truly living in them.

Clearly, then, it is not feasible to think of God as the world-principle on the basis of which the world and our own existence along with the world becomes comprehensible. For then God would be seen from outside and the affirmation of his existence would be a general truth with its place in a system of cognitions (universal truths), in a self-supporting system that was also meant to support our existence – instead of being an expression of our existence. For God would be objectively given; and knowledge of that *given object* would be accessible to us and could be achieved at will. God or his existence would be something *in respect of which* we could establish an attitude of one kind or another. But this is again the primary falsity. For if the idea of God is taken seriously, God is nothing *in respect of which* anything at all can be undertaken. For then he would be seen from outside and we should equally have been looking at ourselves from outside.

We cannot say, for example, that because God rules reality, he is also my Lord. Only when a man knows himself in his own existence to be claimed by God, has he reason to speak of God as the Lord of reality. For all talk of reality which ignores the element in which alone we can have reality – that is, talk which ignores our own existence – is self-deceit. God can never be seen from without, can never be something at our disposal, can never be a 'something in respect of which'.

Since it is a fact that the world seen from outside is godless and that we, since we see ourselves as a part of the world, are godless, it is again clear that God is the 'Wholly Other', not because he is somewhere outside the world but because this world, being godless, is sinful. This world seen from outside, the world in which we move around as subjects, is our world. We take it seriously and thereby we declare it sinful.

Only one double truth of our existence is clear: (1) We do worry about our existence and must exercise responsibility for it: 'It is *your* business' (*Tua res agitur*). (2) Our existence is wholly insecure and we cannot make it secure – to do that we should have to stand outside it and ourselves be God. We cannot talk about our existence since we cannot talk about God. And we cannot talk about God since we cannot talk about our existence. We could do the one only along with the other. If we could talk of God from *God*, then we could talk of our existence, or vice versa. In any case, talking of God, *if* it were possible, would necessarily be talking at the same time of ourselves. Therefore the truth holds that when the question is raised of how any speaking of God can be possible, the answer must be, it is only possible as talk of ourselves.

IV

But does it not follow from the situation just depicted, from the recognition that we are sinners and therefore wholly other than God, that we ought not to speak at all? That would necessarily also mean that we ought not to act at all! Does not the belief that God is the 'Wholly Other', that he is the annulment of men, lead to *Quietism?* Anyone who thought this would be making the old mistake – that is, he would be regarding the idea of God as something *in respect of which* a specific attitude is possible or appropriate. This would be the mistaken assumption that the concept of God can be entered on the credit side of a ledger, that we have it as something objectively given which we can utilize.

If the ideas of God as the Almighty and the 'Wholly Other' are taken seriously in their strict relation to each other, they clearly show that we are not given authorization to investigate for ourselves or to decide on intellectual grounds whether we ought to speak or be silent, act or be quiet. The decision is God's. And his decision is simply a question of *must* for us. We *must* speak or we *must* keep silent. We *must* act or we *must* not-act. The only true answer to the question of whether and when we can speak of God is: if we *must*.

But we shall do well to consider the true meaning of that 'must'. For according to our established pattern of thought, we still see this 'must' from outside. We see ourselves, who *must*, as the object which lies under the causal compulsion of a subject; here specifically we see God who gives the command as the subject. This means that we see men's being determined by God, of whom they *must* speak, as a natural process observable from outside. But the only *must* which can be meant here is a free act. For only a free act springs from our essential being; it is only in a free act that we are ourselves and are completely whole. Such a free act is obedience. For obedience means freely to put one's self under a 'must'. This does not mean a work which we must decide to undertake as the will of God.

For in that case God would really be seen from outside and we should not be really ourselves in the work which we accomplish and present to God; we should be standing outside it. Obedience means complete dependence – not as a religious emotion but as a free *act*, since only in act are we ourselves. Therefore this *must* means obedience.

Consequently, one can never ask in general when such a *must* may confront us. Nor can one have beforehand any knowledge of this *must*. For such knowledge would require a position outside the compulsion, and hence outside the self of those who *must*. The meaning of this existential *must* would then be completely misunderstood. The act which is done because a compulsion preceded it cannot be done as a free act. The act can be free only if it is *simultaneous* with the *must*.

It need hardly be said that this does not mean that the act arises from a compulsive enthusiasm or any other emotion, or out of a secret depth in our inner self. In that case the *must* would signify a natural necessity. A greater or lesser degree of enthusiasm has as little to do with a free act as has greater or lesser resistance, greater or lesser self-mastery, which may make an act appear to be a greater or a lesser sacrifice in human eyes. We are not discussing psychological compulsions. The *must* is a word spoken by God and is wholly outside our control. Only the free act is ours.

We are, of course, speaking hypothetically when we say that there is the possibility for us to speak and act from within God *if* that possibility is a *must*. We cannot know beforehand whether such a *must* may become a reality for us. We can only make clear to ourselves the meaning of such a *must*. We have to understand that on our part it can be only a free act, because otherwise it would not involve our existential being. We can only *believe in faith* that the *must* is a reality.

v

This and nothing else is the meaning of *faith*. But belief in the *must* does not exhaust the meaning of faith. For when we say that only the free act is ours, that statement – or rather the conviction that some specific deed is our free act – is itself only faith. For the free act which is truly the expression of our existence (in the proper sense we exist only in such action and not otherwise and such action is really nothing other than our existence itself), the truly free act can never be known in the sense of being objectively proven. It cannot be offered for investigation as something 'to be proved' (*probandum*). For in that case we should be objectifying it and putting ourselves outside it. A free act can only be *done* and in so far as we *speak* of such doing, the possibility of it can only be believed.

Thus we find ourselves led to the conclusion that our own existence, since it depends on our free act, can never be known by us. Is this existence illusion? Unreality? Certainly it is nothing about which we have knowledge, about which we can speak. And yet it is only our existence which can, if it is really present in our speaking and acting, give reality to that speaking and acting. *We* can only believe it in faith. And does this faith lie within our powers so that we can decide to adhere to it? Obviously faith must also be a free act, the primary act in which we become certain of our existence. But this basic act is not an optional affirmation which we decide to make. It is obedience, a *must* – it is, in truth, faith.

The question of how to attain such faith is insoluble if it is understood as a question about a process which takes place while we look at ourselves from outside. It makes no difference whether the process is conceived rationalistically or psychologically, dogmatically or pietistically. The question has meaning only when it asks what faith means – and in this sense it is unavoidable.

Faith can be only the affirmation of God's action upon us, the answer to his Word directed to us. For if the realization of our own existence is involved in faith and if our existence is grounded in God and is non-existent outside God, then to apprehend our existence means to apprehend God. But if God is not universal law, nor a principle, nor anything objectively given, obviously we can know his reality only because he speaks to us, only because he acts upon us. We can speak of him only in so far as we are speaking of his Word spoken to us, of his act done to us. 'Of God we can only tell what he does to us.'[2]

The meaning of this Word of God to us, this act of God upon us, would then clearly be that God, granting us existence, makes righteous men of us sinners, that he, forgiving our sins,

[2] W. Herrmann, *Die Wirklichkeit Gottes*, Tübingen, 1914, p. 42.

justifies us. This would not mean that he overlooks this or that trivial or serious misdeed, but that he gives us freedom to speak and act from God. For only in action as the free expression of a person – or rather in the free act in which alone a person really exists – can persons come into a relationship with persons. Such relationship is totally destroyed if the action is brought under the category of conformity to law.

But this statement cannot be interpreted to mean that God inspires us, making us into ecstatics or miracle workers. It means that he accepts us as justified even while we are separated from him and can only talk *about* him or ask questions about him. It is not that some special, demonstrable change happens in our lives, that we are imbued with special qualities and can do special things or speak special words which are of a non-human kind. What could we ever do or say that would *not* be human! But *this* has happened: all our acts and words are freed from the curse of dividing us from God. Our speech or action always remains sinful, since it is always something undertaken by us. But as *sinful* it is justified; that is, justified *by grace*. We never possess *certain knowledge* of God; neither do we *know* our own reality. We have both certainties only in our faith in God's grace.

Could faith then be the Archimedean point from which the world is moved off its axis and is transformed from the world of sin into the world of God? Yes! That is the message of faith. But anyone who wanted to question further on the necessity of faith, on its correctness, on its basis, would get only an answer referring him to the message of faith which comes to him with the claim to be believed. He would receive no answer which would demonstrate the rightness of faith before any authority. If there were such an answer, the Word would not be *God's* Word. God would be made answerable to man's judgment. Faith would not be obedience.

Wholly fortuitously, wholly contingently, wholly as specific event, the Word enters our world. No guarantee comes with it by virtue of which it is to be believed. No appeal to authority can have a preferential claim on the belief of others, whether it be made for Paul or for Luther. Even for ourselves, our own faith can never be a standing ground on which we can establish ourselves. Faith is continually a fresh act, a new obedience.

It always becomes uncertain again as soon as we observe ourselves from outside as men and begin to question ourselves.
It is always uncertain as soon as we reason about it, as soon
as we talk about it. Only in act is it sure. It is always sure as
faith in the grace of God who forgives sin and who, if he pleases,
justifies me who cannot speak from God but can only undertake to speak about God. All our action and speech has meaning only under the grace of the forgiveness of sins. And that is
not within our control. We can only have faith in it.

Even this lecture is a speaking about God and as such, if
God is, it is sin, and if God is not, it is meaningless. Whether
it has meaning and whether it is justified – none of us can judge.

3

KARL BARTH, *THE RESURRECTION OF THE DEAD*[12]

[1926]

KARL BARTH'S book is a brief commentary on the First Epistle to the Corinthians. Chapter 15, as the climax of the Epistle, is discussed in detail. The primary characteristic of Barth's interpretation is his insistence on *understanding the whole letter as a unity*, in contrast to the usual view which sees in it a chance conglomeration of passages, the themes of which were determined by the needs and demands of the moment.

Barth does not dispute either 'the largely fortuitous character of the specific topics treated in I Cor. 1–14' nor 'the absence of an explicit connective relating I Cor. 15 and its new theme to the preceding sequence' (pp. 1f.; ET p. 6). Rather, the unity which he finds emerges out of the question, 'first, whether Paul's decisions on the topics treated in I Cor. 1–14 are as unrelated as the topics themselves, or whether there is not discernible a single train of thought which binds them intrinsically together. And second, is I Cor. 15 to be understood as only one topic among others? Does not rather a central thought which ran through chs. 1–14 now emerge in full clarity, so that the theme of ch. 15, even though it may appear as one theme among others, is really to be accepted as *the* theme of the whole letter?' (p. 2; ET p. 6). The unity to be looked for is therefore a material unity, i.e. one grounded in the subject-matter, not some sort of 'spiritual' unity which would depend on the unity and individuality of the one author's personality.

No one will want to deny that this method of inquiry is both appropriate to the content of the Epistle and fruitful for de-

[1] *TB*, V (1926), pp. 1–14.
[2] K. Barth, *Die Auferstehung der Toten.* University Lectures on I Cor. 15. Munich, 1924 (I have not yet seen the second edition). English translation by H. J. Stenning, *The Resurrection of the Dead*, London, 1933. Page references to the translation are marked ET.

tailed exegesis. The inner unity so defined could even be present if the composition of the Epistle were not only the result of the accidental circumstances attending its writing, but also if the Epistle as a whole were the composition of a redactor who combined sections out of various letters of Paul, as B. J. Weiss believed. If such a material unity is really present, then it will certainly have left its mark in all exegesis which is at all true to the content of the Epistle. But there is great gain in every way when the question of such unity is consciously raised and is accepted as the guiding line for exegesis.

Barth, however, does not present this idea merely in the general form in which it is, in my opinion, indisputable. He gives the particular interpretation that the basic theme, the real purpose of the letter, finds explicit expression in the words of ch. 15. Therefore the whole commentary can be given the title *The Resurrection of the Dead*. This title, too, seems to me to be fully appropriate to the content. In it is expressed the fact that Paul's preaching is eschatological proclamation. That of which he is continually speaking is the end of this earthly man and his world. In other words, Paul defines the life of the believer as life characterized by faith in Christ's resurrection and hope for his own resurrection.

If this faith and hope are sincerely held, they are not something that a man can *also* have along with other ideas as an adornment or a comfort of life. They determine the *whole* of the Christian's existence and bring him into a particular relation to the world. Consequently every question which arises in the area of his existence in the world can be rightly dealt with only from the point of view of eschatology. If Paul can really hold this faith and this hope steadfastly, then everything he says about man must belong under the title, *The Resurrection of the Dead*.

Of course this concept can be used for exegesis only as a *question*, not as a recipe. As a question it provides a *critical standard* gained from Paul himself for use in interpreting separate statements. Exegesis would thus have gained the possibility of being in a real sense material criticism. How far Barth himself uses the leading theme as a guide for his interpretation must therefore be the object of investigation. And at the same time another question must be considered. Is this specific judgment that the theme of I Corinthians find its most authentic expression in ch. 15 exegetically justified?

This is all that I have to say by way of introduction. The question of the relation between historical and theological exegesis, so much discussed in connection with Barth's *Commentary on Romans*, need not be interjected here. Barth's own statement in the Preface makes it unnecessary. If the aim in both kinds of interpretation is the understanding of the content, they belong together in a unity. And 'when exegesis with a preponderantly historical interest and one with a preponderantly theological interest are kept separate, the result is certainly defective' (p. 1; ET p. 4). Barth's commentary on I Corinthians does not stand in opposition to historical-philological interpretation, but uses it or supplements it. Consequently a discussion of the book has value only if it follows the course of Barth's interpretation, emphasizing what is important and debating what is questionable.

The *first part* of the book (pp. 2–56; ET pp. 5–100) presents a masterly exegetical survey of chs. 1–14. The treatment of chs. 1–4 (the rival parties in the Corinthian community) is most illuminating. The 'from God' (4.5) 'is obviously the hidden nerve of this whole section (and perhaps not of this section alone)' (p. 4; ET p. 16). The contending parties in Corinth rob God of what is his, of his right of judgment, his majesty, his freedom, in order to deify instead religious personalities or party programmes. Paul does not support one party (his own), and he makes no effort to settle the dispute by a consideration of the question of which party is relatively more in the right. He will not permit the Gospel to be made into a debatable programme, into an idea, into an occasion for the development of spiritual power. The *first lie* (πρῶτον ψεῦδος) of the Corinthians is their substitution of a belief in their own faith either in God or in particular leaders for faith in God. They confuse faith with human knowledge and convictions. Against this, Paul preaches the power of *God* and the wisdom of *God* (cf. 1.24, 31; 3.21).

Here one of Paul's main ideas is, I think, rightly given. In my judgment, however, a false colouring is added when Barth, misled by a side glance at the contemporary world, interprets the party divisions of the Corinthians as parallel to modern 'personality cults'. Actually the Corinthians seem to have regarded the party heads as mystagogues (cf. 1.14–17) and as gnostics. They evidently expected to attain salvation (σωτηρία) by means of the sacraments and knowledge (gnosis).

In meeting this situation, Paul does not merely deal with the question of parties in itself. With equal force he opposes the delusion that knowledge is a way to God. God's saving act of the cross (σταυρός) cannot in any way be *comprehended* as a possibility of salvation; if it could be, it would not be an act of *God*. For men the Christian proclamation is 'folly' (μωρία), and it cannot be legitimatized to men's reason as 'wisdom' (σοφία). As a *comprehensible* possibility, it would necessarily be no more than a possibility within the scope of man. Therefore no relation to God is given in knowledge, in gnosis, as a human quality. Or as Barth says, God can be only subject, never the object in man's relation to God.

But it seems to me that the dialectic inherent in the situation now needs to be recognized. The Corinthian parties think that by their party slogans they are representing the 'from God' (4.5). That they have instead bound themselves to men is Paul's judgment, not their intention. The dialectic of the situation lies in the fact that the 'from God' can in any particular case of human reality only be expressed by taking a specific stand; that is, such a party slogan can in certain circumstances be duty.

Of course, the 'from God' can be rightly pronounced only as a corrective, as a warning. 'God always remains subject in the relation created by that testimony. God is never transformed into the object, into the possession of man, giving man a right to speak, to speak a final word' (p. 4; ET p. 16). That is true – but when we speak, when we are obliged to try to speak, therefore even when we are speaking in order to validate the 'from God', God is the object.

Not that Barth is unaware of that! But it seems to me here, as on other occasions, that the presentation of his exegetical insights lacks a certain clarity and intellectual precision. So I believe that I am in fundamental agreement with Barth if I carry his explanation a little further. The solution of the problem here lies in recognizing that the *freedom* of leader and programme does not mean the proclamation of subjectivity (whether that is understood rationally as autonomy or romantically as immediacy) and individualism. Such freedom means freedom from one's self and at the same time from an individualism of motives and opinions based in the self. But this surrender of self is not a mere waiting, nor is it a silence (however holy) nor mysticism. It is laying hold of the Word of God.

Now this laying hold of the Word of God must not be mere dogmatism or speculation; it must be an act in which lies the reality of my existence. By this act declaration is made that at this very moment I must speak, must act, must affirm, because my 'now', being claimed by God, is made the moment of decision. (Paul so acts, disregarding the consideration that what he is saying could become another party slogan.) But in understanding the character of my 'now' as demanding decision, I am also freed from taking *my* speaking and action as a system or programme. I confront it in freedom, so far as it is something to hand, done and said. But again, this is not the freedom of relativism, as if here was something needing improvement when measured against an aim or a goal (though this will, of course, happen). I am free in the knowledge that my speaking or acting has meaning (reality) (even if it is 'correct'), only if it springs from decision; beyond that it has no objective validity.

If what has been said is true (that is, if Paul's conception of the matter is correctly interpreted), as Barth also believes, then it is clear that Barth is right in calling Paul's 'standpoint' eschatological. If at the end of all that we can comprehend stands death, then it follows that every human standpoint, held as a position *beyond the decision*, is only a *situation* and is therefore temporary, is already past, is death. Consequently we *know* nothing of a life 'which we can comprehend as the life of *God* – since the most we have is an empty concept of it – apart from the fullness given by God alone and his revelation in the *resurrection*' (p. 7; ET p. 20).

But, on the other hand, it is in my judgment also clear that Barth's interpretation of 2.6–3.2 is not acceptable. For here Paul speaks of the 'cross' (σταυρός) as 'wisdom' (σοφία), not in a paradoxical sense (cf. 1.24, 30), but as an announcement which is intelligible to the human understanding as 'wisdom'. Granted, this is true only for the 'perfect' (τέλειοι), the spiritual (πνευματικοί). But what does the concept *spirit* (πνεῦμα) mean here? It seems to me certain that these terms, and *natural* (ψυχικός) in 2.24, indicate that Paul is here thinking along the lines of the mystery cults. In fact, ch. 2.7 describes wisdom (σοφία) as 'secret and hidden'. Here, therefore, wisdom is not 'the word of the cross' (λόγος τοῦ σταυροῦ) in the sense of 1.18ff., for that word is from henceforth revealed. That is true, even if one should apply *the hidden* (τὴν ἀποκεκρυμμένην) of 2.7 to the past and should say, according to v. 10, that for Christians it is hidden no longer; yet it remains hidden for others who do not belong to *us*. But 'the word of the cross' is being preached to *all*. An element in this λόγος is now stressed, by virtue of which it is 'wisdom' – and not only paradoxically as in 1.24, 30! There is therefore a way of regarding this word and a way of speaking it which proclaims it as wisdom. That such a view of the saving act is intended, is also shown in v. 8: if the rulers had been wiser, they would have perceived the plan of salvation.

Now Paul (according to 3.1) has not yet been able to impart this wisdom in Corinth. The ethical immaturity of the Corinthians is asserted, not as a judgment against them, but as a reason for this inability. It is impossible to interpret 3.1–3 with Barth as a lament 'that he had clearly not succeeded in being understood by them as "from the Spirit" ', that they 'were not yet in the position to hear his word as the Word of God' (p. 10; ET p. 25). The text says very plainly that Paul has not imparted to them the 'wisdom' defined in 2.6–3.2.

Actually in 2.6–3.2 specifically Pauline ideas are amalgamated with ideas peculiar to the mysteries. Chapter 2.10–12 emphasizes strongly that only God himself can be the subject of the knowledge of God. In the light of this, the important question is not that of the categories (which are, in fact, animistic) used in formulating the statement, but what is meant here as the content of the knowledge of God. The answer is truly Pauline, 'His free gifts to us' (τὰ χαρισθέντα ἡμῖν). (Here Paul is no longer thinking of the 'perfect' but of Christians in general.) But Paul does not hold to this idea consistently. For according to 2.6–9, the content of the 'wisdom' is myth, speculation *about* the 'word of the cross', *about* God; and therefore also *about* man (viewed as an entity of the cosmos).

But in the recounting of the myth, nothing at all is said

about my existence, about the reality within which alone I can hear God. For from what source do I get the knowledge of all that the myth tells (the rulers, the veiling of the nature of God, the deception of the demons, etc.)? Since Paul departs from his fundamental idea here, he falls into a contradiction which has often been commented upon. Particular chosen Christians, the 'perfect', are here described as the possessors of the Spirit, whereas in Paul's usual way of thinking, all Christians have the Spirit.

But the contradiction is not (as Lietzmann, for example, thinks) the one which is also (apparently) to be found in Gal. 5. 16f., 25; Rom. 8.12f. There the Spirit is not a possession given to us and under our control, to which an appeal can be made; the Spirit is present only where there is an appropriate way of life. In this passage, however, the Spirit is a possession which we can utilize, which justifies our claim to 'wisdom'. But the real contradiction is not that a Christian 'has' the Spirit, yet does not have it (as a possession). It is that all Christians as baptized persons have the Spirit yet only special individuals count as 'spiritual'. Thus it is not contradictory for the Corinthians in 3.1–3 to be called 'carnal' (σαρχιχοί) although they are baptized – on the ground of Gal. 5.16f., 25; Rom. 8.12f. that could be possible – but for the 'spiritual' as such, those who have control over the Spirit, to be set over against the others in the community.

Therefore is is clear that material criticism rightly objects to the use of the concept of 'wisdom' in 1.18–26 as a basis for the interpretation of the concept of 'wisdom' in 2.6ff. In 2.5–3.2, it is Paul's pride which declares that Christians, too, have a 'gnosis' which can compete with the gnosis of the heathen.

Therefore we are, I think, much indebted to Barth for bringing the interpretation of I Cor. 1–4 out of the area of explanation in terms of its historical context into the sphere of material discussion of its content. I also think that he has rightly seen the decisive point. But by a more exact exegesis which starts out from the determination of the meaning of the text in its own period, it is in my judgment possible to attain a still sharper conceptual comprehension of the result. Thus I myself cannot forgo the use of material criticism, which stems from the text itself.

The formulation which Barth offers for the contents of chs. 5–6 and their relation to chs. 1–4 seems to me outstanding. The Christian community by its (word *and*) ethos represents the crisis for natural man. Here, the guiding thought is the observation that Paul does not direct his moralizing to individuals but towards the community as such. 'The flaming sword of the "from God", which was there suddenly lifted as Christian truth over the religious vagaries of the Corinthians, here is raised in accusation and threat over their natural way of life, which they feel to be assured or even required by Paul's words "all things are lawful for me". Christianity brings not rest but unrest into the natural life' (pp. 14f.; ET p. 33).

There is, of course, need of a clearer explanation of the statement: 'Chs. 1–4 are *also* to be understood ethically and what is denounced in chs. 5–6 is *also* a lack of knowledge' (p. 11; ET p. 33). The 'all things are lawful for me' of 6.12ff. also deserves a more exact interpretation. In Stoicism, the criterion for the limit of 'all things are lawful' is the ideal man; that is, the correct understanding of our nature as being human. The self, for which the 'all things are lawful' holds, is defined by the inter-related concepts of reason (λόγος) and nature (φύσις). What is Paul's criterion? He accepts the 'all things are lawful' and qualifies it in his own way. The limit is set by the fact that the self belongs to the 'body of Christ'. But what is meant by that?

The body is the spiritual body, but Paul does not explain this concept (6.17). On the contrary, a new argument begins at v. 18, which emphasizes the importance of the 'body' in such a way that the concept *body* is given a physical character. Paul is not concerned, as e.g. Bousset thought, with the contrast between sensual and intellectual. In v. 19, the 'spirit' is emphasized and its nature is indicated at least so far as to declare it to be something outside the control of men, 'you are not your own'.

This much may be inferred in principle: there are no actions which are indifferent (though the point is not, of course, developed consistently, cf. 13a with 18), and the criterion by which actions are differentiated is neither the ideal *man* nor the spiritual *man*, but *God*. Man appears therefore as *claimed* and claimed radically, so that all the claims of the world must fall silent. It is this – the negation of the *claims* of the world – that is for Paul the real meaning of 'all things are lawful for me'.

Therefore Barth is in fact right when he closes his summary of chs. 5–6: '*Again* from a new angle there has become visible in outline something of what he [Paul] in ch. 15 will proclaim as "the resurrection of the dead" ' (p. 15; ET p. 33). For Barth, the meaning of ch. 7 reveals itself as: '*Above* his own well-grounded judgment on this point and *against* the enthusiasm of those who would make out of it a principle, stands again for Paul the "from God" of v. 7. Furthermore, from the rejection of the pleasures of life, from asceticism, no principle can be established separate from the glory of God; nothing true in itself can be established' (cf. v. 19). Therefore he can conclude: ch. 7 'makes it clear that the force of the "from God" affects not only the wicked man, but also the good man, even the over-good; that the meaning of the goal towards which the whole letter aims will be the glory of God – in truth only the glory of God' (p. 17; ET pp. 36f.).

This approach is vindicated as it becomes clear that Paul is treating every theme from the standpoint of eschatology. According to Paul, the Christian stands in a peculiarly broken relation to the world. The existence of the Christian is in the world but does not belong to the world. It belongs to the future which is God's (7.29–31). The Christian's manner of existence is to be developed again, in clearer concepts, in what Paul says about 'calling' in the section 7.17–24 – a section which Barth barely touches. If according to v. 19 neither uncircumcision nor circumcision means anything (before God), it follows that no concrete situation in which a man may happen to be means anything. In that case, of course, 'remaining' in a situation can be required only in a dialectical sense. For obviously, under specific circumstances, even uncircumcision or circumcision can be an object of command (ἐντολή) – for example, uncircumcision for the Galatians – though not as in itself a qualification but only as an act which has its meaning in the doing.

So the Christian way of life is never a definite situation, given or established, and anyone who becomes a Christian does not need to alter anything in the external situation of his life as such; he must remain in his 'calling'. The calling as such is a matter of indifference, as is a person's married status. This is not a demand for quietism; it is merely the emphatic denial that there are external signs by which being a Christian can be identified as quality to hand. What is required is 'keeping the commands of God' (v. 19). The Christian is claimed by God. Therefore the Christian can continually adopt different appearances, for he stands under the future, he belongs to the future; and any specific situation would be already disintegrating, would belong to the past.

However, for Paul in this passage, the 'calling' is clearly not the instant claim of God here and now, but (improperly) the circumstances of the individual when God's call comes to him; it is therefore a continuing situation. Now since being a Christian is not a situation, the 'calling', too, seems not to be a removal into a new situation but a claim upon the man called within his concrete historical existence. And this claim puts the man beyond the demands of his specific situation. The mark which characterizes a Christian is simply the mark of being called.

Here I am interpreting in agreement with Barth's understanding, as is proved by a statement which he makes on chs. 8–10. 'It is as if Paul took a sponge and would wipe out the counsel he has just given, when he writes (10.31): "whether you eat or drink or whatever you do – do all to the glory of God". That is the sole intent of this section' (p. 18; ET p. 38).

Freedom (ἐξουσία) is the theme of chs. 8–10. The Corinthians believe that their 'freedom' is given with their 'gnosis'. The statement is true, but their understanding of both gnosis and freedom is false. Knowledge (gnosis) in itself does not exist; or, to state it differently, there is no knowledge which gives results on which man can clearly rely. The principle of monotheism cannot be utilized as a basis from which conclusions can be drawn. For in the first place, God is not an object which exists in the same way as earthly things and which can be observed like them. And secondly, the Christian knowledge of God is present only as a determination of life (as obedience to the claim of God) which expresses itself as love (ἀγάπη). In other words, it is clear that God is not object but subject of the Christian's knowledge.

This truth Paul expresses by the use of a formula of Hellenistic gnosis (8.3). Therefore there is no contradiction between

8.1, 'we know that we all have knowledge', and 8.7, 'but this knowledge is not in all'. The gnosis in v. 1 is to be understood as the possession of a universal truth, a dogma; but in v. 7 it is an existential knowing. The possession of the former does not guarantee that a man is now living in this existential knowing. The Corinthians do not understand that, and therefore they also do not understand what Christian 'freedom' is.

Chapter 9.15–18 may also be explained somewhat more pointedly than Barth has done. The point of the section lies in the 'I am entrusted with a commission' (οἰκονομία). Paul finds it unthinkable that he should use the 'freedom', which he has as an apostle, for its own sake (or for himself!); and therefore he renounces it altogether. For him the renunciation is a demonstration that he is an apostle and that the 'freedom' only exists because the 'necessity' (ἀνάγκη) is laid upon him. It depends on that wholly and only. It is not like being a government official who has a railroad pass and then uses his freedom for pleasure trips. 'The exercise of that freedom has no positive value in itself' (p. 27; ET p. 54). 'Reward' (μισθός) and 'boasting' (καύχημα) are primitive ideas to express the fact that Paul acts, looking only towards God.

Then the unity with vv. 19–23 is also clear. The 'freedom' is not something that we have for our personal use; it is 'God's freedom' (p. 24; ET p. 49). Accordingly, the end of the section can follow (10.31–33): 'Whether you eat or drink, etc.' 'This naturally has no relation to the modern cliché that the whole of life, even eating and drinking, can be service to God. Paul is not discussing eating and drinking nor any other human activities; he is dealing with the use or misuse of the freedom founded on the knowledge of God. Whatever is done in the freedom which is dependent, *really* dependent on God, and that means done in the knowledge which is in no way a self-exaltation of men but rather a being known by God (8.3), is done to the *glory of God*' (p. 28; ET p. 56).

It is therefore evident throughout that the life of the Christian stands under the 'end' (ἔσχατον), under the future of God. 'Paul is concerned equally for the Corinthians who are on the *better* way and for those on the worse. The former, as well as the latter, must experience the encounter with God as the end of *their own* way' (p. 29; ET p. 57).

Barth's comments on 11.2–16 are also excellent. The actual subject-matter here is not important; that is, the particular custom of wearing a veil is of no significance. The essential point is that there is in Corinth (as Paul sees the situation) a tendency to deny the authority of the husband over the wife. This tendency involves a view of life which Paul attacks, defending his own conservative position. The question how far his view can be disputed is not raised. But in his view a third consideration is important. In the order of nature we run against impassable barriers which direct us upwards, towards that which remains wholly different, wholly incomprehensible – towards God. Repudiation of this natural order is the folly of the Corinthian tendency. The reference to the differences of the sexes as given in the natural order implies no difference in their relation to God. (Christianity does not hallow earthly ordinances!) But the order must be respected as a sign pointing towards the order of God of which it is indicative.

Therefore – so I think the interpretation should continue – natural relations are not reasoned away (still less human existence within them). It cannot be said: natural relations mean nothing before God, therefore we will ignore them. (That would assign a very dubious meaning to them.) The actual man is still circumscribed by nature. It is not a self-evident fact that natural differences mean nothing in the sight of God; nor is it something to be demonstrated by man himself. It is valid only 'in the Lord' (ἐν κυρίῳ, v. 11).

Chapter 11.17–34, like 11.2–16, sets forth 'the disparagement of the natural man who was flourishing mightily in the Corinthian community, with his drive for self-willed, self-seeking self-assertion and self-vindication' (p. 33; ET p. 63). This characterization of the section by Barth is, of course, somewhat too general; his commentary does not do justice to all the twists of the text. But the meaning of the instruction in v. 26 is rightly interpreted: 'Paul's interest is focused on the act as such, not as in later periods on the relation between the elements and the significance of the sacrament. Those who partake announce by their participation . . . that they know their Lord and know that He is outwardly invisible but yet is as immediately present with them as that which they eat and drink. . . . In this ceremony, verily, the shadow which Christ casts over the whole of this earthly life cannot be forgotten. Is it possible to perform this act without trembling before the great precariousness with which this world of ours was forever branded in the night when our Lord was betrayed?' (p. 35; ET pp. 66f.).

A climax is reached in the interpretation of chs. 12–14 as containing 'in the picture that they reveal, something of the end of history or, more accurately, something on the boundary of the end of history' (p. 37; ET p. 70). In the central section, ch. 13, 'the actions and the struggles of men are viewed in the same way as in the chapters already discussed – only here the judgement is expressed without ambiguity. Even the acts of the gifted, the inspired, the "spiritual" man terminate at the point where an end is made of man as man, where the best gifts must be judged as fragmentary (ἐκ μέρους, in part) and where "they shall pass away" ' (p. 38; ET p. 72).

Though in ch. 13, 'a human possibility is shown to be the ultimate possibility of all, beyond the last', it is clear that '*this* human possibility is *God's* possibility for men' (p. 39; ET p. 72). Love (ἀγάπη) is not an ethical ideal but an eschatological event. Nor, however, is the enthusiasm present in the spiritually gifted something that can be classed with primitive manifestations or psychic excitement or understood through analogies from the history of religion and the analyses of the psychology of religion. Such manifestations are of course divorced from any clear ethical connotation. On the contrary (however much truth there may be in such comparisons), love is to be understood only as the ultimate human possibility, absolutely beyond the area of healthy, bourgeois religious mediocrity.

These enthusiastic manifestations are to be taken seriously – but they are in fact ambiguous. All such phenomena can, as the parallels in the history of religions prove, arise outside the Christian community. But *within* the community they all stand under an affirmative sign. 'The significance lies actually not in the manifestations themselves but in their source and goal, in that to which they point, of which they bear witness' (p. 40; ET p. 75). But as soon as they are accepted 'for themselves' within the community (for example, when their relative values are compared), they have lost all relation to their source.

But then it follows that 'within the community' does not

provide a decisive criterion for historical judgment. The identification of these manifestations as spiritual gifts cannot be made by observation. Whatever is 'divine' in them is not something objective to which man can point. Their 'divine character' depends on their origin. The gift is unidentifiable apart from its origin; nor can the origin be recognized apart from the gift. The divine origin is therefore not a structural element but is present only as a vivifying force. In other words, one does not *possess* spirit, one *is* spirit or one is not.

How does this affect the criterion that these gifts are gifts of the Spirit when they are present in the Christian community? The community is not just a bunch of enthusiasts: it is constituted not by its members but by Christ. It is the 'body of Christ' (12.12f.). The relationship with what *we are not*, with the act of God consummated in the sacrament (12.13), is our only legitimation. But this relationship to the act of God is naturally nothing other than faith. Paul is speaking to Christians, to those who have faith. The real question to which ch. 12 leads is this: how can those who believe, experience the reality of the Spirit in their lives, how can they be certain that in their action and refraining from action the Spirit is made manifest? To that question the answer reads: there is one possibility only, and it lies beyond the 'gifts' ($\chi\alpha\rho(\sigma\mu\alpha\tau\alpha$); it is love. The puzzling sequence of thought (ch. 13 between 12 and 14) now becomes clear. Chapter 12 concludes: a usable criterion for the divine character of the gifts does not exist. The gifts are present in the community and their divine character depends on the act of God (the sacrament) on which man relies. But what is the way of life of the man who is a member of the community by which he may know himself to be a believer? Love!

Certainly, one cannot say to the unbeliever, 'You must pursue love' (14.1, Goodspeed's translation). But Paul is writing to a Christian community. In that community the indescribable eschatological event becomes real, so far as love is really present in it. And in the description of love (13.4–8) in which 'the predicates of love there heaped up simply negate man as subject' (p. 47; ET p. 86), it becomes clear that the preaching of 'love' is preaching the resurrection of the dead.

I said earlier that Barth's interpretation of chs. 12–14 is the climax of his book. That emphasis is no accident, but corresponds to the fact that chs. 12–14 constitute the climax of the letter if the unity of its contents is accepted. If the theme of I Corinthians is the 'last things' – not as an object of speculation but as a reality in the life of Christians – then the climax of the letter is actually ch. 13 with the interpretation just given. Barth, however, takes ch. 15 to be the climax, for there the resurrection of the dead is the explicit theme. What then should be said of Barth's treatment of ch. 15 (pp. 56–125; ET pp. 101–213)?

'The doctrine of the last things is the content of I Cor. 15' (p. 56; ET p. 101). 'Last *things*, however great and significant they might be, are as such not *last* things. He who would speak of *last* things can only be he who speaks of the *end* of all things, speaks of their end understood so radically and so fundamentally, speaks of a reality so absolutely above all things that the existence of all is wholly grounded in that reality alone. Therefore he would be speaking of an end of all things which in truth would be nothing other than their beginning. And of final history and ultimate time only he would speak who would speak of the end of history, of the end of time. And he would speak of their end understood so fundamentally, so absolutely, he would speak of a reality so radically above all happening and all temporality, that while he speaks of the ending of history, of the ending of time, he would at the same time be speaking of that which is the foundation of all time and of all that happens in time' (pp. 57f.; ET p. 144).

Is Paul in I Cor. 15 speaking in this sense of *last* things, of the end of history? Actually he does speak of that, but at the same time he is speaking of last *things*, of the 'closing scene of history' which Barth very rightly distinguishes from the real end of history in the sense just defined. The closing scene of history is, namely, 'history which comes at the close of history, at the close of the life history of individuals as well as of world history or church history or even of natural history. It is outside the possibilities known to us, but yet is always, although it is new and unknown, wider, still a possibility which follows the known in an unbroken sequence, even if perhaps accompanied by unprecedented catastrophes. It takes over the known and continues it on a higher level' (p. 56; ET p. 102).

Now it seems to me certain that Paul in I Cor. 15 is speaking of such a closing scene of history, although such speaking is really outside his legitimate concern and his intention. In other words, full, exact understanding of I Cor. 15 is not to be attained without a thorough critical study of the content. (This Barth gives only intermittently, as for example on v. 29). However little Paul proclaims any kind of 'world-view', like every one else he is unable to avoid having one; and he has to say whatever he says using terms intelligible within the context of his world-view. It is not allowable to explain away the components of this world-view (in Paul's case mythological components) as simply figurative; or to by-pass them by a re-interpretation. The charge made by Barth against later Christian eschatologists, that they constructed out of the biblical material a closing scene for history which was not the real end of history, holds also against Paul. For Paul takes his material from Jewish or Jewish-gnostic apocalyptic; Paul also 'stopped halfway' (p. 59; ET p. 105). That we as critics, perhaps, come no farther than Paul, does not release us from the duty of criticism.

But it must be emphasized still more strongly that criticism is *analysis* and that the exegesis of I Cor. 15 must not remain stuck fast in the reconstruction of an interesting phenomenon of a past period, but must understand the chapter as the 'attempt to say the impossible' (p. 61; ET p. 106). Barth says rightly: 'Of the real end of history it is possible at every time to say: the end is near!' (p. 59; ET p. 106). It is therefore true that Paul is actually speaking of the end of history, for he sees men actually standing before God, as chs. 1–14 showed. And it is also true that when Paul speaks of the resurrection of the dead, he is not speaking of the 'non-existent, the unknown, the unattainable, nor of a second existence, of something further to be learned, of a higher future possession. He is speaking of the source and the truth of all that is existent, all that is known to us and possessed by us' (p. 60; ET p. 108). For when Paul speaks of the resurrection of the dead, it is clear that he means to speak of *us*, of our reality, of our existence, of a reality in which *we* stand. He is not discussing something about which we can speculate and to which access could be gained by knowledge or by some kind of human behaviour – either by moral action or sacrament, asceticism or mysticism.

Our resurrection *is*, with the resurrection of Christ, a reality (15.20–22). But it is not unimportant that Paul in expressing this truth uses the oriental salvation myth of the Original Man, since knowledge of the myth helps us to explain his separate statements more accurately. On the other hand, it is false to imagine that he liquidates our own existence in myth; for chs. 1–14 showed how he understood our existence.

Now Barth is entirely right when he emphasizes that for Paul the 'body' is inherent in the reality of man and that Paul therefore can speak only of a resurrection of the body. Any such concept as immortality of the soul is not only alien to him as an historically limited Jewish Christian but would also be wholly inadmissable for him. By using it he would abandon all that he says about the reality of men. If the resurrection of the body is denied, the *whole* of Paul is denied and one cannot then salvage Rom. 8.28 or I Cor. 13 as true and edifying (p. 69; ET pp. 122f.).

It also follows that Paul knows nothing of a 'Christian monism'. 'The idea of a soul surviving after death fits so neatly into a monistic view of the world – although perhaps it does not prove the possession of such a view. The resurrection of the body, however, of the same body which we see die before our eyes and which then ceases to exist, does not affirm a duality of this world and the beyond, but an identity between the two. That identity is not something already given; it cannot be established directly. It can only be hoped for, can only be believed in. Such an affirmation is the pitiless disruption of monism, is the "stumbling-block" and unreason and religious materialism' (p. 66; ET p. 117). Now, however, we are confronted with the necessity to investigate carefully what Paul understands by 'body' (σῶμα). (Barth failed to do this and his exegesis pays the penalty.)

Chapter 15.12–19 is rightly explained. Faith (πίστις) is vain if the uniqueness of Christ is denied. The kerygma rests on revelation and where this revelation is denied, the proclamation is vain. The miracle of Christ's rising from the dead means for Paul the establishing of the unique category, Christ. For if Christ stands only as a perfect manifestation of personal life (that was certainly not the idea of the Corinthians; for them Christ is a kind of mystery-cult deity), then he remains within the framework of humanity. Then there can be 'dogmatics' but not a kerygma. Christian monism, since it cancels the revelation, is trying 'to pull itself out of the bog by its own hair'. Naturally, the argument of vv. 12–19 is not trying to prove or postulate the truth of the revelation or of the resurrection of Christ. It confronts the reader with the Either-Or.

But it is evidently not correct (in this context) to interpret vv. 1–11 as Barth does: Paul is here defending himself against the accusation of the Corinthians that he had preached to them not the original gospel but his 'Paulinism'. According to Barth, Paul means to say: 'It was not and is not *my own* preference to impart to you the gospel with this strictly defined content . . . but I transmitted it as I myself received it. In other words, the gospel of the original community is in no way different from my gospel. You will gain nothing by trying to go behind Paul in order to find for yourselves a supposedly simpler and more acceptable gospel. For if you go behind Paul, then with your first steps you will come up against the same enigma which you think only Paul and Paulinism sets before you' (pp. 74f.; ET p. 139).

With this interpretation, Barth has supported his contention that vv. 3f. are not intended to be an historical account. In an historical account, 'in accordance with the Scriptures' would have no meaning! (But in the mind of Paul and of the whole Christian community, just the contrary was true!) For what kind of historical datum could there be, the truth of which depended on the resurrection of the dead? (But it is plain that for Paul the resurrection of the dead was accepted *also* as an historical fact!) The witnesses are said to be witnesses for the gospel and not for the historical fact; the place and time of the 'was seen' (ὀφθῆναι) are irrelevant; Christ's appearance is possible always and everywhere. (But how does that accord, in spite of Barth (pp. 81f.; ET p. 132ff.), with the 'most of whom are still alive' [v. 6] and the 'last of all' [v. 7]?) Neither vision nor objective fact can be deduced from the 'was seen'.

All of that interpretation seems to me (for better or worse) unacceptable. I can understand the text only as an attempt to make the resurrection of Christ credible as an objective historical fact. And I see only that Paul is betrayed by his apologetic into contradicting himself. For what Paul says in vv. 20–22 of the death and resurrection of Christ cannot be said of an objective historical fact.

I will not now discuss the point that Barth, in my judgment, has given a false image of the Corinthians for whom obviously Christianity was a mystery religion, so that his view of the historical situation leads him to some false interpretations of details. He is right, however, that vv. 20–22 definitively characterize the real situation of Christians. Consequently he can say: 'The coming of the Risen Christ (the Parousia) is not a different, second happening apart from His resurrection, but is only the final, visible, overt stage of the same hidden movement which in the revelation first became known within time. It is the fulfilment of all that which in time can only be grasped as *promise*' (p. 97; ET p. 167). Precisely when the gnostic salvation myth on the basis of which vv. 20–22 are formulated is known, it becomes clear that Barth's exegesis is correct here. For the fundamental idea in that myth is the inner unity of the cosmic events. The one *is* only so far as the other also is. But correct as Barth's interpretation is, it still cannot be denied that for Paul the parousia is a different, second event apart from the resurrection, since for him the resurrection and the coming are two temporal occurrences, are objective, 'historical' events.

Paul's view comes to clear expression in vv. 23–28. These verses are intended to support the *future* 'they shall be made alive' (v. 22) against the belief of the Corinthian gnostics who cancel the future and claim (cf. II Tim. 2.18) to have 'life' as a present possession as a result of the resurrection of Christ. Paul develops the futurity of the resurrection life (not the future situation!) in vv. 23–28. But he does it in a way which includes several statements from traditional Jewish–Christian speculation or from dogmatics (cf. the δεῖ in v. 25). And these statements, which are a part of the world-view that he takes for granted, describe the different dramatic events of the closing scene of history. A typical scriptural citation is meant to demonstrate this fact (that the conquest of death is the *last* event), which is most important for interpreting the passage.

Barth evades this by an impossible translation and interpretation. (He follows Hofmann of Erlangen.) The 'then' (εἶτα) of v. 24 is to be referred to the 'at his coming' (v. 23). 'At that time, at the end, is death, the last enemy, destroyed.' But apart from the impossibility of taking the intervening sentences [between 24a and 26] as a parenthesis, the text reads εἶτα (=*'after* this'), not τότε ('at that time'; cf. vv. 28, 54). The εἶτα (v. 24) therefore adds the third member to the first two ('first fruits' and 'afterwards'). And (for better or worse) Paul is speaking about different, temporally successive events. In Barth's translation of v. 24, 'for he has destroyed all separate origin', a most important idea has been arbitrarily injected and the meaning of ἀρχή has been misunderstood. Co-ordinated as it is in the sentence with 'authority' (ἐξουσία) and 'power' (δύναμις), it can only mean the ruling power of this world. In v. 27 it is impossible to make 'Christ' the subject of ὅταν δὲ εἴπῃ. We have here a typical exegetical formula, like δῆλον ὅτι in the following clause, so that it cannot be an independent parenthesis. In that case, a δὲ or a γάρ would be required. Finally, the ἵνα clause (v. 28), cannot depend on the τῷ ὑποτάξαντι but only on the ὑποταγήσεται, for that is the point of the sentence.

Why obscure the fundamental idea of the passage by so many artificial and tortuous experiments? For Barth has correctly recognized Paul's main point. Against all Christian monism, against mysticism and a spiritualistic belief in immortality, Paul is emphasizing that 'the present world situation and even our present relation to God – even the Christian's relation to God – is wholly provisional, an episode, is in fact an episode in the transition and the struggle' (p. 97; ET p. 168). Death is not overcome by us by means of a pious frame of mind or in any spiritual–religious–ethical kingdom of God on earth. Death is in the world as the pinnacle of all rebellion against God; and death will be overcome some day. The meaning of the kingdom of Christ and therefore also the meaning of Christian faith is never in any way encompassed in what is present and given. 'Rather, it is in its essence a hope and a waiting for that which in every time is only what is to come, only what is promised' (p. 99; ET p. 171).

It is in fact certain that for Paul 'life is not a given objective entity', but is future; and he does not speak of 'life after death' as an existing situation. 'The kingdom of God, however, is not, as it is often so easily supposed to be, an exalted continuation of this life – it is just the resurrection of the dead. To believe, to stand in the kingdom of God, means to be waiting for the *resurrection*. . . . A Christianity which does not accept *this* meaning of the kingdom of *Christ*, which is the kingdom of *God*, which is *the end of death*, – such a Christianity is nonsense' (pp. 99f.; ET p. 172).

It is also important to understand the relativity of the Christian religion. 'Relativity means dependence. The dependence is on God, who speaks His decisive Word in the resurrection of the dead. The presence or absence of this dependence decides the question of whether Christianity has a full true meaning or is complete unreason' (p. 105; ET p. 181). Hence we can understand that the words 'resurrection of the dead' are for Paul nothing but 'a paraphrase for the word, *God*' (p. 112; ET p. 192).

I accept all that as correctly interpreting Paul. But I regret Barth's failure to recognize that this meaning can be ascribed to Paul only on the basis of a critical study of the content. Barth himself involuntarily employs such criticism in his own ingenious paraphrases. But I do not think this kind of criticism, this analysis, is so easy to practise. However much I admire Barth's sure grasp of the central ideas of the text, I cannot proceed by his method. We are not dealing here with a mere juxtaposition of genuine Pauline concepts and ideas which belong to the area of the thought of his time. The two interlace and interpenetrate. In my judgment there is need of much more rigorous exegetical work and of closer analysis of the text if assured results are to be attained.

But even then the *hazard* of such exegesis must be much more strongly emphasized (and such critical considerations do indeed lie behind Barth's printed commentaries). It is no small matter when *the* ideas of Paul which are particularly plain and which were certainly important to Paul (the whole 'closing scene of history', for example) are so to speak explained away – whether it be by re-interpretation or by critical analysis.

The conclusions from the exegesis of 15.1–34 may be summarized as follows:

1. Paul knows nothing of an immortality of the soul. For him, 'life' is not the endless continuation of man's given present life (or even of the life conferred in a mystery). Therefore it is not something present, something 'natural'.

2. For Paul, earthly life is characterized by death. If he were speaking of the immortality of the soul that would not be true; death would then become just one event *within* life, something like a sleep from which man wakes again or like a journey which takes him to another place. This would be the case equally if the immortality is not ours from the beginning but is created by some 'medicine of immortality' (φάρμακον ἀθανασίας).

3. Accordingly 'life' for Paul can only be a future miracle which remains future so long as man is man, that is to say so long as man exists as a temporal being.

4. Nevertheless, 'life' for Paul does in a certain sense exist in the present, so far as through revelation the future has become reality in the present, or so far as man is himself future. There is therefore a peculiar identity between the present man and the future man; and Paul definitely names the 'body' as the bearer of this identity.

5. Therefore the being of man as such is characterized by the 'body' and by 'death'; the being of the Christian man by the 'body' and by the future of 'life'.

Now all of the above depends on the exact determination of the concept *body* (σῶμα) – perhaps it might be translated 'corporeality' – and vv. 35–44a can be, in a way, used for that purpose. What these verses intend to provide is an elucidation of Paul's *purpose*; actually they obscure his thought by their apologetic. Here Barth is again able to evade the necessary critical analysis by a very ingenious, but to my mind untenable, exegesis. According to him, the general sense of vv. 35–44a must be: 'Between life and life of the same entity there stands, if not the resurrection, at least something analogous. It could even be said: the enigma of the resurrection, between the seed and the plant, is death' (p. 108; ET p. 185). 'Take this (v. 36) to be the general answer and the examples may be found in vv. 37–41. In nature the same entity is met, (a) vv. 37f. in sequence, (b) vv. 39–41 simultaneously, in a totally different form without losing its identity. Then follows in vv. 42–44a the application of the double analogy: as in nature this change of predicates occurs without loss of identity, so also in the resurrection' (p. 108; ET p. 186).

The general characterization is correct. These analogies are not offered as proof; they are only intended to show that the resurrection is conceivable (p. 107; ET p. 186). In vv. 35–44 Paul really 'begs the question' (*petitio principii*) (p. 108; ET p. 186). It is also true that the analogy of the grain of wheat is not intended to present the resurrection as a natural process (p. 106; ET p. 183). Certainly the resurrection was not that for Paul – but neither was the germination of the grain of wheat. Paul has no conception of a 'natural process', as v. 38 shows, 'God gives it a body as he has chosen'. But that here one's thought is directed to the *Source* of nature, to its creation and redemption, cannot in my judgment be accepted. The problem of nature as such is not under consideration at all; only by inference is it clear that for Paul nature does not exist as an independent entity alongside God.

Further, it is not true that v. 36 can be taken as a general answer which is exemplified by the two analogies given in vv. 37f. and vv. 42–44a. For vv. 37f. and vv. 42–44a do not stand on the same level and v. 36 and vv. 37f belong immediately together.

The general sense of vv. 36–38 is perhaps correctly reproduced by Barth. The sprouting of the plant gives the image of a pure synthesis; that is, the natural event becomes intelligible when in our thinking we substitute the same subject for the wholly different forms of seed and plant. In the difference of the successive forms the same subject remains. ('The subject persists, the predicates have become different' seems to me an inadmissible formulation; the 'seed' is not a *predicate* of 'plant'). Actually the synthesis is a synthesis of plus and minus aspects which meet together at zero, the critical point which for the seed means death, for the plant sprouting. 'In the middle, in the wholly hidden critical point between before and after lies a creation, more exactly "a new creation".' With the affirmation of the unity of the subject, death as the middle point between the two forms is affirmed and with it the incomprehensible creative life. The 'one entity in the midst of death is changed into the new form in order in the change to prove itself for the first time as really *one*' (p. 109; ET p. 188). Of course here we 'do not yet have an understanding of God and the resurrection, but we have the possibility of understanding if they are given us to understand' (p. 111; ET p. 190). The resurrection, too, is a change, the subject of which is man. We know only one predicate, the old body; not the other, the new body. But so far as we see death here as we saw it in the seed, the assertion that for men, too, death is the point of transition is an understandable assertion. The critical point is conceivable as a turning point which leads from minus to plus.

But in reality nothing is understood, for the analogy fails precisely at the decisive point. The transition of the seed into the plant is in no sense a dying. When it is so called, then the sprouting process of the plant is being interpreted from human experience; the plant is in truth personified. We have really only a substitution, a *quid pro quo*. One cannot talk seriously of the death of a grain of wheat. The seed is already the plant (in direct, not indirect, identity). And the formulation of two different predicates for the one continuing subject is untrue, for in the case of the plant we have two forms of appearance which are indeed impossible simultaneously but do not in any way contradict each other. With man, on the contrary, it is not a matter of different forms of appearance of a subject which can be interchanged, but of the being of man which is defined in two mutually exclusive ways, since that being is first dead and then alive.

Paul, of course, can see an analogy here, because he names as subject the 'body', which can have two different forms of appearance, transient and eternal. But that leads to a wrong road, for now transitoriness and eternality appear as inherent qualities, as 'flesh' (σάρξ) and 'glory' (δόξα). (N.B. It is especially misleading if one proceeds from this apologetic passage, I Cor. 15.35ff., to the interpretation of Paul's concept of 'body' and of his anthropological concepts in general).

Barth's interpretation of vv. 39–41 is therefore also wrong. In his view, here too, Paul is describing a synthesis in which the same subject, 'flesh' or 'body' or 'glory' can appear simultaneously and separately in different forms. Here also, in the change of predicates (bird, fish, etc.), a passing away and a becoming new takes place, in that different things are included in one concept. But apart from the fact that it is extremely artificial to label the 'change' of the concept 'a passing away and becoming new' (the *concept* itself does not change at all!), there is a further misunderstanding. Paul does not co-ordinate 'body' with the entities, 'flesh' and 'glory'. What Paul means to say is rather that besides the 'terrestrial bodies' whose different kinds of 'flesh' (σάρξ) are described in v. 39, there are also the 'celestial bodies' which differ among themselves in glory (δόξα). 'Flesh' and 'glory' are therefore the materials, the natural qualities, which can acquire form in the 'body' (σῶμα).

The point of the passage is then that the resurrection of the 'body' is conceivable because there are bodies of different materials. But if the 'body' can equally well be mortal or immortal (in the meaning just given), then death is not taken seriously. Death is then only something appended *to* man, which could be different; it does not characterize men as men. Mortality is a natural quality produced by the accidental character of matter. And so, too, 'life' is only an accidental, natural quality of the 'body'.

Such an interpretation misses entirely Paul's real concern; for the resurrection is then not a miracle, the future of God. *Man* is not transformed in the resurrection, he remains the same; he merely acquires a different kind of material. Nor is the 'life' the life of *this* actual man now existing (that is, it is not resurrection from the dead!), but it is a kind of general divine nature. With this view, the genuine Pauline concept of the 'body' is abandoned. For if the 'body' can equally well be mortal or immortal, if *as body* it belongs equally to all earthly and heavenly beings, then the 'body' is no longer that which determines human existence as such. Into the place of the 'body' (σῶμα) has moved the Greek concept of 'form' (εἶδος), gained from the observation of nature. Many modern scholars have allowed themselves to be led astray by this passage and interpret 'body' in Paul as form, structure.

In 15.44b–49, Barth's understanding of Paul stands out most clearly. 'Resurrection of the dead', a paraphrase of the word 'God'! 'God is Lord.' This assertion could not be made on the basis of the rule of God over the world (that is not within the scope of our knowledge, not even after the best religious observation of nature and history), but only on the ground of God's rule over *me* who am neither world nor nature nor history.[3] 'If I know only this God [God who rules the world],

---

[3] Here Barth means by history the complex of events in space-time which can be 'objectively' observed, not the history in which I really stand.

then I know only so much as I could know of fate. Before this God I could only stand, observing, uninvolved, a spectator' (p. 112; ET p. 193.)

That God is Lord, not of the world which can be objectively observed, but the Lord over *me*, means that he is the Lord of life. But that does not mean that he is Lord of an eternal life known *to us*, the determination of which by God we also know. 'The determining of eternity, of the universality of things, by God is certainly a pious idea. But equally certainly it is not an idea which puts me actually and really under the claim of God' (p. 112; ET p. 193).

If God is *spirit*, we certainly are not spirit. God would, of course, be our Lord so far as we share in the 'spirit'. But how inadequate that would be, even if it were really true! And it is not true. For the concept of spirit in human idealism or dualism cannot possibly be applied to the Spirit of God. It cannot be true, for the Spirit of God is not anything that a man can possess along with other things.

But apart from that untruth, 'what about the rest of myself, which is certainly not spirit, but is earth, body? God is Lord of the *body*! With those words, the question of God confronts me sharply and inescapably. The body is the man; the body is what I am. And this man, this *I*, belongs to God. Now finally I have no refuge concealing me from God; I can no longer raise as a shield any sort of dualism nor retreat into any reality protected against God. I can offer no earthly weakness as an excuse. If God shall be my Lord, He is Lord of exactly this earthly weakness. For this earthly weakness is just what I am as I am bound to God, bound to live in God, to be glorious before God. The "Spirit", not our fragment of spirit and spirituality, but the Spirit of *God* conquers. And the Spirit conquers not in a purely spiritual being but there "is raised a spiritual *body*". The end of God's way is a corporeality' (pp. 112f.; ET pp. 193f.). (Compare p. 115; ET p. 197: 'to desire to belong to God *without* the body is rebellion against the will of God'; p. 123; ET p. 206: for the interpretation of 'this' [τοῦτο], see also p. 68; ET p. 121.)

Here Paul's true meaning finds brilliant expression. And the real meaning of both 'body' and 'spirit', even if not made conceptually clear, is given valid cogency. But Barth did not really derive this meaning from I Cor. 15 44b–49. He took it partly from the first half of the chapter and partly from other statements of Paul such as Rom. 6. To find the concept of the 'spiritual body', as Barth has developed it, in I Cor. 15.44 is not possible. Nowhere in vv. 35–44 is it stated that the spirit is the Spirit of God. And it is significant that Barth does not preserve the inferential sense of 44b but translates the εἰ by 'so far as'. Then he explains the meaning of 'natural' (ψυχικός), not from Paul's terminological use, but from the ordinary language of today when he infers from the elimination of the 'natural body' by the 'spiritual body' that Paul is combating the immortality of the soul (and quite rightly!) (pp. 114f.; ET pp. 195f.).

For the rest, Barth's interpretation of vv. 45–49 and vv. 50–58 can be covered briefly. In general the exegesis here suffers because of the attempt to exclude the expectation 'of catastrophic developments' from Paul's eschatology. So, for example, 'then' (τότε) in v. 54 is explained as 'from this standpoint'; the *shall* of the last trumpet is to be put in quotation marks; the 'mystery' of v. 51 is the simultaneousness of being alive and being dead in the resurrection and so on. I can see all that only as an arbitrary forcing of the meaning.

But I consider entirely right Barth's characterization of the Christian way according to Paul. We who in our own concrete existence actualize the idea of man with 'living being' (ψυχή ζῶσα) also actualize the idea of man with 'life-giving spirit' (πνεῦμα ζωοποιοῦν). In the coming of Christ 'we can and we ought to lay claim to the original, the redeemed creation. But that claim is not to something existent, something objectively given; it is rather to ordinances which are to be understood only as coming from above.' Paul sets man 'between Adam and Christ and says to him "you are both"; or rather "you belong to both". And as both together mark the way of God from the old creature to the new, so your life is also the arena across which this road leads. And you must also cross *from* here *to* there' (pp. 117f.; ET p. 202).

But what, then, does it mean that Barth has set the eternal future (*futurum aeternum*) in place of the future expected by Paul as an impending cosmic event (pp. 122, 124f.; ET pp. 209, 211)? It means interpreting Paul really critically; it means understanding him better than he understood himself! And I can only repeat that the *hazard* of this kind of exegesis must always be explicitly recognized, and the exegesis must be developed on a basis of the most exact knowledge of the contemporary background and by means of careful and penetrating analysis of the content. If previous research has fulfilled the first of these two exegetical tasks with great devotion and astonishingly valuable results, it should be said that the second – since F. C. Baur – has been pushed into the background. Precisely at this point, Barth has shown a new direction. The work is not finished, but we stand at a new beginning.

In conclusion, I should like to point out one peculiarity of Barth's work. Almost always he refuses to make use of the other letters of Paul as an aid to interpretation. I do not see why this help should not be used, and I venture to indicate briefly how the other letters might be fruitful for the understanding of I Corinthians.

While it is true that the eschatological hope of Paul is directed towards a future objective event in time, it is equally true that this event is a definitive event in which time stands still and the past is over (I Cor. 15.20). Therefore it can certainly be said that Paul cannot really mean an objective temporal event, for fundamentally there is nothing 'afterwards'. The parousia does not mark a division between two different times occurring in a temporal sequence one after the other. Therefore Paul gives no picture (this is especially noteworthy in vv. 23–28) of the conditions of life after the resurrection, except in the misleading, polemical section vv. 35–44. Basically, 'to be with Christ' is the only thing he can say of life after the resurrection, cf. I Thess. 4.17; Phil. 1.23.

The meaning of 'to be with Christ' must be determined from what Christ meant to Paul. For that meaning, Rom. 5.1ff., must be mentioned in addition to I Cor. 1.30: 'whom God made our wisdom, our righteousness and consecration and redemption'. There we have the statement of what Christ means for men, *these* actual men who we ourselves are in our temporal situation. Christ is not the cosmic ground of a future condition of existence, but the historical foundation of our present life. In a certain sense, i.e. in so far as we belong to Christ, we *are* the resurrected, are the 'first fruits' (ἀπαρχή), are a 'new creation' (καινὴ κτίσις), cf. II Cor. 5.14–17. But this resurrection life is never something objective. It is between time and eternity. In the judgment *of God* we are the justified, and the 'final possibility' that this may become a reality in our temporal life is 'love'.

Since in the First Letter to the Corinthians the dominant theme is not justification by faith but the temporal life of the believer within time, ch. 13 is the true climax of the letter.

4

HISTORICAL AND SUPRA-HISTORICAL RELIGION IN CHRISTIANITY?[1,2]

[1926]

THE BOOK by the Professor of New Testament at Heidelberg, Martin Dibelius, which is discussed in the following pages, is one of the most significant volumes to appear this year (1926). The book is important not only because of the author's great learning, his acuteness and the variety of gifts which have distinguished him as a scholar in his own field; but also because with these he combines a most modern spirit. Furthermore, he has devoted his learning to the service of practical religion and to the interest of the church.

It is instructive to compare his book (as has already been done elsewhere)[3] with Harnack's *What Is Christianity?* Both books are typical of specific periods of theological thought. The change in the situation today in comparison with the winter semester of 1899/1900 when Harnack's lectures on the nature of Christianity were delivered, finds expression immediately in the title of Dibelius' book, with its antithesis between historical and supra-historical.

With the distinction between history and supra-history, the author by-passes more than a hundred years of development and relates himself in a specific way to the tradition of *Rationalism*. Rationalism – within theology – had sought to justify its pious relation to the original Christian tradition by means of this distinction, the roots of which lie much deeper in the intellectual history of the West.

Hegel's philosophy of history and the application of that

[1] *ZZ*, IV (1926), pp. 385–403.
[2] Martin Dibelius. *Geschichtliche und übergeschichtliche Religion im Christentum*, Göttingen, 1925 (2nd ed., 1929, with the title, *Evangelium und Welt*).
[3] Rade, *CW* (1925), col. 859.

philosophy to the Christian tradition by F. C. Baur represented a magnificent attempt to transcend the distinction between history and supra-history, in the realization that the distinction really makes history a meaningless game. For the timeless-eternal, the 'supra-historical' (the eternal truths of reason in the sense of Rationalism) does not need history; and the individual does not need history either, for he has his real existence in the supra-historical and therefore has at all times the possibility of recourse to the timeless eternal. The fortuitously historical is then, since it is fortuitous, also meaningless. And when it is completely separated from the supra-historical, it can acquire no meaning, even when it is seen in a causal sequence understood as governed by law. The Hegelian view of history and that of Baur, however, include the knowledge that human existence is real only in time and history, that there are eternal truths of reason only as truths in history. Full value is again given to the fortuitously historical and so also to the actual life of man.

Whether such a position was more or less attainable on the basis of underlying idealistic presuppositions is another question. Certainly it is rewarding to read Baur's dispute with Uhlhorn. The latter had accused Baur of seeing in history only the universal, an ideal process in which the particular, the individual and personal, were without meaning. That is exactly what Baur does not mean and he retorts: 'The multiplicity and the diversity of nations and individuals constitute the concrete life of history; yet of course with the essential qualification that one by itself alone would be as one-sided as the other; that the particular can as little exist without the universal as the universal can exist without the particular. Therefore neither of the two factors, which belong essentially together, can be over looked. The multiplicity must be understood as bound into the unity and the particular in its subordination to the universal.'[4]

The questions raised by Hegel and Baur did not influence the historical research of the following generations. Later scholars saw their task essentially as that of achieving the most complete comprehension possible of the causal relations of

[4] F. C. Baur, *Die Tübinger Schule und ihre Stellung zur Gegenwart*, 2nd ed., Tübingen, 1860, pp. 4ff.

historical development. They accomplished stupendous results in collecting factual information and in analysing the material. I shall not consider here individual historians, secular and ecclesiastical, who followed that tradition, but shall limit myself to a discussion of the research into the beginnings of Christianity. That research was ruled by the idea of development, the concept of the law of causality governing historical events. It was believed that in history so understood, the revelation of God was directly visible. Hence the outstanding 'personalities' and 'religious heroes' in whom an undeducible, irrational quality could be discerned, were rated as especially clear phenomena of revelation.

Now it is quite understandable that a scholar like Dibelius rejects this naïve equating of history and revelation and recognizes that history which can be investigated by the historico-critical method is 'world'; consequently God is not to be found in it. Nor is it strange that he should resort to the old distinction between history and supra-history; although it may be regrettable that he ignores the view of history held by Hegel and Baur.

Of course, Dibelius fully believed that he had no need to deal with their view, since for him the supra-historical, the supra-temporal, did not consist of teachings, ideas, eternal truths of reason, as it did in Rationalism. Jesus brought no universally valid teaching, but the ethos of his words is 'in the highest degree supra-temporal' (p. 54). But what is the meaning of *supra-temporal* here? For this is the subject of the author's inquiry and he is expressly rejecting the temporal, psychological view of the last generation. His presentation of the proclamation of Jesus is not to be a psychologizing biography of Jesus (p. 41). Jesus' words are not to be explained merely as the simple expression of an attitude of mind (p. 54). Nor is the preaching of the Kingdom of God to be understood as the emergence of a world-view (pp. 40f.; cf. pp. 46, 61). Rather it is the supra-temporal in the message of Jesus, the ground of life raised above worldly relationships, which is to be investigated (p. 55).

The author thus rejects both the liberal position that the essence of Christianity, the dynamic force of its history, lies in the unique personality of Jesus; and the idealistic view that universal ideas validate the history of Christianity. The transcendent world which is attained in the idealism [of the Stoa] is the only human world idealized (p. 103). In Christianity love is not philanthropy, nor a virtue arising out of the presuppositions of natural law (p. 164). Faith is not any sort of universal truth (p. 134). But the ground of life is *timeless*, supra-temporal (pp. 45, 55). And just as the ground is timeless, so, too, is the goal (p. 45); it is a supra-temporal attitude (p. 59).

Now, what can be timeless except reason (*ratio*)? It is fatal – at least terminologically – that there seem to be several grounds of life. The Stoic teaching on virtue does not spring from the same ground as the Christian ethic, but obviously from a different ground. Therefore man has a choice (p. 102). But what do we learn of the ground from which Christianity speaks?

Man gains the relation to this ground of life, not by any achievement, but through an inner attitude (p. 45). This attitude has nothing to do with an ethic based on reward (p. 57), but is an ethos (pp. 57, 60) which is designated as 'being', 'inmost being' (p. 58), 'supra-temporal' being (p. 63). It is a being which is independent of time and the world (p. 60), which comes from eternity (p. 63); it is rooted outside this world (p. 65). It is also designated as 'new being' (pp. 63, 69, 96). It is 'ultimate, innermost; there are no adequate words for it' (p. 60). Words can only point towards it and give a faint hint of it (p. 60; cf. p. 153).

Therefore, theology, if it is not content with expressing pious emotion, can only speak of that ground indirectly, allusively, or, as Kierkegaard did, in paradoxes (p. 88). Or art can speak of it, for the source of art lies behind reason in the chaos of divine and demonic forces (p. 8). And like art, cult and liturgy speak of it in symbols (p. 88). So, too, the speech and action of religious men have real validity only as symbols (p. 63; cf. p. 66). Only symbolically, and as it were by reflected light, can the new being be proclaimed (p. 100). The holy cannot be expressed in human words; it becomes visible only in symbols (p. 142; cf. p. 144).

The author's position is clear when he designates the ground of life as '*the generating ground*' (p. 64), when the new being is called the '*creative being*' (p. 63), the 'creative life' (p. 64). The names are equivalent (p. 64), but the 'spontaneous' in the child is a picture of the new being. For a child's character is 'creative' because it is 'uninhibited' (p. 64). The new being comes forth from the ground of the 'creative unconscious' (p. 102) and it must be given form in the individual independently and creatively for the transformation of life (p. 163). Some sentences on p. 100 go the farthest in this direction. 'Christianity is differentiated from Judaism in that the Christian revelation is not *ought* but *be*. A piece of history, a man's life which through it gained the force of an archetype, has made this being known – made it known truly in the only way by which all that is deepest can be made known, by hints and by reflected light, symbolically. Therefore, not mere imitation, but rather creative new generation, is required from the believer in Christ. For the Jew, the revelation is given in a book as the clear, unambiguous will of God, so that *faith* means to him a pious life conforming to the *ought* of God's will. But to the Christian, the same word, *faith*, means creative receptivity.' O you lucky Jews!, one might well exclaim. For surely we should be 'of all men most miserable' (I Cor. 15.19) if a new creative fecundity were required of us.

Christianity and the New Testament are now interpreted by this standard. Behind all 'trends' lies the 'religious archetypal creation' (p. 131). In the Gospel a current comes alive (p. 37). The 'genius' of Paul lies in his creative religious force (p. 99). So, too, 'creative powers' were active in Jesus and he was 'a source of the power of God among the people' (p. 44). Not what he says and does, but what he 'means' in relation to the Kingdom of God is of basic importance (p. 44). When Jesus is challenged and responds, he makes no 'demand', but simply 'opens a channel for the power which gushes forth from him' (p. 47).

The essential is 'simply this: to allow the power which comes from the nearness of the kingdom, that is, of eternity, to flow out upon many, in order that in the last hour they may be prepared for the coming of the kingdom, that is, for the coming of God' (p. 47). 'The purpose of Jesus is fulfilled without need for him and his disciples to struggle and organize. Nothing has to be built or created. The meaning of Jesus' work is that men will be caught by the reality of the kingdom, that fires will be

kindled, that powers will be transmitted' (p. 49). In the healings performed by Jesus, powers appeared which from ancient
times were ascribed to the Messianic age. Jesus allows the
powers which have come to him from the future world to
overflow (pp. 52f.).

But there is more! The new being, which breaks forth out of
the depths of the ground of life, exists in *affects* and impulses
(p. 63). It is a human state, in fact an inner disposition, an
inner life, which glimpses a similar inner life in other human
beings (p. 96). Faith is 'the affective relation to some good
which exists above the plane of knowledge and proof' (p. 13).
Religion is the 'affective relation to a supra-world' (p. 21).
An 'affective supra-value' is given with the 'revelation' (p. 22);
even as the purpose of the parables of Jesus is actually the
arousing of affects (p. 57). 'What Jesus gave to his hearers is
therefore not a new world-view, a new basic principle, a newly
disclosed wisdom. It is an affect kindled by the overpowering
nearness of God. And this affect then modifies, ennobles or
expands other affects' (p. 60). Faith never comes into being
'without affect, without the yearning which comes from a
sense of need' and the result therefore is not to overcome but
to ennoble the affects (p. 103).

He who possesses the new being is the 'religious man' (p. 96)
who lives in religious productivity (p. 97). For the inner life
can be given form and can be radiated (p. 95). 'The affect
radiates its power in some degree beyond the single personality, to certain others who are near at hand and are really in
need – to the neighbours. An intuition for help is a component
in the consciousness of the redeemer – it is present actually as a
strong affect, immediately experienced. Where this affect is
not felt, the redeeming consciousness is dim and dull' (p. 164).
In this relation, the affect is love. The essence of Christian love
is just affect (pp. 164f.). It bursts forth from the new ground
of life (p. 61). As Jesus' hearers did not get instruction from him
but kindled their own being at his being (p. 63), as they
'glimpsed' in him the new world; so his inner powers were
shared with them and in the same way their power radiated
out upon others (p. 164). The indwelling of the new being in
Jesus made of the disciples believers in the 'numinous' sense;
and the reality of the new being compelled the Easter faith

(p. 85). Thus Jesus is the Holy One, whose relation to his own is 'numinous' (p. 77).

The concept of *faith*, if it is to be consistent, must also undergo a fatal re-interpretation. Faith is affect, *consciousness* of redemption (p. 164). But for a Christian, it is possible to speak only of *faith in* a redemption which as such is *not* a present reality within any circumstance of human existence.

If the author had rightly understood the concept of 'world' in the Christian sense, then he would be right when he asserts that after the proclamation of the Gospel in the world 'this world [can] no longer be wholly "world", because the sign of the reality of God is present as a constant disturbing thrust, as a requirement of change' (p. 65). But in that case, faith cannot be an affect, a 'religious process' (p. 132). Perhaps this choice of words shows that the author is not discussing faith at all, but is rather describing believing subjects who are being 'observed' and therefore are seen from the outside. Certainly his concept is not proved to be a concept of *faith* by his assertion of the *irrationality* of the religious event. That assertion is wholly immaterial for anyone who is not concerned about the comprehensibility or incomprehensibility of the religious life, but who does need to speak of the incomprehensibility of the revealed grace of God. Of that grace alone may the Christian use the word irrational – if indeed the word must continue in use at all. Really it should be discarded, for nothing in Christianity is incomprehensible in the *rational* sense.

But now apparently, the new being, the inner disposition, the affect of faith, is to be somewhat more clearly defined. Faith was designated (p. 13) an affective relation to a 'good'; elsewhere it appears as a *sense of value*. Faith dares 'to let the highest value which is "believed in" illuminate an uncertain future' (p. 30). The concern of religion is not the problem of the world-view but the question of true human value (p. 46). Faith is interested only in the reality of its world of value (p. 97). Christians are united by the inner possession of a 'world of value which is not of this world. By its standards they decide their lives; by it they feel themselves bound in their everyday existence. And the acceptance of that value-world as absolute means raising their existence above all relativities' (p. 95).

Every sacramental experience in Christianity is determined

by the 'actualization of value' which is 'created by the powers of the new being' (p. 101). The Gospel means a new order of value, in which the highest value is the new being (p. 167). Therefore the author's investigation of the supra-historical does not have as its goal the knowledge of reality, but the quite different goal of penetration into the highest value (p. 170). Apart from the antithesis of reality and world of value, which is painful, at least terminologically, the author is entirely right in emphasizing that faith is not interested in a picture of the world. But he seems to me mistaken in ignoring the fact that a view of an order of value is also a part of a world-view.

Since for the author the new being stands within an order of values, it is not surprising that he can speak of a *pre-religious stage* and that he designates as the question for the present day, whether we shall move beyond the pre-religious into a creative religious era (p. 145). Such a pre-religious force is found, for example, in sexual love (pp. 157f.). 'If by love an affective life is awakened even in the coldest and most calculating of men, a poetic feeling even in the dry Philistine, then it is obvious that man is raised above the limitations of his own nature to some hint of a stronger, higher life than he knew before. This hint, which is certainly not religious, may still serve as a preliminary impulse towards the religious experience which is instigated by the hand of God.' For in the experience of love man comes to understand 'his situation as a blissful dependence on a power which possesses an ultimate cosmic force. He knows himself to be personally bound by it and to it he gratefully submits himself. This feeling of dependence, which comes out of his own experience but which has cosmic dimensions, may serve as a preliminary preparation for the new being which Jesus will create by the Gospel' (p. 158). As if the experience of love could not equally well let loose all the devils! But from the author's standpoint it is consistent to assert that even in the struggle of the workers for independence, a consciousness of value is developed which has pre-religious significance (p. 168).

After all this, it is surprising to find that in Christianity the essential nature of salvation is not simple contact with divinity but the *inner definition of that divinity* (p. 101). This raises a hope of more to follow, especially since it is stated that this definition *has been given in history*. But what does the author mean by that statement? 'It is given in history – this is to be taken in the widest sense of the words – so that not only the events of the classical period but also the rise of all similar thinking and legends are to be included as data of spiritual history' (p. 101). What does that imply? It means that the unique character of the Christian knowledge of God is deducible from the history of Christianity in the world. Christianity is conceived as one historical phenomenon among others. The Christian knowledge of God is accepted as an historical phenomenon in this sense. In fact to the 'essence of Christianity' (here the author agrees with Harnack!) belong also the developments, modifications, and supplements of its original heritage 'which gave it direction in the course of its history' (pp. 31f.). With this point of view, the thesis that Christianity cannot be separated from its historical basis is supported by nothing more than the assertion that the history of Jesus is not reducible to myth (pp. 13f.).

But the question of the specific character of the divine which is peculiar to Christianity must be, on the author's pre-suppositions, actually a question of the nature of the supra-historical. And 'the perception of the supra-historical, that is, of the unconditioned that lies behind relative phenomena, is effected on a plane wholly different from knowledge of the historical' (p. 170).

How far, then, is the definite content of the divine really given in history? At this point I do not understand the author. And I understand as little how the perception of the highest value 'can also be spread abroad and implanted without historical understanding of the facts', and how 'the renewing of this perception, which is necessary for every age' is impossible 'without a knowledge of what preceded', a knowledge which is achieved by the most unprejudiced historical research. For 'only the understanding of historical life in its whole expanse' performs for the investigation of value the service which is required if the whole compass of the supra-historical is to be unlocked for it (p. 170).

Thus, not without knowledge of the processes, but probably without an historical understanding of the facts – how should that be understood? And to what extent does the complex of history, as elaborated and interpreted, represent the Christian

Gospel (p. 33)? It seems to me that history in the usual meaning of actual events is ruled out, when it is said: 'It still was a piece of history from which faith arises. It stems from the irrational meaning of history and from its illumination by the light of another world, – but this is still history, even if supra-historically transposed and given as it were the opposite label' (p. 13).

And how should we understand the statement: 'For before we can begin, in the power of that faith [the Easter faith] and that Spirit [the Spirit of Pentecost], to value supra-historically the historical life into which our own existence is knitted, we must ask: was that interpretation right?' (p. 14). Therefore the critical question, 'Was that interpretation right?', precedes faith. It is a question which, in the context of the author's thought, obviously can be answered only by separating the historical and the supra-historical in relation to Jesus and to the history of Christianity. Must we then analyse critically the historical interpretations of others in order to evaluate afterwards our own historical existence supra-historically in the power of faith? That would be an extraordinary way of getting our own faith to stand upright.

No! *Here history has fully lost its meaning.* 'In the place of the old belief in miracles as the support of our religious life has been substituted the concept of the irrational, of the "Wholly Other", of the divine, which touches us as a possibility in every event and which as a real fulfilment is granted here to one, there to another. It may be connected with the tradition or free from it, but always on our side there is no knowledge of any law or rule for it' (p. 51).

What is termed 'revelation' must be that which God discloses to us. But for the author, 'revelation' means that the creative power of religion, a power which is 'wholly different in kind', breaks into the world with the birth of every great and living religion (p. 22). In history such revelation becomes tradition (p. 23). Now it is presumably clear that if history itself has decisive meaning as revelation, the tradition also has such meaning. For only in the tradition does history really live. It is certainly not alive in the historical picture scientifically reconstructed out of the tradition treated as a 'source'. But, as we have seen, the author does not consider adherence to the essential of tradition. As a result, history is discarded.

To say that the 'Word' subsists not 'in the letter' but 'in the spirit' of God does not present an enlightening antithesis. For if one is speaking seriously of revelation in history, then the written documents are certainly a part of it. We are not helped at all by the reference to the 'current of historical life' (p. 97), which is after all simply the great complex of pure contingencies. The 'new being' merely joins the complex of historical relativities, out of which the author arbitrarily plucks it to use as the illuminating factor for historical phenomena when he declares 'the reality of the new being compelled the Easter faith' (p. 85).

Thus far I have for the most part summarized Dibelius' thought, although I have also expressed my own critical attitude. I would like now to stress all the more that I not only gratefully welcome his presentation of the question, but also agree with him to a considerable extent. I agree with him particularly when he criticizes the chronologically historical, psychological and moralistic approaches common today.

I also believe that our agreement on the positive side goes much farther than at first appears. But I think his concepts are wholly unsuited to bring to clear expression what he perhaps dimly glimpsed. He remains too much involved in the relativity and the psychologizing from which he obviously desires to escape. In my judgment, the responsibility for this lies not so much with the author himself as in the confusion of the contemporary theological situation and in the lack of a body of genuine theological concepts.

Thus far, I have concentrated on the presentation and criticism of the author's concept of the 'new being'. In what follows I shall discuss the corresponding concept, *world*.

Religion, because it is not God, is a piece of the world. This the author plainly states at the very beginning (p. 1). His polemic (pp. 24–8) against the usual apologetic, which tries to preserve an antiquated view of religion's relation to the world instead of the true meaning of religion, is excellent. But it is not made equally clear how far religion as a 'piece of the world oriented to God' may occupy a special position in contrast to the rest of the world.

According to the author's view, religion comes into being in those moments of revelation in which it enters the world with creative force. It is an alien spirit which, from the point of view of the world, appears as monomania (p. 22). Primary religion is accordingly alien to the world and flees the world. Now that statement applies to the side of religion which is turned towards God. On its other side, religion acts upon the world, establishes a relation to the world and must establish such a relation, as the history of the great religions shows (pp. 15–25). The world religions subsist from the combination of primary and secondary elements (p. 17). In its deepest nature, religion has no relation to the world (p. 20), since no third element (such as the world) can intrude into that affect, which represents the relation with the supra-worldly, between the supra-world and men (p. 21). Rilke's lines describe it:

> Thou art the second in his solitude,
> The quiet centre for his monologues
> And every circle drawn around thee
> Spans him the circle beyond time.

Now it is certainly true that religion must establish a *relation to the world*. The author gives indirectly, by the very sense of responsibility and obligation which guides his pen, *the* proof, which is more convincing than all his explanations. In the explanations he presents elaborate expositions showing how the mass of adherents and the children growing to maturity naturally induce such a relation to the world; while the thrust into the depths and the expansive power of religion compel a relation to the world (p. 22f.). Proof of that kind shows only a prior acceptance of religion as a phenomenon of this world.

But such an experience of revelation, when really understood, could establish no world relation at all, nor would it offer any possibility of a relationship to the world, because it cannot enter the historical process and produce a tradition. It is confined to isolated moments. If the founding of the church is attached to such instantaneous experiences in the way the author describes, then it is no longer the primary religion that establishes a relation to the world. This primary religion, indeed, cannot be spoken of or conceived as undergoing historical development. It is simply no longer there!

The author also sees truly that all religious or Christian

institutions are 'world': churches, Christian welfare work, even Christian ethics. One can only regret that he does not think this truth through radically. Does he not realize that what he calls primary religion is also a piece of world? And even though it may be 'world which is oriented to God', it remains world; and as such it stands under the whole curse of world-existence, separation from God! It is absurd to imagine that the world could come as a third party between God and man – or to suppose that it ought not so to come. As if *he*, the man, were not himself 'world'!

What the New Testament, what Christianity calls 'world' is constituted by *men*. Man himself has this affective relation to the supra-world. It is *his* affect which is under discussion. Therefore in the author's presentation of the ground of life, of the new being, etc., God is humanized and made a part of the world. The ground of life is in fact cosmic, part of the 'world'. It is significant that, according to the author's statements, 'world' is something which has intruded as a secondary element into the Christian community (pp. 30, 98). It is as if the curse of the world could, in the sense in which he discusses it, be demonstrated in the 'secularization' of Christian literature. Thus it becomes clear that to the author 'world' signifies 'culture'. Thus his 'primary' approaches dangerously close to Rousseau's romantic 'nature'.

Actually, the author is a romantic; only with his romanticism there is mixed a little modern axiology, philosophy of value. Just as the experience of love possesses its pre-religious character because it produces awareness of dependence on a cosmic power (p. 158), so God is called the 'world-ground' which in Jesus became a person (p. 90). And every dualism is resolved into a final unity for the pious man, since 'for him every stirring of the spiritual life points backward to God at the beginning and points forward again to God at the end' (p. 87). Therefore the symbol, both in art and in the cult, is the fitting expression for the unutterable (p. 88).

The characterization of the 'inter-mixture of dependence and freedom, of crisis and new creation, which is given with the Christian Gospel' as 'the inward activity' of men (p. 172), is wholly romantic. Characteristically romantic, too, is the statement that the 'voluntary impulse' to a 'full life' in the

Youth Movement is to be recognized as the antithesis to the conscious aim at a specific goal which is the norm in a mechanized and specialized existence (pp. 3–5). Here the author has in mind only the antithesis between impulse and goal. But although he also knows that the Youth Movement can achieve an historical result only if its forces 'flow back into the world', if they form a pattern of external life; although, too, he sees that permanence is to be gained only by amalgamation with the changing forces of history (pp. 6f.); there are nevertheless lacking here the essential concepts of authority and obedience through which alone the possibility of historical living can be understood. Those concepts present no universal goals, such as freeing the world from its slavery to business, but only concrete tasks.

A purely formal ideal like the Youth Movement's 'full life' is romantic. And it might be noted that the Youth Movement remains ineffective so long as it does not overcome its reluctance to set for itself concrete, specific tasks. Experience shows very plainly that the Youth Movement has become a real force wherever it has enlisted in concrete undertakings, whether nationalistic, ecclesiastical, Catholic, or proletarian. It is not possible to penetrate and overcome (p. 9) the world by a formal, theoretical ideal, but only by engaging in concrete undertakings, because then one recognizes concrete authorities and acts not on impulse but in obedience.

Consistently the author asserts that eschatology treats not of the end of the world but of its goal (p. 95), that the kingdom of God is a condition (p. 38). The particular relation between history and supra-history in the author's presentation thus becomes comprehensible. For this contrast is not so serious if God is the ultimate ground of human existence and if it is possible to attain to God (p. 15) from a piece of history (history as the author understands it).

Christianity is a world phenomenon. That is certainly true. But the author ought not to say it, since for him Christianity includes direct contact with the supra-world. And faith also, although he defines it as a divine creation, becomes a world phenomenon. Nor does he find it at all incongruous that Christianity is a world phenomenon, yet its message is a judgment upon the world.

Furthermore, for the author, the specific technical knowledge of the science of religion can count as a positive gain of
modern progress. 'Only after Christianity was investigated and
analysed in full freedom by the methods recognized as valid in
the world of scholarship, could it present its claims in that
world of intellectual life which is no longer subject to any
church control' (p. 27). Scientific theology has, through the
historical picture it presents, indirectly promoted Christianity
'since it has established anew and definitely secured its position
in the totality of intellectual culture' (p. 94). Christianity is a
genus of religion in which it is possible to feel at home (p. 97).

Certainly all of that can be said, but only in order to sub-
stantiate that everything human is 'world' and to understand
that the Christian Gospel negates exactly this humanity. But
the author sees the proper relation between Christianity and
the world as a *synthesis* such as is pre-figured in Schleiermacher
(p. 26). In accordance with this view, the task of Protestantism
was to give to a culture which was no longer bound to the
church 'the central life-faith in the Christian sense' (p. 25).
That idea was valid in relation to the culture of Idealism; it no
longer has value in relation to a mechanized and specialized
culture. In relation to such a culture, there is no question of
'uniting a spiritual world through a faith which nourishes and
supports it. Something wholly different has come in the place
of the world of spiritual life (of Idealism), something which by
its very nature denies such a relationship and could have no
centre of life at all in that sense' (p. 26).

That last sentence is characteristic of the author's view of the
world. But is the culture of Idealism, when measured by the
Christian concept of the world, any less 'world' than the present
culture? We are not surprised, then, when the author designates
as *the* question of the present day whether a fresh interpenetra-
tion of the world by the Christian Gospel could guide the inner
history of this time by giving it the centre which it lacks (p.
171). What is said further, that every Christian bears the
responsibility for the way the motives of the Gospel are to be
implanted in the world (pp. 166, 172), makes the whole rather
banal.

Dibelius sees correctly that the expected *Kingdom of God* is
not a situation, political or religious, earthly or transcendent,

secular or spiritual (p. 37). The real significance of Jesus' proclamation of the kingdom of God does not lie in the expectation of cosmic catastrophes; and its real meaning is free from any kind of ideological world-view (pp. 39–40). The statement that the preaching of the kingdom sets before men 'the terrifying Either-Or which in Jewish terminology is called "salvation-judgment" ' is admirable (p. 42). 'Now the reality of God is fully recognized; today or tomorrow, it is affirmed, God will be standing within this life. What will become of you?' (p. 64). Here is the 'confrontation of the human soul, of human life, of all human skills, by the reality of God, the measuring of all things human by God's measure; it is the judgment of time by eternity' (p. 65).

But the author is misled by his formulation when it serves to divide the historical and the supra-historical, so that he can and does see the kingdom of God as a *state*, actually as that state which he calls the new being. Yet where the acceptance of the eschatology is really complete, *every* human situation is, as world, under judgment. For men there is no situation which could be 'independent of time and world. . . because grounded in the supra-temporal world that we call eternity' (p. 60). For man, who is never a supra-temporal being but always stands within time and history, eternity can always be only future. Man is always dependent on time and world in a particular way, even when he also puts himself under the future of God. For he puts himself under that future precisely by undertaking his concrete tasks in time and world. Thereby he makes free for that future, his past and his own nature which was already forfeited to death. (In other words, his situation as such is already doomed to pass away, doomed to death.) Man can never take a leap out of time; he can only choose whether his present is to be determined by the future or by the past.

In that case, it becomes clear that the preaching of the kingdom as an eschatological message cannot promote any particular world organization as the means to a new situation which would be supra-world. As a situation, the new would still be world; that is, it would be a situation qualified by the past and by death. But it is equally evident that religion (to use Dibelius' terminology) has a relation to the world. For religion is the concern of concrete men who stand within time and world and who must so stand and act, in responsibility and decision, in obedience to God.

Since the author overlooks this truth, he cannot deal rightly with *the ethical teachings of Jesus.* He is indeed free from the old error of 'interim ethics'. But he takes Jesus' ethical teachings as a sign and mark of the 'new being' in him, instead of as commands which are authoritative and require obedience – the obedience, that is, of the concrete man standing within a specific time and world. It strikes me as odd when Mark 10.9, 'What therefore God has joined together, let no man put asunder', is understood as 'an illuminating paraphrase for the ideal married state' (p. 153) – an interpretation which also ignores the fact that an 'ideal state' cannot be ascribed to marriage as a temporal-historical event.

For the same reason, Dibelius has not been able to allow full value to Jesus' *concept of the neighbour.* (This point has also been noticed already.[5]) He characterizes neighbour only negatively (p. 61), as without any limitation or calculation of consequences. He cannot do otherwise, simply because a man whose being exists in the 'supra-temporal' has no genuine neighbours. For him there exist only very agreeable subjects over whom he can let the powers of his new being flow. But my neighbour is the man with whom I am constantly associated in my concrete historical existence. This means that the concept of the neighbour depends on the conception of human existence as a mutual inter-relation which conditions my existence from its very beginning, and apart from which 'man' is a pure abstraction. If the real man stands in this inter-relation, then he has a historical existence – an existence which makes its concrete historical demands. This certainly does not suggest that God's requirement from men is not *doing* but *being* (p. 45). The author ignores the fact that a true *being* of man which is a state does not exist (not even if the state is conceived as a supra-temporal relationship) but that the being of man is achieved in his action.

I agree with Dibelius that the Gospel knows nothing of 'social action' with its goals in this world (p. 48), or of any 'system of ethics' (pp. 57, 60–3, 146). But for Dibelius, 'relation to the world' must always appear as decadence, because he

[5] Rade, *CW* (1925), col. 860.

does not see that the 'unconditioned' is never present in man
except within his momentariness, that is, in the *now* of his concrete historical existence in time; and because he thinks it
necessary to keep looking towards a supra-temporal being.
Dibelius has, of course, a different *concept of time*. For according
to p. 1, *limited by time* does not mean to be bound to one's own
time with its demand for a decision at this moment; it means
being contained within the whole course of time understood as
a unity. Conditioned by time, therefore, means for him not
conditioned *for* but dependent *on*. That is, he interprets the
present, not out of the future but out of the past – and such
interpretation is certainly the opposite of Christian eschatology.

Now, when the author examines the relation of religion to
world event in the light of this interpretation of time, he reaches
the consistent conclusion that an investigation limited to one's
own position would constrain 'the divine into the narrowness
of one's own circle of experience' (p. 1), while the divine should
only be perceived by an examination tracing it through the
whole course of time. But in any such examination, one's own
existence is from the first observed from a distance and thereby
relegated to the past. Such an examination of history cannot be
a real questioning of history from the actual present, however
hard the author strives to make it so.

In my judgment the author comes closest to the truth in the
following statement. 'Anyone who, in the midst of the diverse
kinds of witnesses to Christian behaviour, lives under the delusion that he himself is *the* fulfiller of the Gospel is blind to how
much "world" must be combined with the ethics of the Gospel
in order to make it an actual ethical rule of life. "World"
here means the factors which in general determine the life of
the individual – a specific period of time with its relationships,
business obligations, personal position in time and life with its
wide or narrow outlook, the host of good and bad spirits which
we call heredity and environment: race, family, physical body,
landscape, nation, ability, education, profession, way of life.
Who, amid such a complexity of things, would want to measure
his neighbour by his own standard and doubt a neighbour's
Christianity on the basis of difference in behaviour? The active,
ethical power of the Christian Gospel would be felt by us all
more clearly and unitedly if we weaned ourselves from these

world limitations, without which none of us can live, to seek the ultimate ground of conduct, the impulses which flow to the Christian from the Eternal Being revealed by Jesus. It is the inner subjection to these impulses, not their transformation into an ethic conditioned by the world, which is decisive for the Christian quality of conduct' (pp. 163f.).

Here I should like to be able to ignore the disturbing terminology ('the impulses which flow from the Eternal Being'!); for what is meant is clearly the core of the matter. But the situation is not really so complicated; it is truly very simple. It looks complicated only when the 'Christian ethos' is included as one motive among others, so that there seems to be an interlacing of motives. What the author has seen and has expressed here ought to lead him further and make him sceptical of his concepts of 'new being' and 'world'.

Moreover, his argument with Buddhism (p. 106) shows how near the author is to the right view. For here he rightly affirms that Christianity is distinguished from Buddhism by a more resolute and fuller grasp of *reality*. The wording again seems to me inadequate. But it is true that the Christian does not seek to escape from the paradox of life and suffering as from something above which he can finally raise himself. He recognizes it as the reality in which he lives and which therefore determines his existence. He will not cleave to the life of another world as an escape from the tensions of reality and its contradictions. (If he did so, he would not really have accepted reality as *reality*!) For this tension belongs to one's own human nature; beyond it stands only God who redeems this contradictory life because he forgives the sinner. Within these tensions, however, there is nothing which as such can be called divine. At this point the ideas of a Platonizing dualism (cf. p. 87) modify the author's pantheism.

In accord with the author's view, the meaning of the *Cross of Christ* remains symbolic. Specifically, it is the symbol for 'the collision of two worlds' 'in their original purity and intrinsic nature' (p. 106). So, too, for the author the Christ-myth is a symbol (p. 82) or interpreted history (pp. 32f.). The Cross expresses symbolically the relation of God to the world (p. 100). That is, it is the relation of the *concepts* of God and of the world which in a Platonizing thought pattern appears as an ontic relation. (Cf. the statement, p. 64, that Jesus 'wills' nothing in time!) That is to say, the author, since he views the real existence of man not as truly historical but as supra-temporal, can only see the relation between God and man as also supra-temporal, i.e. as timeless, and that means as a relation of concepts or substances.

The New Testament thinking about God rejects precisely this (Greek) concept of God and knows only a relation between God and man which is achieved in the historical event as an act of God. In the New Testament, the Cross of Christ as an historical fact in all its ambiguity is an act of God, not as *interpreted* history, therefore not as the symbol *for* the relation of God to man, but as the act of God in which that relation is achieved. The New Testament knows sin and forgiveness as temporal experiences – in Dibelius' thinking they have almost no place. Dibelius knows (if not by intention, by the nature of his concepts) only a Christianity transformed into a romantic pantheism.

For the same reason, too, the author opposes *reality* to *value*. As if our concern were not knowing the reality in which alone (as the author was in fact aware in his argument with Buddhism) God is to be found! Therefore even the relation between the new being (or faith) and *thinking* is so distorted. Dibelius does not understand thinking as the effort to disentangle the facts themselves and so bring one's own existence into clear comprehension. He does not understand it as an act of living, but as an avocation. Thinking is for him a specific kind of scientific (that is, rational) reflection upon things, the objective character of which is preserved by observing them from a distance. Thinking is therefore isolated from the reality of one's own existence, in which the things are encountered.

Consequently he cannot accept theology as cogitation on the existence of the Christian, but only as rational investigation of the objects of faith, as a support for the content of faith (p. 86), and as a part of social science which sets the phenomenon of (Christian) religion in its relation to other social phenomena (p. 87). He himself sees that this kind of thinking is not suited to faith. But he does not see that the deficiency in this kind of thinking in relation to the divine world does *not* lie in any inadequacy peculiar to the thinking. He does not see that nothing at all can be said of the divine world in the way objective entities can be spoken of, so that myth, in spite of its greater naïveté, is not better than rational theology when it speaks of the divine world as a kind of objective thing.

The assertion that the Christian heritage cannot be formulated in propositions (p. 95) only shows that to the author the connection between thinking (speaking) and life has wholly vanished. If man's existence is an historical existence, then it is inherent in it that man in his thinking discovers for himself the world and his own existence and shares his discoveries in talk with others. The irrational has no significance for him and the unutterable for him is really a nothing – though for an animal it might be the supreme good. Rather, the chief duty of man is to achieve clarity in thinking and speaking about his own situation. The problem of the church for contemporary Protestantism is not a *cult-problem* (p. 144), but a problem of *theology*.

5

ON THE QUESTION OF CHRISTOLOGY[1]
[1927]

I

THE FOLLOWING discussion is concerned with the book *Jesus Christus der Herr* by Emanuel Hirsch.[2] However, since this is not a review of the book but rather a discussion of some of its ideas, I am also including Hirsch's review of my book, *Jesus and the Word*,[3] since that review is both valuable for its content and concerned with better understanding of the problem.

The first part of Hirsch's book, entitled 'The Report Given to Us', presents a historical account of the message and the activity of Jesus and of 'the earliest witness' to him. The second part, 'The Recognition Required from Us' develops the basic ideas of a christology. The author's real interest lies in the second part. Here he expresses his fundamental ideas on the method and aim of historical work. The discussion therefore must begin there. A substantial part of the argument is, I think, common to us both. For Hirsch is also seeking to turn theology away from the false paths of idealism (p. 59) and mysticism (pp. 77f., 81, 90f.), and thereby to make fruitful the theological work of Kierkegaard.

The author begins with a critical judgment upon the methods of theology generally followed since Schleiermacher. 'We cannot accept a mistaken procedure which . . . sees in the pious consciousness of the Christian the specific object of theological knowledge' (p. 43). This fundamental judgment must be considered more closely to discover how far the two of us are really in agreement.

[1] *ZZ*, V (1927), pp. 41–69.
[2] Emanuel Hirsch, *Jesus Christus der Herr*, Theologische Vorlesungen, Göttingen, 1926.
[3] *Zeitwende*, 2 Jahrg. (1926) No. 9, pp. 309–13.

Formerly, in *genuine orthodoxy*, theology was the science *of* faith in the sense of the 'faith *which* is believed' (*fides quae creditur*), *for* faith as the 'faith *by which* one believes' (*fides qua creditur*). Certainly the 'faith which is believed' (*fides quae creditur*) is a legitimate subject for scientific investigation. Such an investigation may, on the one hand, serve as a kind of rational 'natural' theology and may furnish a basis for dogma; on the other hand, by means of logic, it may bring the ideas drawn from Scripture and dogma, accepted as a formal authority, into a system in which the revelationary character of the relevant ideas is seen as guaranteed by their supernatural origin. It views the 'faith which is believed' as something which is known and is elaborated by means of scientific inquiry (cf. p. 45). In that case, there remains for the 'faith by which one believes' (*fides qua creditur*) only the role of accepting the conclusions of theology. (That holds even though faith may be quite differently defined, as in the doctrine of justification.) Thus faith itself becomes theology in so far as it makes a judgment and it becomes a matter of a resolve in so far as it submits without judgment. For the 'faith which is believed' in the final analysis deals with 'supernatural' truths which are by no means self-evident.

In reality, however, these truths – no matter how strongly one may emphasize their supra-rationality and anti-rationality – never lose their rational character. For if revelation is seen only in the anti-rational, then it becomes the private concept of an individual; that is, its teachings have the character of revelation only in so far as their rational character has a negative sign. The 'faith by which we believe' is therefore ultimately the resolve to hold as 'true' 'truths' which are not rational. This is self-deception, for one cannot consider as 'true' what is contrary to reason, as W. Herrmann was never tired of insisting.

In contrast, the belief in authority (*fides implicita*) of Roman Catholic doctrine is not only more practical but also more honest. For when faith admits its inability to judge and believes on the authority of the church, then trust can be real and living. In Protestant orthodoxy, on the other hand, the 'faith by which one believes' has become a wholly formal and wholly human attitude. It is not related to the object of faith, God, but to doctrines about him. Faith in a doctrine is an impossibility. One can only understand a doctrine (critically) or submit to it by a deliberate resolve. In so far as we speak of faith as 'trust' (*fiducia*), the knowledge and acceptance of 'pure doctrine' are subsequent to it. This kind of theology forgets that the only possible access to the 'faith which is believed' is the 'faith by which one believes'; and that the 'pure doctrine' can be developed only as a doctrine seen in faith.

Thus it is understandable that *theology since Schleiermacher* rejects this confusion of faith with theology and the actual elimination of faith from theology which resulted, and sees the object of theology as faith, the 'faith by which one believes'. But it goes to the other extreme. In opposition to the orthodox view that faith follows theology, it affirms the reverse: 'religious faith precedes theology and produces it' (so J. Wendland, RGG, V, col. 1197). The 'faith by which we believe' is made independent of theology.

This is understandable as a reaction against orthodoxy. But it is an absurd procedure. The senselessness becomes clear at once with the question 'What, then, is theology to be?' Religious faith can subsequently be made an object of reflection! (*ibid.*, col. 1202). Of course; but for what purpose? Curiosity – even if it is labelled 'interest' – is not a legitimate motive for theology. And reasons like the assertion that theology aids the mutual understanding of believers (*ibid.*, col. 1198) seem comic when related to actual experiences. No, if theology does not belong essentially to faith, if it is not itself an act of faith (and here I agree wholly with Hirsch, cf. p. 42), then it has no sense at all.

What then is the conclusion? We have seen that the old theology was a science *of* faith as the 'faith which is believed' *for* faith as the 'faith by which one believes'; that the new theology is a science of faith as the 'faith by which one believes' and has therefore lost the 'faith which is believed'; at the same time, it has also lost all reason for existing. For it is now included in the social sciences (Troeltsch) and has gained 'universal validity' at the cost of no longer mattering to anyone.

This new theology states not what the true faith is but what it is *truly to have faith* (cf. the popular formulation, what matters is *that* a man believes, not *what* he believes). The believer, however, is concerned only with the first question. This theology

sees the believing subject as the object of analysis, understands
'faith' as a human attitude and elaborates a purely formal
concept of 'faith' in which Christianity and all other religions
agree. Then as J. Wendland glibly says (following Troeltsch),
theology as apologetics and philosophy of religion must 'first
show why religious faith is natural, necessary and normal for
men at all; then, by demonstrating a series of upward steps,
that is, by a 'comparison of religious and different kinds of
faith', it must show 'why the Christian religion is superior to all
other kinds of faith' (*RGG*, V, col. 1202). The idealistic or
romantic conviction of the immanence of the deity in spiritual
or cultural life helps to obscure the fatal mistake that here
'religion' and Christianity are presented definitively as functions of the human mind, as cultural phenomena. Faith will
reject any such apologetic – which is like pulling one's self
out of a swamp by one's own hair.

Actually, the absurdity of the situation is revealed by the
question of truth. If faith is accepted beforehand as a given world
phenomenon and is so explained, and if the 'reality' of the
faith (the religion) is first demonstrated and then subsequently
the question of truth is raised, that question cannot be rightly
faced. For it can only be dealt with within the faith (Hirsch, p.
44). What court of appeal outside faith is to decide whether
the belief is correct or not? Perhaps the philosophy of religion?
But faith is in a hurry and cannot wait for the work of the
philosophers of religion. And if a man answers magniloquently
that naïve faith has no need of such a question because it is
certain of itself, then he confesses that he himself is merely
playing with the question of truth. For unless a man seeks the
truth because he *needs* it, he certainly does not seek for it at all.

The actual situation is this. When theology has abandoned
its particular object, the 'faith which is believed', it *can* then no
longer understand the 'faith by which one believes'. It assumes
that faith to be a human attitude which can be seen without
seeing the object of faith. It misjudges the *intentionality of faith.*
For the 'faith by which one believes' is what it is only in relation
to its object, the 'faith which is believed'. Plato long ago knew
that love (ἔρως) can only be defined as love of something (ἔρως
τινός). Faith which is conceived as a human attitude, as a
spiritual function, as a pious frame of mind, as a sense of the

numinous, and the like, is *not* faith at all. Faith exists only as
faith *in*, that is as faith in its object, in God known in revelation.

Anyone who ignores that fact, necessarily misunderstands
the concept of revelation. In the old orthodoxy, revelation is
the 'supernatural' doctrine, identified as revelation by its
astonishing origin; but in other respects it is a doctrine which
can be preserved and expanded like other kinds of knowledge.
Hence the concept of revelation is deprived of the contemporary impetus essential to it. In the new theology, however,
the contemporary impetus is preserved at the cost of reducing
the revelation to an experience, to something which occurs in
a pious subject – nothing is any longer revealed by it.

In all this, I find myself in agreement with Hirsch – but we
must press on. Hirsch sees quite rightly that the conclusion to
be drawn from what has been said is that the knowledge inherent in faith is the only *theological knowledge* there is (p. 41).
This means, first, that theology, the object of which is God,
must be aware that the only access to this object is faith and
therefore theology speaks under the presupposition of faith.
Second, all faith includes theology. 'We Protestant Christians
are all theologians' (p. 42). Theology is nothing other than
rational reflection about our own existence as that existence is
determined by God. Theology is accordingly the scientific
elaboration of what is already present in simple faith.

But this is not to be understood as if faith were a lower stage
above which one could mount by scientific reasoning and
arrive at gnosis. For *science* is not an esoteric art with its own
canons which can be applied to selected objects and so also to
faith. Science, in the sense of disciplined thinking, is a possibility inherent in the original relation to the object. It therefore
does nothing more than explore our relation to the object and
thereby make us cognizant of the object. Therefore anyone
who (I agree with Schlatter) cuts the connection between
thinking and living, who understands science to be a mysterious
art which deduces all the possibilities of objective knowledge
from a single principle, who therefore determines the nature
of objects from the concepts of science instead of determining
the science by the objects, inevitably creates such a contradiction between knowledge and faith that a scientific theology
becomes impossible.

For faith cannot permit (as theology since Schleiermacher more or less definitely demands) the nature of its content to be dictated to it by a 'scientific doctrine' or a 'system of reason'. True *science* itself can only be one element of our relation to the object itself. And *theology* is nothing other than an activity of faith itself. It can be elaborated more by one believer and less by another, but it can never be wholly absent from Protestant faith – provided Protestant faith is faith in its object. So Hirsch rightly declares: 'Scientific theological thinking . . . does not establish a new intellectual movement; it only purifies and completes what is already implanted in everyone who has that faith' (p. 42).

But we must not go on to say that 'the activity of theological cognition which we have to pursue is *identical* with the activity of a faith personally accepted' (p. 42). It is no more than a single separable facet of the activity of faith. The *movement of faith* is the existential action itself, the obedient listening to the Word. Such hearing can never be an observable possession for me; I cannot set it working. I cannot even resolve that I will hear – because as a free act the decision is already decided. But *theology* as scientific thinking is a human enterprise which I can resolve to undertake. It has meaning as theology, however, only when it is really an impulse of faith, only when obedient hearing protracts itself in the undertaking of theology. But I cannot control whether that happens; and that is the insight upon which what is usually called dialectical theology depends.

Like all science, theology carries within itself the possibility of taking the wrong road – the possibility, that is, not of saying something false but of losing all relationships to its object and of saying only the 'correct' thing or of becoming a system of concepts. This possibility is much more serious in theology, because for all other sciences, access to their object lies within the area of human possibilities. They can therefore always be criticized and corrected by reference to the freely accessible object. But God is the subject of theology; therefore the subject of theology is not within man's control and theology has no store of knowledge which can be verified by reference to the object.

Thus theology is a hazardous undertaking; but it is at the same time indispensable, because faith is not something apart from us. Faith determines our existence and is expressed in our thought, speech, and action. If we refused to think theologically we should be imagining ourselves as angels instead of sinful men. Because God claims us who are human beings, because he is gracious to us who are sinners, theology exists. 'Accordingly, because God desires living communion in which his Word becomes our own inner possession, therefore beyond perception there is theological knowledge' (p. 42).

Theology therefore is always under the temptation to forget the real possibility of access to its object, and dialectical theology endeavours to be a perpetual reminder of that possibility – although of course it can offer no guarantee of access. But anyone who forgets the dialectical faces two dangers. The first is the danger of proceeding dogmatically, that is, of taking the statements of Scripture and dogma as universal truths and bringing them into systematic cohesion, or at least making them as conceivable as possible.[4] The second danger is that of proceeding historically, that is, presenting the scriptural faith as an historical phenomenon and assuming at the same time (so far as one remains conscious at all of the task of theology) that *this* historical presentation is the knowledge which reveals the object of faith. It is this second error into which I think Hirsch has slipped.

II

Misconception appears first in Hirsch's discussion of the 'theology of paradox'. Here (pp. 49f.), he attacks the view that the 'Word' confronts the natural man only as paradox or offence; that faith in itself is neither mediated nor demonstrated. His polemic is based on a misunderstanding. Actually the only paradox with which theology can legitimately be concerned is not a paradox of unintelligible and absurd ideas nor of irrational statements. It is a paradox of *event*, of the act of God who forgives sins.

---

[4] This course Hirsch definitely rejects. Whether in such a context his polemic against Kierkegaard (pp. 45f., 51f.) is just, I doubt. It seems to me that he has not given sufficient attention to what Kierkegaard himself says about 'communication' and that he has misunderstood, the bold parody on the speculative system, turning Christianity into an intellectual experiment' in the same way as did the reviewer of the *Brocken* (*Ges. Werke* 6, Jena, 1925, p. 321). There can be no possibility of such a *tour de force* (p. 51) by the Kierkegaard who wrote *Fear and Trembling*.

In this event there is nothing which is offensive or paradoxical to the intellect. For anyone can understand what forgiveness is, if he wants to understand it. But it is certainly not an observable fact that God really has forgiven us; it can only be believed in faith. Therefore faith 'understands' the 'Word' very well and Hirsch is correct so far when he says that faith in this sense is 'mediated' – that is, that in its content the ground which produces faith can be known. 'For the Christian truly needs an indestructible ground which inwardly constrains him, because his faith is *not* something which he can procure for himself at his own pleasure. It is a certainty which is created in him while his natural life rebels against the terror of what is disclosed to him therein'. (Herrmann, *Die mit der Theologie verknupfte Not*, Tübingen, 1914, pp. 18f.). 'Faith is engendered solely by that which is its content' (Herrmann, *Gesammelte Aufsätze*, ed. F. W. Schmidt, Tübingen, 1923, p. 268). If it were otherwise, if faith were belief in an incomprehensible X, then faith would be an action dependent on a specific resolve; it would be a purely arbitrary accidental occurrence. And it would be, as Hirsch quite correctly states (p. 51) in agreement with Herrmann, the beginning of justification by works.

But whom is Hirsch attacking when he characterizes the 'theology of paradox' as entangled in such a misunderstanding? The charge certainly does not apply to the contents of this periodical [*ZZ*]. We are seeking only to guard against the assumption that faith is intellectually comprehensible from *outside* the faith. We certainly would not characterize faith as unreason. When Hirsch says (p. 50) that faith is a new beginning in the sense of an historical decision, that is exactly Herrmann's view, and also ours. However, Hirsch must be asked whether he sees the mediation and the ground of faith as given *only* through the object of faith, in its content (and therefore only discernible for faith itself); or whether he does not take a leap out of the circle so drawn, in order to look for verification outside it.

What does his christology involve? To speak theologically of Jesus Christ means, according to all that has been said, to speak of him as he is seen by faith and only by faith. This, therefore, is Hirsch's aim, if for him Jesus is the 'Word'. For that means that Jesus is the revelation of God, making God present with us. How is this theme developed?

III

We are rightly referred to the *experiences* which we actually have of Jesus. But in what sense are we referred to them? That is, what role is ascribed to them? What kind of experiences are actually meant?

The appeal to experience would be legitimate if the experience were really identical with faith, since the questioning faith would then really be referred to its object. But with Hirsch, the experiences and the faith fall apart, and the experiences are supposed to be the foundation of faith and to certify it. According to his view, christology must 'include *genetically* the confession of faith in the deity of Jesus Christ. It must show how the Gospel portrayal of Jesus Christ as God's all-conquering Word is a living presence in our hearts. It must show in what *inner experiences* faith is *assured* that its submission to Jesus as the Christ, as the Word of God, is justified' (p. 54). Thus the experience we have of Jesus is represented as an emotion of the heart. But if my emotion is the witness for my communion with God, then I am appealing to my experience when I ought to appeal to the Word of God. Faith which is born of such an emotion is ultimately a faith in myself.

Hirsch would presumably answer: the entity which stirred our heart, by which our faith was kindled, is the historical fact, Jesus Christ, which is *given* objectively, which we ourselves did not create. But the obvious question arises of how this fact is seen. 'Faith is enkindled by the picture of Jesus Christ which speaks to us through the Gospel records' (p. 9). But the picture which Hirsch draws is the reconstruction of a historian who 'seeks to depict a real, individual man' (p. 73) and who achieves this by psychological analysis. Hirsch explores the personality of Jesus; he wants to know 'how Jesus felt in his heart' (p. 74) and he 'understands a little of the trials which Jesus had to bear' (p. 89). He is able even to speak of Jesus' faith. The result is 'Christ after the flesh'.

This is good old liberal tradition. J. Weiss and W. Bousset also approached the question this way. 'The confession of Christ as Lord is empty if we do not, when we encounter him, look into the specific face of an individual man' (p. 9). Keim and Holtzmann might easily have written: 'The records of his

long nights of prayer (e.g. Mark 1.35; 6.46) and of his battle
with the Tempter, the secret of his path of suffering which
included temptation, all teach us that he appropriated God
and God's will to himself in personal intercourse with God.
He stood, like us, in a relation of confrontation by God and he
found unity with the Father by the surrender of his own will in
this confrontation' (p. 73).

In agreement with this liberalism, the name *Son* is interpreted
(p. 74) as if it were the expression of a personal relation of Jesus
with the Father, an 'attitude of the inner life'. With this interpretation, understanding of what the New Testament says
of the death of Jesus as a sacrifice becomes impossible. Instead
there is merely the concept of sacrifice, which is equally
applicable to the Spartans at Thermopylae.

The interpretation of the *account of the baptism* is typical.
Hirsch, in common with the whole liberal tradition, conducts
his investigation on the presupposition that in the narrative
something must be disclosed about Jesus and about his development if he is observed in isolation (that is, observed in the
manner of objective, psychologizing historicism and apart from
his real relation to history). According to Hirsch's view, the
name Son was given him by the voice from heaven for a rightful possession 'as clarification of the attitude of inner life already
present, not as the first establishment of communion' (p. 85).
Keim and Zahn interpret in similar fashion.

The New Testament knows nothing of a Jesus seen in isolation as a world phenomenon explicable through the conception
of development. Such a Jesus is just a reconstruction. In the
view of the Gospels, the community which tells the story of the
baptism is thereby rejecting the question of Jesus' human
development and personality. They deliberately put the
account at the beginning of Jesus' work with the intention of
showing that Jesus, of whom the following narrative is told, is
not a man, but the Son of God, the messianic king. The community sees in the baptism of Jesus, not the source for a *fact*
which can be proved to others but the source of a manner of
their own existence. It makes no difference, therefore, whether
the supposed fact is understood, in the sense of ancient demono-
logy, as possession by a spiritual power or, according to modern
psychology, as Jesus' spiritual state. Yet Hirsch in other con-

texts knows that Christ is not an entity objectively present like the objects of the world. (He says [p. 48] that Christ is 'no tangible presence'.) But something that is 'objectively present' is not merely a metaphysical 'substance' in the sense of the dogma of the ancient church; it also includes a soul-picture such as Hirsch paints.

What Hirsch paints is the 'Christ after the flesh'. Christ is not seen with the eyes of faith but is viewed in a way which belongs to *rationalism and pietism*. For what is it that is concretely experienced in relation to him? In the first place, we experience in him his lordship over our conscience; 'he rules the conscience with a kingly power' (p. 57). His presence becomes decisive for me over my whole inner life (p. 59); and as I experience that domination, I become his contemporary – or rather he becomes contemporary and present with me (p. 59). But does this mean 'contemporary' as Kierkegaard meant it? Does it really mean comtemporaneous in the present time? No, it is merely timelessness. For Hirsch can say no more than that Jesus' call to repentance can make us aware of the demand of conscience, as can the voice of every prophet. At best Jesus is portrayed as giving me the occasion to recognize the demand of which I always had the knowledge and which Hirsch in any case characterizes as timeless (pp. 62f.). The demand which I thus come to accept does not have its ground in Jesus but in my own existence.

In what way, then, does Jesus become Lord? Become judgment? Does not the 'judgment of conscience' mean that we ourselves must pronounce the verdict upon ourselves? Hirsch makes this unmistakable when he says that the judgment we experience in Jesus does not break our evil will (p. 66). Therefore what Hirsch is discussing is not the judgment of God.

Jesus so regarded never confronts us as 'Thou'. A *Thou* who demands something of us with a concrete claim upon our conscience can only be a Thou confronting us in today's concrete present. In relation to a *Thou* in the past, the most that is possible is the perception of a moral demand that is timeless – the recognition of the fact that for us there is a law. The historical Jesus does not make any direct demand on us, nor does he condemn us for any deed we have committed against him. When Jesus is so regarded that his call to repentance merely makes us conscious of a moral demand – whatever the vehemence – then every *Thou* in our daily association is more important. For actually he is only seen making demands on others and pronouncing judgment on others. And if I find inducement to consider the demand valid for me – even then Jesus becomes neither *Thou* nor Lord *in this way*.

Yet I think I see evidence that Hirsch wants to go beyond this rationalism. He thinks that Jesus' call to repentance reveals to us more than we already know in our conscience (p. 64). But what is this *more*? It cannot be the attack against legalism and compensatory morality (pp. 63f.) – even though every man may be secretly ten times a Pharisee. The *more* seems to consist in the fact that Jesus continually gave a concrete content to the general requirement. 'We yield ourselves to his call to repentance only when we gaze upon him, upon Jesus himself, as the exemplifier of his demand, when we bring him into the particular personal life allotted to us, when we seek to live like him as his disciples' (p. 65). This formulation seems to show clearly that the tendency to go beyond rationalism is trapped in pietism.

The influence of pietism is especially obvious when Hirsch speaks of the *passion of Jesus*, emphasizing how Jesus had to struggle against temptation until his last breath. Of the *cross*, he writes: 'When he as the Holy One has once shattered our conscience with his words, it becomes inconceivable to us that men condemned him to a shameful death' (p. 65). Why? That is quite understandable, and Hirsch himself so presents it in the historical account of the first part of the book. He says truly, 'the will to kill him is born out of the kind of heart which his call to repentance has exposed as at enmity with God, the kind of heart which beats also in us' (p. 65). 'That completes the condemnation.' But does it? Yes, as man gives the verdict on himself in his conscience. But such a verdict is given equally when we are confronted, for example, with the death of Socrates.

Furthermore, in regard to the attempt to immerse one's self 'in the heart of the crucified' (p. 75), I must say bluntly: it is impossible to see what more was done by the historical Jesus who goes to his death in obedient love than was done by all those who, for example, in the World War took the same road, also in obedient love. Their road actually means more to us, not only because we see it more clearly, but chiefly because we were associated with them as with a living *Thou*. To try to create such experiences of encounter with a person of the past seems to me to be artificial and to lead to sentimentality.

Jesus Christ who has the full power *to forgive sin* is not to be found in this fashion. I have done him no wrong and he has nothing to forgive me. And since the forgiveness cannot be verified as a discernible objective event, I am not at all helped by reading touching stories of how Jesus forgave the sinful woman or Zacchaeus (p. 71). Hirsch, however, thinks he can show that Jesus can become inwardly known to us as our forgiver (p. 67). We believe his word of forgiveness because the power of his call to repentance so deeply affects us (p. 67). Yet this call only makes us aware of what was already alive in us as the, perhaps unheard, voice of conscience. Do we also perceive the certainty of forgiveness in the same way within ourselves? Certainly any one who has understood the call to repentance can know that only grace can deliver him. But does that knowledge give him a certainty of grace? Such certainty cannot be based on the fact that someone whose call to repentance moved him speaks also of grace.

How far does Jesus teach us 'trust'? A personal trust in the reliability of a person makes no sense here. Furthermore, it is not possible in relation to Jesus, for 'after the flesh' he is dead. In what sense, then, can he 'personally be very close' to us so that we 'engage in live dialogue with him'? It is clear that he cannot be a *Thou* for us in the same sense as a man with whom we are associated in daily life. So nothing is left for Hirsch except to give play to the imagination, which he rejects in general but yet does not wholly exclude (p. 60), and to make the picture of the Crucified as impressive as possible. The result is that the word of forgiveness is presented as something which can be known as truth before one has received it. But just as man can only know love to be real by loving; so too only he who has been forgiven can know the truth of forgiveness.

In short, speaking of Jesus in such a way is certainly not speaking of him theologically. It is the 'Christ after the flesh' who is portrayed before our eyes, and even that portrait is wholly abstract. For since this Jesus is manifestly separated

from us by a great distance, all the features are heightened to
the absolute and thus lose their individual character. What
finally results is a wholly formal ideal which has been coloured
by a kind of aesthetic contemplation. An 'always prayerful,
always obedient surrender' (p. 80) is an *abstraction*. 'A perfect
manifestation of the character of God in man' (p. 79) is something which we cannot even imagine, but it is equally an
abstraction.

If Jesus is to be understood, as Hirsch explicitly intends
(pp. 78–82), according to the analogy of our own personal life,
then obviously what is presented to us by the statement that the
history of his inner life was a history of the good only, is an
abstraction. His inner life, as Hirsch portrays it, was without
break or spot, always and only a continual living activity of
good and blessed decision. Quite apart from its original com-
pleteness and purity, it was kept inviolate by the acceptance of
wonderful divine guidance and was fulfilled and deepened
(p. 87). Such a picture is merely an ideal carried to the extreme
limit; it has no actuality whatever. And the New Testament
knows nothing at all of it. The close kinship of rationalism and
pietism has never shown itself to me so vividly as in this portrayal by Hirsch.

IV

I cannot admit, therefore, that Hirsch is really speaking
theologically about Jesus. And I find that in his presentation he
has abandoned his own fundamental position and has reverted
to a form of the discredited Life-of-Jesus theology. Consequently I do not care to say more on the first part of the book.
The particular shadings which appear in the portrait presented
are subordinate to the general view. A discussion of details
would only be possible after a consideration of the source-
criticism presupposed. I will only express my regret that the
author was compelled to keep the first part so brief. Important
ideas are not developed, important passages in the text do not
receive penetrating interpretation. This lack could certainly
be remedied in a second edition.

But what has already been said must suffice, while I turn to
a defence against the charge which Hirsch has brought against

me. My criticism of his position would remain entirely negative if I could give no positive answers to his questions.

Hirsch feels bound to charge me with having reverted to the belief in authority and thereby to the justification by works of orthodoxy, which he has so effectively criticized. If I repudiate his theory of mediation and his basis for faith, how can I myself then show how faith is grounded in its content? That is the question Hirsch asks in his review of my book, *Jesus and the Word*.

'If the Word, even as it calls us to decision, is to . . . lead us into a personal relation with God, then it is not a matter of indifference to us that it did not fall from heaven as a printed book, but is spoken by a living man' (*Zeitwende*, 1926, p. 312). 'One is not the bearer of a word to another in the way a porter carries a sack. It makes no difference to the porter whether the sack holds iron or coal or something else; and the sack does not care whether Hans Schulz or Willi Müller is dragging it. But a word is borne as an apple tree bears an apple. It is self-evident that on this apple tree there can be no other fruit and for this apple no other kind of tree, because the same life, the same sap, flows in both. This means that God always in *one* way proclaims to us a Word which witnesses to him; he creates the living man in whom it flowers' (*ibid.*).

I should like to put the counter question. *By whose authority, then, is the Word proclaimed among us?* Does the right to stand before the community and the world as a preacher of the Word depend on the personal qualities of the preacher? That does not seem to be Luther's opinion, according to the statement of Gogarten which is cited (*ibid.*, p. 287). Can I justify my unbelief in the Word by saying that I do not know the state of the proclaimer's heart? Or that in fact I know that all is not in good order there? Does the Christian message really depend on anything except the printed book fallen from heaven? Must we first as personalities make our hearts into a pedestal for the Word of God?

Certainly it is true that 'it is wholly impossible to speak of God and divine things without disclosing one's self' (Hirsch, p. 312). But that fact can serve only as a warning against substituting our faith (as a discernible situation) for the proclamation, and guiding the hearers to it as a substitute. We are required to proclaim the 'faith which is believed', not the 'faith by which one believes'! The latter can be directed only to its object and must not be diverted by the proclaimer towards the 'faith by which one believes'. In order to proclaim the 'faith which is believed' so that it becomes manifest to the 'faith by which it is believed', the proclaimer must attend not to his personality but to his theological training. We may well be amazed, but the concrete situation for the preacher actually is that when he goes up into the pulpit, a printed book lies before him. And that book must be the basis for his preaching, exactly as if it had 'fallen from heaven'. (Its origin as established through historical criticism obviously does not concern him at that moment.)

Therefore *the inner relation between Word and bearer of the Word is irrelevant to the claim of the Word.* Certainly it can become impossible to misunderstand a word because of a person who exemplifies it in his life; but it can equally well be misunderstood because of a human example. The preacher, therefore, in order to make misunderstanding impossible, can only point steadily away from himself towards the Word.

But what kind of Word is it? It is 'the Word pointing to God', and as such it is 'always testimony to a personal will which in itself is unknown to me' (p. 313). For that reason it is a matter for decision and the question, 'how is such testimony to be validated for me?' (p. 313), must be answered by 'in no way at all' – if the question means that through attending to anything whatever apart from the Word I could be relieved of the decision. 'But I trust the witness of another personal will, hitherto unknown to me, only so far as I believe (!) that I have in him evidence of a living union with that will' (p. 313). That seems to me too little in a matter of life and death. For who is to tell me that the other person is not living in an illusion? In that way every belief may be justified. For in the life of a Buddhist or of a Moslem, cannot faith have attained full unity with will? No, the truth of a man cannot guarantee the truth of his message – there is only the 'printed book'. And in that book the question can truly have a positive answer – none other than John 7.17.

Now the kind of question with which Hirsch and many others confront my book is entirely understandable. They want to know how I rescue myself from the situation created by my *critical radicalism;* how much I can still save from the fire. Wiser people, like P. Althaus[5] and Friedrich Traub[6], have even discovered that I saved myself from my scepticism by taking refuge in Barth and Gogarten. They must pardon me for finding their wisdom comical. I have never yet felt uncomfortable with my critical radicalism; on the contrary, I have been entirely comfortable. But I often have the impression that my conservative New Testament colleagues feel very uncomfortable, for I see them perpetually engaged in salvage operations. I calmly let the fire burn, for I see that what is consumed is only the fanciful portraits of Life-of-Jesus theology, and that means nothing other than 'Christ after the flesh' (Χριστὸς κατὰ σάρκα).

But the 'Christ after the flesh' is no concern of ours. How things looked in the heart of Jesus I do not know and do not want to know. Nevertheless, it seems to me that there is a profound truth, not in what Hirsch says but in what he really means. If I am to discuss this point with Hirsch, the discussion must also include my truly honoured teacher, Wilhelm Herrmann. To him I wish to relate myself directly. For in his work the tendency which I deem right is clearer and more pronounced, since he saw the mistakes made by the usual Liberalism. In what follows there should be no suggestion of personal antagonism between Hirsch and me. Rather, we are both concerned with a pressing theological problem.

v

Faith (the 'faith by which one believes') is obedient hearing of the Word – that is, of the Word which tells me that I am a sinner and that God in Christ forgives my sins – and such faith is a *free act* of decision. For only in the free act of decision is the being of man as a historical being achieved. Here I think I am in agreement with Hirsch (cf. his book, p. 50). Then follows the theological task of guarding this act of faith against the misunderstanding of it as a work. This task, Herrmann declared (*Gesammelte Aufsätze*, pp. 105f.), had still to be accomplished. And he sees the task as such to be simple when faith is defined as trust. 'If faith is pure trust, then it is for us a free surrender

---

[5] *ZST*, I (1923/24), p. 765, line 3.
[6] *Glaube und Geschichte*, Gotha, 1926, p. 38.

which is the exact opposite of a voluntary undertaking (the latter would be a "work"). Accordingly it is, in its depths, *our own work.*' (I should prefer for the sake of clear terminology to say 'act'.) 'But then equally it is experienced as the work of one stronger than us, who inwardly compels us. This experienced union of dependence and freedom characterizes true religion. It creates an inwardly independent nature; it is a wholly incomprehensible event' (*ibid.*).

The question, then, is this: if faith is act, does it not follow that we wish to be saved by our own act? If faith is decision, does not our salvation depend on our own resolve? When the tradition of the church refers to the Holy Spirit who works this act in us, the answer has no meaning if the Holy Spirit is conceived as some mysterious entity which is operating behind our resolves. That would result, as Herrmann says, 'in thinking according to Augustine and living according to Pelagius' (*ibid.*, p. 46). But if the Spirit is the manner of the new historical existence of the Christian, then in the traditional answer the problem is defined, although it is not solved. We are reminded by it that 'in Christ' (ἐν Χριστῷ) our action is 'a being driven by the Spirit' (ἄγεσθαι πνεύματι, cf. Rom. 8.14) and yet the action does not cease to be ours. The task, then, is to make this act understandable.

Herrmann therefore demands that dogmatics elucidate the *genesis of faith* (e.g. *ibid.*, pp. 116–18); not, of course, as a process to be interpreted psychologically, but by showing that 'faith is engendered by that which then forms its content' (*ibid.*, p. 268). Since faith is not a knowledge of propositions but an act of historical living, it must be presented as such. This Herrmann thought he could accomplish if he characterized the act as '*experience*'. In spite of many easily misunderstood turns of expression and some which are themselves the result of misunderstanding, Herrmann did not mean a state of soul, or a soul-condition which we could have in our possession, but a real historical event, the experience of trust which is at once act and effect. And he did not misjudge the intentional character of the experience. 'Our trust lives always through the power of that which created trust in us' (*Die mit der Theologie verknüpfte Not der evangelischen Kirche und ihre Überwindung*, Tübingen, 1913, p. 24). No cult of experience is asked of us, but rather integrity in confronting our own experiences (*ibid.*, p. 22). That is to say, we are to relate ourselves, not to our experience as a soul-condition but to that in which, in the experience of trusting, I put my trust. This integrity also involves the complete accept-ance of the claim under which we always stand, acceptance of the existential knowledge of the precariousness of our present moment, acceptance of living historically. That is what is meant by the statement: 'Nothing in history can belong to us except what we ourselves experience' (*ibid.*, p. 24).

But what is this *experience of trust*? It exists 'when a personal life touches us to which we can cleave in trust and reverence. Such experiences become for us revelations of him by whom alone we can know ourselves to be absolutely governed in free surrender. In them is revealed to us each time in a special way something of the only Being whom we can rightly call God. But certainly we find our God in this spiritual power only when we will to put ourselves in the relation of trust to that power as we have experienced it. If we clearly see how it brought us to full surrender and thereby created true life in us, then we should be dishonest and untrue if we were not ready to obey it alone and to seek the conquest of our difficulties through it alone. The real value-content of all historical living is the experience of justice and mercy, the spiritual power felt when trust is created. For the man who is truly sincere, it becomes the living God' (*ibid.*, p. 22f.). We are thus led to the genuine historical en-counter of *Thou* and *I*. And we can understand that in the encounter the unity of act and gift, of freedom and necessity, of independence and obedience is real precisely in the experience of trust.

Herrmann also makes it clear that this is not an experience of seeing a revelation which is objectively present in the in-dividuality of the other person. The revelation is only in the historical process of the creation of trust. For 'he who bows down before the moral goodness of any one man does not relate himself to that single man only when he is moved to reverence. Through the impression he has received there is born in his thinking the conception of a higher power which is acting upon us in this particular phenomenon. We feel ourselves gripped by this higher power in the depths of our life and know our-selves to be wholly and entirely dependent upon it as we undergo that simple ethical experience. Therefore, reverence for persons, inner obeisance before the phenomenon of moral force and goodness, is the root of all true religion' (*Gesammelte Aufsätze*, pp. 52f.).

But such trust and reverence for moral strength and goodness is clearly not the Christian faith. For such an experience is possible and actual within every human life and it loses its power when the experience changes to disappointment and mistrust. *Without* power, however, there is no real trust; that is, trust *by itself* cannot change us from sinners to righteous men. Our mistrust is always standing close beside the hate in which we are actually imprisoned; and this hate forces us to misuse the experience of trust. We always attach ourselves to the individual and put our trust in him instead of in God; we hold to the visible, the objective, instead of to the invisible. Therefore we always become uncertain of those whom we trust. And so far as, in spite of disappointments, we try to hold firmly to what was given us in the experience of trusting (as Herrmann tries to do), we hold *either* to an *idea* of goodness as the power of history *or* to a *demand*, the authority of which we admit, so that we then stand under the *law*. Thus what is essential is attributed to man. For it is indeed true that we find God in the power confronting us in the experience of trust *only* when we remain related to it as we experienced it. But here we inevitably fail and such a revelation becomes therefore uncertain to us. It ultimately shows us only what is required of us and that we live in hate.

This Herrmann also knows, for he continues: 'The faith which sustains a Christian is not, of course, yet complete. But certainly, the Christian faith, when it is genuine, is simply the completion of this beginning' (*ibid.*, p. 53). That statement is true. There remains only the question of how this completion is conceived. Here the church tradition, functioning as law (for law and gospel belong together) will refer us to Jesus. But in what sense?

According to Herrmann, it is *the impression made upon us by Jesus*, the person, that redeems us. Jesus is the 'manifestation of personal goodness' which grips 'men as a revelation' and makes them 'gaze in reverence upon the domination of reality by goodness'. 'The personal life of this man has the power to create for itself an incomparable instrument in a rich tradition. From this tradition, the receptive man can discover in astonishing freshness the spiritual activity of the soul of Jesus, how he thought and felt, what he desired and accomplished; and can thus experience its overwhelming force. Only he who can so find Jesus receives the complete revelation of God and is thereby raised above the anxiety of this world and above the misery to which the law as revealed by Jesus reduces men. By this unlimited power of Jesus' will to good, we not only are made certain of God; we also are reconciled to God by the way in which Jesus related himself to sinful men'. (*ibid.*, pp. 54f.).

Our relation to the person, Jesus, is unlike our relation to other men. With them, the ethical demand that we experience through them gives us at the same time a critical insight into whatever is misplaced in them. The ideal which we thought they embodied grows beyond them. Jesus becomes the interpreter of our conscience, becomes a conscience for us, becomes our judge. But 'while by the simple power of his personal life, he makes the sinner insecure; at the same time, by his friendliness, he gives him support'. As he long ago forgave the sinners who came to him, so now all men when they look back to his person are freed from their inward anxiety, from the whole burden of their guilt. 'When this is the effect of the impression that Jesus makes on us, then our faith is born. The man who undergoes that experience of the person, Jesus, understands the experience, with no need of anything further, as the impact of an overwhelming power, full of love and truth. . . . Thus through what the Christian experiences, he becomes certain that the power of the good not only judges him but also redeems him. Thus the Christian faith is created. That faith is simply the trust which Jesus won from us by his personal life, followed by joyful submission under the God who appears to us in Jesus and who acts upon us through him' (*ibid.*, pp. 15–17).

It is clear that this is what Hirsch is also saying. *But what is affirmed here is an impossibility.* Basically, the assertion is that the experience of trust, which in relation to other men is never possible for us except as a broken and insecure experience, in relation to the person, Jesus, can be unbroken, victorious – an experience to which we can always return.

But such an analogous relation of trust in Jesus is no longer possible for us. As a *Thou*, in the sense of a fellow man, he has vanished – as every such *Thou* vanishes when the man dies. Furthermore, there is no discoverable reason why, in a relation of trust in Jesus, our own will to be obedient should not be quite as uncertain as in the relation of trust in others; nor – if there really were such a difference – why the redemption would not then be accomplished by our own power to obey the demand of the good.

Since it is wholly impossible to enter into such an *I-Thou* relation with Jesus, Herrmann, against his will, succumbs to the danger of describing the *'inner life of Jesus'* as a historical datum present to hand in world history, which can be clearly seen with a little honest effort. He is obviously trying to guard himself against that danger when he says that the historical Jesus as Redeemer is not demonstrable as an indubitable historical fact to every man (e.g. *Gesammelte Aufsätze*, p. 24). But though the inner life of Jesus may not be a surely demonstrable fact for historical research, yet it can be a fact of experience for us (e.g. *Die mit der Theologie verknüpfte Not*, p. 26). That can be the case when the man through the experience of trust is really led to a genuine act of will, to reverence, and repentance.

But since the man still cannot come in any way into an *I-Thou* relation with Jesus, the course of Herrmann's thought finally leads to presenting the 'inner life of Jesus' as an objective fact – although it is nonsense to try to see the faith and the love of a man as objective facts.

What Herrmann has forgotten is twofold. First, the eschatological position which according to the New Testament Jesus holds as the One who is the crisis (κρίσις), the turning point, of the ages, through whom the human race has won the possibility of being conditioned by love instead of by hate. That is a truth which in itself can neither be demonstrated nor experienced; it can only be believed.

And second, he has also forgotten that the ground of faith is solely the Word of proclamation (Rom. 10.17). Therefore Herrmann denies Scripture its unique position. He wants to 'broaden' Luther's designation of Scripture as the Word which can rescue every man from his miseries when he seeks and finds Christ in it. 'The Creator of a new life is near to us, acting in everything which brings us a conviction of the One Invisible

God. This conviction we experience *above all* in the faith which becomes known to us in wonderful diversity and unity through the Holy Scripture. Here again the Christ of the New Testament is exalted above every other God-filled and God-supported life' (*ibid.*, p. 32). But in all this, Scripture is not regarded by Herrmann as the proclaimed Word which demands 'faith's obedience' (ὑπακοὴ πίστεως!) but as a document which furnishes information about the faith of persons whose faith was strong.

Finally, all this stems from the fact that Herrmann, because of his front-line position in the revolt against orthodoxy, overlooks in the concept of faith the *moment of obedience to the proclamation*. He is rightly concerned to avoid the misunderstanding that faith is obedient, unintelligent acceptance of doctrine and he wants to show clearly how far one can speak of a true obedience which is not a work performed. But he ignores the truth that the proclamation presents Jesus as an historical fact through which our own historical existence is decisively conditioned – although that fact is not verifiable by historical science. He is therefore continually seeking for something which we can use as a proof for the scriptural promise of forgiveness. He does not see that if the Word declares our existence to be conditioned by an historical event, that Word can be spoken only from beyond our existence; for we ourselves do not rationally comprehend our existence. We can only acknowledge the Word, only believe it in obedience.

It is therefore necessary to abandon absolutely the search for proof of the Word of proclamation, either external proof or proof within ourselves (in 'experiences'). We must really accept in earnest Rom. 10.17: 'So faith comes from what is heard, and what is heard comes by the Word of God'. *Faith is directed to the Word and to the authorized proclamation of the Word.* Therefore, no other validation can be demanded for the Word and no other basis created for it than the Word itself. When it comes to us, it asks us whether or not we will hear it.

'Therefore we must be on guard, for if we try to preserve the Gospel, not by its own power, but by our own strength, then the cause is lost. For whatever is most ably defended by men, crumbles. Let us stop worrying. The Gospel does not need our help. It has strength enough of its own. Let God take care of it by himself. It is his and he will protect and maintain it. Therefore I leave it to him, however many and great are the attacks against us. But so far as the Gospel is concerned, all that does not trouble me at all and I have no anxiety about how I shall defend it. I and all of us together are too weak to defend such a Word. I have entrusted it to the dear God. It is his Word and he is strong enough to defend it and protect it, however much they rage and storm. . . . In all these troubles there is no better counsel than to preach the Gospel purely and simply and ask God to direct and lead us' (Luther, *EA*, vol. 15, p. 538).

But, then, how do we meet the objection that in the proclamation a myth is presented to me which does not at all relate to myself, to my existence? That therefore I must accept a fact which is no part of the reality of my life? That faith therefore becomes a fortuitous choice of a fortuitous possibility, that it is subject to my preference and is therefore only pseudo-obedience? That I obey an authority which is actually constituted an authority by my obedience? 'Faith in God sticks to the Word, which is God himself; trusts and honours the Word, not because of the person who speaks it, but because faith feels it to be so certain and true that no one could tear faith away from it. . . . The Word in itself, without respect to person, must be enough to move the heart, must so capture and hold a man that he is imprisoned in it, feels how true and right it is – even if all the world, yes even if God himself says otherwise' (Luther, *EA*, vol. 10, pp. 162f.).

The objection that the authority is of my own making proceeds from the presupposition that I must myself make a resolve to have faith, as if I had been offered an option. But faith does not depend on a resolution about which I can deliberate. Faith is immediate decision; that is, in hearing I *have* already *decided how* I hear. The objection overlooks the fact that I am a historical being, that *the Word of the proclamation does not confront me in a detached situation as a fortuitous happening, but confronts me as I live within a definite historical situation*. It directs me to nothing other than my history. This Herrmann sees rightly at first; but he does not maintain the thought. However, he is entirely right when he says that the Word presupposes that I am living within the experiences which he describes and also assumes that I face those experiences honestly. Briefly, the Gospel presupposes the law which is a given part of my historical existence.

Now all these 'experiences', trust and reverence, distrust and repudiation, love and gratitude, hate and ingratitude, loyalty and honour, disloyalty and remorse – in short, our genuine historical existence in the intercourse of *I* and *Thou* – all these are really disclosed to us for the first time in the Word of the proclamation. This Word (just by the speaking) teaches us to see what kind of being we are in those experiences; how in them we stand before God. The proclamation does not effect a magical change in our life by demanding our obedience and giving us forgiveness. It brings nothing into our life as a new entity. It only opens our eyes to ourselves – though not, of course, for the purpose of self-observation. The hearing is an event in our historical living and becomes an act of decision for this or for that. The decision conditions our life anew – this way or that, for 'life' or for death.

In these 'experiences' we are always being questioned, being put to the test. We cannot possess them; we 'have' them only in action. But in that act, the more genuinely we grasp the experiences, the more uncertain and doubtful of ourselves do we become. We do *not* have faith in the experiences, nor do we obey them. The proclamation asks us whether we are ready to believe the experiences as a possibility which God has injected into our history. It commands us to believe in that possibility on the ground of forgiveness, that is, we must believe because our history is so conditioned, is so re-cast by the historical fact, Jesus Christ, that we may grasp love as its possibility.

The proclamation therefore comes to us each time within our historical existence, not outside it. It proclaims *forgiveness*. It does not detach us from our historical situation but propels us into it. It gives us no new possession – neither knowledge, gnosis, nor moods and emotions, nor mystic experiences. It proclaims the justification of the sinner; it directs man to his own humanity. For *this* humanity, grace is valid. And the grace of forgiveness is simply the fact that the history in which we live is conditioned by the 'crisis' in Jesus Christ. We are asked whether we will to belong to the new age of love and life, or whether we will to remain in hate and in death.

The question, therefore, does not come to us as a fortuitous inquiry from the outside and its answer does not depend on a preference which is subject to our deliberation and choice.

The question confronts us with the disclosure of how in those 'experiences' we are always *radically* questioned. It is distinguished from our own questionings under the law not only because it questions radically but also because it simultaneously gives the answer. What is really asked is whether we are willing to hear the answer that we are sinners and must accept grace. We are questioned the more forcibly, the more our history in general is characterized by those 'experiences' in the intercourse of *I* and *Thou;* but with still greater force when that history includes the encounter with the *Thou* which is qualified by Christian faith and Christian love – that is, the more we stand within the history of the Christian church.

'The more' is required, for today it no longer seems possible to say simply *that* we stand within the church. For where is the Christian church? Where is the Word proclaimed? But even if we really had to say that the Christian church has vanished, it would still be no less possible to believe the Word of Scripture (which at least exists as a 'printed book'); for certainly the law cannot vanish. And thus it would be possible for the Christian church to arise again.

It is also clear that in the church there is a *dual proclamation of the Word: preaching* and *conduct.* For historical living under the Gospel demands more than historical living under the law. Here I come back, with a justifiable bias, to Hirsch's attack against me. And again I cite Herrmann in support.

'We can help them [the others] only in one way. By what we see there [in the New Testament] we must be made to reverse our course and we must have found there a happiness which can, without our talking much about it, give joy to men who come in contact with us' (*Die mit der Theologie verknüpfte Not,* p. 270). 'The Social Democrat declares that there is nothing but self-interest in the world. Now we show him that there is love. Our faith knows that the power over all things rests with love. Whether the love will rescue our enemy or harden his heart we do not know. But it acts. It has an ally in his own thoughts' (*Gesammelte Aufsätze,* p. 487).

Of course, in the proclamation by conduct we do not point to ourselves. This proclamation is not direct but indirect; that is, it is achieved by our action in the strict historical sense. We do not exhibit our personalities in a shop window, we do not put our experiences on display. We *act* in faith and love. We do not build a foundation for the Word of God and we do not point to anything as a ground on which faith could be accepted. All our action can only *question* the other man and the result can easily be to make him more obdurate. But we are conscious of our own responsibility, because faith is not a *general* possibility but an *historical* possibility. Consequently, faith can be made easier or harder and it lies within our power to make faith easier or harder for others. In this kind of action we are not engaging in some special kind of activity such as social welfare or home missions. There are no particular 'professions' which perform works of faith and love; but all our acts in fulfilling our everyday obligations can become such works.

None of the above, however, applies to the proclamation of the Word through preaching. In preaching we have only to proclaim the 'faith which is believed'. We do not have to produce faith, or to talk of personalities strong in faith and love – neither the personalities of others nor our own. Least of all may we talk of our own! Here the excellent word of old Achelis holds good: 'Do not preach of yourself; rather preach to yourself.'

Faith is not directed towards something which lies outside the reality of life, outside historical existence, nor towards anything which is established by a supernatural authority (the church as it is misunderstood) or by any process of reasoning. Faith is in reality directed towards something which *confronts* me; that is, something which does not lie within those possibilities of life under my control. Faith makes it manifest that the existence of man does not in fact stand under man's control. We are exposed to powers which determine history and we are always being tested about the way in which we will grasp the possibilities of our historical existence. Since the historical fact of Jesus Christ, we are asked: will we listen to God or to the devil?

There remains to be clarified the question of the assurance of salvation. Faith is certain of salvation only when it looks, not at itself but at him on whom it believes. 'For it would be a lamentable delusion if we should try to rely on the strength of our faith instead of on that which gives faith validity' (*Gesammelte Aufsätze*, p. 267). And in discussion with Frank, Herrmann says pertinently: 'I consider much more dangerous [than the artificial erection of dogmatic tradition into statements of faith] Frank's assumption that the ultimate support for the thinking of the believer is found in a fact of the subjective life, in the spiritual experiences of the reborn. That assumption does not correspond to the true relation. The thinking of the believer will never find its ultimate support in what God has made out of him. The support is in the objective fact of the revelation which God put into the world for him' (*ibid.*, pp. 290f.).

Earlier Protestant dogmatics expressed this in its own way by saying that faith, considered in itself as a work, does not assure salvation. 'Faith does not make a man pious and justified before God by being itself our work and belonging to us but by accepting the promised and proffered grace which is given unearned from the rich treasure'. (*Fides non ideo iustificat aut salvat quia ipsa sit opus per se dignum, sed tantum quia acceptit misericordiam promissum. Apol. Conf.*, II, p. 56). According to Luther, faith is insensibility (*insensibilitas*). 'It sees nothing; it is the dark road' (*EA*, vol. 37, p. 437). It can depend on nothing else than 'the bare word' (*nudum verbum*). 'Faith holds to that which it neither sees, feels, nor experiences, either in body or in soul. But it has a good confidence in God, hence it surrenders itself to that and supports itself upon that; it does not doubt that the outcome will happen as it expects. Therefore it certainly does so happen, and the feeling and experience come unsought and undemanded, just in and through such expecting and believing' (*EA*, vol. 14, p. 47).

In a sermon on Matt. 15.21–28, Luther says: 'But this is written for the comfort and instruction of us all, so that we cannot fail to understand how deeply God buries his grace for us and how we are not to picture him according to our feeling and thinking but strictly according to his Word. . . . Therefore the heart must reject such feeling, must grasp and hold fast the deep and secret *yes* which is above and below the *no*, with firm faith in God, like the little woman. We must confess God's rightness in his judgment against us; then we have prevailed with him and caught him in his own words' (*EA*, vol. 11, p. 125).

If the question of certainty for faith means anything other than a question concerning the Word of God, then it is surely a question of doubt. And doubt has no certainty at all; it can be mastered only through faith. In the relation of trust between *I* and *Thou*, I am asked only whether I believe the *Thou*. I cannot through my own feeling validate for myself the trust I have given him. This is equally true in man's relation to God. A faith which concentrates on itself is no more faith than a love which concentrates on itself is love.

Faith is act and is certain only in the consummating of the act. To make its certainty subsequently into a problem for investigation is to ignore its historical character and to look for faith in something objectively present instead of in action. And anyone who seeks a faith in the objectively present is punished with doubt.

6

THE SIGNIFICANCE OF 'DIALECTICAL THEOLOGY' FOR THE SCIENTIFIC STUDY OF THE NEW TESTAMENT[1]

[1928]

I

THE DESIGNATION 'dialectical theology' does *not* refer to a *theological system* presenting particular formulations of dogma which might be relevant for New Testament study – such as statements about sin and grace, revelation and Christ – and might be deduced from a dogmatic principle. Such statements actually would have no relevance whatever to New Testament science, the aim of which can only be to understand what the New Testament says.[2]

For example, suppose it were said: dialectical theology has asserted and established the dogma of the radical antithesis between God and man; hence the concepts of God and man in the New Testament must be understood consistently with that dogma. The answer would be: The New Testament alone can

[1] *TB*, VII (1928), pp. 57–67. (A lecture given at the Theological Conference in Eisenach, October 19, 1927, provided the basis for these observations.)

[2] The lectures which were given at the Theological Conference on the preceding day, October 18, by Dr Staerk and Dr Hempel on the significance of 'dialectical theology' for Old Testament study were based on the misconception that dialectical theology is a system of dogmatics. Both speakers understood their task to be the testing of such statements by the Old Testament, on the assumption that the Old Testament may be correctly understood apart from dialectical theology. Here the theme 'Dialectical Theology and Biblical Scholarship' loses its real meaning. For that meaning depends on the validity of the assertion made by dialectical theology that the motifs pursued in it are already verified in the interpretation of Scripture itself. A report on these lectures appeared in the publication of the work of the Conference, *Deutsche Theologie*, Göttingen, 1928. Staerk's lecture was printed in full in the *Allg. Ev. Luth. Kirchenzeitung*, 1927, no. 51.

give evidence on that point. Above all, it should be emphasized that the statement, 'God is not man and man is not God', is not a theological statement in any sense.[3] This statement speaks of God *in general* in contrast to man *in general*. It does not speak of God in *his relation to the individual man* – a relation temporally conditioned and recurring at specific moments. It therefore does not speak of God; it speaks of the *concept* of God. Theological statements which are truly theological are statements which speak of God and his revelation, not of the concepts of God and revelation. They are statements such, as for example, that God became man in Jesus Christ, that in Jesus Christ he forgives us our sins.

Nor, however, does the term 'dialectical theology' denote a *method of investigation* which ought to displace, say, the historical method. In the area of philosophy there might be a kind of 'dialectical method'; but for the New Testament there can be only *one* method, the *historical*. However, insight into what is really meant by dialectical theology could lead to a deeper insight into the nature of history and thus modify, enrich or clarify the method of historical investigation.

What, then, is meant by *dialectic*? Undeniably it is a *specific way of speaking* which recognizes that there exists no ultimate knowledge which can be encompassed and preserved in a single statement. For the sake of clarity, I offer an illustration of how a method of *philosophical dialectic* may proceed from this recognition. The dialectical method in philosophy depends on the conviction that every truth expressed is a partial truth and that the whole truth which is its basis can best be found by first setting beside it the contrary statement. For the contrary statement, so far as anything can be said in support of it, must also contain a portion of the truth. By setting the two partial truths against each other and combining them, it may be possible to grasp the underlying principle.[4]

If, however, we are speaking of *dialectical theology*, then what is meant is a dialectic in which the concept of truth is not determined by the concept of true statement but by the concept of

---

[3] The same holds, of course, for the other statements which Staerk cited as alleged dogmas of dialectical theology and tested by the Old Testament: 'eternity is not time', 'revelation and redemption are not history'.

[4] Cf. also ZZ, IV (1926), pp. 40ff.

reality. That is, a theological statement is not true because it can be based on a timeless principle of truth which exists in infinity and can at any specific time serve to prove the truth of a single particular statement. Consequently a theological statement is not true because its content expresses something which is timelessly valid. It is true when it gives the answer to the question posed by the concrete situation in time to which the sentence itself belongs when it is being spoken. Its truth is not the truth of a statement valid irrespective of time; its truth applies to the specific time of the speaking. The act of speaking, and not the content of what is said in isolation, is questioned as to its truth.[5]

Therefore, the statement that God is merciful to the sinner may express a truth and may be substantiated by an analysis of the conception of God, as, for example, in Scholasticism – i.e. a God who is not merciful would not be God. But, according to the dialectical *method*, there could also be set against it the contrary statement that God is angry at the sinner. This statement could be equally well substantiated and out of the two statements a deepened concept of God could be gained, since it would be understood that in God, wrath and grace for the sinner belong together as a unity – as the Scholastics tried to show. But obviously this would not be dialectical *theology*. For here only the *concept* of God was discussed, and theology must speak of *God*, even though it also speaks in concepts and has the responsibility to be clear in its concepts.

The *theological* statement that God is merciful to the sinner is not a general assertion about the concept of God, but declares that the real God is really merciful to real sinners, to you and to me. It contains, when it is really understood, a twofold insight: (1) I can know it and therefore say it only if God really *is* merciful to *me*. And this I can know only if he shows me or tells me that I cannot speak at all of his grace as inherent in his eternal nature, that I can speak only of his concrete act or

---

[5] I offer a simple example outside theology for such dialectic. The statement that the child owes his parents gratitude is meaningless when taken as an assertion of timeless validity. Only the individual child can assert it truly and meaningfully; the parents cannot. Conversely, the statement that the parents have an obligation to the child can be asserted only by the parents and not by the child, who in the act of saying it would dissolve the relation of sonship.

word. (2) Therefore, I can never speak of this mercy except in relation to such act or word. That is, this act or word is never merely the occasion which made me understand that God is eternally merciful; the act would then become a part of the past, the word would be a timeless doctrine. The act is always actual performance, the word is always true as it speaks to me.

That means that *the concept of the grace of God* is a dialectical one, or more accurately – not the concept of grace but the *statement* that *God is gracious to me*. It is dialectical, not in the sense that it would be completed and qualified by the opposing statement of the wrath of God against the sinner (although that, too, is true), but because, in one word, it is a *historical* statement. The 'knowledge' of God's grace is not knowledge of a timeless truth or of a fact of the past; it is the acceptance of the gracious act of God. Such knowledge is not gained by philosophical reasoning (θεωρεῖν) but by intimate relation (*yāda'*). That is, it is the acknowledgement of the claim of the lordship of God. This knowledge is therefore never a dead possession, something merely known. It is true where it is a reality, where God *is* merciful; that is, where he is merciful to *me*, and where I accept this grace.

Equally, this means that the grace of God is never an *entity objectively present to me;* it is not a characteristic, a quality. Rather, when I look at myself I see nothing but sin; grace I see only when I look at God – not when I entertain a correct idea of God, but when I set myself before and under God's act of grace.

II

But why do we believe that theological insight and knowledge must have such a dialectical character? If theology is not to speculate about God, if it is not to speak about the *concept* of God but of the real God, then in speaking of God theology must at the same time speak of man.[6] In its statements, therefore, theology presupposes a specific understanding of man. Just what is that relevant understanding? For the realization that when theology speaks of God it speaks at the same time of man is not new in itself.

From the point of view of idealism, the being of man is con-

[6] See above, pp. 53–65.

stituted by the Logos, reason, the eternal and absolute.[7] An *idealistic theology* therefore assumes that it is speaking simultaneously of God and man because, following ancient and classical tradition, it is accustomed to think of God and the absolute together. But actually such a theology speaks only of man.

According to the *romantic-naturalistic* view, the being of man is constituted by the soul as a centre of life, which emanates forces, receives and shapes experiences. A theology so oriented, which equates the 'creative' life and experience with God, of course believes that it is speaking simultaneously of God and man. It speaks only of man.

We believe that we understand the being of man more truly when we designate it as *historical*. And we understand by the historical nature of man's being that his being is a *potentiality to be*. That is to say, the being of man is removed from his own control, it is risked continually in the concrete situations of life and goes through decisions in which man does not choose *something for himself*, but chooses *himself* as his *possibility*.

The meaning of the slogan 'dialectical theology' can be briefly expressed in this way. It is the insight into the historical nature of man's being or – since theology is concerned with one specific mode of man's being, namely with his speaking – it is the insight into the historical nature of speaking about God. Obviously, then, dialectical theology is not a method of investigation, in so far as method is a way of investigation dependent on the character of the object investigated. It is rather the perception of the peculiar character of the object which precedes every investigation and makes it possible. In this case it is the perception of the historical nature of man and of his speaking of God.

Now what is the result when this insight is applied to the scientific study of the New Testament? There is no result which is in any

---

[7] I am not speaking, as D. Rudolf Paulus assumed in the Eisenach discussion, of a *dead* idealism. On the contrary, I find it very much alive. The recognition that idealism's view of human existence is not relevant to theology is not like the discovery, for example, that one has boarded the wrong train. In that case one gets off and boards the right one. But idealism's view of man's existence arises perennially out of existence itself and therefore its claim must be perennially challenged. For that very reason, the knowledge of faith is dialectical.

way different from the result of applying the same insight into the historical nature of man to scientific historical investigation as a whole. Because of this insight we shall always interpret every historical source as a genuine historical phenomenon, that is, with the presupposition that in it a possibility of human existence has been grasped and expressed. We shall therefore achieve a final understanding of the text only when we reach final clarity on the possibilities of human existence. But since as human possibilities these are at the same time our possibilities and therefore are not within our control, they cannot be classified under topical headings. The statements of the source cannot be fitted into a topical scheme. Rather, they can be understood only so far as we comprehend our own existence.

Therefore, it must be recognized in relation to exegesis, as in relation to any historical phenomenon, that the exegete is always realizing his own potentiality-to-be, grasping his own possibility in the exegesis. Thus we may not presume to interpret any statements which are made about God and man on the assumption that we are master of a final understanding of man and his possibilities. We can neither naïvely assume that this final understanding is that presented in the text nor naïvely use it as a standard for criticizing the text.

For example, a statement like the rabbinic pronouncement that the invisible God shows himself to man in the hour of his death is obviously understandable only to one who knows what 'death' is: it presupposes a specific conception of death. We do in fact bring to the interpretation a naïve conception of what death is, but is our conception the same as that in the pronouncement? What do we understand by 'death'? A mere cessation of life? A natural event? Perhaps impressions made upon the exegete by his own contacts with death are inescapably associated with his conception of it. It is certainly true that no one *knows* what death is except one who has died – and he is silent. One may perhaps know something more about it, before it comes, the more it obtrudes into one's life. The more a man knows of it, the more he will understand such a statement as that of the rabbis, what meaning of death is presupposed in it and what there is to say about it.

If an exegesis so oriented aims at understanding in its historical character what is said in the sources, it will realize the difference between statements in which something is reported about facts of nature or events in space and time and such statements as treat of the being of man. The latter obviously cannot be tested in the same way as the former, by available or readily discoverable facts. For man is not something objectively present in nature; his existence is lived, it is historical and exists in flux. All statements about man's being must, therefore, always correspond to the particular extent to which it is disclosed to the speaker, and the understanding of the exegete is in turn limited by the particular extent to which his own existence is disclosed to him. Furthermore this openness is always the understanding of *my* existence; it never has the character of a result achieved by investigation, of a truth of knowledge which can be tested, be possessed and given currency; which can then become the foundation of further new knowledge.

This knowledge always has a 'dialectical' character – not because it would be limited and completed by an antithetical statement, but because it must always be freshly won. I can never say, for example: now I *know* what Paul or John understood by 'death', because I can never say: now I *know* what death is. A statement which was once the adequate expression of an existential knowledge of death can, if it is conserved as something known, as a possession, hide from me an understanding of death, of my death. If I think I have fully 'penetrated' that statement, think that I now know what death is, I can still discover when death actually is threatening my life that I have known nothing about it all along.

III

Certain conclusions follow from what has been said.

1. When a statement concerning existence, concerning life and death, love and hate, sin and grace, good and evil, God and world, is to be interpreted, the interpretation will always need to ask: Out of what conception of existence did the statement originate? It must ask what understanding of existence underlay the concepts used in such statements. And it asks these questions because of the recognition that the existence of man is an unsolved question. It is not at all an unambiguous, objective fact but is susceptible to a number of interpretations. The exegesis will set beside the text which is to be understood the

naïve conception in which the exegesis is itself involved and will question its own conceptuality. For it knows that it has a possibility of understanding only if it keeps the question open for itself.

2. This exegesis will no longer understand history according to the idea of development. Certainly the concepts used in discussion are developed according to the laws of logic; certainly there is a development of institutions. But what is never developed anywhere is the solution of the problem of existence. Certainly the understanding of the problem can become richer and deeper; but not as though a particular insight established a level on the basis of which a higher insight is 'developed'. Rather, every insight must always be freshly won (as every act of mutual understanding in trust and love between men is essentially new). And every insight is maintained only so long as it continues to stand the test of being lost, of fallenness. No one ever 'has' the solution. No one 'knows' what death is, or happiness, or love, or hate, in the way one knows that $2 \times 2 = 4$, or that the Council of Nicea met in 325.

It is, for instance, possible that insight into human existence is more true at a primitive stage of culture and science than at a more highly developed level. The concept of power, *mana* or *orenda*, which is found in 'primitive' religions, is customarily investigated in scientific accounts on the basis of a particular scientific view of nature and accordingly is explained as a concept of primitive science which has been superseded. Then, for example, statements of the New Testament in which this concept of power plays a role are customarily judged in the same way. But the question we ought to ask is what understanding of human existence finds expression in the concept of *mana*. Obviously (though with the provision that we, too, are speaking from a definite conception of existence) it is the understanding of human life as surrounded by the enigmatic and the uncanny; as at the mercy of nature and of other men. And at the same time the temptation inherent in human life is expressed in this concept, since there appears in it the will to escape from what imprisons man, to make one's self secure by outwitting the enigmatic powers through making them useful to one's self. Perhaps a much truer conception of human existence is expressed there than in the Stoic view of the world or in that of modern science – irrespective of how much more highly developed the science may be in comparison to that of the 'primitive' world.

Or consider the characterization of the 'Word of God' in Oriental religions as the Creator's Word which calls the world into being, and as the oracle which illuminates present and future and gives counsels for action. What is meant is plainly not understood when one speaks of an anthropomorphic concept appearing here, or of a primitive idea of the magic of the spoken word – however 'correct' all such comments may be from a specific angle of inquiry. But certainly there is to be seen in that concept of the 'Word of God' a recognition of the truth that man knows himself to be limited by and dependent on a power which puts the world and himself beyond his control, which relegates him to the position of a creature; a power which removes his own action from the direction of his arbitrary will and prescribes what he ought to do.

In other words, man knows himself dependent on God as the marvellous power which sets him simultaneously in darkness and in light. In darkness, for it puts the world and himself outside his control. In light, for this power is in a certain sense understandable; consequently man is understandable to himself and light falls for him on what he ought to do. Therefore, he calls this power the 'Word of God'; the word of *God* because it is the word of the dark power which stands over him, to which he knows himself to be surrendered; the *Word* of God because it is not wholly incomprehensible to him, but 'says' something to him – something about himself.

A 'more developed' conception, like, for example, the Logos of the Stoics, perhaps corresponds to a view of the world which is more advanced scientifically. But the question is whether man's existence is as truly comprehended when man is understood as a piece of the cosmos which is ruled by law and which can be rationally understood in its conformity to law.

3. This interpretation will also no longer describe its own development as parallel to the development of the natural sciences. For the interpretation itself is dependent on the degree of the disclosure of its own existence at any given time; the concepts it uses can be developed, but not its own fundamental understanding. A statement like that made above on the con-

cept of *mana,* i.e. that in it is expressed the understanding of existence as surrounded by the uncanny, can certainly be transmitted by science. But at any given time it is understood only according to the degree in which the eeriness of existence is understood by the interpreter himself.

Scientific development is unending, and therefore only a science wholly estranged from life can fail to hear the question, of the meaning that such science has when it reaches definitive results only in infinity. Certainly such a science, which always produces conclusions that are only relative, would be useless for theology and for the church, when theology and the church must demand absolutely certain pronouncements.

Hence it seems absurd even to the laity that the scientific exegesis of the New Testament must continually be on the move. Why, for instance, can one not be content with Luther's translation and interpretation of Scripture? In fact, an exegesis of the New Testament, as a really historical science, would become meaningless unless it has within itself the possibility of a definitive understanding of the text. But if the interpretation of a text involves the understanding of its comprehension of human existence and such understanding depends on the exegete's awareness of his own existence and its possibilities, then a definitive interpretation is in principle possible at any time. Of course, such an interpretation is never a 'scientific result', a sure possession which can be transmitted. It has always a 'dialectical' character; that is, the possession of the 'correct' interpretation can prevent a true understanding of the text, because true understanding must derive from the question of the specific man whose own existence is at stake.

Scientific work is, of course, unending, because our concepts develop endlessly. Therefore, the task of interpretation is set afresh in every generation; that is, to be intelligible, interpretation must use new concepts. Though Luther's exegesis of St Paul may rest on a genuine understanding, yet we cannot rest content with it, for the simple reason that we must first reinterpret Luther.

4. From all this it is clear that the real task of historical science, and hence of exegesis, does not consist in reconstructing a piece of the past and fitting it into the great complex of inter-relations called history (i.e. world history). For an investigation

of that kind the documents serve as 'sources'. Out of them, by a reciprocal process, first a picture of the time that produced them is constructed; and then from that picture the documents are to be understood as phenomena to be fixed at that specific time and place. Such a procedure presupposes a final and available understanding of human existence; it assumes without proof whatever naïve understanding the historian of the moment happens to hold. The historian *knows* basically the nature of all the matters of which the text speaks: God and world, life and death, sin and grace, etc. He does not submit his own existence to question in the light of the text, but listens to what the texts say about these matters in order to assign them their proper place in the 'development' of thought. Naturally, all statements then appear as part of a great inter-related complex which culminates in the understanding accepted as self-evident by the historian.

The construction of this complex, however, (which in itself can be understood idealistically, materialistically or otherwise) is not the result of historical research but is the presupposition for it. But this presupposition is untenable when I realize that my understanding of man is always provisional, unproved, perhaps wholly wrong. In that case, the text always offers the possibility that I could gain a new understanding of myself from it. It is not a 'source' for what has been in the past; it is speaking of *me*, since it speaks of my existence; and I confront it, not to observe and confirm, but as truly questioning it, as willing to learn from it. It can become an authority for me.[8]

IV

All that has been said hangs in the air unless it is made clear how such turning back to history can really disclose to us the possibilities of our own existence, and how it is really possible to reach an understanding of an alien – in this case of a past – understanding of existence.

---

[8] How far the work of the historian also includes the task of reconstruc-tion of the past can only be hinted at here, since my purpose now is simply to show that such reconstruction is not the *goal* of his work. It certainly belongs within the scope of the work and its real significance consists in criticism of the tradition in which the historian himself stands at any parti-cular time and through which he must cut a clear view to the text and the concepts used in it.

If the text presents statements dealing with natural objects or with events in the world of space-time, the matter is relatively simple. The condition for the possibility of understanding is that the author of the text and I live in the same world, in which things and events such as are mentioned appear and in which they are generally accessible in principle. In that case I can understand even when the things or events were previously unknown to me. I can understand information about antediluvian or exotic animals because I have enough knowledge of the world to know what an animal is and what possibilities there are for the way animals look and live. If someone presents an object which does not conform to those possibilities, then I declare that it is not an animal. I can understand information about Egyptian fashions in hair-styles and beards because such fashions play a role in the world in which I live. I can understand accounts of a battle or of the founding of an empire because such events occur in the world in which I live, and I am involved in them.

The case is very different when the text deals, not with objects and temporal events within the world, but with the world itself, which is neither object nor event and of which I am myself a part, when it deals with my own existence, with life and death, or when it treats not some objectively present entity or occurrence, but existence itself. For existence never has the character of neutral objectivity like things in the world. What kind of instruction does the text give when there is no reference to anything objective?

Obviously, I can understand such a text only if I bring to it a *pre-understanding* of the subjects there discussed. For example, in order to understand what life and death mean in the text, I must already have a pre-knowledge of what life is and of what death is. Or in order to ask what is meant in the New Testament by revelation, I must already have some knowledge of revelation. Yet in what concerns the possibilities of my existence there is never a definitive knowledge which is possessed. What, then, is the nature of this pre-knowledge? It cannot be a fragmentary knowledge, like the knowledge belonging to the natural sciences; for such a fragment would have the character of definitive, possessed knowledge.

Idealism explains this pre-knowledge on the theory that I

already have a basic knowledge of everything which pertains to my existence and that all that is needed is the occasion which makes actual the knowledge already potentially given in reason. Historical learning acquires the character of 'recall' (ἀνάμνησις) in which the text plays the role of the occasion; that is, it does not really tell me anything additional in the true sense; it only brings to my consciousness what I already knew, since I am a reasoning being. But if man is understood in his historical character, then it follows that he does not *a priori* have his possibilities within his grasp, but grasps them in genuine decision.

A text can reveal to me a possibility of my understanding of existence *because* I have a pre-knowledge of my possibilities. I do not actually know what death and life are, for that could be truly known only when life is at its end – the end, when death is there, also belongs to it. Yet we have a peculiar pre-knowledge that death is not a mere natural event, not simply the cessation of life, but that it is the test of our life; that it is something unnatural, enigmatic, against which we struggle and in the shadow of which our whole life stands.

We know of it as one can know of love and friendship even if he has not found love, has never met a friend. We know of it as the blind know of light and the deaf know of sound. We know of it – and yet we only really know it when love is given us, when a friend comes to us. But for us truly to know it, there is the precondition that it should already be a possibility of life – not something to be idealistically interpreted or to be reduced to an objective entity, not a 'capability', but always a pure possibility, because our being is always a 'potentiality to be'. We know – overtly or covertly – about our possibilities because knowing what we are inheres in our living.[9]

It is impossible to tell anyone what death and life, sin and grace are, in the same way as it is possible to inform him that there are flesh-eating plants or varieties of fish that produce living young. Rather, when we speak to him about death and life, about sin and grace, we are speaking to him about his own

[9] I ignore here the fact that we always have this understanding already embodied in a certain interpretation since we stand in a tradition which speaks of these subjects and has developed concepts for them. The preconception which I have of death and life at any given time can even conceal the true pre-understanding.

life to which all these belong, just as light and darkness, love and friendship belong to it. Only on the basis of this pre-supposition can he understand what we say and only on the basis of this presupposition can we understand the contents of a text.

The text does not give me knowledge of any astonishing dis-coveries, nor of things already existent but hitherto unknown to me; it imparts no knowledge of unknown incidents. But possibilities of my own self are disclosed to me which I can understand only in so far as I am open to my possibilities and will to let myself be open. I cannot simply accept what is said as information;[10] for I understand it only by affirming or denying. This does not mean that I first understand and then take a position. The understanding comes about only in affirm-ing or denying. For this is a matter of the disclosure of my own possibilities which I understand as mine only by grasping them or by rejecting them as a perversion of myself. Understanding, therefore, is always simultaneously resolve, decision.

This is what is really meant when one speaks of '*spiritual*' (*pneumatic*) *exegesis*. This detestable expression is, of course, only likely to pervert a true understanding of the problem. For nothing is involved which is in the least analogous to some mysterious entity, the Spirit (*pneuma*) acting as interpreter and whispering the meaning of a text to me. Nor am I required to be a spiritual personality, in which or to which the Spirit attaches itself as a 'religious-ethical' quality.[11]

What is meant – what can only ever be meant – is that historical understanding is not achieved as an appropriation of knowledge, an acquiring of unknown 'facts'. It is an under-standing which is at the same time one's own decision about one's self. This understanding is neither irrational nor un-scientific. But the concept of science as derived from the natural sciences must not be transferred to history. On what is that prohibition based? In any science the nature of understanding

[10] The appearance of so doing exists only when I fail to question critically my preconceptions arising from the tradition in which I stand and instead interpret the text according to them.

[11] The statement that the prerequisite for a proper exegesis is prayer (H. Frick, *Wissenschaftliche und Pneumatische Verständnis der Bibel*, Tübingen 1927, pp. 32f.) is as true and as false as that prayer is a prerequisite for every good work.

can be determined only by its object; in this case, therefore, it is determined by history. Hence it is simply a question of the historical understanding of the science of history.[12] This requirement is as valid in relation to the New Testament as it is in relation to historical documents in general. All historical comprehension depends on the fact that the content to be interpreted pertains to my own existence, that my existence is characterized by openness, that I know more or less clearly about my possibilities. I can evade this knowledge, can hide it from myself, can forget it; but I still have it. Yet such knowledge is always a preunderstanding, a knowledge which does not know. For an individual existence never knows itself conclusively; it is always coming to know itself afresh and differently, because it is never finished. As every new situation in my life puts me in question and gives me the possibility of a new understanding of myself, so also does every text. It assumes my unknowing knowledge, a knowledge which has the character of a question. Unless I ask, I cannot hear; for man is not a *tabula rasa*, a photographic plate. But to be able to question, I must in some fashion already know.

For example, what is the meaning of the Johannine concept 'joy' (χαρά)? 'These things I have spoken to you, that my joy may be in you, and that your joy may be full' (John 15.11; cf. 16.22, 24; 17.13). What is promised is 'joy'; but this joy is the joy of Jesus and is a joy which the 'world' does not know. What kind of joy is that? Man does not know it; and yet he clearly has a pre-understanding of it, a question about it. Otherwise he would not understand the sentence at all. Obviously this joy is not gratification or pleasure, for those the world also knows. And yet the joy of the world must already bear within it the possibility of that supra-worldly joy.

v

In principle, then, there is nothing new to be said about the 'dialectical' interpretation of the New Testament. It simply requires the exercise of the historical understanding.

[12] I hope all talk of 'spiritual exegesis' will soon cease. Either it is relevant, in which case it is the duty of every exegete to announce himself as 'spiritual' or to forgo exegesis, or it is nonsense. I cannot believe that pastors will permit spiritual exegesis to be assigned to them as their domain and taken out of the hands of 'scientific' exegetes.

If interpretation must be governed by the question of how a particular statement of the text is *now* to be dealt with according to its understanding of human existence, and this question must challenge the naïve understanding in the traditional conceptuality of our time, then it is necessary to recognize that our traditional understanding of existence is determined by the modern development of thought, that is, by rationalism, the classical period and romanticism, by modern natural science and psychology, and by the Greek understanding of being and individual human existence which permeates all these sectors. As a result, we have to put the critical question, how far our own understanding of existence and the concepts we use are appropriate for the exegesis of the New Testament.

Since this does not usually happen, the meaning of many statements of the New Testament will remain shut away from us. Or else we understand statements which really speak of existence as statements speaking about man as an objective entity in the world, as a natural object. Hence – with a few exceptions such as the interpretations of Albert Ritschl and Adolf Schlatter – the concepts of Pauline anthropology are interpreted on the basis of a conception of existence wholly different from that out of which they came.

For example, 'world' (κόσμος) is understood as the world in which man stands as an object, as the natural world, as a *what*. But for Paul 'world' is meant in an existential sense, as the way in which an actual existing individual lives as such.[13] 'World', therefore, is not to be interpreted as an object but as a manner of man's existence.

Similarly, 'body' (σῶμα) and 'flesh' (σάρξ) are understood as an object attached to man.[14] This is especially clear in the distinction accepted from Holsten and Lüdemann to Holtzmann, the distinction between a 'physical' and an 'ethical' (or a secular and a religious) anthropology in Paul. This is to suppose that the concepts 'body' and 'flesh' primarily characterized men as natural objects in the world and that their meaning in

---

[13] M. Heidegger, *Sein und Zeit*, Tübingen, 1927, p. 65; ET, *Being and Time*, New York and London, 1962, p. 93.

[14] Strictly speaking, 'body' is usually interpreted as the 'form' of the 'flesh' which is understood as 'matter', a conception which is wholly Greek. In that case 'body of flesh' (σῶμα τῆς σαρκός) is in fact understood as 'formed matter', as an object from which man must be freed (cf. Rom. 7.24).

Paul could be determined independently of what they mean in relation to sin, to death, to the Holy Spirit, to the resurrection.

The result is that the relation asserted by Paul between 'flesh' and 'sin' (ἁμαρτία) can no longer be seen, and sin must be equated with sensuality. But from the beginning, 'body' and 'flesh' must be defined as the body and flesh of *the specific man* about whom Paul makes other statements. Anyone who insists on understanding 'body' as if it were a concept that applied to all entities which can have bodies (though Paul himself, of course, slips into that usage in I Cor. 15.38ff.) has decided beforehand that Paul viewed men in the category of objects in the world. To understand 'body' as 'form' is wrong because the Greek concept 'form' is derived from the product (ἔργον) of a craft (τέχνη) and, when applied to man, puts him in the category of an object in the world. Man is therefore seen as the Greeks saw him, but as Paul certainly did not.

Obviously the concept of the 'body' must also include the possibility of the Greek meaning; otherwise Paul and the Greeks could never have reached a mutual understanding by the use of the word.[15] Conversely, the possibility of the Pauline understanding must lie in what comprises the Greek concept of 'body'. A real understanding of the Pauline concept, as of the Greek, is therefore possible only through the search for the understanding of existence basic to the text. Such an investigation is made by a scrupulous consideration of the possible ontological meaning of 'body' in general as the term is actually used and of its possible modifications. Only then will the statements about the resurrection of the 'body' and the 'body of Christ' be intelligible.

Paul's conception may be briefly stated. 'Body' designates the being of man, in so far as it is not under man's control, man's historical existence which, according to Paul's thinking has two possibilities – it can be determined by God or by sin. The mode of existence of the body determined by sin is 'flesh'; that of the new man is 'spirit'. If the meaning of 'flesh' and

---

[15] So Paul (I Cor. 15.38ff.) lets himself be influenced by the Greek meaning. But to interpret the Pauline concept of the 'body' from that passage is methodologically false because there Paul is writing controversially. Where he uses 'body' in his own sense, it is clear that body does not mean form. See, for example, Rom. 8.10; here the meaning is '*you*, since you *are* body' – not 'since you *have* a body'.

'spirit' in Paul is now defined according to the naïve thinking which hypostasizes a mode into an object, Paul's statements become incomprehensible, since the meaning of matter or substance is assumed as the primary sense of 'flesh' and 'spirit'. How should Rom. 7.14–25 be understood? Lüdemann, who continued to work with sharply defined concepts, discovered here the conception of an anthropological dualism in agreement with the Greek view. 'Flesh' is not the *whole* of man, for in man the 'mind' (νοῦς) can be differentiated from the 'flesh'. Man does indeed stand under the domination of 'sin' (ἁμαρτία) which inheres in the 'flesh'; but since in the 'mind' he can distinguish himself as subject from the 'flesh', the possibility exists that the human power of the 'mind' may be strengthened through the 'spirit' so that the man may free himself from the flesh and overcome it. For if the flesh and sin were the whole of human nature, where would there be any possibility of salvation? All this is formulated in Greek concepts and accordingly that which for Paul is a mode appears as an object. Lüdemann, therefore, can think of the continuing subject, man, which must persist in the process of the history of salvation (if the redemption is to be understood as my redemption) only as an object, a substance. He cannot see man's being as historical.

A similar criticism applies to Bousset. He sees that for Paul the 'spiritual man' (ἄνθρωπος πνευματικός) is 'a being of a different and higher kind than the ordinary man'. He explains this superiority from the dual consciousness of the spiritual man; in other words, psychologically. Paul's supernaturalism, he thinks, is so strong that 'he threatens to split the unity and continuity of the human self completely. The Pauline Christian, like an ecstatic, has lost his real self, not only intermittently but permanently [!]. The self of man is nothing; the powers which determine this self, whether spirit or flesh, are all.' The opposite view of Rom. 7 has no significance, for here the human mind (νοῦς) is thought of, in Platonizing fashion, as man's better self. But this way of thinking is a concession to the natural self of man, or in the interest of a coherent psychology. So Bousset, too, can conceive man only as a substantive unity. He conceives this unity to be a unity of the mental process, psychologically understood. He, too, does not understand man's being as a historical being.

Actually, he misunderstands Rom. 7 because he interprets 'mind' or 'inner man' (ἔσω ἄνθρωπος) in the Greek sense as man's better self and hence he cannot combine with it statements about the 'flesh'. He cannot see that man is thought of by Paul from the beginning as subject to the claim of God. That is the *only reason* why Paul can speak of man's 'mind' and why for Paul it is just because of man's mind that his flesh is what it is.

But that means that Paul sees the 'unity of the subject' as grounded in the fact that God's claim goes out to man. From the beginning, the self is not seen as an isolated or isolatable entity, which is first objectively present and which God then claims. It is what it is, a self, only in so far as God's claim encounters it. Man's unity, therefore, is not a unity of substance, nor does it consist in the context of a psychologically comprehensible mental process, nor in the continuity of a rationally understandable development. It must rather be seen as historical; that is, as a unity which is given through man's being claimed by a *Thou*.

Man's being is not thought of as a phenomenon of nature, nor as a substance; it is achieved in his response to God's claim on him, and therefore in his action. But this action is understood, not as process going on in time (like the action of a machine) but as deliberate and responsible act. Just for that reason, man does not have his being at his own disposal, for at every moment it is being risked. That is, for Paul, man's being stands under the possibility of being determined by God or by sin.

VI

The significance of 'dialectical theology', therefore, does not consist in definite theological propositions presented to the investigator either for criticism or as the basis for exegesis. The insight into the dialectic of man's existence, that is, into the historical nature of man and of his statements, opens to the investigator a new road which is not a substitute for the old historical method, but which deepens it.

It is therefore basically incorrect to speak of the significance of dialectical *theology* in this context. So to speak only contributes to the misunderstanding that we have here a theological system. We must rather speak of the significance of the insight into the dialectic of existence, into the *historical nature of man's existence*. There is nothing theological in that.

The work of the exegete becomes theological, not because of his presuppositions and methods, but because of its subject, the New Testament. His character as a theologian is due to the fact that the church has sent him to the New Testament which he is to interpret. It is not what *he* can accomplish on the basis of his presuppositions, his methods of work, or even his degree of spirituality, that makes his work theological work. The task of investigating the New Testament is just as secular as the investigation of any other historical source. The responsibility for the theological character of the investigator's work is borne by the New Testament itself, which he merely serves. His hearing as an investigator is secular. Only the Word that is written there is holy.

7

THE ESCHATOLOGY OF THE GOSPEL
OF JOHN[1]
[1928]

THE Gospel of John (5.21ff.) describes *the mission of Jesus as eschatological*. His work is 'to give life' and 'to judge'. But these verses do not refer to the 'last judgment' or to the 'parousia' as a vivid cosmic event which is to come sooner or later. The eschatological event is already being consummated.

He who hears my word and believes him who sent me
   has eternal life;
He does not come into judgment,
   but has passed from death to life (5.24).

The hour is coming, and now is,
   when the dead will hear the voice of the Son of God,
   and those who hear will live (5.25).

He who believes in him is not condemned,
   he who does not believe is condemned already . . .
And this is the judgment, that the light has come into the
   world, and men loved darkness rather than light (3.18f.).

If anyone keeps my word,
   he will never see death (8.51).

I am the resurrection and the life;
   he who believes in me, though he die, yet shall he live,
   and whoever lives and believes in me, shall never die
   (11.25f.).

[1] ZZ, VI (1928), pp. 4–22.

It is usually said that in such sayings the old eschatological concepts have been transformed. Life is already here, the unbeliever is already judged. Is this not *spiritualization or even mysticism*? Is not life understood as purely 'spiritual', 'inward'? It is illegitimate to cite in contrast to this passages like 5.25f.; 6.54 which are evidently meant in the sense of the ancient eschatological drama, for these passages are suspected to be the result of redaction.[2] What must be investigated is the meaning of the concept of 'life' in the Gospel of John. An understanding of that concept can be gained from an insight into the so-called 'dualism' of the Gospel. Life belongs to the realm of God; death to the realm of the world. But what does *world* mean in the Gospel of John?

I

In the first place, 'world' (κόσμος) is not to be understood as 'the complex of gods and men and the entities brought into existence on their account'.[3] Rather, for John, as for the New Testament in general, God does not belong to the world; nor is he the world in totality. He stands over against the world. But the world is created by him through his 'Word' (1.1ff.). Here the 'cause' of the world should not be designated in the same way as that of an objective phenomenon; that is, the world is not to be derived as an objective entity from another objective entity, God, in order to be made theoretically understandable. The prologue makes this clear. The intent is rather to *qualify* the world as 'created'; it has the *character* of createdness. It is not conceived at all as an objective phenomenon. The 'world' – is primarily mankind.[4]

[2] That is in fact my own opinion. But the redactor must himself have understood these statements as consistent with the eschatology of the Gospel as it is to be developed above. However, I would prefer not to deal with this problem now. It can only be discussed when the recurrent, basic view of the Gospel is understood.

[3] Chrysippus, p. 257 (v. Arnim, *Stoic. vet. fr.* II, 168) 'The world, Chrysippus says, is the system of heaven and earth and the creatures in them. Or it is the system of gods and men and of those entities existing because of them. But from another viewpoint the world is called God, through whom its orderly arrangement is begun and completed.'

[4] Compare the alternation of 'all' with 'men', 'darkness', 'the world' (1.1, 3, 4, 5, 10). And compare the predicates used with 'the world'. The world 'knows' (or 'does not know') (1.10; 14.31; 17.23). The world 'loves' (15.19) or 'hates' (7.7; 15.18f.; 17.14); it 'receives' (or 'does not receive') (14.17); it 'sees' (or 'does not see') (14.19); it rejoices (16.20);

Man does not stand *over against* the world; he *is* world. That is, the world is not some objective entity, appearing separately in itself, in relation to which man can assume the position of an observer. (Any such observing would be a part of the world, would itself be 'world'.) But 'to be world' means first of all for men that they are created. And according to the prologue, the fact that man *is* world, i.e. that he is created, implies that man *can understand* himself in his createdness. For the 'Word' through whom the world came into being is from the beginning in the world as 'the light of men' (1.3–5).

This knowledge which man can therefore have of himself is not 'the light of reason and conscience' (at least not directly). It is primarily *acknowledgement*, for it is the knowledge of man's *createdness*. This knowledge has indeed been rejected by 'the world' (1.5). 'The world' also has a knowledge and it imagines that it sees (9.41). As the Gospel shows throughout all the first part, the world has its own point of view, its ethic, its orthodoxy. But in spite of all, the world does not understand itself. On the contrary, with its knowledge the world perverts its own nature; for the 'world' becomes what men make of it. Men fashion it, and it fashions men. It does not thereby lose its character as creation – rather, just because it is creation, the possibility has been given to it of misunderstanding itself, of setting itself against God. And further, because it is creation, its blindness, in which it fashions itself as world, takes the character of rebellion against God. The real 'dualism' of John, far from being based on a cosmological theory, springs directly from his idea of creation.

The individual man's place in the world is expressed by saying that he is 'of the world' (ἐκ τοῦ κόσμου 8.23; 15.19; 17.14). Compare 'from below' (ἐκ τῶν κάτω 8.23). 'From the world' has the sense of defining man's origin. 'From the world' man comes to all that he does, comes 'from the world' as one who is himself world. The world is humanity, meaning the 'they' that is every man and yet is no man.[5]

---

it 'believes' (or 'does not believe') (17.21), and 'knows' (or 'does not know') (17.23, 25). Obviously the 'world' is invariably men. The same holds of the assertions that God loves the world (3.16), that it is to be saved (3.17), that the Son speaks to the world (8.26).

[5] Cf. M. Heidegger, *Sein und Zeit*, pp. 126–30; ET, *Being and Time*, pp. 163–8.

The world has its tradition (Moses) of which it is proud; it has its forms of society, takes precautions and guards its security (esp. 5.41ff.: 'receive glory from one another'). It has its freedom (8.33) and its ideals (12.5: instead of squandering, one ought to assist the poor). A man keeps the law; he considers his decisions; he does not immediately reject all that is new but tests it on the basis of the old tradition (7.52) and investigates its authentication ('testimony', 5.31ff.). He believes in God – of course! He has his experts who provide the terms for expressing what everybody thinks; and according to their judgment a verdict is given. These experts are the spokesmen for 'sound human wisdom' and the representatives of established positions (the 'Jews' and the 'Pharisees') who naturally do not differ much from the 'common people' (ὄχλος 'crowd').

Such is the world of sound human wisdom, of manageable possibilities which can be controlled. The characteristic question of that world is: 'How can this be?' (3.9; 6.42, 52; 7.15). Whatever lies outside its boundaries appears as 'singularity' (7.15) or – more usually – it appears laughable, absurd or godless. (The writer of the Gospel brings all this into sharp relief in the disputes of the first part, especially in the constantly recurring 'misunderstandings'.) Actually the 'world' is not conscious of its limits. Of course, an upper level is conceded for the world; the existence of God is accepted. But the world has not the faintest conception of what the limitation of its own being set by God means. It has not the faintest understanding of God (5.37f.; 7.28; 8.19, 55; 15.21; 16.3).

Men do not *know* God; for knowing God does not mean to have ideas (perhaps correct ideas) about him. To know him is to see him as really made manifest, and that means to recognize him as Creator, to submit one's self to be determined by him. Those who are 'of the world' certainly know much that is 'right'; but it all turns in their mouths to falsity, to a lie, because they do not understand that it is limited. Moses, to whom they appeal, will accuse them (5.45), for even within their world they must face the limits of their possibilities, must become aware of their limitedness. So it is understandable that, when confronted by revelation, they become untrue even to their own law in which they take pride (7.49f.). Their obedience is manifestly not genuine.

Therefore it is clear that there can be no question of a cosmological dualism in the Gospel. The nature of the world, since it is always being fashioned through those who are in the world and are responsible for it, is not a condition, a situation, which may be viewed as a fate that man must endure (as it appears in gnostic mythology). And the liberation from the world which is experienced in faith is not the deliverance of the soul from matter or from demonic powers. Nor, on the other hand, is the world the prevailing culture, against which an individual could set himself in opposition with the aim of finding his way back to his real self. Being-in-the-world (or 'of' the world) is thought of as a quality of human existence. To be man is *to be world*.

This 'being-of-the-world' is 'being from below', 'being in sin' (8.21–24), because it is being without God. The apparent freedom of the world is only the abandonment of the world to itself and is therefore bondage to sin (8.31–34). Of course, this quality of being world only acquires the character of *sin* through the fact of revelation. 'If I had not come and spoken to them, they would have no sin' (15.22–24; cf. 9.39–41). *The real sin is unbelief* (16.7f.).

But sin does not consist in one specific act committed alongside others, say, in the fact that the world put Jesus to death. For then unbelief would be a 'work' like other 'works'. Sin is, rather, to hold fast to being-world when confronted by the revelation which puts in question the world in its 'being as world'. Sin, therefore, is to remain in what one is, in what proves to be darkness now that it is confronted by light. Sin is *to remain* in the darkness (12.46). 'Now they have no excuse for their sins' (15.22). 'If you were blind, you would have no sin. But now that you say, "we see", your sin *remains*' (9.41). It is clear then that *man's 'being-world'* is always his own chosen possibility – not a natural state but a fallenness.

There is indeed no possibility of escape from it as a *human* undertaking (for if it were human, it would itself still be world). But the world can know of its fallenness – not explicitly, but clearly enough to be able to understand when revelation speaks to it. The light shines in the darkness, even before the Word became flesh (1.5). In the possibility of knowing itself as created, the world would always have had the possibility of receiving the Word. It has not grasped this possibility. 'You do not have his word abiding in you.' And that becomes manifest when it is confronted by the revelation: 'for you do not believe him whom he has sent' (5.38).

Through the *event of revelation*, therefore, *two possibilities* become actual for the world.

1. To be world in the new sense of *remaining* world. To press down the seal on fallenness; deliberately to appropriate it, to cling firmly to one's self.

2. Not to be world, not to be 'of the world'; and thereby in a new sense to be 'out of' the world – really outside it, no longer to belong to it (15.19; 17.6, 16). This is valid for 'his own', for the 'friends' who are chosen out of the world (15.16); who are no longer 'world' (14.19, 22; 15.19; 16.20). For them the world has in a certain sense come to an end; 'the ruler of this world is judged' (12.31; 16.11).

Therefore with the coming of the Revealer a *crisis* occurs. Crisis (κρίσις) is in one sense a division. No particular event constitutes the crisis; apart from the revelation nothing happens – the revelation merely discloses what existed already. It makes actual in a new way the two possibilities which being-world always had; and in this way it characterizes clinging to the world as sin. The Son does not judge, but the world as it were judges itself (3.17–21; 12.46–48). The Word which Jesus speaks judges (12.48). For the two possibilities are distinguished in the way in which the Word is heard. The crisis is brought about in the nature of the reaction to the revelation. The hour comes and is already here: in the very act of its being proclaimed.

But with such a separation crisis is also *judgment*, for in it the sin becomes actual. The crisis thus becomes the judgment in the sense of condemnation by the wrath of God (3.36). The two possibilities are therefore the grasping of death and of life.

II

When a man *commits himself to his fallenness*, he surrenders his authentic possibility. The world's view is that man *has* possibilities at all times. The world forgets that man *is* at all times himself possibility, that his being is potentiality-to-be. Man is at all times called to decision, to risk himself. The world rejects such decision – and in the rejection it has already made the decision and has cut off its existence as a potentiality-to-be. So it has cut off its future; for to exist as a potentiality-to-be is to have a future. Therefore the world is always already the past. All that the world has is unreal and a lie; it has already passed away, since it remains always with the old and never leads into the future. The world lies dead.

This *clinging to self*, characteristic of the *world*, is illustrated, for example, in the two sections, 5.31–40 and 5.41–44, the themes of which are authentication (the witness, μαρτυρία) and glory.[6] The repudiation of faith expresses itself in the demand for an authentication of the Word. That is, those who demand it are the sort who criticize the Word from their own standpoint and desire that it be validated for them. They cling to themselves, they attach themselves firmly to the world. Quite consistently with this, they prize 'glory from one another'. That is, by their desire for an authentication they reveal where they find their security – in being honoured by one another. Therefore they refuse the security that God gives. It is again consistent with this attitude when elsewhere they refuse to understand how to judge (7.24; 8.15). For only by this refusal can they justify themselves.

But to choose God means to let the world go and to let one's security go with it. There is nothing enticing about that! On the contrary, that demand is a 'hard saying', a 'stumbling-block' which terrifies because it is the end of man (6.60f.). But just that end is *life :* to win back one's self as possibility, once again to be in the potentiality of being and to have a future.

What then does *life* mean? It is clear from what has already been said that life is *not inwardness, not even the inwardness of the mystic.* As death is the grasping of a possibility of man himself, so also is life. It is not a transposition into a transcendent sphere, the exaltation of the 'soul' into a divine being. It is true that in the language of the Gospel some well known mystic formulae and phrases appear, such as a peculiar use of the word 'know'

---

[6] The two passages are expanded by the redactor. In 5.33–6a the reference to John the Baptist is inserted and in the last clause of v. 39 ('and it is they that . . . '), as in vv. 45–7, the reference to the witness of Scripture is added. Note 2 on p. 166 applies here also.

or a variant of the so-called immanence-formula of the mystic, 'I in thee and thou in me'. This usage will be discussed later. But it is immediately obvious that all the mystic predicates of God (without origin, without attributes and the like) are lacking. Lacking, too, is the anthropological dualism which is so important for Hellenistic mysticism. There are no reflections on the fate of the soul, on soul-guidance. There is not the slightest trace of 'religious experience'.

Nor is life an ideal state, attainable by man as a 'spiritual' being and within his control. Idealism and humanism are wholly alien to the content of the Gospel. Only the man whom the Father draws can come to the Son (6.37, 44), only he to whom it is granted by the Father (6.65), only he who is 'of the truth' (8.47; 18.37). 'His own' have not chosen him; but he has chosen them (15.16). No man as such has qualities which vouch for him before God and which he needs only to recollect. All human thinking is impotent before the revelation which is an offence to all sound human wisdom (cf. the misunderstandings emphasized in the Gospel). A man must be 'born anew' (3.1ff.). Indeed, even 'his own' do not *understand* the revelation, in the sense of human understanding; they have only to believe.

Therefore, *life* for man is in no sense ever under his control. It is no phenomenon of the world; it belongs solely to God and his Revealer:

For as the Father has life in himself,
so he has granted the Son also to have life in himself (5.26).

Of course, anyone who *believes*, *has* life (5.24, 40; 6.57; 8.12; 11.25f.; *et al.*); indeed he has it in himself (6.53f.). But his existence is never an independent existence of his own ('of himself', ἀφ' ἑαυτοῦ 15.4; cf. v. 5 'apart from me you can do nothing'). Life remains a *gift*, received only in faith whenever the Word is heard.

But *hearing* is not a question of understanding a particular content. No timeless value is disclosed in the Word which can be perceived, possessed and then transmitted. The desire for information in order to satisfy curiosity is banned. Jesus does not submit to interrogation 'in respect to his teaching'. It can be received only as it is preached (18.19f.). Even 'his own' do not understand him, as we have already said.

In the farewell discourses, the disciples are not given any kind of esoteric knowledge. Jesus does not bring them a gnosis which communicates information and his followers do not apply to him, as to a teacher or hierophant, *for* knowledge; they come to *him*. Nor will he later become unnecessary to them when they 'know' what he has taught. God cannot be seen apart from the revelation; but that does not mean that he can be known only through some mysterious teaching from a super-natural source and that he *is* known when this teaching is accepted. It means rather that *always* God can be reached only through his revelation, through his Revealer. There is no 'short cut'.[7]

Actually, the assertion is made that *apart from the revelation God is not here and is never here*. No one has seen God except the Son and 'he has made him known' (1.18). The knowledge of God claimed by the world is no knowledge, for true knowledge is demonstrated when those who claim it believe the Revealer (5.38; 7.28f.; 8.19, 54f.). But these claimants subordinate the Word of God to the wisdom pursued by the scribes (5.39; 7.52).

Only through the Son does one have the Father; but who-ever sees the Son actually sees the Father (14.8–10). This is what is tirelessly emphasized in the formulae which speak of the unity of the Father and the Son. Such statements are a long way from any kind of mysticism (10.14f., 30, 38; 17.10f., 21), for the proof of the unity is just the Son's words and works (10.38: 14.10f.).

Therefore no concept of God is taught as a general truth; but *faith* has only become a possibility for men because God has sent his Son. Prior to that there can be no talk of faith. The word of the Son does not consist in universal truths which should be 'understood', but in the incredible Word of revelation, that he has been sent. There is no way to this by means of a medi-ated insight.

'My teaching is not mine, but his who sent me; if any man's will is to do his will, he shall know whether the teaching is from God or whether I am speaking on my own authority' (7.16f.).

The meaning is not that one should begin with the 'ethic' as

[7] Cf. Kierkegaard, *Einübung im Christentum*, 2nd ed. Jena, 1924, pp. 178ff.; ET, *Training in Christianity*, New York and London, 1941.

something generally intelligible in order to arrive automatically at the 'dogmatic'. The only course of action is the obedience of faith. There is no validation of the Word existing alongside the Word. It is its own validation.[8]

III

Accordingly, if the *crisis* is consummated *in the present* (that is, at the definite time when the response is made to the sending of the Son, in the answer to the Word, then it is not consummated *at any time one chooses to take a position* in relation to the concept of God, to the idea of a redeemer, to eternal norms and orders, to the 'intellectual content' of the Word, to concepts which 'interpret' the world or the 'meaning of life' or the like. On the contrary, it is consummated in a *specific* present, a specific *now*, as the response to *an historical fact*.

'But this is the crisis, that the light *has come* into the world' (3.19). The crisis is truly brought about in the present, faith truly gives life *now*. But not in any *now* whatever, only in the *now* distinguished by the proclamation of that historical fact. The crisis is linked, not to any general truth but strictly to one particular event, that is, the coming of Jesus.

Hence it is false to talk of the spiritualizing of the eschatology and of its inwardness. The event which as a fact in time transforms the world (because it judges) is the sending of Jesus. The judgment is an event occurring in the world and in world history; it is not a process in the soul.

The concept of faith is therefore defined eschatologically; that is, faith does not denote a human attitude which could be timeless and could be assumed at will, which a man could have at any time; perhaps when he withdraws into himself. For the *eternal* God is not within the circle of perceivable possibilities; within that circle stands only the incarnate one, whose Word is heard in time and by whose Word man is confronted in time, in a *now*. It can be *too late*! Then men will seek him and not find him (7.34; 8.21). Just as John 7.17f. ties the true knowledge of God – in contrast to a 'natural' idea of God – strictly to the idea of

---

[8] Some passages of the Gospel sound as though *the miracles* were a validation. As the question of the miracles in John is complex; however, it is enough to say here that the context shows with increasing clarity that the miracles are *ambiguous* signs. A miracle finally brings Jesus to the cross (11.45ff.). A strange validation!

revelation (the unity of Father and Son), so that he who does not know the Revealer does not know God, so 7.33f. asserts forcibly the uniqueness and contingency of the revelation. It is stressed that the revelation is not available at any moment it might be desired. It is not true that because Jesus was once here, the revelation could be obtained whenever one wanted it. The revelation exists only where the Word is confronting an individual. The possibility is open only when a man is addressed, not before and not after.

Thus to the *now* of the coming of the Revealer there corresponds exactly the *now* of the proclamation of the Word, as the *now* of a historical fact of a definite time, the *now* of opportunity, the *moment*. That is, Jesus, since 'the Word became flesh', is not the Revealer because of his 'influence on history' which obviously affects all men and which is always available to men to be estimated and evaluated. Jesus is the Revealer in the preaching of the Word as a concrete event at a given time.

This *now* of being addressed at a specific time, this moment, is *the eschatological now* because in it is made the decision between life and death. It is the hour which 'is coming and now is' here at the moment of being addressed. But it is this eschatological *now* only when it is strictly bound to the 'Word become flesh'. For the Word which speaks to me and is heard is simply the Word which proclaims that fact. Since that fact came to pass, the possibility of this Word exists, so that the fact divides all history into two halves, into two aeons.

Therefore it is not true that the *parousia* expected by others as an event to occur in time is denied by John or transformed into an event in the soul, an experience. John rather opens the reader's eyes to see that the *parousia has already occurred!* The naïve division into a first and a second coming which we find elsewhere has been discarded.[9] If a real coming were still expected in the future, then the actual coming would have been misunderstood. It is understood only where it is recognized that *this* very coming is the turning point of the ages. Whatever cosmic catastrophes may come, they cannot be radically different from what happens every day in the world. If something

---

[9] Cf. the conception of 'the day' of Jesus (8.56) and also the polemic against a naïve cosmological eschatology which represents the Son of Man after his 'coming' as permanently, objectively present (12.34–36).

like a resurrection of bodies from their graves (5.28f.; cf. above, p. 166, note 2) should happen, that could be nothing more unnatural than the way one wakes from sleep every morning. The decisive event *has* already happened. The hour is *here*, for the dead hear the voice of the Son of God. And he who hears it *has* passed out of death into life (5.24f.). He who does not believe *is* judged (3.18f.). The ruler of this world *is* judged (16.11).

But that means that the world is no longer the same as before. It can no longer be seen as it appeared formerly, between the creation and the incarnation of the Word. It no longer makes sense to direct men to the Creator God who is revealed in nature and human life. For now there are only two possibilities for men: to be in life or to be in death, in heaven or in hell. Truly – in hell. For life in the world without faith in the revelation is henceforth hell.[10]

IV

But *life* would be misunderstood if it were thought of as from now on an established *state*, as a *fate* permanently won; if it were forgotten that life is only real as a grasped possibility of man's self. That means that a man does not axiomatically now live under the new historical conditions, under the 'effects' of Jesus, as he can live under the effects of the Thirty Years' War, of the Enlightenment, of the French Revolution or of Goethe. For then the coming of Jesus would not be the *eschatological fact*.

The truth is rather that human existence has regained its authenticity in its potentiality to be. It exists, so far as it exists *in life*, always as potential being; therefore always as a fresh decision which is never under man's control (else it would be already past), but future. Life can be taken for granted by no

---

[10] Furthermore, all of this is not fundamentally different from *Paul*, although Paul does not question the dramatic eschatology of apocalyptic. Cf. Gal. 4.4, 'But when the fullness of the time (= the turning point of the ages) was come, God sent forth his Son'. Rom. 5.1, 'Therefore since we are justified by faith we have peace with God . . . '. Rom. 8.1f., 'There is therefore now no condemnation for them who are in Christ Jesus'. (The eschatological judgment has already occurred.) II Cor. 5.17, 'Therefore if any one is in Christ, he is a new creation. The old has passed away; behold the new has come.' II Cor. 6.2, 'Behold *now* is the acceptable time, behold now is the day of salvation'.

one; it must always be chosen anew. Therefore that *now* of 'the Word became flesh' is always present in the *now* of the proclamation, in the *moment*.

The historical fact of the *sending of Jesus* is therefore an ambiguous fact. So far as it is a fact of concrete history, it has – like every historical event – the possibility of being understood as a past event which existed in the past and which enters the present through memory. Yet this fact also has the possibility of being present. It can be spoken of in the *aorist*, that is as something done in the past, and it can be spoken of in the perfect as still present.[11]

Because Jesus has come, he *is here*. But this perfect of his being here is made into the aorist of a past event, into an objective fact of the past, by unbelief. And it is characteristic of John that Jesus as a fact of history is not an objective fact of the past which would be present only in its effects on history or in the memory which recalls it. He is not to be seen as an object. Therefore his coming is not understood when it is critically attested and a 'position' taken in regard to it. Then it would be seen as an object, understood as 'world' instead of as an eschatological event. A reconstructed 'life of Jesus' is 'world'. As the fact, 'Jesus', which is universally demonstrable, Jesus is made into world. But the living Jesus – that is, Jesus as eschatological fact – is not visible at all to the world (14.22). In the 'world's' discussions the crisis is reflected only as a 'split' (so Luther translates σχίσμα), 7.43; 9.16; 10.19; 11.45f.

The true way of making present the historical fact of Jesus is therefore not historical recollection and reconstruction, but the *proclamation*. In the proclamation Jesus is, so to speak, duplicated. He comes again; he is always coming again. Duplicated: 'I will pray the Father and he shall give you *another* helper' (14.26). The helper, the Paraclete, who continues Jesus' revelation in the world, is the Word preached in the Christian community. His teaching continues the teaching of Jesus.[12] His work is 'to bear witness to me' (15.26; cf. 8.14, 18).

---

[11] For the aorist cf. 1.11; 8.14; 9.39; 10.8, 10; 2.47. For the perfect, 3.2, 19; 5.43; 7.28; 8.42; 12.46. Gogarten's usage where, relying on Grisebach, he speaks of the perfect (for example, *Ich Glaube an den Dreieinigen Gott*, Jena, 1926, p. 66) is incorrect. It would have to be past.

[12] The same assertions are made of the Paraclete as are made of Jesus. He proceeds from the Father, 14.16, 26; 15.26 (cf. 8.42 *et al.*); he speaks,

His work is to 'convince' (16.8–11; cf. 3.20). He will lead the community into all truth (16.13), i.e. he will continue the revelation.

But that 'leading' does not mean providing some necessary supplementary teaching. For he will not speak 'on his own authority', but will 'take what is mine' (16.13, 15); he will 'bring to your remembrance all that I have said to you' (14.26). Therefore the Paraclete marks no new stage of development in the history of dogma. Nor is he even an 'inner light' or anything of the sort. He is the 'other helper' as Jesus was the first. He is Jesus himself who will come to 'his own' in the Paraclete (14.18–20, continuing 14.15–17). The promise of the Paraclete is nothing other than the promise that the revelation will be continued in the community's proclamation of the Word. The 'witness' of the Paraclete is the authorized witness-bearing of the community (15.26f.).

Jesus himself is therefore present in his Word. The believers of all times repeat the 'we have beheld his glory' (1.14). And that is exactly the meaning of the Gospel of John; the revelation is made contemporary. But the Word does not become 'idea' and as such enter into the 'history of thought'. On the contrary, it is the authorized Word, of which the source is the historic fact of Jesus and which proclaims that fact. In so far as the Word is at any time proclaimed, the eschatological *now* stands over every present; and in every such *now*, the judgment and the giving of life is consummated.

The *character of life* is then fully clear. The contemporaneousness of the historical Jesus does not lie in the historical effects of his work, nor in any historical reconstruction of that work. It is therefore neither something demonstrable in the present nor an objective fact of the past. He is present in the authorized Word. Likewise life is nothing demonstrable or objective; it is no inwardness, no experience. It is the determining of a particular *now* by the Word, in so far as the Word is heard in faith. That is, in so far as the new possibility of my being is understood as potentiality to be, as having a future. Life is not a situation, not a present secure possession; it is not timeless. But being at the moment is determined out of the future as a true

---

not from himself, 14.17 (cf. 7.16; 14.24 *et al.*); the world does not know him, 14.17 (cf. 1.10; 17.8 *et al.*). See also the passages mentioned above.

present. Life is a way of being, just as 'world' or 'death' is a way. But in contrast to world and death, life is always, even now, a being-in-the-future.

It therefore follows that faith – as becomes continually more clear – does not have the unequivocal character of a spiritual or psychological attitude. It is not being convinced of general ('eternal') truths nor is it the once for all acceptance of a dogma. Man does not through faith acquire a quality on which he can depend; he cannot appeal to the fact that he believes. He can only believe again and again – he *may* always believe again and again. For life is exactly that. Being finished, being concluded (i.e. the fact that the world is always already past) ceases. Man himself is always being given himself back as his possibility. He is not bound; he is *free*, no longer the slave of sin.

Only in listening to the revelation, to the Word, does faith exist. Only in such listening is the possibility of the future opened. In faith, because we recognize the revelation, the *now* becomes free from the past, from death; the future is opened. Life is therefore life because out of the future a true present is given.

v

The *theme of the farewell discourses* is this: the revelation is *here*, is present, however far in the past it may seem, however far past it is for the unbelievers. But this *here* does not mean that it is possessed here as knowledge or as an attitude of mind. Therefore a vast *distance* persists between the glorified one and his own – a distance which precludes all familiarity, all mysticism. The evangelist evidently chooses mystical formulae here deliberately (as elsewhere he chose mythological) in order to interpret them. And he *so* interprets them that the real question, which lies hidden in mythology and mysticism, now takes its rightful place.

There is *no direct sight of his glory* for those who believe. The believers certainly no longer belong to the world (15.17–20); but they still remain in the world and are not taken away from it (17.14–17). Only *in* the world does the possibility exist for them to be 'not of the world'. Therefore they always live in hope. Jesus for them is always departing and always the promise stands valid: 'I will come again and will take you to myself' (14.3). Only at his departure is Jesus the Glorified; '*now* the Son of Man has been glorified'. This *now* makes it possible for the first time to say, looking at the past, 'He *has been* glorified'; because in this *now* begins the future which breaks loose from the past, being past and gone: 'and God *will* glorify him' (13.31). In this *now*, past and future are uniquely bound together.

'His own' are to rejoice that he is going from them to the Father; for only so does it become clear that he is for them nothing other than the Word. Only so can the Paraclete come (14.28; 16.7). Only so can Jesus appear as the Revealer, without the misunderstanding that all depends on personal relations with him – as if the revelation were given in the objective figure. Heretofore the disciples always needed to question him and his words were riddles (16.23, 25); now for the first time there is clarity, openness (παρρησία).

Therefore only *the exalted one* is the Revealer; but he is Revealer only as he is at the same time the *lowly one*. All the decisive words spoken of the exalted one are said also of the lowly one. And as the 'lifting up' is called the saving act in 3.14f., so also is the sending down to the world in 3.16. To believe in the glorified one, therefore, does not mean to stand on the same level with him, to be intimate with him in mystic experiences. What Jesus said to the Jews, he said also to the disciples: they will seek him and cannot come where he is (13.33; cf. 7.34; 8.21). Therefore it is manifest that from a certain angle both the world and 'his own' are in the same situation in relation to Jesus. The disciples have no assurance that that is under their own control. They come to the glorified one only through the incarnate one. That sets the real distance between him and them. The revelation is *an indirect revelation*. The *now* of the disciples always keeps the character of the crisis, of the Either-Or – either to fall into the world or to grasp life.

Therefore the essential thing is *to abide in him*. And this concept shows again the strange conjunction of past and future. Primarily this abiding is not a piece of futurity possessed in the present (this is what the world thinks – as when it insists on the immortality of the soul); it is having the past in the *now*. It is neither a convinced acceptance of dogma nor a new quality, but a holding fast to the decision of faith, to fidelity in the true sense, when confronted with the future which is opened in every *now* and which puts the *now* to the test.

The commandment of love makes this clear. 'Abide in me' and 'abide in love' (15.1–8, 9-17) stand together. This 'abiding in love' means primarily 'abiding in being loved'. But this is immediately defined in such a way that the abiding is actual only if it is at the same time an abiding in loving. The love which Jesus commands as he says farewell is founded on the revelation: 'As' – that is, corresponding to the way that – 'I have loved you' (13.34; 15.12; cf. I John 4.7-10). *Therefore* this command is a *new commandment* – not because of its relative newness in 'spiritual history', but because it is the eschatological commandment which can become real only where the revelation is believed. 'Beloved, I am writing you no new commandment, but an old commandment which you had from the beginning; the old commandment is the word which you have heard. Yet I am writing you a new commandment, which is true in him and in you, because the darkness is passing away and the true light is already shining' (I John 2.7f.).

The obedient love which has become a possibility through the historical fact of Jesus designates *the concrete course into the future*. The Word is not actually *heard* unless there is also *action*. But *the* act which does not, like achievements in the world, belong to the past, *the* act which is free from the past and grasps the future, is the act of love. Therefore the decision each time is a decision concerned with the encountered *Thou*.

This decision of love, however, is not a second decision alongside faith; it is precisely faith itself. For the man who believes is indeed the living man whose *now* is never a fleeting moment, for his *now* has life, has future. He believes, and so he already loves. For faith is truly the seizing of his potentiality of being, the anticipating of his future beforehand in resoluteness. To some extent the believer anticipates in faith the concrete individual decisions of love for the future – but not abstractly as ideals. It is rather that in each individual concrete case a true decision of love now takes place and it alone proves whether that decision of faith, prior in time, was authentic.

The decision of faith is not an experience which is confined to a single moment! *I am not*, in fact, the person that I am as the object of an isolating, psychological observation at an isolatable moment; and my existence is not constituted by the sum of single moments. For the world it appears like that because the world knows no real future and consequently also knows no real present. But life is just this: the world's sham life (in which the moments have always fallen into the past, into death) has ceased; and man can now live in the future. That is, he can love.

The 'abiding' is therefore not something that is appended to faith. Rather, there is no authentic faith where there is no abiding. The abiding is really a structural element of faith. It connotes faith because in faith the future is grasped on the basis of the historical revelation. It is a fidelity which is always new.

Now the 'abiding in me' is not only an abiding in love but also an 'abiding in the Word'. And it is to this latter abiding that *knowing* is promised. 'If you continue in my Word you are my disciples. And you will know the truth and the truth will make you free' (8.31f.). Of course, the 'truth' is not rational knowledge nor doctrine, but is the openness, the reality of God. And 'freedom' is not understood as a formal concept, but as freedom from sin. Therefore the knowing is not intellectual, nor, of course, is it mystical. It is an existential knowing, not to be tested by objective observation and investigating scrutiny but by reality (not *objective et speculative sed realiter experiri*).

We have already seen that Jesus did not bring revelation as a mysterious, all-illuminating doctrine, with a profound meaning which can be probed and accepted. One does not go to him for the sake of knowledge; one comes to *him*. Yet the relation to him is only indirect.

Now when *faith* and *knowledge* are distinguished, this is not to differentiate them according to their objects. For the object is always the same – the revelation or the 'truth'. Nor does the distinction mean that the knowledge would be the goal of a development beginning with faith. In that case, knowing would be a final *state*, which as a state would no longer be a grasping of the revelation. It is true that in 8.30–32, faith is described as the first turning to Jesus. But knowing is not the final phenomenon of the developing of faith, of abiding in faith; knowledge is this abiding itself. Hence the sequence of faith and knowledge is interchangeable.[13]

[13] Cf. 6.69; 8.31f.; 10.38. The opposite: 17.8; I John 4.16. Cf. also

Faith, therefore, *is* knowledge in so far as it endures; if it does not endure it is not real faith. So knowledge proves to be, not the highest level or the goal of faith, but a structural element of faith. It can be differentiated from faith so that it becomes clear that faith does not have the character of a knowledge which is the result of investigation and of intellectual conviction, but always bears within itself a moment of uncertainty since it always depends solely on decision.

Only a knowledge of God and Jesus can be presented in testimony; a faith cannot be so presented. For faith is always in danger, exposed to doubt; it has its certainty only as the positive correlative to uncertainty. But this certainty, as *authentic* certainty, requires uncertainty as *its* correlative. It is certainty only as faith beset by attack and doubt, and yet maintained. Therefore, as there can be no knowledge which would not be faith, so also there can be no faith which would not be knowledge.

This knowledge is therefore not the comprehension of the meaning of a particular content; yet it is truly in a different sense an *understanding* – that is as the *'full joy'* (15.11; 16.23f.). It is understanding *as* the *self-understanding* in which one comprehends the Revealer and one's self. There is no further need to question; the believer stands in 'openness' (παρρησία). At the same time he stands in 'life', in 'peace' (14.27; 16.23), in 'glory' (ch. 17); and the world is overcome (I John 5.4f.).

I John 2.4, 'He who says, "I know him" ' with 2.6, 'He who says he abides in him'.

8

CHURCH AND TEACHING IN THE NEW TESTAMENT[1]

[1929]

I

WHEN we inquire into the meaning of church and teaching in the New Testament and their reciprocal relationship, what is our special concern? It can best be clarified by first making clear to ourselves what general conception we have in our minds when we speak of 'church' and of 'teaching'. From the New Testament we certainly expect to gain enlightenment about church and teaching; and we therefore already have some concept of both 'church' and 'teaching', even though it may be extremely vague. We do certainly know something already about the possibilities of 'church' and 'teaching'. Perhaps there lies hidden in such preliminary concepts a real pre-understanding which needs to be clarified, deepened, or corrected by the investigation of the New Testament.

In any case, our understanding of the New Testament pronouncements will be the more accurate, the clearer we are about our own previous ideas. Nobody can read a text without having presuppositions, but these can be made to some degree harmless, or even fruitful, if we look at them honestly, so that they become preliminary questions instead of pre-judgments.

1. When we speak of 'church', what picture, more or less definite, do we have in mind? We may perhaps say that the concept of the church is constituted by three elements which are always more or less clearly assumed when we speak of the church.

(*a*) A church is a religious association, the distinguishing mark of which is that it is *a cultic community*. As a cultic com-

[1] *ZZ*, VII (1929), pp. 9–43.

munity, it has God present in a particular setting of place and time and specific, traditional forms of behaviour.

(*b*) The church is an '*eschatological*' fact. That is, the cultic community does not regard itself as a phenomenon of the world – not, for example, as a fraternity nor as an organization formed for any purposes of this world. It understands itself as 'other- *N B* worldly'. Thus, for example, the 'today' in its liturgy or 'this is the day which the Lord has made' is not meant as a piece of chronological information, but as the eschatological *now*.

(*c*) The church, as an organization not made by men, is a community called into being by the deeds and words of the deity. It is therefore bound to a *history*; and it provides in a *tradition* an account of the history of its calling.

2. What is meant when we speak of '*teaching*'? There are various connotations. To begin with the most general interpretation: teaching is information given in words about something which is not yet known. But the mere consideration that, as the teaching of the church consists in communicating tradition, it is a continual repetition of what the hearer already 'knows', means that further consideration of the meaning of *know* is needed. In one sense the teaching of a church is evidently not 'known' in any way that makes the repeated communication of it superfluous – even when it has been learned by heart.

In any case, in communicating teaching it is always assumed that the hearer *understands* it. But that means that before he hears it, he already has a certain relation to it, that there exists some possibility of his discovering it or that he has been made aware of it, that he is asking about it. (For questioning, of course, is evidence that the questioner has some relation to what he asks about.)

Now there appears to be *one* immediately obvious difference about a previous relation to what can be communicated.

(*a*) The communication may be a presentation of *facts which I cannot know of myself*: for example, that Caesar crossed the Rubicon, that Columbus discovered America, that an aviator has crossed the ocean. Or perhaps that in Australia there are such and such races of men or such and such kinds of animals and plants. In short, the communication is of factual information about objects or events in the world, past or contemporary.

(*b*) Alternatively, the communication may *disclose a knowledge which I have always had*, which merely becomes conscious and explicit through the 'instruction'. This is true of the teaching of arithmetic to children. In general, instruction in mathematics is of this nature; so, too, in the natural sciences when the instruction is not merely the collection of material but also 'explains' – that is, when the teacher uses the collected material as the occasion for presenting explicitly a picture of the world as ordered by law, one which has already been presupposed. This is also the procedure, say, of psychology, which is not interested in what a particular individual actually feels or thinks but in stating what laws the thinking or feeling follows, what 'types' or 'patterns' exist, etc. Logic, the philosophy of history, systematic ethics, etc., proceed in similar fashion. Research and teaching here is a process of 'recall' (ἀνάμνησις).

The two kinds of communication or knowledge – let us call them 'factual knowledge' and 'knowledge of principles' – really belong together, however, and form a *unity*. For I understand the 'facts', the 'data', only in so far as I understand the world in which they occur. A knowledge of principles is always included in the knowledge of facts; and, conversely, a knowledge of principles is always related to a knowledge of 'facts'. Order, conformity to law, is always the order, the conformity of the factual. In any communication of factual knowledge, the knowledge of principles is validated, extended or modified. And by every modification of the knowledge of principles, my understanding of the factual is modified.

Now since the basis of all knowledge and every possibility of communicating the factual is understanding, communication of the factual does not tell me anything that is *new in a fundamental sense*. That is, I am told nothing which I could not also discover for myself – provided I made the necessary journeys or investigated the proper sources. I am given no information which is in principle unavailable to me. Thus, whether I am dealing with facts bounded by space and time or with timeless abstract 'truths', communication of the one kind always results in communication of the other, although now one is explicit and now the other. And in every case the communication relates to the world that I already know in principle. In no case am I told anything which is fundamentally new.

In what sense, then, can anything really new be said to me? All understanding of anything (that is, of anything in the world) is always ultimately an understanding of myself, a 'finding my own place in my world'. In all such factual knowledge or knowledge of principles, the world is presumed to have the character of something objective, passive, accessible to simple observation. That is, the world is conceived in conformity with the Greek understanding of being. Research into facts and principles has not altered fundamentally since it was developed by the Greeks. In such a conception of the world as an objective entity, man himself is regarded as an object (as a fragment of the cosmos); his self-understanding is achieved along with the understanding of the world (and vice versa). That is, it is assumed that man has himself fundamentally under his own control and completely under observation ('know thyself', γνῶθι σαυτόν); he can learn to understand himself better and better, but not in any basically new way. His original self-understanding can merely become explicit.

If the statement that something new can be known and can be meaningful at all, that can only be in the sense that man learns to understand himself in a new way. That is, such an assertion can be made only where it is recognized that the existence of man does not have the character of an objective entity but is a *historic* existence; where it is recognized that man in his history can *become* a new person and *consequently* can also newly *understand* himself; where, therefore, it is recognized that the being of man is a potentiality to be. That potentiality to be is always at risk; its possibilities are grasped each time by man in resolve, in decision.

An understanding of these possibilities of man's existence here and now would obviously be a new understanding each time, since a historical situation with its character of possibility is not understood if it is conceived as a 'case' illustrating a general law. The historical situation cannot possibly be 'seen' in the Greek sense as an objective fact; it can only be heard as a summons. For the situation demands resolve and is only understood when the resolve is taken.

It is certainly clear that *the possibilities of existence* are disclosed *in 'life' itself*. But is this disclosure also given through 'teaching'? That it is given by 'life' is shown by the experiences

188 *Faith and Understanding*

of remorse, gratitude, shame, trust, etc., in which I always
become a new person and newly understand myself (whether
explicitly or not) as corrupt or pure, as happy or unhappy,
etc. ('One face appears before the act, the accomplished deed
another shows.')

Can 'teaching' also disclose to me the possibilities of my existence?
Can it say something new to me by opening up to me a new
understanding of myself? It certainly can in the sense that as
theoretical reflection and the communication of that reflection
it *makes explicit my implicit understanding of myself*. That is, it
brings clearly to my consciousness what guilt, conscience,
remorse, shame, duty and gratitude, trust and love, are. Does it
thereby impart to me something new? Yes, in so far as self-
understanding is a part of existence itself; and as understanding
becomes explicit, existence comes closer to its own potentiality.

This explication is not objective, neutral instruction. Just
as it can be *given* only through the self-explication of the
teacher, so it can be *received* only by one who holds fast to his
own experiences and acknowledges them. But that means that
in such acceptance, the original life persists and is developed
further. In such 'instruction', I am not hearing about remorse,
gratitude, etc., as interesting psychological facts without personal involvement. I am myself involved; only as a man who
is remorseful and grateful can I understand.[2] My self-understanding given in my experiences never has the character of a
knowledge of something present at hand, and therefore self-
understanding itself does not have the character of being
present at hand, but is seized only in resolve.

But can teaching in itself disclose new possibilities of existence?
If teaching is understood in the most general sense as communication through words, then teaching as the expression of a command or a request, as thanks or as a declaration of love or hate,
does obviously open a new possibility. For such words are not
an expression of 'seeing' from a distance, they do not convey
information gained by observation or orientation; the words
themselves are a part of the situation which they disclose and

---

[2] Nobody who understands what is involved here will think of saying
'was' instead of 'is'. For, if the experiences of remorse, gratitude, etc.,
are understood as genuinely historical, as my own experiences, then they
cannot become given facts of the past.

which is disclosed in them. A word of thanks is itself gratitude, a word of love is itself love, a word of hate is itself hate.[3]

In this sense, therefore, the disclosure of the understanding of existence is obviously accomplished by teaching; and teaching then has the character of direct address.

The *liturgical language* of the church plainly has that character when it is a call to repentance, an exhortation, a proclamation of the forgiveness of sin, etc. The 'teaching' which the church transmits to the community on repentance, forgiveness of sin, etc., as its content shows, is not intended to provide information for the curious or 'interested' observer (a student of the philosophy of religion or a Buddhist). Such 'teaching' is a call to repentance, or accords the forgiveness of sin in such a way that as it is proclaimed and heard repentance results or impenitence becomes an actuality; sins are forgiven or imputed.

Such examples do not, however, fully define the content of the church's kerygma, for it also includes (linked always with the content already described) the *communication of facts*. But the communication of facts does not serve, as it does elsewhere, simply to enrich the old understanding of the world which I, the hearer, have already. On the contrary, its intent is to dispel that understanding, since it communicates to me facts which have their meaning as divine acts, as events in a history of salvation. They are, in a word, *eschatological* facts. They are events the reality of which is incomprehensible on the basis of a given understanding of the world taken as a matter of principle. And as such they are undiscoverable by any investigation of the world.

But there is clearly nothing anomalous in the fact that information can be communicated, not for the purpose of increasing knowledge and enlarging the understanding of the world, but to bring about commitment; in other words, to

[3] This can be made clearer by noting that the situation is altered if such words have to be translated to a hearer who does not understand the language, or if they have to be shouted to a deaf person. A bellowed declaration of love is an obvious fatality. This point could also be more accurately presented if the character of human existence as co-existence with one another were made clear and the original meaning of the 'word' clarified on this basis. Only an understanding of existence as *individualistic* finds a difficulty in the statement that 'teaching' can disclose possibilities of existence; and only from such a point of view can the well-known antithesis of 'teaching' (knowledge) and 'life' arise.

disclose to me a new possibility of my existence. Indeed, when the direct address specifies something that I ought to do, it always does so on the basis of some fact which is kept in view. The communication of what must be done can occupy the foreground, or, if the fact is self-evident, what must be done can be stated separately by itself. Otherwise, the fact can occupy the foreground or be mentioned separately, if what must be done is plainly bound up with it. The communication of the fact can then acquire the character of address; it can be *indirect* summons. For example, I can be told that my mother has secretly made a sacrifice in order to give me pleasure or to make my career possible. If I take that as a mere statement of fact, I have not really understood it. I understand it only if, on the basis of the information, I comprehend my relation to my mother and hence myself also in a new way. Or my life could be reshaped should I learn that my father carried a heavy burden of guilt (cf. Kierkegaard).

This use of factual content underlies the teaching of history in the schools and can be the only real basis for it. For if the aim is only to give the pupil orientation into a certain sector of scientific knowledge, Mexican history would serve as well as German. But the purpose is to teach the pupil to understand himself to be bound by obligations to his nation, to teach him to grasp possibilities of resolve and action.

In such cases, the teaching has a peculiar ambivalence about it. It can, of course, be understood as mere communication of a knowledge that enriches my old understanding of the world. Confronted by the communicated facts, I have the possibility of viewing them as objective events in the world, past or present. Basically, I have that possibility with every expression of gratitude and petition, of joy and love, etc., that I encounter. I can, for example, consider them psychologically or sociologically; for every human relation carries with it the hidden temptation to engage in interested psychological or aesthetic consideration. But I also have the possibility of 'hearing' such expressions and such factual communications.

We call understanding by such appropriate 'hearing' *historical understanding*, because here the understanding is itself a historical action in which I grasp my own possibility. Communication, like understanding, does not have the same character here as when the aim is simply enriching the understanding of the world by the communication of facts or principles. In the latter case, the communication is incidental and of secondary importance since basically I have the possibility of discovering the world by myself. But, in the former, the communication is a necessity. In the one case, the communication merely gives me some information or offers me an opportunity to know something; in the other, *the communication is itself a part of what is communicated.* When the communication is a word of thanks, a request or the like, as we have already remarked, the word is a part of what it expresses. It is also clear that the language of the church's liturgy, the call to repentance, the forgiving of sins, etc., is not a communication of information but is itself, as a summons, the decisive word in which the divine call and the forgiveness are brought about.

At the same time, even when the address is indirect and communicates facts, it is clear that the communicating is a part of the matter communicated. It has the character of *tradition*, which is itself part of the history it narrates. The tradition is actually a part of the event which it preserves, celebrates, laments, or even merely describes. This tradition *speaks to me*, because I belong to this family or to this nation to which the tradition also belongs as a part of its life. Naturally it confronts me with its peculiar ambivalence; but truly understood it is the summons of the history of which it speaks and to which I belong.

The conclusion to be drawn is, therefore, that '*teaching*' may be the exposition of the understanding of the world which I already share: the world is an objective entity for me and I am an object in the world. In that case, teaching is accomplished by the communication and reception of factual knowledge or of the knowledge of principles. In relation to this teaching, which is incidental and of secondary importance for the pupil, understanding has the character of 'seeing', of observing from a distance.

Or, on the other hand, 'teaching' discloses the possibility of my existence which I must resolutely grasp, and so teaches me to understand myself anew. This it does, as direct summons or indirectly, whether through theoretical explanation of my self-understanding or through the communication of facts. In relation to this teaching, which is essential to the one taught, understanding has the character of 'hearing', of knowing one's self to be summoned, of decision.

But there is one further question! We said that a presupposition for teaching as a communication of the knowledge of facts and principles, is the *possibility of understanding*, and that the ability to understand such teaching is dependent on the fact that I already understand the world to which the teaching relates. Consequently, the teaching never tells me anything that is fundamentally new. Does the same condition apply to the possibility of understanding the teaching that discloses a new understanding of myself? *Does it not also presuppose a previous self-understanding*, so that here, too, nothing really new would be taught? That I understand myself as summoned when confronted by a summons, and can thereby understand the summons, surely also presupposes that this understanding was my possibility to begin with.

In actual fact, I must have a *pre-understanding* of gratitude and duty, of hate and love, etc., as possibilities of my own existence, if the possibility for gratitude and duty, etc., is to be opened for me by a word. I must have a *pre-understanding* of sin and forgiveness if I am to understand when someone speaks to me about them.[4] But the decisive element is this: here it is not a matter of understanding possibilities which are, if I so desire, under my own control, so that I can choose this way or that or can refuse to make a choice and thereby remain the same. Here *my own possibility* is at stake, a possibility which I cannot select at my own pleasure, but into which I am put in my *historical situation*. In choosing it I *choose myself* and therefore become a new person. Facing such a possibility, I do not have the freedom to refuse to choose and so to remain my old self; facing this possibility I am forced to a decision. And this decision is new each time; each time my self-understanding is put to the test by it.

Thus the word of teaching, which discloses this situation to me and which, as we have seen, is a part of the situation, is

---

[4] Such a pre-understanding need not, of course, be in the form of an explicitly formulated concept. It is existential, given in and with my existence. I can have it in conceptual clarity, but such explicitness, which as a rule I have accepted uncritically from tradition, can also conceal true understanding from me.

therefore equally new. Its significance does not consist in giving me instruction, informing me about the phenomena of gratitude and duty, of hate and love, etc., but in making actual to me the concrete possibility of gratitude and duty, hate and love. The 'newness' thus consists, not in *what* is said, what can be understood as a 'timeless' expression of meaning, as an 'eternal truth', but in the fact *that* it is said. Just because it is said, my situation becomes a new situation and I myself – deciding this way or that – become a new person. Because the *saying* here is newly spoken and the *hearing* as self-decision is always new, the result is a 'new' teaching.

II

The New Testament concept of the church, the community (ἐκκλησία) continues the Old Testament concept of the *qāhāl*. The *qāhāl* is primarily the cultic community in which God is invoked at a fixed place, at fixed times and in fixed ways, such as sacrifice, prayer, song, etc. In the *qāhāl* God acts with men in whatever they do. They undertake nothing of themselves and initiate nothing; they obediently fulfil what God has commanded for the cult, and in such obedience they are certain of the nearness and the favour of God.[5]

The essential character of the cult, therefore, is neither that of a national festival nor of an act of magic which is supposed either to exercise a direct influence on vegetation or the like, or to confer a higher nature on the worshipper through sacramental mysteries. Nor is it basically an exercise in meditation to induce religious feelings, mystic experiences or ecstasy. The *qāhāl* is an 'eschatological fact', since in it the activity of man (his everyday anxieties and his daily work) comes to an end and God acts. This is most clearly expressed in psalms like Pss. 47;93; 96–99, in which, the 'now' which determines the cult (Yahweh has become king) is not a chronological datum but the eschatological *now* of the cult.[6]

---

[5] There is no resemblance to the *qāhāl*, therefore, when today a city 'arranges' a formal worship period for a theological conference meeting there and 'honours' it by attending.

[6] Cf. the recent discussions on the 'Enthronement Psalms' and on the relation between cult and eschatology, especially S. Mowinckel, *Psalmenstudien II, Das Thronbesteigungsfest Jahwähs und der Ursprung der Eschatologie,*

Israel gathers for the *qāhāl* as the chosen people called by God. To their fathers God gave the promise; he led them out of Egypt. To Israel he has given the law through Moses. Therefore the *qāhāl* is at the same time the community of the obedient who submit themselves to the law. That means that the members do not merely share this history 'by nature'; each individual must make his own decision. The consciousness of being called and chosen involves a conscious resolve to be bound to a quite specific history with its blessings and its duties. The act of worship is then itself an element in the history of salvation.

The cult therefore communicates at the same time the tradition of this history. This aspect of the cult is very early, since the tradition tells how, for example, the celebration of the Passover is based on a specific historical event. It is characteristic especially for Israel that the agricultural festivals have a historical basis, and that in the course of time other celebrations of historical events are added, e.g. Hanukkah and Nicanor's Day. The festival legends which are transmitted in the tradition exhibit a characteristic difference from the Greek cult legends. In the Israelite tradition, the story centres not on the fortune of a deity but on the history of a people.

Cult, eschatology, and the consciousness of history thus determine the concept of the *qāhāl*. In the *Jewish synagogue*, the third motif is the most prominent. The tradition is fixed in writing; the reading and the exposition of the tradition constitute the service. The cultic element is not lacking, since God is thought of as present in the Torah; among the Diaspora and especially after the destruction of the temple, it became more prominent. In a certain sense, the cult then lost its eschatological character. The more the temple worship receded from the centre of religion in Judaism, the more Judaism became a religion of the law, and, at the same time, the more the unity of nation and cult community was lost, so much the more strongly did the idea of 'the true Israel' develop. The true Israel, 'the community of the just', would 'appear' hereafter – at the end of the days. The community which now exists knows itself as the community of the 'poor' and 'pious', surrounded by the

Kristiania, 1922; Hans Schmidt, *Die Thronfahrt Jahwes*, Tübingen, 1927; H. Gunkel, *Einleitung in die Psalmen*, Göttingen, 1928, pp. 100–16.

godless and scornful. It sees itself as a *waiting* community now, waiting for the fulfilment. The old concept of the *qāhāl* is therefore still preserved. But the contemporary waiting community does not consider itself the real *qāhāl*. That will become actual only when the final fulfilment comes.

This concept of the church (ἐκκλησία = *qāhāl*) *has been taken over by the New Testament.*[7] It is not the *concept* of the church that is new in the New Testament. What is new is the conviction that the *qāhāl* has now *become a reality*, that the community of the righteous has appeared, that the true Israel is here, called by Jesus Christ, the Messiah, the Lord of the community. The true *qāhāl* is visibly present in the separate communities (ἐκκλησίαι) which belong to the community as a whole, the church (ἐκκλησία). But they belong to it, not as parts or limbs which, when joined together, constitute the whole; for the whole is present in each single community. Here the eschatological character of the church is most clearly revealed. The church is not a phenomenon of this world, but is the beginning of the new.

That assertion was actually made by Paul and by Hellenistic Christianity. How far, if at all, it holds for the first company of disciples or for the *original Palestinian community* is very questionable. Evidently the Palestinian community felt itself still to be a waiting community in which the old future eschatology of Judaism persisted. It instituted no new cult, but continued steadfastly in the old temple worship. Its understanding of itself as the messianic community only became explicit in the beginning because of the expectation that Jesus, the crucified prophet, would come again as the Messiah. But he was not understood as the One who had already come as the Messiah, had died and risen, and had thereby brought the new creation.

In this respect, the original community kept wholly to the *proclamation of Jesus* himself, who preached the *coming* of the Kingdom of God. But Paul and John preach that the new age *has* already dawned, that judgment and justification, death and life are already present, unaffected by whatever may still be expected in the future. There is therefore no reason to look

---

[7] How the Greek idea of ἐκκλησία influenced the early Christian concept of the church in other ways can be ignored at this point.

for a special concept of the church in the preaching of Jesus. Jesus obviously shared the concept of Judaism.[8]

The real development of the idea of the church begins in Hellenistic Christianity through and after Paul. This concept of the church shows three characteristic elements.

1. *The 'church' is the cultic assembly of the community* (cf. I Cor. 11.18, 'when you assemble in church' [ἐν ἐκκλησίᾳ] (that is, 'as a church'), in which the Lord (κύριος) is present, as is proven by the Spirit (πνεῦμα) and the gifts of grace (χαρίσματα). Indeed, God himself is present as the one who 'works all in all' (I Cor. 12.6). And if any outsider who is there in the assembly is confronted by the prophetic word, he must confess 'God is really among you' (I Cor. 14.25). The fact that the community apart from the cultic assembly is also called 'church', simply shows that the cultic assembly is the genuine expression of the essence of the community and that the whole life of the community is dominated by it. The community as such has been liberated from the world. It is the community of the holy, the community of 'saints' which considers the 'unrighteous' (ἄδικοι I Cor. 6.1), 'those outside' (οἱ ἔξω I Cor. 5.12f.; I Thess. 4.12) as strangers.

2. Because it is such a community, *the 'church' is also the eschatological community*, for 'holy' is an eschatological as well as a cultic predicate. As the community of the 'end time', as the messianic community, it has the 'Spirit', the gift expected at the end. (Cf. e.g. also I Cor. 14.21, where the gift of speaking with tongues is understood as the fulfilment of the predictions of the 'end'.)

3. The 'church' is *the fellowship of those called by God.*

(*a*) It is called by the prophecies of the Old Testament; the community is the Israel of God (Gal. 6.16), in contrast to the Israel after the flesh (I Cor. 10.18). The history of Israel is its history; Abraham is its father (Rom. 4.16; Gal. 3.7–29); the Christians are the nation of the twelve tribes (James 1.1), the chosen people (I Peter 2.9f.), etc. The community is thus *bound to the Old Testament history* and takes over the Old Testament *tradition*. (The efforts of Paul to preserve the unity of the

[8] Moreover, the few sayings of Jesus in which the word 'church' (ἐκκλησία) occurs were composed in the community and then put in his mouth (Matt. 16.18; 18.17).

Gentile Christian communities with the Jerusalem church are special evidence of this concern.)

(*b*) It is called by Jesus Christ (I Cor. 7.22) or by the preaching that proclaims him, by his death and his resurrection, through which God has instituted the 'message of reconciliation' (II Cor. 5.19). *As the culmination of the old acts of salvation, the new last decisive act has been achieved.* 'In the fullness of time, God sent his Son' (Gal. 4.4). The sending, his obedience even to the cross, is the event, crowned by the resurrection, through which the new community is founded.

So the church is *the 'body of Christ'* (σῶμα Χριστοῦ). And in the 'body of Christ' all three elements of the concept of the church are present: the *cultic*, since the sacraments of Baptism and the Lord's Supper determine the community (I Cor. 12.13); the *eschatological*, since the unity of the community as the 'body of Christ' is the work of the Spirit who is the Lord. But for evidence that this cultic-eschatological fellowship of the body of Christ is also *a community determined by history*, a more searching investigation of the concept 'body of Christ' is required.

1. In the concept 'body of Christ', 'body' does not have the *simple meaning of an organism* which exists by the conjoining of single parts, like organs and limbs. Certainly, in I Cor. 12.12–30, Paul uses the figure of the body as an organism, a figure which comes from the ancient tradition. But the first verses immediately show that the idea of an organism is secondary for him. This idea requires the parts to be *different*, so that their differences constitute the whole; precisely in their differences they are equally essential to the body. Paul uses this idea in vv. 14–30. But first he says in vv. 12f. that the members of the community (ἐκκλησία), because and in so far as they belong to Christ, are *alike*, so that *no* differences exist. They are alike, not because in their differences they are all equally important for the whole, but because, since they all belong to Christ, their differences are of no consequence.[9] The body is not constituted by its

---

[9] So Paul never designates the community simply as a body but always (and this is significant) as 'the body of Christ' (I Cor. 12.27). And he can also say 'so we, though many, are one body in Christ' (Rom. 12.5). It is clear that for him the idea of *Christ's* body is primary and that in I Cor. 12 it is the particular situation in Corinth which provides the occasion for making use of the concept of the body as an organism as well.

members but by Christ.[10] Consequently the body exists before
or above the members; it does not first come into existence
through them and in them. Now since the individual members
come into the body through baptism (v. 13), and since baptism
is baptism into the death and resurrection of Christ (Rom. 6.3ff.),
it follows that the saving event which is *prior* to the empirical
community constitutes the community. And further, since the
Lord's Supper maintains the fellowship with Christ (I Cor.
10.16; also 12.13?), and since the members share in the death
of Christ and so proclaim his death (I Cor. 11.23–26), that,
too, means that the saving event creates the community.

2. The saving event which the community appropriates in
the sacraments is not, however, thought of as a fact of nature,
as the prescription for producing a medicine which gives
immortality (φάρμακον ἀθανασίας, Ignatius, *Eph.* 20.2), in which
case the body of Christ would be a *sacramental fellowship* bound
together by *the magic of a supernatural food*.

Paul does, of course, use the sacramental ideas of the
mysteries (Rom. 6.2ff.; I Cor. 10.16f.; 11.24f., 27, 29), but he
modifies them. He uses them because they provide him with the
means to express the truth that the Christian who places
himself within the continuity of the history of salvation is
removed from his own control, and can therefore trust himself
wholly to the power of the Lord, who now has dominion over
him, just as he is to be at the Lord's disposal (παραστῆσαι,
Rom. 6.13ff.).[11] Partaking of the sacraments gives no guarantee, as the Midrash on the generation of the Exodus (I Cor.
10.1–13) makes plain. 'Let anyone who thinks that he stands
take heed lest he fall' (v. 12). Every one must examine himself
to see whether he has partaken worthily of the Lord's Supper;

---

[10] In Col. 1.18, Christ is called the *head* of the church.

[11] I do not think that Paul used the ideas of the mysteries, say for paedago-
gic reasons, as figurative descriptions. As a man of the ancient world, he
thought quite realistically. Therefore he actually thinks that the sacrament instills a substance, a dynamic substance, into the Christian – and
it even has its physical effects. But the decisive point is this, that he understands the being of Christians not as a natural being but as historical being.
However, he can represent this being to himself only in the inappropriate
concepts of natural phenomena. Thus it is clear, for example, that he conceives of the 'Spirit' as a dynamic substance which is instilled into a man.
But it is equally clear that 'to have the Spirit' or 'to be in the Spirit' or the
like, means for him a *mode* of historical existence; it means to live without
anxiety, to act continuously in love, etc.

for if not, he takes it to condemnation. But 'worthily' does not so much mean being ritually clean, as being ethically worthy (I Cor. 11.27–29). It is not because of the 'elements' that the sacrament is effective for salvation. It is effective as action, as an act of confession, affirming the history that is made contemporary in the sacrament, and affirming the grace assured in the sacrament (but it is the grace of the Lord!). Therefore, the sacrament is effective for salvation as an act of obedience. In consequence, the New Testament knows nothing of Christian 'priests'.

As an *act of confession*! For the receiving of baptism is the pre-condition of faith. But the confession is this: 'For if you confess with your lips that Jesus is the Lord, and believe with your heart that God has raised him from the dead, you shall be saved' (Rom. 10.9). This confession of faith in the Lord or in the fact of salvation, which is made in baptism, is an act of obedience. Faith is obedience.[12]

The imperative of obedient action is therefore joined to the indicative of the affirmation of salvation (Rom. 6). To be brought by baptism into communion with the resurrection of Christ means, therefore, at the same time to know one's action to be under the imperative: 'Yield yourselves to God as men who have been brought from death to life, and your members to God as instruments of righteousness' (Rom. 6.13); or 'As many of you as were baptized into Christ have put on Christ' (Gal. 3.27). But this 'put on Christ' has equally the sense of an imperative, 'walk honestly . . . put on the Lord Jesus Christ' (Rom. 13.13f.).

Gal. 3.29 shows plainly that baptism does not confer a being in a new magical quality of life, but that through baptism the baptized are ingrafted into the history of salvation: the baptized are sons of Abraham. Paul is not thinking here of the baptismal experience of the individual but of the historical fellowship instituted through baptism.[13] It is not as individuals that Christians become Christ's through baptism (say, by becoming 'deified' as in the mysteries); but *all* become *one*; 'you are all

---

[12] Cf. Rom. 1.8 and I Thess. 1.8 with Rom. 16.19. Cf. further Rom. 1.5; 10.3; 11.30f.; 15.31; Gal. 5.7; also, Rom. 15.18; II Cor. 9.13; 10.5f., 15.
[13] It should be noted that in Gal. 3 Paul is not thinking at all of the individual and his 'development', but of the history of salvation.

one in Christ Jesus' (Gal. 3.28f.). The possession of the Spirit
which manifests itself in ecstasy is not an end in itself, for the
enjoyment of the individual who experiences it. For all, it is
the sign of their new position within the history of salvation,
the sign that the Christians are 'sons' and no longer slaves
(Gal. 4.6f.).

This view of Paul's depends on the fact that he *does not see
man as an isolated individual*, who can command his own destiny,
who – as the Greeks taught – can begin afresh at any time and
make a masterpiece of himself. For Paul, *man stands from the
beginning and continuously in a historical context* from which he
comes to his 'now' and by which he is determined. This does
not mean that Paul understands the 'now' as causally determined by the past, that he sees the individual as 'the product
of his historical environment'. He understands man as one
who has always already made his decision with reference to
the past, from which he comes, and who has been moulded
by this.

According to this conception, man is not, so to speak,
merely himself, as the Greeks would understand that 'self'.
That is, man is more than that which is discernible in him by
observing him in any isolated moment. He is also what he was
and what he will be. He has only the possibility of letting himself be determined either by what he always was (by the
'flesh', by death), or by what he ought to be (by the 'Spirit',
by life). But this decision becomes actual for him at the moment
when the Christian proclamation confronts him. For that
announces to him the possibility of becoming free from his
past. Such freedom does not mean, however, that he no longer
has any past whatever.[14] But he has won the power of free
decision upon his past. He may take it with him as that for
which he has been forgiven. If he looks only at himself, his
past is 'flesh', is sin and death. But forgiveness for this past has
already been pronounced by the saving event which has
annulled 'flesh', sin and death. This forgiveness he must

[14] That kind of thinking belongs to the mystery religions. Paul understands that the decision with reference to the past is always at the same time
a decision with reference to the future, and *vice versa*. The deified mystic
in the mystery for whom the past is simply blotted out no longer has a
future, and he finds it difficult to know what he is to do until he dies. At
most he can be careful that nothing happens to him.

appropriate in the obedience of faith, in order to become free for a future determined by the promise.

That man is viewed historically, becomes clear from the fact that through his decision he has a share in the possibilities which determine all historical life: 'flesh' or 'Spirit'. Faith is therefore obedience.

As obedience, faith is confession, not in the sense of a single act, done once for all like a declaration of church membership. It is a placing of one's self at God's disposal, for the act to which God summons a man at any given moment. Thus it means being determined by the future. The church (ἐκκλησία), as the fellowship of the called and obedient, is a historical entity. 'To be in Christ' is accomplished in 'care for one another', in 'suffering with one another' and 'rejoicing with one another' (I Cor. 12.25f.; cf. Rom. 12.15), as mutual service (διακονεῖν).

Romans 6 shows specifically how such obedience determines the life of the individual. Following ideas of sacramental magic, Paul says: 'We know that our old self was crucified with him so that the sinful body might be destroyed, and we might no longer be enslaved to sin' (v. 6). 'Buried with' (v. 4) is replaced by 'crucified with'. The cultic act of baptism is therefore understood as only the beginning. By virtue of its power the whole life becomes the 'sacrament' of those who share in the death, the sacrament of the community, which is founded on the fact of salvation enacted by God, but which manifests itself in the 'no more enslaved to sin' and the 'yielding yourselves to God' (v. 13).

Thus according to II Cor. 1.5, the *'sufferings of Christ'* 'are shared abundantly' by Paul. The 'sufferings of Christ' are neither sufferings *such as* Christ endured, nor are they simply sufferings endured for Christ's sake. Still less are they sufferings in 'imitation of Christ'. Nor do the sufferings, as sufferings of a special kind, establish the relation with Christ; it is because of the relation with Christ that the sufferings become the 'sufferings of Christ'. They are sufferings of any kind, sufferings which may befall anyone, although they will come in special number upon the followers of Christ. But for the believer, because of his relation with Christ, they have gained a new meaning, since living and dying are encountered in his allegiance to the Lord (Rom. 14.7–9; Phil. 1.21).

The suffering and death of Jesus is not, therefore, a mere fact of the past; it is contemporary. To be united with Christ means to be standing in a new historical context, as is proved by the fact that the sufferer does not have and bear his share in the 'suffering of Christ' for himself but for the sake of others. Comfort abounds for the Corinthians because Paul shares in the 'suffering of Christ' and can therefore comfort them (II Cor. 1.4). So Paul's sufferings also come under the 'for one another' (II Cor. 1.6f.). He comforts them and they pray for him (vv. 10f.).

Now Paul can also, in exactly the same way, describe communion with Christ as a *sharing in the life of Jesus* (II Cor. 4.7–18). Paradoxically, the 'life of Jesus' becomes manifest in that Paul is 'carrying in [his] body the death of Jesus'. Such 'carrying' certainly does not consist in any 'imitation', but in Paul's willing acceptance of the sufferings which befall him in the service of Jesus. Accordingly, 'life' is not a quality or disposition created by the magic of the sacrament. Nor does it consist in mystic 'experiences'. It has no existence *apart from* Paul's resolute perseverance in the work of an apostle, so that the 'life of Jesus' which is manifested in his body is at the same time the 'life' which is at work in his hearers (v. 12).

Since 'life' is made manifest paradoxically in death and since only the 'death' is visible to the eyes of the world, it becomes clear that the 'revelation 'that takes place here is accessible only to faith. 'Life' is not, therefore, an objective phenomenon of the world; it takes place in history and is visible only to the man who in faith, in obedience, shares in achieving this history.

The meaning of the Pauline '*in Christ*' (ἐν Χριστῷ) has already been clarified by the preceding statements. To be 'in Christ' means to stand within this new history, which is not world history and the history of sin, but is eschatological event. Therefore it means to belong to the new world: 'if anyone is in Christ, then he is a new creation' (II Cor. 5.17). 'In Christ' does not designate a personal or mystical relation to Christ, but an eschatological fact.[15] 'In Christ', one has the eschatological

---

[15] 'New creation' (καινὴ κτίσις) is an eschatological term. It should also be noted that 'to be in Christ' (ἐν Χριστῷ εἶναι) has the same meaning as 'to be Christ's' (Χριστοῦ εἶναι) = to *belong to* Christ, to be owned by him

blessings of 'righteousness', of 'justification' (II Cor. 5.21; cf. Gal. 2.16) and of 'freedom' (Gal. 2.4).

The phrase 'in Christ' has no exact analogies in the history of religions and was evidently coined by Paul himself after the broader analogy of 'in the Spirit' (ἐν πνεύματι). For that very reason, 'in the Spirit' must be interpreted in accordance with 'in Christ' and not *vice versa*. That is, for Paul, 'in the Spirit' does not mean an ecstatic or mystic state but describes the Christian's new mode of being, the manner of his historical existence as an existence in the New Age. (The Spirit is, in fact, the gift belonging to the 'last days'.) The phrase has the same meaning as 'in Christ' (the 'Lord' is in fact synonymous with the 'Spirit': II Cor. 3–17).

'Spirit' is correlative to 'flesh'. Just as 'flesh' characterizes the manner of the old existence as a 'walking' (περιπατεῖν) in sin, so the new existence is characterized by the 'Spirit' as a 'walking' in righteousness. The meaning of Gal. 6.15; 5.6 and I Cor. 7.19 when taken together is unmistakable. Each time, the new existence is first described negatively. It is not determined by the question: circumcision or uncircumcision? Gal. 6.15 then designates it positively: 'But [it is] a new creation'; Gal. 5.6: 'but [it is] faith working in love', and I Cor. 7.19: 'but [it is] keeping the commandments of God'. The 'way of life', the 'desires' of the Christian are determined by the Spirit (Rom. 8.4–11). 'To have the Spirit' means 'to be led by the Spirit' (Rom. 8.14), and so to have no more fear (Rom. 8.15). 'If we live in the Spirit, let us also walk by the Spirit' (Gal. 5.25).

Everywhere the same thought is expressed. Man is not his own master. Therefore the Christian is not under his own control, but he can – confronted through the proclamation with the question – choose his Lord. The possibility of choice is founded on God's saving act and on that act the new existence of the Christian is founded. But the new being does not exist as an objective entity in a static situation. As it is grasped in obedience, so also it is achieved in obedience.

Thus Paul's *concept of the church* has finally become clear.

(Gal. 3.28f.; 5.24; II Cor. 10.7; Rom. 8.9; 14.8). The Christian no longer belongs to himself; he is no longer at his own disposal (I Cor. 6.19; Rom. 14.17f.).

The church is the empirical, *visible* community of those who believe the Gospel. Hence Jesus Christ is the Lord of the church and is honoured as such in the church's worship. But as God of the cult he is at the same time the eschatological Lord. He is the eschatological Lord, not primarily because he will come again, but because he has been in this place and has called the community into life as a new creation. The church is therefore an eschatological entity. But it is such because it constitutes the end of the history of salvation, not as a phenomenon extracted from the world, but as a historical entity. The church is therefore at the same time *invisible*. For it is visible only for faith, that is, for the obedience which grasps the new historical possibility.

III

With these observations, we have already given some indication of the meaning which *teaching* has in the New Testament and of how it is related to the church.

The proclamation of Jesus can only be called kerygma. It is in no respect theoretical or reflective. It is primarily *direct address*: a call to repentance and a promise of coming salvation for those who are ready to repent. It does have relation to facts in so far as it proclaims a future fact, the coming of the kingdom of God. But this coming of the kingdom is not to be understood as the sort of fact in the world which can be observed and which can be investigated when observed (Luke 17.21, 23f.). A man cannot be on the look-out for it as he can for a worldly opportunity (Mark 4.26–29). It is a fact which forces a man to look out for himself, a fact which confronts him with his ultimate possibility and demands his decision.

In so far as Jesus 'teaches' the coming of the kingdom of God, this 'teaching' is indirect summons. But his proclamation also contains *indirect teaching*, in that the call to repentance, that is the imperative which is implicit in the 'teaching' of the coming of the kingdom of God, is developed in the context of a *dispute with Jewish legalism*. This relation is clear, for example, in the sayings preserved in Matt. 5.21–48, where the will of God is contrasted with the Law, or when Jesus argues about the Sabbath, or cleanness, or the greatest commandment. His words do not have the character of theoretical considerations; they present a summons to right action. In such teaching, thinking is obviously intended to serve action. That is, by the consideration of a theoretical case, man's understanding of himself as he stands before God is made explicit. Such thinking is far from 'talking something over'. In it, the resolve for obedience to the will of God which has already been pre-supposed, and which opponents or questioners also claim to have, is in fact made. The resolve must be proved true by bringing this thinking to realization and judging and acting accordingly.

The use of examples and parables – a use which Jesus shares with Judaism – demonstrates how little the scientific character of theoretical reasoning is developed. Here it is plain that the *understanding* of teaching as direct address is presupposed. Even in the disputes, it becomes explicit that the thinking or the 'teaching' does not add anything over and above the direct call. There is only summons and hearing with the concomitant achievement of understanding, of more or less explicit thinking. (In Schlatter's words: the act of thinking and the act of living are one.)

In the kerygma, therefore, 'theology', as man's theoretical reflection upon his confrontation with God, is applied to action. Conversely, it is clear that thinking is not self-orientation nor disinterested 'observation' of the world and men as objects. Man is understood in his historical nature so that the facts of which he is apprised – whether the coming of the kingdom of God or the man who fell among thieves – demand a resolve force him to decision.

Concerning his own person, Jesus presented no specific teaching. On the other hand, he stressed the fact of his presence as significant, even as decisive, since he is the bearer of the Word in the final and decisive hour and since, therefore, it has come to pass *that* his Word confronts the hearer here and now. Jesus also regarded John the Baptist in the same way (Matt 21.32; cf. Luke 7.29f.) and to that extent also 'taught' about the Baptist. That 'teaching' also has the character of indirect summons, of the call to repentance (Matt. 11.7–19; Luke 7.24–35). In the same sense, he 'teaches' about his own person: 'Blessed is he who takes no offence at me' (Matt. 11.4–6).

Or:

> Everyone who acknowledges me before men,
> The Son of man will acknowledge before the angels of God;
> But he who denies me before men
> Will be denied before the angels of God (Luke 12.8f.; cf. Mark 8.38)

And the same sense is expressed in 'and there is more than Jonah here! . . . and there is more than Solomon here!' (Matt. 12.41f.; Luke 11.31f.).

Just as Jesus 'teaches' concerning the Baptist, so a christology is implicitly contained in the call to decision in respect of his own person; but Jesus does not develop it. *If it is to be made explicit*, its meaning can only be that the decision for or against him is made in it, and not in theoretical speculation. Therefore, a christology is fundamentally false if it is an attempt to reconstruct the 'messianic consciousness' of Jesus as an observable phenomenon with objective existence,[16] instead of being the confession of faith: He *is* the Messiah.

Now this means that whenever Jesus refers to his person, he is referring, not to an unambiguous fact of the world which can be observed by anyone and which can therefore be reconstructed by historical research, but to an *ambiguous* fact, the true character of which is understoood only in the act of *hearing*. He repudiates any unambiguous sign of authentication (Mark 8.11f.; Matt. 12.38–40; Luke 11.29f.), consistently with his repudiation of 'observation' (παρατήρησις) in general (Luke 17.20f.). He does point to the 'signs of the times' (Luke 12.54–56); to his equally ambiguous casting out of demons (Matt 12.28; Luke 11.20; Mark 3.27); to his preaching and also to the preaching of the Baptist (Matt. 12.41f.; Luke 11.31f.).

How this kerygma with its implicit 'teaching' relates to the church is no problem. For Jesus knows himself to be within the history of his people. So he takes the cult and the law for granted as valid, just as he presupposes the Old Testament tradition as a whole; and he continues the kerygma of the prophets. He proclaims simply that their predictions and promises are now

---

[16] All the modern studies of the messianic consciousness of Jesus which are known to me belong in this category. Even E. Brunner, *Der Mittler*, Tübingen, 1927 [ET, *The Mediator*, London, 1934; Philadelphia, 1941] does not succeed in radically transcending it.

finding their fulfilment. Since this kind of proclamation belonged to the essence of the Jewish 'church' from its beginning, the preaching of Jesus, both as direct summons and as theological exposition,[17] stands within the Jewish church.

With *Paul* the problem of church and teaching at once becomes prominent. Paul's own personality as well as his particular historical task compelled him to make the knowledge given in faith explicit. And he had to do so on two fronts.

1. *Against Judaism.* For although Judaism provided the concept of Messiah for the understanding of the fact of Jesus in its true significance, yet it was also the source of many difficulties, since the fate of Jesus does not correspond to the usual picture of the Messiah.[18] Similarly, in opposition to Judaism the absolute claim of the tradition had to be reduced to a relative claim.

2. *Against Gnosticism.* Here it was essential to demonstrate that gnosis in the Christian sense is legitimate only if the obedience of faith is achieved in it. Christian knowledge may not be self-orientation or any speculative consideration of man as a being who is under his own control. For Christian knowledge has a genuinely historical character. It is therefore an understanding which is consummated in resolve and is an understanding of one's self.

---

[17] The nature of the content of the proclamation of Jesus is fairly clearly expressed in the terminology of the Synoptics.

The inclusive term for the proclamation, which expresses its character as summons, is κηρύσσειν ('preaching'): Mark 1.14, 38f.; Matt. 4.17; 9.35; 11.1; Luke 4.18f. (following Isaiah 61.1f.); 8.1. But the usage is not strictly followed. 'Teach' (διδάσκειν) is used similarly: Mark 2.13; 6.6; 10.1; 12.35; 14.49; Luke 4.15; 13.22, 26; 19.47. Matthew combines 'preach' and 'teach' in 4.13; 9.35; 11.1.

On the other hand, 'teach' is used consistently when the words of the preacher relate to a specific case: Mark 1.21f.; 4.2; 6.2, 34; 8.31; 9.31; 11.17; 12.14; Matt. 5.1; 21.23; Luke 5.3, 17; 6.6.; (11.1); 13.10; 20.1 (in combination with 'preach the gospel', εὐαγγελίζεσθαι). So also the 'teaching' of Jesus (διδαχή) is mentioned: Mark 1.22, 27; 4.2; 11.18; 12.38, corresponding to the usual designation of Jesus as 'teacher' (διδάσκαλος or ῥαββεί).

For the preaching of the Baptist and of the disciples 'preach' (κηρύσσειν) is used: Mark 1.4, 7; 3.14; 6.12 (13.10; 14.9); Matt. 10.27; Luke 24.47. 'Teach' is used of the disciples in Mark 6.30 and Matt. 28.20.

[18] Cf. Schlatter, *Der Glaube im Neuen Testament*, 4th ed., Stuttgart, 1927, p. 142.

With Paul, then, there is a clear distinction between the kerygma as direct address and theology as indirect address; that is, Paul is really a *theologian*. It is indicative of this distinction that the kerygma presents 'folly' (μωρία) which is only para-doxically 'wisdom' (σοφία) from the standpoint of God, while theology presents wisdom directly (I Cor. 1-4).

First of all, clearly, *the kerygma of Paul*[19] *proclaims a fact*: Jesus Christ, whom God sent when the time was full, who was put to death and rose again 'for our trespasses' or 'for our justification' (Rom. 4.25). Through him 'redemption' (ἀπολύτρωσις) is given (Rom. 3.24f.), 'reconciliation' (καταλλαγή) is achieved (II Cor. 5.18f.). Therefore, Paul's 'teaching' is not at all 'enlightenment' in the sense of an exposition of principles; it is primarily the communication of a fact. What is proclaimed is not a new concept of God, such as that God is really gracious and not wrathful, but an *act* of God. God's wrath (ὀργή) still persists, and his *grace* (χάρις) is not his eternal attribute but his saving act.[20] Accordingly, God's *love* (ἀγάπη) is his act of love which is accomplished in the death and resurrection of Jesus Christ.[21]

Similarly, *faith* (πίστις) is not a human mood or attitude as such – for example, trusting God or the like – but understood strictly in accordance with its intention, is faith *in*, that is, faith in the saving act. Hence faith is obedience (see above p. 199).

The designation of the saving act as God's 'grace' and 'love', and of faith as 'obedience' shows that *the fact of salvation* is not to be understood *as an objective fact of the world* – not even a fact of the greatest cosmic dimensions.[22] The saving act is not something objectively present, nor is it perceived by scientific observation as objective entities or events which occur or have

---

[19] I am limiting myself to Paul. But what holds for him holds with appropriate modifications for the early Christian proclamation as a whole.

[20] Cf. Rom. 3.24f; 5.15–21; Gal. 1.6; 2.21 (cf. v. 20!); II Cor. 6.1 ('not to receive the grace of God in vain': 'grace' is the 'reconciliation' of 5.18f.).

[21] Cf. Rom. 5.8; 8.34f., 37, 39: also Gal. 2.20; II Cor. 5.14f. and II Cor. 13.11, 13; Rom. 15.30.

[22] How far this intention is consistently carried through (cf. for example, I Cor. 2.8; Phil. 2.6–11), is another question. Paul's presentation often strays into the inappropriate conceptuality prevalent in the ancient world. Cf. note 11 on p. 198 above.

occurred in the world are perceived. As the cross of Christ, it is certainly *also* a fact of the world – that is exactly what constitutes its ambiguity. Just for that reason the 'word of the cross' appears as 'folly', for that word declares this cross to be the saving fact (I Cor. 1.18–25).

The Word is understood only when the cross is seen as 'grace' and 'love'; it is understood only in the obedience of faith. Therefore, the proclamation is not a mere factual communication which could be given once for all. It is preached again and again, continually. For in the communication of the fact of salvation there is a summons, a question to be decided, an invitation. 'Now we are ambassadors for Christ [in Christ's stead?], as though God did beseech you by us; we pray you in Christ's stead, be ye reconciled to God' (II Cor. 5.20).

Here it is assumed that those addressed can truly hear the proclamation, since they can *understand* it. *Understanding* does not mean the ability to deduce from it an explanation for fitting what is proclaimed into the previously held world picture. That is exactly what *cannot* be done. The proclamation is a 'stumbling-block' and 'folly'; but 'so it pleased God' (I Cor. 1.21). *Understanding* means rather that under the impact of hearing the proclamation, the individual has learned to understand himself anew, to understand himself as the sinner to whom God is giving justification.

The *pre-understanding* which is thereby pre-supposed as a necessary condition is expressly noted by Paul. It is given in the law which is the 'custodian' 'on our way to Christ' (Gal. 3.24). 'The scriptures consigned all things to sin, that what was promised to faith in Jesus Christ might be given to those who believe' (Gal. 3.22). The law had to lead into sin in order that grace could come to reign (Rom. 5.20f.).[23]

Understanding is achieved in decision, in obedience. Since (1) God's saving act is an action and not enlightenment, and since (2) the hearing of the proclamation involves under-

[23] In such statements Paul developed only the pre-understanding given to the *Jews*. Romans 1–3 shows plainly that he assumed a pre-understanding also among the *Gentiles*, for the situations of Jews and Gentiles are described as fundamentally alike. This is clear also from his conviction that the kerygma is also addressed to the active conscience (II Cor. 4.2) also to be found among the Gentiles (Rom. 2.14f.). Cf. also, e.g. I Cor. 14.24f.

standing, Paul's *concept of revelation* is clearly defined. God's revelation is primarily an event, not a communication of knowledge. But the event is a basis for both a knowledge and a teaching, since it makes possible a new self-understanding.

Rom. 2.5; 8.18f.; I Cor. 1.7; 3.13 use 'reveal' and 'revelation' (ἀποκαλύπτειν, ἀποκαλύψις) in referring to the future eschatological event. The eschatological event of the present is described in exactly the same terms:

Rom. 1.17f.: 'For in it [the Gospel] the righteousness of God is revealed through faith for faith . . . the wrath of God is revealed from heaven against all ungodliness . . . .'

Gal. 3.23: 'Now before faith came, we were confined under the law, kept under restraint until faith should be revealed.'

God's revelation, then, is effected even when no one is aware of it (Rom. 1.18ff.). And the 'revelation' of faith (Gal. 3.23) is certainly not the communication of a doctrine, a dogma, but the opening up, through God's act, of the possibility of having faith. Faith would be 'revealed' (in the sense of the saving act described in Gal. 4.4), even if nobody believed.

The possibility of understanding is, of course, based on the operation of the divine act, as it is an event which happens to men; for self-understanding belongs to human being as such. When the revelation occurs, something happens of which man can become aware, something of which he necessarily becomes aware under certain circumstances (for example, in the Last Judgment). But 'revelation' ('unveiling', ἀποκάλυψις) designates not the knowledge communicated but the event which puts the man in a new situation.

The same conception appears in the use of 'manifest,' 'manifestation' (φανεροῦν, φανέρωσις), since here the element of the basis of knowledge given by the event is more strongly emphasized, in such a way that the 'becoming manifest' (φανερωθῆναι) is effected primarily as an event. When Paul says in Rom. 3.21 'but now the righteousness of God has been manifested', he is simply referring to the saving act described in vv. 24f. II Cor. 4.10f. is to be understood in the same way:

Always carrying in the body the death of Jesus,
so that the life of Jesus may also be manifested in our bodies.

For while we live we are always being given up to death
for Jesus' sake,
so that the life of Jesus may be manifested in our mortal
flesh.

What is spoken of here is an *event* (see above p. 204ff and cf.
the 'at work in us' ἐνεργεῖσθαι of v. 12). But *the possibility
of being understood* is inherent in the event, and understanding
is incumbent on man.

Thus in II Cor. 2.14–6.10, Paul develops the thought that
the Gospel which he preaches is characterized by clarity.
It is understandable precisely because it is the Gospel of life.
It appears 'veiled' only to the lost (4.3). Since the 'new covenant'
gives life (3.6), it is correspondingly open, while the 'old
covenant' was characterized by a veil.[24] But the understanding
can be grasped only in resolve.

Therefore the preaching which brings life carries also the
possibility of spreading death and darkness (2.14–16). In the
sight of God, the 'manifestation' which is consummated in the
proclamation is unequivocal; but to the sight of men it is
ambiguous (5.11), just because man is questioned by the
proclamation and must himself decide for life or for death.
The proclamation is addressed to man's conscience (4.1–6).

It therefore follows that since the revelation as event gives
life and does not allow man to remain his old self, nor does it
present itself to him for neutral observation, a *knowing*
(γινώσκειν) is also included, for the *revelation is effected precisely
in the proclamation*. The proclamation is not simply the communication of knowledge about a fact so that one could go
back and ought to go back to the fact which gave rise to the
proclamation. But the proclamation, the occurrence of the
proclamation as event, is itself a part of the revelation. Here the
decision is made – one way or the other since the word puts
the question and forces man to decision. Thus the apostle
brings death and life.

As a consequence the preaching apostle, with his authority,
with his claim to the obedience of the community (II Cor. 2.9;
7.15; 10.6; Phil. 2.12; Philemon 21), also belongs to the Gospel;

[24] II Cor. 3.7–18 affirms this open character of the Christian preaching.
II Cor. 2.14–16 and 4.7–15 show that the openness is paradoxical.

he is a part of it. He actually speaks 'for Christ', so that God himself is 'appealing' through him (II Cor. 5.20). Paul thus justifies (II Cor. 2.14–6.10) his own 'plainness of speech' (παρρησία) together with the clarity of the Gospel. In Rom. 10.13–17 he shows also that faith is the result of preaching (ἀκοή, hearing). In II Cor. 5.18f. he calls God's institution of the 'ministry' or the 'word' of reconciliation God's act of salvation. So, according to Rom. 1.16, the Gospel (εὐαγγέλιον) is 'the power of God for salvation to every one that has faith'; in the Gospel that power is 'revealed' (1.17).

The kerygma, the summons, is therefore teaching in so far as it implies a specific understanding. It gives instruction concerning a fact – but a fact which must not be regarded as an objective fact of the world. Therefore the factual communication is not merely the imparting of information which is incidental and secondary; it is itself a part, as the preaching authorized by the saving act is a part, of the saving fact itself. And conversely, the fact of salvation is not such without the preaching. There is no way of going behind the preaching to a saving fact separable from the preaching – whether to a 'historical Jesus' or to a cosmic drama. Access to Jesus Christ exists only in the preaching.

For exactly this reason, 'teaching' is summons, indirect in that it informs, direct in that it becomes appeal (II Cor. 5.20ff.). In the summons, a specific understanding is communicated to the obedient hearer. Or rather, obedient listening implicitly includes the understanding, and obedience can be achieved only with explicit understanding.

Now since 'teaching' is such kerygma, the *essential inter-relation between church and teaching* is fully clear: *The church is constituted by this kerygma.* It cannot exist at all without the 'ministry' (διακονία) of the word. And this 'ministry,' which makes the saving fact an actuality in the church, makes the church an eschatological fact, makes it the community of the saints, of the called. Where the preaching sounds, there the day of salvation dawns: 'Behold *now* is the acceptable time, behold *now* is the day of salvation' (II Cor. 6.2). Therefore, the cult is primarily the proclamation of the word and the answering confession of faith, the faith which acclaims the act of salvation.

When the service also includes the ministration of the sacraments, it still remains under the domination of the word. The sacraments stand beside the word as the 'word made visible' (*verbum visibile*). They achieve nothing which differs from what is achieved by the spoken word. Like the word, they make the saving act a present act; like the word, they demand obedience; and like the word, they include, together with the possibility of giving life, the other possibility of bringing condemnation (I Cor. 11.29 and cf. above p. 199). Thus Paul can even call the celebration of the Lord's Supper a 'proclaiming' (I Cor. 11.26).

Church and word therefore belong together. The word is what it is, not because of any content of timeless meaning, but as authorized preaching continuing the tradition. It follows, conversely, that *the word is also constituted by the church*. Consequently, one cannot appeal to the church to settle a doubt about the word since the church is constituted by the receiving and transmitting of the word. Nor, however, can one appeal to the word to settle a doubt about the church, as if the word carried its import timelessly in itself and as if the fact that it is being spoken here and now were not an integral part of it. The summons is transmitted in its delivery. The church cannot be played off against the word, for it is constituted by the word. And the word cannot be played off against the church, for the word possesses its meaning as authorized tradition. The preacher does not proclaim himself (II Cor. 4.5); hence his personal qualities, the strength of his faith or the quality of his ethical life, have no relevance. As a religious or ethical personality, he does not concern his hearers (I Cor. 3.5–9; Phil. 1.15–18).

Naturally it is not possible to state in general terms *how far at any given time the hearer's understanding must be explicit* in order to find expression in the confession of faith or in the transmission of the summons. On the one hand, every utterance of the word is a specific interpretation; it therefore contains theological elements and at any given time it is formulated in the concepts current at that time. On the other hand, conceptual interpretation of the understanding of the word can be a task undertaken consciously and intentionally. If such theological, theoretical, doctrinal work is not to lose its way, if it is to remain indirect summons and is to be achieved in the obedience of faith, then the venture to accept the task may only be made if it becomes a duty. It is not to be attempted because of any 'conception of the scientific discipline' to which theology allegedly belongs. Therefore, to be legitimate, theology must always be critical and polemical.

With Paul, in fact, it is exactly that.

1. *Against Judaism or Judaizing*.

(*a*) The Jewish picture of the Messiah had to be corrected. The stumbling-block of the *crucified Messiah* had to be affirmed as divine wisdom. Here Paul's theological work is only indirectly visible, for in his letters he did not argue directly with his christological opponents. Indeed, we do not know whether he ever had to do so. But he certainly had to carry through, at least for himself, the argument against the Jewish conception of the Messiah.

Paul's *christology* cannot be presented in detail here. It need only be noted that it is not theoretical speculation but is developed in unity with the self-explication of Christian existence. As the Christian existence proceeds through judgment to grace, so Christ is the crucified and the risen. The cross was not the fulfilment of a tragic destiny, and no cosmic drama was played to its end there, providing a spectacle for sympathetic or reflective observation. The cross is truly seen only when it is understood that God's judgment upon all self-righteousness and 'boasting' (καυχᾶσθαι). has been given in it There must come a 'being crucified with him', a fellowship in his suffering and a sharing in his death (Rom. 6.6; Phil. 3.10). For those who believe in the cross of Christ, the world also is crucified (Gal. 6.14).

The resurrection of Christ is not an anomalous cosmic event, but the beginning of a new creation. The risen Christ is the 'firstborn among many brethren' (Rom. 8.29), 'the second Adam' (Rom. 5.12f.; I Cor. 15.21f., 45). What has happened in the resurrection is achieved in all those who believe.

(*b*) Paul's *teaching on the law* is explicitly developed against the Judaizers in Galatians, against the Jews in Romans. In it Paul shows what faith and obedience really are. He shows how the law is, on the one hand, the eternal will of God and how, on the other hand, it has been misused by the Jews who wish to make it their 'boast' (καύχημα, καύχησιςλ, an instrument of 'their own righteousness' (Rom. 10.3; Phil. 3.9). It therefore becomes in God's hand the means of stripping away man's 'boasting' and driving him into sin, so that he learns to understand what 'grace' (χάρις) is. This teaching is supported by Paul's anthropological teaching on 'body' and 'flesh'.

2. Against Gnosticism.

At this point, the question of 'teaching' becomes critical, and here the inner unity of Paul's thinking becomes especially clear. The refutation of the Gnostics runs exactly parallel to the refutation of the legalists.[25] *The Gnostics* misunderstand the Gospel in taking it as an occasion for 'boasting'; they think that as 'spiritual men' (πνευματικοί) in whom 'Christ speaks' they possess a new quality; they understand Christian 'liberty' (ἐξουσία) as the right to arbitrary personal preference. So they boast of their 'wisdom' (σοφία). They thereby make themselves independent of God and set up their own wisdom, which they exhibit as a possession of their own and deduce regulations for conduct from it. Obedience is not fulfilled in their 'theology'.

They forget that above the 'all is yours' stands the 'but you are Christ's, and Christ is God's' (I Cor. 3.21-23). They forget the 'what have you that you did not receive? If then you received it, why do you boast as if it were not a gift?' (I Cor. 4.7). They are 'already filled' ('satiated', κεκορεσμένοι, I Cor. 4.8), and they forget that above the 'all things are lawful for me' stands the 'but not all things are helpful' and the 'but I will not forfeit my freedom for anything' (I Cor. 6.12). They forget the 'you are not your own' (I Cor. 6.19).

Thus they misunderstand the historical character of Christian knowing. That is, they do not recognize that it is an *understanding of one's self in the obedience of faith*, that consequently one can never have wisdom as a possession and can never make it perfect.[26] Therefore they boast and construct as it were a divine wisdom through their own. But they here commit the original sin of the world, which refused to understand itself

[25] Cf. Schlatter, *Der Glaube im Neuen Testament*, 4th ed., 1927, pp. 388f.
[26] Phil. 3.12-14 teaches the paradoxical character of Christian 'perfection' (cf. v. 15, 'as many as are perfect', ὅσοι οὖν τέλειοι).

as created and did not give honour to God (I Cor. 1.21; Rom. 1.19–21), and the original sin of the Jews, who wished to set up their own righteousness by means of the law in order to have a 'boast'.

The Gospel, however, is the 'word of the cross'. It requires the relinquishment of every human claim, of all 'boasting', so that the word may be understood as the 'power and wisdom' of God (I Cor. 1.14). That word is 'folly' until a man has learned to understand himself as 'a fool' (I Cor. 3.18), and no longer thinks that he can understand it as wisdom by himself. The Gospel can be known as wisdom only by the man who 'boasts only of the Lord' (I Cor. 1.31) and knows himself to be a fool; only by the man to whom the 'Spirit' is given and who knows himself the possessor of such knowledge only because he has received it as a gift (I Cor. 2.6–16; note especially v. 12, 'understand the gifts bestowed on us by God', i.e. that we may understand ourselves as recipients of a gift).

Christian 'wisdom' (which certainly exists) therefore presupposes living in faith, no longer being a 'babe' or a 'man of the flesh' (I Cor. 3.1–3). Thus it can only be the interpretation of the faith itself, which is preserved or newly achieved in the interpretation. If wisdom shifts from this foundation and becomes speculation, then it is turned into folly. It is legitimate only *when obedience is fulfilled in it*, as I Cor. 8.1–3 shows. Our knowledge is grounded in 'being known by God' (cf. I Cor. 13.12; Gal. 4.9), and is manifested as such in the love which involves man's self-surrender, the sacrifice of his liberty (I Cor. 8.9), in 'mutual service'. This inner connection between knowledge and love shows plainly that legitimate theological knowledge implies the obedience of faith, even as faith lays the foundation of knowledge.

The same point is made in Phil. 3.8–11. Knowledge is founded in the righteousness accepted in faith and therefore has as its goal 'to gain Christ' and 'to be found in him'. But this goal is reached by 'becoming like him in his death' and thus knowing the 'power of his resurrection' and 'sharing his sufferings'. The relation between knowledge and obedience is therefore plain. Knowledge is founded on the relinquishment of all self-confidence (cf. vv. 3f.), but it consequently has the positive effect of leading further into the Christian fellowship.

The independent gnosis which relies on itself and which lacks 'obedience' inevitably sees *its objects as phenomena which are present to hand*. It does not need to submit itself to them, to 'hear' them; they remain silent and are 'seen' by it. Paul can describe this character of objectivity, in which the 'facts' appear to the unbelieving observer, in different ways. In Rom. 2.28f. he speaks of 'a Jew outwardly' (ὁ ἐν τῷ φανερῷ 'Ιουδαῖος) and of 'circumcision which is outward in the flesh' (ἡ ἐν τῷ φανερῷ ἐν σαρκὶ περιτομή), in contrast to a 'Jew, inwardly' (ὁ ἐν τῷ κρυπτῷ 'Ιουδαῖος) and the 'circumcision of the heart in the spirit and not in the letter' (περιτομὴ καρδίας ἐν πνεύματι οὐ γράμματι).

What is here called 'outwardly' in contrast to 'inwardly' and what is at the same time called 'fleshly', is elsewhere designated *'according to the flesh'* (κατὰ σάρκα, II Cor. 1.12). The clearest statement, because it employs the term 'know' (γινώσκειν), is II Cor. 5.16: 'Therefore from now on we know no man after the flesh; even though we have known Christ after the flesh we [so] know him no more'. The old dispute whether 'after the flesh; modifies *Christ* or *have known* is unimportant. For to know anyone from the standpoint that he is flesh, that is, to know him in mere, generally observable objectivity, means to know him in the manner of 'fleshly' knowledge.

Christ can also be seen in that way. He is a Jew 'according to the flesh' (Rom. 9.5), just as Abraham is the ancestor of the Jews also 'according to the flesh' (Rom. 4.1). That is, it is possible to regard either as an object. But when in I Cor. 1.26, the wise of this age are called 'wise according to the flesh', this does not mean that they exist objectively, but that they are wise in the way of the flesh. 'According to the flesh' therefore has a peculiar double meaning (as has *flesh* in general with Paul). The two meanings are certainly inter-related, since to perceive something in its character as flesh is itself a 'fleshly' procedure.

If inward circumcision (Rom. 2.28f.) is also called circumcision 'in the spirit and not in the letter', then it is also clear that 'letter' here has the sense of an objective phenomenon, of what can be perceived by merely looking at it. This is exactly the delusion of the Jews. They understand the law, the will of God, as 'letter' and therefore see their own obedience as an achievement which can satisfy the limited requirements they find in the law; they do not see that God's will can be known and fulfilled only by obeying. The letter kills (II Cor. 3.6) just because the man who is content with objective phenomena has lapsed into death. The believer looks not at 'the things seen' (τὰ βλεπόμενα) but at 'the things that are unseen (τὰ μὴ βλεπόμενα, II Cor. 4.18). He guides his life not 'by sight' (διὰ εἴδους), not by observing the objective, but 'by faith' (διὰ πίστεως, II Cor. 5.7).[27]

Church and Teaching for Paul. The church is constituted by the kerygma and the kerygma by the church. Upon the kerygma is based a theology which, as critical, polemic teaching, must become explicit to meet the demands on it. Since the theology itself is based on obedience and must itself be the fulfilment of obedience, as such fulfilment it extends obedience and consummates the fellowship with Christ based on obedience.

Since Christian theology according to Paul has this character, it is an indirect *summons* precisely when it is critical and polemical. But it is *indirect* summons since the kerygma is contained in it in the form of a discussion of the teaching. It is therefore clear that *this theology itself is continually subject to criticism* – but only to the criticism which is itself based on obedience. Otherwise, 'the spiritual man judges all things but is himself judged by no one' (I Cor. 2.15). But the *kerygma* in itself is not open to any criticism, since as a summons demanding obedience it cannot be judged from a neutral position. Its precise demand is relinquishment of one's own judgment.

The kerygma, however, is always expressed in the conceptuality of human intercourse. Therefore, although kerygma and theology are fundamentally different, they are not separable in practice. That means that the exact content of the kerygma, how many and what affirmations it must contain, can never be definitely stated. But this impossibility simply corresponds to the nature of the kerygma, to the fact that it can be understood only in obedience and that therefore the understanding must always be newly achieved. Precisely on that fact depends

---

[27] Cf. also, the use of 'face' (πρόσωπον) as 'external circumstance' (ἐν προσώπῳ καυχᾶσθαι); for example, 'pride themselves on a man's position and not on his heart' (II Cor. 5.12).

the necessity of theology as the deliberate completion of the interpretation of the understanding of faith.[28]

[28] Here, too, the New Testament terminology is consistent. The word of summons, which demands the obedience of faith, is κήρυγμα, proclamation; to proclaim it is κηρύσσειν. Teaching in the narrower sense of the interpretation of the understanding of faith is διδαχή (or διδάσκειν). This distinction is not strictly observed since 'proclaim' and 'teach' are also used in parallelism (Rom. 2.21). But 'apostle' and 'teacher' are differentiated. The apostles 'call' the community and establish it; the teachers work in the established community to give interpretations of Christian knowledge (I Cor. 12.28f.). 'Teaching' (διδαχή) is a 'gift' in the community and communicates knowledge (γνῶσις) and wisdom (σοφία) (I Cor. 12.8; cf. 14.6, 26).

The character of κηρύσσειν ('proclaim') as summons (also καταγγέλλειν, 'announce') is made clear by the fact that μαρτυρεῖν, ('testify'), a term used for the most part in connection with exhortation, can stand in its stead (I Cor. 15.15; cf. Gal. 5.3), and testimony (μαρτύριον) is used instead of kergyma (κήρυγμα) (I Cor. 1.6; 2.1). Likewise, παρακαλεῖν, 'summon', also a term of exhortation, can mean the proclamation (II Cor. 5.20; 6.1) or παράκλησις, 'appeal', can stand for κήρυγμα (cf. I Thess. 2.3 with I Cor. 2.4).

The character of 'teaching' (διδάσκειν) as (indirect) summons becomes clear in that it can be replaced by 'command, ordain' (διατασσεθαε cf. I Cor. 7.17 with 4.17). Accordingly, speaking within the community is most often called παράκλησις, 'exhort, exhortation'. 'Exhortation' (παρακλησις) leads to 'up-building' (οἰκοδομή: I Thess. 2.11; 4.18; 5.11; I Cor. 14.3, etc.).

9

THE SIGNIFICANCE OF THE HISTORICAL
JESUS FOR THE THEOLOGY OF PAUL[1]
[1929]

THE PROBLEM 'Jesus and Paul' may be stated in three ways:

1. Is the development of Paul's thought determined by the historical Jesus; either directly, or indirectly through the medium of the primitive community? If so, how far did this influence extend?

2. How is the theology of Paul related in its content to Jesus' proclamation, quite apart from whatever causal significance Jesus' proclamation had for Paul?

3. What significance has the fact of the historical Jesus for the theology of Paul?

The third question is our concern here. But the specific meaning of this question and the problems it raises appear more clearly if we look first at the other two.

I. *How far is Paul dependent on Jesus?*

Paul was not influenced *directly* by the historical Jesus. He was neither a disciple of Jesus nor one of his opponents in Palestine in Jesus' lifetime. It is possible that Paul had never been in Jerusalem before his conversion, and that the account of his participation in the stoning of Stephen (Acts 7.58–8.3) is legendary, as is also the statement (Acts 22.3) that he had been a pupil of Gamaliel.[2] The conclusion that Paul knew Jesus personally and had made his own estimate of him can certainly

---

[1] *TB*, VIII (1929), pp. 137–51.
[2] Heitmüller, in agreement with Mommsen, so concluded (I think rightly) from Gal. 1.22, 'And I was still not known by sight to the churches of Christ in Judea'. Bousset (*Kyrios Christos*, 2nd ed., Göttingen, 1921, p. 75, 2) did not find this conclusion convincing.

not be drawn from II Cor. 5.16 ('though we have known Christ after the flesh, yet now we know him so no more').

Furthermore, there is almost nothing which can serve as evidence of *indirect* dependence. Paul denied such dependence. He is 'an apostle – not from men nor through man, but through Jesus Christ and God the Father' (Gal. 1.1). And of his gospel he asserts that it 'is not man's gospel. For I did not receive it from man, nor was I taught it, but it came through a revelation of Jesus Christ' (Gal. 1.11f.). He emphasizes the fact that he first came to Jerusalem three years after his conversion, remained there only a short time, seeing only Peter and James, the Lord's brother (Gal. 1.18f.), and that he did not again come to Jerusalem until fourteen (eleven?) years later (Gal. 2.1).[3]

Of course Paul must have had some knowledge of Christianity before his conversion; otherwise he could not have become its persecutor. He must have heard specifically that the Christians were expecting the recently crucified Jesus to return as Messiah. Paul does not state this explicitly as the ground of his hostility, but according to I Cor. 1.23 the cross is the 'stumbling-block' for the Jews. He gives as the reason for his own attitude (Gal. 1.13f.) that he was 'extremely zealous for the traditions of the fathers' (cf. Phil. 3.4–6; II Cor. 11.22). That this was actually his reason is plain, since for him the *either-or*, Jesus Christ or the law, was self-evident (Gal. 2.15ff.; Phil. 3.4ff.).

He must therefore have come to know Christianity in a form which was already critical of the law, which had in a measure transcended it. That is, he made the acquaintance of Christianity in the form of the Hellenistic Christianity which had arisen in Syria as a result of the propaganda of the Hellenistic Jewish Christians driven from Jerusalem by the death of Stephen (cf. Acts 8.1ff.; 11.19ff.). The 'tradition' cited by Paul (I Cor. 11.23–25; 15.1–7) is also Hellenistic in character. In addition, his concept of baptism (Rom. 6.1; I Cor. 12.13) and of the Lord's Supper (I Cor. 10.16) and also the fact that he takes for granted the title Kyrios and the worship of the Kyrios shows that he accepted without question the Syrian Hellenistic

[3] Cf. W. Heitmüller, 'Zum Problem Paulus und Jesus', *ZNW*, 13 (1912), pp. 320–7.

type of Christianity with which he was affiliated. This, in spite of all objection, seems to me an assured result of the research of Bousset and Heitmüller.

Obviously this Hellenistic Christianity had also taken over *Palestinian traditions*. All our Gospels, in which those traditions were collected and preserved, were in fact written in an Hellenistic environment. But not much of the tradition is identifiable in Paul's writings. If he found it current in the Hellenistic communities known to him, he ignored it for the most part – entirely, for instance, in the discussion of the law. From Judaism comes e.g. the dogma of the Davidic descent of Jesus (Rom. 1.3); from the Palestinian-Jewish tradition comes the substance of the 'word of the Lord' on the future coming and the resurrection of the dead (I Thess. 4.15–17). But it must remain uncertain whether these statements reached Paul as transmitted words of the Lord or whether he did not himself first receive them as a revelation of the exalted Lord.

Apart from the passage in Thessalonians and the words of institution at the Last Supper (I Cor. 11.23–25), Paul cites only *two sayings of the Lord*: I Cor. 7.10f.: 'To the married I give charge, not I but the Lord, that the wife should not separate from her husband . . .'; and I Cor. 9.14: 'In the same way, the Lord commanded that those who proclaim the gospel should get their living by the gospel.' Both these are part of the *regulations of the community* and neither is in this form an earlier saying of Jesus. In fact, I Cor. 7.10, which has its parallel in Mark 10.12 or in Q (Matt. 5.32; Luke 16.18), assumes the wife's right of divorce which is not recognized in Judaism.[4]

The passage in Q (Matt. 10.10; Luke 10.7) which supports I Cor. 9.14 is itself a community formulation. Paul certainly thought it important to have a word of the Lord on a matter of discipline or of community regulation, as is clear from I Cor. 7.25, 'now concerning the unmarried I have no command of the Lord'. This attitude makes it the more certain that when Paul does not cite such a word where it would be expected, he knows of none.

---

[4] In spite of H. L. Strack and P. Billerbeck, *Kommentar zum Neuen Testament aus Talmud und Midrasch*, II, München, 1924, pp. 23f. For that section deals with exceptions, while I Cor. 7.10f. assumes that the same law applies to men and women.

But it is most obvious that he does not appeal to the words of the Lord in support of his strictly theological, anthropological, and soteriological views. It is debatable whether his *ethical exhortations* are at times influenced by sayings of Jesus or not. Is Rom. 12.14, for example, an echo of the command to love one's enemies (Matt. 5.14; Luke 6.27f.)? Does the summary of the content of the law in the command to love (Rom. 13.9f.) depend on a word of the Lord (Mark 12.31 or Matt. 22.39)? Does 'I would have you wise as to what is good and guileless as to what is evil' (Rom. 16.19) go back to the saying about serpents and doves (Matt. 10.16)? Are the words of the Lord in Mark 11.23 or in Matt. 17.20; Luke 17.16 reflected in I Cor. 13.2 ('If I have all faith so as to remove mountains')? All these are at most possibilities.

Even if these passages were accepted as proof of dependence, they would show that it is only the ethical teaching of Jesus which is echoed in the exhortations of Paul. But the real significance of Jesus for Paul does not lie there. Furthermore, it is entirely possible that the similarity in such statements is due to the fact that Jesus and Paul both drew on Jewish tradition. But when the essentially Pauline conceptions are considered, it is clear that there Paul is not dependent on Jesus. Jesus' teaching is – to all intents and purposes – irrelevant for Paul.

II. *The Relation of the Theology of Paul to the Proclamation of Jesus*

A far-reaching agreement in content between the theology of Paul and Jesus' proclamation lies in an area where it would be least expected: in their *teaching on the law*. What kind of agreement? Did not Paul explain the law as an ordinance of salvation belonging to the past, from which Christians are freed? Was not the purpose of the law, according to Paul, to lead men into sin so that God's ordinance of salvation by grace might prevail? Jesus said nothing of that sort, but he assumed the validity of the law.[5] The polemic of Jesus is not directed against the law as such, but against the scribal tradition of interpretation and practice.

[5] I am, however, certain that in Matt. 5.17–19 we do not have the words of Jesus but a product of the polemic of the community.

But Jesus preached the kingdom of God as *coming*. When it is come, what will be the function of the law? It cannot then have for Jesus simply the meaning it had in the former age. Jesus might have shared, perhaps, the view which did exist in Judaism, that in the time of salvation the law will become obsolete – at least for the most part.[6] In any case, the words of Jesus present only the view that the law is valid now, for this age. Does Paul dispute that? On the contrary!

But still, Jesus did not have the same idea as Paul about the purpose of the law in this age! Jesus says nothing about the law being an impulse to sin. Obviously, there is a real difference here, but to understand it, the attitude of Jesus and Paul to the law must be examined somewhat more closely.

1. *For Jesus, the validity of the law is self-evident.* In the law, man finds the will of God revealed and therefore the answer to the question: 'What must I do to inherit eternal life?' 'You know the commandments' (Mark 10.17–19). When Jesus is asked for 'the first commandment of all', he quotes Deut. 6.4f. and Lev. 19.18 (Mark 12.29–31). And in support of his position on divorce he appeals to Gen. 1.27; 2.24 (Mark 10.6–8) (cf. further Mark 2.25f.; 12.26; Matt. 9.13; 12.7).

Certainly it is not only Jesus' practice in the observance of the Sabbath and of ritual cleanness which goes beyond the law. There is also an occasional saying like Mark 7.15, 'There is nothing outside a man which by going into him can defile him; but the things which come out of a man are what defile him.' With these words he repudiates a basic tenet on which the Old Testament laws of purity rest. However, when Jesus says this, he need not necessarily think that he is rejecting the law, but that he is only interpreting it. And although his interpretation does in fact annul the law in the sense which it had when it was given, the primary question remains simply whether or not he *intended* to annul the law. That he did *not* so intend is fully clear. Equally clear is the reason for his understanding the law as the expression of God's will and the kind of commandments in which he found it – in *the ethical demands.* For the right view of marriage he appeals to the Old Testament for support and on

─────────

[6] Cf. for example, G. Klein, *Der Älteste christliche Katechismus und die jüdische Propaganda-Literatur*, Berlin, 1909, pp. 214f.; Strack-Billerbeck, *Kommentar zum Neuen Testament*, I, pp. 246f.

cleanness he cites the word of the prophet (Isa. 29.13):

> This people honours me with their lips,
> But their heart is far from me;
> In vain do they worship me,
> Teaching as doctrines the precepts of men (Mark 7.6).

He sets the commandment to honour parents (Ex. 20.12) against the Jewish practice of the Corban (Mark 7.9–13). Obviously, Jesus discriminated within the Old Testament law, usually naïvely and implicitly, but on occasion explicitly (Matt. 23.23):

> Woe to you, scribes and Pharisees, hypocrites!
> For you tithe mint and dill and cummin,
> And have neglected *the weightier matters of the law,*
> Justice and mercy and faith;
> These you ought to have done,
> Without neglecting the others.

The distinction is even clearer in Mark 10.2–9 where he calls the provision for divorce (Deut. 24.1) Moses' concession 'to your hardness of heart', while the true will of God, according to Gen. 1.27; 2.24, requires the indissolubility of marriage.[7]

The great antitheses of Matt. 5.21–48 show clearly what is at issue. The true will of God is set against what is legally right. And for Jesus, the scribal tradition has the character of law. The mistake of the scribes is their conception of the Old Testament law as a legal code with limited provisions which a man can fulfil by the proper actions. For Jesus, on the other hand, the Old Testament law has the character of the true will of God which demands of man, not a limited but a radical obedience. Such obedience cannot be viewed as an achievement which establishes a claim (cf. Luke 17.7–10; Matt. 20.1–15).

It can of course be said that the problem of rabbinic piety and rabbinic discussion is exactly this problem of the relation between a legal code and ethics; and that the problem is very much alive in rabbinical Judaism, so that there are numerous rabbinic parallels to the words of Jesus. But for rabbinic theo-

---

[7] I have disregarded critical doubts about the authenticity of the tradition in this interpretation. For the words cited, even if their form may be the work of the community, in content (in my judgment) accurately record Jesus' position on this point.

logy the problem remains the co-ordination of law and ethics
or their amalgamation, while Jesus radically separates the will
of God from the law.

Jesus' position becomes clear through a comparison with
the *Old Testament prophets*, who, because they set the law and
righteousness against the religion of the cult, are in large measure responsible for the development of the law and its pre-
dominance in Judaism. The prophetic message is rooted in the
insight that cultic worship does not justify a man before God,
because man acquires his authentic character by his behaviour
in mutual dealings between men. If a man would be pure before God, it is important for him to keep these mutual transactions pure; and for that, the law is a help.

But the law can also be misused and made an end in itself.
It can be put to the service of the *I* instead of the *Thou*. This
happens when formal legality becomes the goal of action and is
counted as an achievement which establishes a claim in the
sight of God. It happens, for example, when a requirement
which was originally intended as a check on man and a limit
on his personal will (like the requirement of a formal divorce,
like the *ius talionis*, like limiting hate to hatred of enemies) is
interpreted in reverse as a permission granted to men, as a
concession to him. In that case, the real meaning of the law as
the demand of God which requires radical obedience is abandoned. Therefore the polemic of Jesus, which sets ethical
behaviour over against the law, originates from the same
motive as the prophetic polemic which sets the law over against
the worship of the cult.

2. When Paul's thought is compared with this, it becomes
clear first of all that for Paul *the law is the expression of the holy
will of God* and that he understands *the law as the embodiment
of moral demand*. This is evident from the way in which he thinks
of the 'conscience' (συνείδησις) of the Gentiles as a substitute for
the law (Rom. 2.14f.). Just as the Jew has in the law 'the embodiment of knowledge and truth' (Rom. 2.20), so man's
'inmost self' must assent to the law (Rom. 7.22). In fact the
teaching that the law as the old way of salvation is abrogated
is *not* to be understood to mean that the content of the law is to
be rejected! 'What then shall we say? That the law is sin? By
no means. . . . So the law is holy, and the commandment is

holy and just and good. . . . We know that the law is spiritual'
(Rom. 7.7–14). To him who fulfils it, the law brings life (Rom.
2.10; 10.5).

In fact the basic section of the letter to the Romans (that is,
1.18–3.20) is built on the foundation of the conception of God
as the judge who demands good works from men. The preaching of faith does not introduce a new concept of God with the
content that God is not the judge but only the gracious God.
On the contrary, according to Paul, faith and grace can be
understood only on the basis of the firmly held concept that
God is the judge.[8] Therefore Paul can emphasize to Christians
that this God is a God of judgment and that his judgment is
given according to man's works.[9] The situation of men 'before
faith came' is desperate, not because man has a false law which
he mistakenly accepts as the will of God, but because he does
not fulfil the law which is the will of God. Therefore it is man
who is responsible when the effect of the law is to bring death
(Rom. 7.7ff.).

The proclamation of freedom from the law is therefore not
the proclamation of any new ethical ideal. And there is no
suggestion that for the Christian the law is abrogated in the
sense that the valid expression of God's will in the law has now
become invalid. Its requirement is still valid even for Christians: 'Owe no one anything . . . love is the fulfilling of the law'
(Rom. 13.8–10). 'For the whole law is fulfilled in one word,
"You shall love your neighbour as yourself"' (Gal. 5.14). And,
according to Rom. 12.2, the Christian has, through 'the re-
newal' of his 'mind', the possibility of proving 'what is the will
of God, what is good and acceptable and perfect'. Therefore
the Christian is required to understand the demand that the
Jew learned from the law: 'You know his will and approve
what is excellent, because you are instructed in the law'
(Rom. 2.18).

Thus *Jesus and Paul are in complete agreement so far in their view
of the law.* And the clearest proof of their unity is that, for both,
the commandment of love is the fundamental content of the law. For
Jesus, too, the commandment to love one's neighbour stands
inseparable from the commandment to love God (Mark

---

[8] Cf. Käte Oltmanns, *TB* (1929), no. 5, cols. 110f.
[9] I Cor. 3.12–15; 4.4f.; I Thess. 3.13; 5.23 *et al.* (esp. II Cor. 5.10).

12.29–31). And even though the antitheses of the Sermon on the Mount measure the law negatively by the will of God, there is also the positive meaning of the demand that the service of God must include the neighbour in whom God's claim is concretely present for me. Anger at a brother and covetous desire must be abandoned; fidelity in marriage and honesty in human intercourse must prevail; revenge and hate must be banished. And it is love of neighbour, radically fulfilled as love of enemies, which proves a man to be a true son of God his Father.

Where then does the difference between Paul and Jesus begin? Is it that for Paul the *purpose of the law is to drive men into sin*? But how far is that for Paul the true purpose of the law? Obviously the purpose of the law is God's purpose; and God's intention cannot, of course, be measured by the standards of modern pedagogy. Paul certainly did not imagine that the law was not given by God to be fulfilled. Naturally, as the holy will of God it was meant to be fulfilled. That it forces men to sin is not a consequence to be derived from its own nature; it is an observed result, and the result must then be recognized as God's intention. But that intention can never be understood in such a way that the obligatory validity of the law is disclaimed. From the human point of view it is to be understood that the law of God is a demand on man, and that man under the law became a sinner.

But then the question must be asked, what did Paul consider to be the real sin of man? There is no doubt as to the answer. The *real sin of man* is that he himself takes his will and his life into his own hands, makes himself secure and so has his self-confidence, his 'boast'.[10] That was the primal sin of the Gentiles who did not understand that they were created and did not give honour to God (Rom. 1.20). That is the offence of the Gnostics who set up their own wisdom and despise the folly of the preaching of the cross, which is the wisdom of God, because they wish to 'boast' of themselves (I Cor. 1.18–31). That is the sin of the Jews who wish to set up 'their own righteousness'

---

[10] Cf. my writing, *Der Begriff der Offenbarung im Neuen Testament*, Tübingen, 1929, pp. 32–4; ET, 'The Concept of Revelation in the New Testament,' *Existence and Faith*, ed. Schubert M. Ogden, New York and London, 1960, pp. 8off.

(Rom. 10.3f.; Phil. 3.9), who claim a right to 'boast' before God (Rom. 2.23; 3.27; 4.2).

Since that sin is 'confidence in the flesh', a seeking for security in the 'flesh' (Phil. 3.4), it would be the sin of apostasy from Christ to try to establish man's own righteousness again through the law. That means 'ending with the flesh' (Gal. 3.3) and so nullifying the work of Christ (Gal. 2.21). The will to assert one's self before God is the primal sin; and for that purpose the law has been misused by the Jews because they wish to establish 'their own righteousness' and do not submit themselves to the righteousness of God (Rom. 10.3f.).

There is only *one* legitimate 'boast' and 'confidence' for men – 'to boast of the Lord' (I Cor. 1.29; II Cor. 10.17; Phil. 3.7–10). Paradoxically, that means to boast of one's weakness (II Cor. 12.19), to boast of the cross (Gal. 6.14). But to boast in this way is to pronounce the sentence of death upon one's self and to put confidence, not in one's self but in God who makes the dead alive (II Cor. 1.9).

But that is really to assert that *not* 'the works of the law' *but only* the 'grace of God' can rescue men. And it means that 'the works of the law' are to be rejected, not because they were contrary to God's will and demand, but because they are misunderstood as man's achievements. The law as God's will is holy and inviolably valid. The law as it confronts man *prior* to 'faith' – or rather as man insists on confronting the law, that is to say the law understood as a ground for man's 'boasting' – is not God's will. It becomes the 'custodian', holding man in restraint under sin (Gal. 3.22ff.). Therefore God's law must bring men to humility.

'Now we know that whatever the law says it speaks to those who are under the law, so that every mouth may be stopped, and the whole world may be held accountable to God. For no human being will be justified in his sight by the works of the law, since through the law comes knowledge of sin' (Rom. 3.19f.). The same meaning is expressed in the characterization of the plan of salvation (I Cor. 1.18–31). What the law means for the Jews, the judgment of the proclamation of the cross as 'folly' means for the Greeks. The wisdom of the world will be put to shame; God has chosen the foolish, the weak, the despised, that which is nothing, to bring to naught that which is something, 'so that no human being might boast in the presence of God . . . as it is written "let him who boasts, boast in the Lord" '.

It is clear that *Jesus did not present this kind of explicit theological reasoning*. But it seems to me equally clear that by it Paul simply explains and clarifies the thought of Jesus by the use of specific historical antitheses. The reasoning is certainly *based on the same fundamental motive*, which was the foundation of Jesus' polemic: the opposition between legal right and the true will of God. That opposition is the reason for Jesus' polemic; God's will cannot be enshrined in legal enactments which man can discharge, so that he could exhibit his achievements before God and present a claim. The servant who has done his proper work has nothing to 'boast' of (Luke 17.7–10). And the answer to the question, 'is seven times enough?', must be, 'there is no *enough* in God's sight' (Matt. 18.21f.). In entire agreement with Paul, although not with the same theological explicitness, Jesus says that the law is not God's will when it is treated as man insists on treating it, when it is understood according to the scribal interpretation as a code which presents single acts to be performed. And Jesus knows also that for the pious legalist the mercy of God is an offence (Matt. 20.14f.).

What Jesus does not state is that from the beginning it is impossible for the law at any time to confront the man who desires to gain security by his own achievements in any other way than as his 'custodian'. But however remote this theological idea may be from Jesus' preaching, that preaching *does actually imply it*. This can be recognized in the fact that Jesus sees and says that the officially religious, the 'righteous', are not willing to listen either to the Baptist's call to repentance or to his own, while the tax-collectors and harlots, the 'sinners', listen (Matt. 21.32; Luke 7.29). The son in the parable who refuses to go is the one who actually does his father's will, while the son who said 'I go' despises his father (Matt. 21.28–30). The 'lost' son, who has fallen into sin, comes finally to confess 'I have sinned against heaven and before you' and receives the father's forgiving love; while the correct son, who has done his duty at home, is not in the position to see his father's real love and is therefore in truth the lost son (Luke 15.11–32). So Jesus knows himself called to the sick (Mark 2.17) and has to accept censure as the friend of tax-collectors and sinners (Mark 2.16; Matt. 11.25f.).

What is it, if not a parallel to Romans 2, when Jesus rebukes the scribes and Pharisees as hypocrites who clean the outside but are 'full of extortion and rapacity' within, white-washed tombs, who appear righteous to men, but within are full of vileness and iniquity (Matt. 23.25–28)? What is it, if not a parallel to I Cor. 1.18–31, when in the Beatitudes the poor, the weeping, the hungry are praised? They are those who have nothing in themselves to exhibit, who have no 'boast', who are, in a radical sense, in God's sight, simply those who wait. And if Jesus did not state definitely, as Paul did, that all men are sinners and did not begin by presenting a theological-anthropological basis for that judgment, *do not his words actually reveal the situation of man as sinner before God just as effectively as does Paul's theological exposition?*

For although it is correct and understandable that legal right stands in opposition to the will of God and that divorce, the use of oaths and the *lex talionis* are in contradiction to God's will – can any one actually dispense with this legal code? Who can fail to see that this law code is a real necessity for us and that without it our timid attempts to love God and neighbour could not really begin? For no one will suppose that in order to fulfil the will of God as Jesus understood it, he must become an anarchist.

But if we need the law, what can this connote except that we are all sinners and 'fall short of the glory of God' (Rom. 3.23)? And if it is right and understandable that anger, lust and hate are transgressions against God's will, what is left to say except the declaration:

> All have turned aside,
> Together they have gone wrong;
> No one does good,
> Not even one (Rom. 3.12)?

Jesus' proclamation is certainly not a theoretical ethic which provides illumination and which has become an inalienable possession of human cultural history, nor anything of that sort. It is a summons. And as such, it is understood only by the one who hears it as a summons and who through it lets himself discover his own situation. But is the position of man before God as it is represented in the words of Jesus in any way different from that in the theology of Paul?[11]

3. Where, then, does the difference lie? It seems to vanish and yet it is still there. But the genuine difference only becomes really visible when the temptations to seek it in the wrong places are removed. The difference *does not lie in eschatological views.* It is true that the central thought of the eschatological preaching of Jesus, the concept of the 'kingdom of God', plays only a small role with Paul (Rom. 14.17; I Cor. 6.9f.; 15.20; Gal. 5.21). But that does not mean that Paul did not expect the coming judgment of God and the coming glory (cf. esp. Rom. 8.18–39). The preaching of Paul is eschatological through and through. *The* concept which could be called the main theme of Paul's preaching is eschatological – the concept of the 'righteousness of God', of 'justification' (δικαιοσύνη θεοῦ); and this concept corresponds to the 'kingdom of God'.

But it is exactly this concept which shows where the difference lies. It is not in the conceptual meaning of the 'righteousness of God'. That is exactly the same as in Judaism. But what Paul says about the actualization of this righteousness is different: the righteousness, the justification, is already achieved and has

---

[11] I fear that by such interpretations I shall bring upon myself the ill-will of H. Windisch who has so lucidly presented 'the practicability of the teaching of Jesus' (in *Der Sinn der Bergpredigt. Ein Beitrag zum Problem der richtigen Exegese*, Leipzig, 1929, pp. 69–91). I do not disagree at all with his view – or rather the view of E. Peterson on whom he depends – when he regards the statement that the demands of the Sermon on the Mount are presented only for the purpose of making man aware of his incapacity to fulfil them as a modern misinterpretation. The demands are to be fulfilled. But Paul's view of the law is exactly the same. The law ought to have been and ought to be fulfilled. But when Paul asserts the impossibility of fulfilling the law he is not thinking in terms of the 'practicability' for which Windisch is arguing. The 'practicability' in Windisch's sense is granted by Jesus and by Paul. Only because they assume it, can they see sin in the actual non-fulfilment of the law. The question raised by the demands of Jesus, and also by the demands of the law, is: *are the demands actually fulfilled?* In spite of his defence of the practicability of the demands of Jesus, will Windisch be ready to claim that he fulfils them? Or does he assume that there is someone else who is fulfilling them? But why not?

And is not the attempt to explain what the summons actually means to the one summoned, how his own situation is revealed through it, a part of 'correct' exegesis? I still think, and I assert it as a fact, that the position in which the hearers of the Sermon on the Mount were actually placed becomes explicit in the theology of Paul.

become available to faith because of the work of salvation which was accomplished in Jesus Christ.

Paul is waiting for the fulfilment, but in a sense different from that of Jesus. Jesus looks to the future, to the *coming* kingdom of God – which is coming or dawning *now*. But Paul looks back; *the turning point of the ages has already come*. 'But when the time had fully come, God sent forth his Son, born of woman, born under the law, to redeem those who were under the law, so that we might receive adoption as sons' (Gal. 4.4f.). God *has already* bestowed reconciliation through Christ. 'Therefore if anyone is in Christ, he is a new creation; the old has passed away, behold, the new has come. . . . Behold, now is the acceptable time; behold, now is the day of salvation' (II Cor. 5.17; 6.2). The decisive event which Jesus *expects*, has for Paul already taken place.

Now the time of the law is past. Christ *has* made us free from the law and also from 'this present evil age' (Gal. 1.4; 3.13). He *has* freed us from 'the law of sin and death' (Rom. 8.2). And put positively – the Spirit, the gift of the End, is already here. The Spirit is working in the community; he is working in individuals. 'But you are not in the flesh, you are in the Spirit if the Spirit of God really dwells in you' (Rom. 8.9). 'For you did not receive the spirit of slavery to fall back into fear, but you have received the spirit of sonship' (Rom. 8.15; Gal. 4.5). We *are* sons (Rom. 8.16; Gal. 3.26–4.7); the time of bondage is past. The 'church' of the righteous, for the appearance of which the Jewish apocalyptists are waiting, *is* here.[12] Paul can address the believers as the holy, the chosen, the called. The 'righteousness' which Israel sought, the believers have already attained (Rom. 9.30f.; cf. 10.4–10). The believers are the justified, the righteous (Rom. 5.1, 9, 17, 21; 8.10, 30, 33; I Cor. 6.11). 'There is therefore now no condemnation for those who are in Christ Jesus' (Rom. 8.1).

Here lies the difference. But it will never be really understood by the methods of cultural history or the history of ideas. For the difference does not lie in the dissimilarities of ideas or concepts but in the fact that what is for Jesus future, Paul saw as present or as the present which has broken into the past. But this difference exists, not because Paul judges the contemporary

[12] Cf. 'Church and Teaching in the New Testament', pp. 184–219 above.

situation differently from Jesus on account of some general –
perhaps some 'religious' – point of view, but because he is convinced that a decisive event has created a new age. The difference is not that Paul sees the relation between God and man
as *in itself* other than Jesus saw it; he sees it as exactly the same.
But Jesus, since he is himself still waiting for the kingdom, in
his proclamation discloses the situation of man as that of one
who waits, while Paul discloses the situation of man as that of
one who receives, though of course this also shows his situation
as one who waits; for the receiving cannot be understood without the waiting.

The difference could be expressed in this way: Jesus preaches
the law and the promise; Paul preaches the Gospel in its relation to the law. Law and Gospel together form a unity. The
law is rightly understood only together with the promise; the
Gospel only together with the law.[13]

*This new element in Paul's thought must not be interpreted with any
idea of a 'development'*, as, for example, W. Wrede or A. Jülicher
try to do. They assume that the theology of Paul naturally
progressed beyond the proclamation of Jesus because of the
events which occurred between the two and which provided
new theological concerns for Paul and stimulated him to formulate them. That statement in itself is correct; but it ignores the
decisive fact that here it is not a question of the development
of theological concepts and views under the impact of events.
The truth is that the judgment has been executed, that the
situation of the world is fundamentally different; it is a new
situation since Jesus was here.

The primary task, therefore, is not to interpret the events as
causal factors for the formation of Paul's teaching, but to
clarify the material understanding of the event itself, through
Paul. The significance of Pauline theology is not that the views

[13] Luther recognized rightly that Jesus preaches the law. One example
out of many is taken from his *Commentary on Galatians* (ed. von Schubert,
p. 36, lines 4ff.). 'Law and Gospel differ specifically in this way. The law
presents what ought to be done and what left undone, or rather things committed and uncommitted, and by this it gives only knowledge of sin.
But the Gospel declares remission of sin and the fulfilment of the law truly
through Christ. . . . It follows that Christ in the Gospel has taught many
things, has given a clear understanding of the law and through this a
greater knowledge of sin so that grace might be more eagerly sought and
more bountifully given and more carefully preserved, the more deeply
sin was understood.'

of Jesus are further developed in it. Pauline theology is significant because in it the fact that Jesus has been present in this world is understood in a particular way. Therefore it is wrong to say that, for example, the concept of the Messiah is further developed by Paul. Even though that statement may have some validity, it certainly ignores the decisive fact; for Paul retains the basic content of the concept of the Messiah, that the Messiah brings the time of salvation, the new age. What is 'new' in Paul is simply the affirmation that the Messiah *has been here*, that *Jesus* is the Messiah.

Paul did not think of himself as presenting new ideas but as proclaiming a fact which is decisive for men. The Gospel differs from the law not because it is a new stage of spiritual development, but because it proclaims an historical fact, Jesus, as the fulfilment of the promise.

This brings us to the third question, the question of the significance of the historical Jesus for the theology of Paul.

III. *The Significance of the Historical Person of Jesus for the Theology of Paul*

That significance can be expressed in one sentence. *It is the historical person of Jesus that makes Paul's proclamation the Gospel.* For Paul proclaims neither a new idea of God nor a new concept of the Messiah; he proclaims an act of God in history, the coming of the Messiah who is identical with the person of Jesus. The conviction that Jesus is Messiah is primary, and as some modification of the old picture of the Messiah follows from that, the decisive factor in this process is not perfecting the development of an idea, but the achievement of a *resolve*.

And what is this resolve? The resolve to recognize Jesus, the prophet and teacher, the crucified, as the Messiah. This resolve had been made by the primitive community when it saw in Jesus the One to whom God had assigned the office of Messiah and the One who will come again to be the judge and to bring salvation. The community proclaimed him as such and therefore confronted Paul with the question of whether or not he would acknowledge this Messiah.

Paul says that Jesus was made known to him as Messiah by

a *revelation* (Gal. 1.12–16). That this 'revelation' (ἀποκάλυψις) was not simply a supernatural communication of information is self-evident. One does not acquire knowledge about the Messiah; one either acknowledges him or repudiates him. So Paul designates as 'obedience' the faith which acknowledges Jesus as Messiah; he calls Jesus the Lord (κύριος) and knows himself to be a 'slave' (δοῦλος). The *acknowledgement* of Jesus as the Messiah is the substantive content of the 'revelation'; it means that henceforth Paul *understands* Jesus as the Messiah, for without understanding there is no obedience. To understand another person as Lord correspondingly means *to have a new understanding of oneself*, as standing in the service of that Lord and attaining one's own identity in such service. Such understanding, such self-understanding, is a matter of resolve, of decision – it can be nothing else (cf. Phil. 3.7f.).

Paul had persecuted the community of Jesus' disciples because he did not understand that Jesus is the Messiah; because, in the light of such a belief, he could no longer have had the same self-understanding he had previously had, that is, the understanding of himself as 'seeking to establish [his] own righteousness' (Rom. 10.3). Such understanding was jeopardized by the Christian proclamation.

How far this question became explicit at a given moment is a separate consideration; evidently no clear formulation was developed in the primitive community. But it is quite clear that for Paul the question was acute. He sees not only that the 'stumbling-block' of the crucified Messiah is an absurdity in itself, but also that it puts in question the 'traditions of the fathers' (Gal. 1.14). Though the *conversion* may be a psychic event (as it always is), its material significance is clearly that Paul let himself actually face the question presented by the proclamation. He therefore risked his own understanding of himself as a Jew against the unimaginable new possibility of understanding himself, and he grasped the new possibility by a resolve. And he grasped it because of the Christian proclamation which put the question.

The primitive community, too, proclaimed no new apocalyptic fantasy and no new messianic idea; it simply proclaimed Jesus as the Messiah. For the decisive affirmation in the proclamation is not the announcement that the Messiah is really coming and that he is coming soon, but that this Jesus, the crucified, is coming as the Messiah. Now this means that for them, too, the decisive event had occurred in the past in the historical person of Jesus. For them, too, the historic person of Jesus was the decisive saving act of God, regardless of how far they themselves were fully clear about it. What remained implicit in their proclamation became explicit with Paul: the new age has begun in the historic Jesus.

How this resolve of the primitive community is to be understood is a separate problem. But at least this much may be said. Jesus presented no teaching about his person, but he emphasized that the fact of his person was significant, even decisive, since he claimed to be the bearer of the definitive word of God in the last hour. *What* he says, he does not say as something new, as something not heard before. But *that* he says it, that he is saying it *now*, is the decisive event; and the saying changes the situation for all who hear him into a new and decisive situation. 'Blessed is he who takes no offence at me' (Matt. 11.6).

> Everyone who acknowledges me before men,
> The Son of man also will acknowledge before the angels of God;
> But he who denies me before men
> Will be denied before the angels of God (Luke 12.8f.; cf. Mark 8.38).

Such a call to decision in the light of his person *implies a christology* – but not as speculation about a heavenly being nor as the fabrication of a so-called 'messianic consciousness'.[14] This christology cannot be theoretical speculation; it can only be the interpretation of the answer given in the decision for him, in the obedience under his word, the obedience which makes possible the discovery that the situation is a new situation. In the primitive community the christology has become explicit to the extent that it confesses: Jesus has been made Messiah by God and will come as Messiah. That confession shows that Jesus' word – not any timeless ideas it may contain, but the fact that it is spoken by him and that the community is addressed by it – is understood as the decisive act of God. This in turn means that the further transmission of Jesus' proclama-

[14] A 'messianic consciousness' would be only a psychological phenomenon and the decisive question which Jesus puts would not be answered. For a discussion of this point, see 'Church and Teaching in the New Testament', pp. 205f. above.

tion could not be a simple reproduction of his ideas. Christ the proclaimer had to become the proclaimed. It is the *fact that he proclaimed* which is decisive.

But the christology of the primitive community also implies something more. The question of the decision was made even more pressing for its members through the *death of Jesus on the cross*. Consequently the answer also meant overcoming the offence of the crucified Messiah. It is not the *what*, the content, of his proclamation that is put in question by his death on the cross. What is put in question is his legitimacy as the proclaimer, the *that*, the fact that it is really he who is the messenger of God bringing the final decisive word. Therefore what is important is the acknowledgment of the *crucified* as the coming Messiah. To adhere to his person thus also involves adherence to his death and the recognition of it as an essential part of the saving act – not as something appended to that act, but as something that decisively determines everything else.

Again it is clear that the meaning of the cross was not necessarily made explicit in the primitive community; but it does become explicit with Paul. But because the primitive community believes in the crucified Christ as the risen Christ, the 'stumbling-block' of the cross is actually overcome by the community. And the task is set to understand the 'stumbling-block' as divine 'wisdom', to understand one's self anew under this act of God by proclaiming the crucified Messiah.

Thus *the proclamation of the primitive community set Paul the question* of whether he would acknowledge the historical Jesus, the crucified, as Messiah, whether he would affirm him as the decisive saving act of God which brings in the new creation. The question was really a double one; (1) whether he would see in an ambiguous historical fact the dawn of the new creation; (2) whether he would acknowledge in the cross of Christ as a historical fact the judgment of God upon man's prior self-understanding. In other words, the question was whether he would understand himself in a new way which pronounced the sentence of 'sin and death' on his former self-understanding.

Paul answered the question with a *yes*. Psychological theories of how this may have happened are profitless in view of the sources which are available. Furthermore, such theories serve only to obscure the essential problem of the real meaning of the affirmation, the question whether we ourselves can achieve Paul's new understanding again for ourselves. All that can be discussed is how the question of new self-understanding is raised by the fact of the crucified Messiah. In other words, exactly what is the nature of this new self-understanding?

Negatively it means:

1. For Paul, *Christ is not the teacher* who has taught a new concept of God, a new view of the world, a new morality, as timeless truths. When Paul cites Jesus Christ as teacher (see above pp. 222f.), he is not appealing to the earthly Jesus, but to the exalted 'Lord', the Lord of the community. Christ can indeed become the 'teacher', but only for those for whom he is already the Lord. He is not their Lord because he is a teacher.

2. *Christ is not an exemplar.* Again, he can become the pattern for serving one another, for 'lowliness' (Rom. 15.3; II Cor. 8.9; Phil. 2.5ff.). But it is always the pre-existent Christ who is the pattern. And this means that he can be the pattern only as the already acknowledged Lord – it is not the exemplary character of the historical Jesus that makes him Lord.

3. *Christ is not a hero.* Any idea of the life and death of Jesus as a heroic achievement is not only alien to Paul but is absolutely excluded by the fact that it is the crucified Lord who is preached. For when the crucified Lord is preached (I Cor. 1.18f.) and portrayed before our eyes (Gal. 3.1), this certainly does not mean that a heroic conqueror of suffering or a 'sacred head now wounded' is preached. What is proclaimed is that the cross of Christ is a negative judgment upon every human achievement in work or in wisdom, upon every 'boast', upon all heroism; and that in this very judgment comes the liberating act of God.

Any 'evaluation' of the 'personality' of Jesus is wrong and must be wrong, for it would be only a 'knowing after the flesh' in the double sense: (1) that such 'knowing' would see the Christ only as a Christ 'after the flesh', that is as a world phenomenon; and (2) that it would be a 'knowing after the flesh', a fleshly understanding, a mere reckoning with the objects of the world.[15]

The judgment upon all mankind is consummated in the cross, and in the cross as an actual historical event. The cross for Paul is not a symbol, an effective image for an eternal idea. The naked

[15] See above, p. 217.

fact of the cross of Jesus means that man is asked the question whether he will relinquish his secure self, his 'boasting'; the question whether that fact is to be the decisive saving fact for him; whether he will boast only of the cross of Christ, because through this cross the world is crucified to him and he to the world (Gal. 6.14). The Gospel is the 'word of the cross' (I Cor. 1.17f.); the enemies of the Gospel are the 'enemies of the cross' (Phil. 3.18). Christ is not proclaimed except as the Crucified (I Cor. 1.17, 23; 2.8; Gal. 3.1). He who does not let himself be crucified with Christ; he for whom the world is not dead and who is not himself dead to the world; he who does not see that Christ 'gave himself for me' so that I have died and 'now live in faith' (Gal. 2.19f.); that man does not understand the cross. That is, the cross is understood by no one who will not allow himself through this historical fact to accept resolutely a new understanding of himself, an understanding which he can grasp only by a resolve, by a resolve which means the radical sacrifice of himself.

But in such self-relinquishment, even as in the acknowledgment of God's judgment upon the 'old man' as sinner, man now understands himself as freed from himself, as risen with Christ. The *resurrection* of Christ is proclaimed simultaneously with the cross of Christ. And though the Gospel is the 'word of the cross', yet the confession of faith affirms: Jesus is the Lord and God has raised him from the dead (Rom. 10.9).

The cross cannot be understood as a world phenomenon, as human achievement or suffering, any more than the resurrection can be (even though Paul himself in I Cor. 15 is almost misled into so describing it). For only through the understanding of the cross, that is, through the acknowledgment of the judgment pronounced in the cross, does the road lead to a knowledge of the resurrection and to fellowship in it (Phil. 3.8–10).

Cross and resurrection do differ in so far as the cross is an ambiguous phenomenon. The cross is a world event which can be seen as such; that is, it can be seen in the context of cause and effect, and as human achievement or suffering. To see the cross is therefore to see the 'stumbling-block'; whether the seeing becomes faith or not requires a decision. But to see the resurrection at all requires faith, for the resurrection is in no sense visible to the unbeliever. Only the *assertion* that Jesus has risen confronts the unbeliever. That is, just as a world phenomenon in all its ambiguity corresponds to God's judgment in the cross, so also to God's saving act in the resurrection there corresponds a world phenomenon – the Christian kerygma, which remains a 'stumbling-block' and 'folly' until the judgment of the cross is acknowledged and accepted.

Now this means that *Jesus Christ confronts men in the kerygma and nowhere else*; just as he confronted Paul himself and forced him to the decision. The kerygma does not proclaim universal truths, or a timeless idea – whether it is an idea of God or of a redeemer – but a historical fact. Now that fact is not proclaimed in any way which makes the kerygma superfluous once it has communicated knowledge of this fact to the hearer, for in that case the proclamation would have only the function of communication; rather, the kerygma is itself a part of the fact.[16] It is a part of the fact in the same way that becoming 'flesh' belongs essentially to Christ. He became 'flesh', not in order that a heavenly being might find it possible to impart teaching and establish holy rites, but because the *that*, the *here and now*, the factuality of his person, constituted the revelation. Therefore the kerygma, too, is neither a vehicle for timeless ideas, nor communication of historical information. The decisive fact is that the kerygma is his *that*, his *here and now*; a 'here and now' which becomes contemporary in the address itself.

It is therefore illegitimate to go behind the kerygma, using it as a 'source', in order to reconstruct a 'historical Jesus' with his 'messianic consciousness', his 'inner life' or his 'heroism'. That would be merely 'Christ after the flesh', who is no longer. It is not the historical Jesus, but Jesus Christ, the Christ, preached, who is the Lord.

Therefore Paul can also term the preaching of the Gospel *the saving act of God*, just as he does the death and resurrection of Jesus. He can call the institution of 'mutual service' or of the 'word of reconciliation' the beginning of the time of salvation (II Cor. 5.17–20). The eschatological *now* of the death and resurrection of Jesus is therefore not a past moment in the vanishing sequence of time; it is marked out as the eschatological *now* by being always contemporary wherever the preach-

[16] See above, pp. 205–9.

ing sounds. 'Behold, *now* is the acceptable time, behold, *now* is the day of salvation' (II Cor. 6.2).[17]

The preaching is the saving event because it is not merely a communication of history; it is, as it was when Paul was confronted with it, the decisive question for men. Therefore it is itself revelation and it brings death and life to the world, because the decision for death or for life is made when it is heard (II Cor. 2.14–16; 4.1–6). It is addressed, not to the curiosity or the 'interest' of the hearers, but to their conscience (II Cor. 4.2; 5.11). Like the death and resurrection of Jesus, so also the preaching, the 'Gospel', is a 'power of God for salvation to every one who has faith', for in the Gospel the 'righteousness of God' is revealed (Rom. 1.16f.). The saving fact is therefore the Word (Rom. 10.13–17). Not the word as the vehicle of ideas or as a communication of historical information, but the Word as preaching, validated by the person Jesus Christ who is one with it – but in such a way that it, too, is one with him and is encountered only in him.

It could be said that because Paul had to combine the fact of the historicity of Jesus and his death with the conception of the Messiah, he developed the *Jewish concept of the Messiah* further and transformed it. But that is not correct if it means that Paul's thought is a logically consistent development from the ideas present in the Jewish concept of the Messiah. For in Paul's mind there was only the question which forced him to decide whether he was willing to recognize the Crucified as the Messiah.

Furthermore, it is not the case that Paul has amalgamated two heterogeneous notions (those of a heavenly being and of an historical man) by a compromise. It could be said rather that he has simply taken the Jewish concept of Messiah radically. For Judaism, the Messiah is not an abstract idea but a concrete

---

[17] In my judgment, it is clear that Paul in I Cor. 15 (esp. vv. 20–8 and 44–9) is endeavouring to express the idea that the resurrection of Jesus is not an isolated objective fact of the past. He is trying, with the help of the cosmological myth of the Gnostics, to express the contemporaneousness of the fact of salvation. Exegesis therefore may not stop at the reproduction of the mythical presentation but must seek to penetrate to the real purpose of the writer. In this case it must let itself be guided by the explanations in II Cor. 2.14–6.10. (See also above pp. 8off.; 205–9. And cf. *Der Begriff der Offenbarung im Neuen Testament*, pp. 27f; ET, 'The Concept of Revelation in the New Testament', pp. 76f.)

embodiment of hope. The Messiah is the king of the last age and as such he brings the salvation given by God. Hence the Messiah is certainly expected as a fact, as an event which will actually happen. For Paul, the Messiah is in no way different. But the Jewish figure of the Messiah can remain an imaginary figure so long as the expectation of the event is not taken seriously, so long as men expect merely the fulfilment of their own desires and are not ready to recognize a contingent fact, a historic person as Messiah.[18] Paul found the willingness to do this; and to this extent his christology is consistently Jewish – not as the conceptual development of the Jewish messianic belief, but on the contrary as its real consummation in the recognition of a pure fact.

But in this very recognition the declaration was made that *the new age has begun*. The 'advance' of Pauline theology consists, not in a more or less improved mythological portrayal of the messianic figure, but in that Paul takes quite seriously the fact that Jesus is the Messiah. This means that he submitted himself to the judgment of the cross and so learned to understand himself as a 'new creation'. Since he is a 'new creation' he belongs to the new age. Christ is indeed the new Adam (Rom. 5.12ff.; I Cor. 15.21f., 45f.), the first-born among many brethren (Rom. 8.29). Anyone who belongs to him belongs to the new world; has the Spirit, the sonship; is justified, glorified and holy.

But how is Paul to be secure against the attack that such statement are only fantasies and speculations? Can he show as a reality of life the effects which he claims? Naturally, the evidence of the reality can be visible only to those who have faith. But faith does see *first: that the new age is real in that Christ is being preached*. Life becomes manifest in Paul's preaching of Christ as the 'minister of reconciliation' (cf. II Cor. 5.18). Outwardly he bears around in his body only the 'death of

[18] The view of Oscar A. H. Schmitz ('Der jüdisch-christliche Komplex' [The Jewish-Christian Complex] in *Der Jude*, IX, Sonderheft III, p. 60) seems to me to be quite correct. He defends (against Buber) the statement that the 'Pharisee takes pains to prevent anything, even the Messiah, from taking a specific form'. He has rightly recognized that it is the contingent happening which is decisive. 'From the viewpoint of the law, the Messiah *must* be misjudged. For, empirically, he is first of all a member of the community who is different and unprecedented. In order to recognize him, one must face reality without inhibitions.'

Christ'; but by this he proves himself crucified and risen with Christ. This means specifically that what is outwardly present and verifiable by observation has been consigned to death. 'Though our outward man perish, yet the inward man is renewed day by day' (II Cor. 4.7–16). So the eschatological *now* becomes actual in the preaching. So the apostle carries life and death through the world.

The result does not depend at all on the apostle as a person. 'For what we preach is not ourselves, but Jesus Christ as Lord, with ourselves as your servants for Christ's sake' (II Cor. 4.5). Indeed even the 'ethical' qualities, the integrity of the apostle – all such considerations – are basically no concern of his hearers. He is their 'slave' as authorized preacher and as 'steward of the mysteries of God' (I Cor. 4.1). The community does not have the right to judge him, nor may he vindicate himself as a faithful servant by his good conscience, even if he has one. 'It is the Lord who judges me' (I Cor. 4.1–4). No one is to be known 'after the flesh', that is, known as he may be assessed in human terms (II Cor. 5.16). Such judging is exactly the error of the Corinthians who gave their allegiance to parties. But it is the preaching alone that matters. 'What then? Only that in every way, whether in pretence or in truth, Christ is proclaimed' (Phil. 1.18).

History is radically transformed, because God has ordained this 'Word of reconciliation', sounding for everyone, and because this 'Word' does not proclaim an idea of the grace of God but proclaims an *act* of God which has already been done and which is being done again now while the word is being spoken to us. *That* this word is said, the fact of the *saying*, makes the new age present. In this way, we stand within a history over which the 'Word' already sounds continuously. We meet our present moment as those to whom forgiveness has already been accorded in the cross and resurrection.

The question, 'Is this all?', would be the very question which Paul rejected in Romans 5 and to which he replied in Rom. 8.31f., 'If God is for us, who is against us? He who did not spare his own Son but gave him up for us all, will he not also give us all things with him?'

The new age is visible only for believers. But just here the *second* reality appears: *there can be and there is faith*. There is faith in the sense of 'obedience' which submits to learning man's situation through the kerygma, which relinquishes all 'confidence' in man (cf. Phil. 3.3) and all 'boasting', which pronounces the sentence of death upon itself in order to put its trust only in him who raises the dead (II Cor. 1.9). In faith, forgiveness is grasped and justification is received. But this faith is not an attitude of mind, a general feeling of confidence in God; it is faith in Jesus Christ, obedience under the kerygma; and it is also confidence because it is freedom from self and communion with him on whom it believes. This faith is 'confession' (ὁμολογία) (Rom. 10.9), and in the 'confession' the believer turns away from himself and confesses that all that he is and has, he is and has through what God has done and is doing in the kerygma.

Therefore, *such faith is itself a part of the saving event, is itself revelation.* 'Now before faith came, we were confined under the law, kept under restraint until faith should be revealed' (Gal. 3.23). Just as the 'preaching' (ἀκοή, 'hearing' = 'preaching'), which is the word authorized 'by the speaking' (διὰ ῥήματος) of Christ, belongs to the history of salvation, so, too, does 'the faith which comes from what is heard' (Rom. 10.17). Faith is not an achievement but a gift (Phil. 1.29; Rom. 15.13). For 'faith' as true decision, as new self-understanding, is not a simply 'having been convinced' or 'having' accepted, so that a man at some time or other 'is converted to Christianity'. As new self-understanding it is a *how*, a way of life itself, and it becomes valid – though again the validity is only to be known to faith itself – in the 'walking' (περιπατεῖν). Paul expresses this with the concept of the 'Spirit'. The believer receives the 'Spirit', that is the new way of his life. He 'walks in the Spirit' or 'according to the Spirit'; and the first fruit of the 'Spirit' is love (Gal. 5.22; cf. Rom. 15.30).

If the new age is a reality in the kerygma and in the 'faith working through love' (Gal. 5.6), that means precisely that it is a reality *through the historical Jesus.* But it is not reached through his 'personality', whether that 'personality' is understood as his human character or as a 'figure' which embodies an ideal; the new age would then be simply a new epoch of spiritual development. Only through the kerygma is Christ accessible and the new age is seen only in faith.

Therefore, when Paul says that *the decisive saving act of Christ is 'obedience' and 'love'*, he is not thinking of the personal character-istics of the historical Jesus (Phil. 2.6ff.; II Cor. 8.9; Rom. 5.18f.; 15.1f.) which are not really visible as obedience and love. The relevant passages all speak rather of the pre-existent Christ. Are his 'obedience' and 'love' visible? No! 'Obedience' and 'love' are never visible as such, but are only experienced as a man experiences the service of others in such a way that he knows himself to be renewed through such service, renewed to a new understanding of self in 'obedience' and 'love'.

That Jesus, the historical person, has done this service for us and has done it, not from personal sympathy and benevolence to us personally; but because God has acted in him, by 'show-ing his love for us in that while we were yet sinners Christ died for us' (Rom. 5.6–8) – all this Paul asserts when he speaks of the pre-existent Christ. The 'obedience' and 'love' of Christ are revealed in the fact that we, confronted by the kerygma, actually have the possibility of 'obedience' and 'love'; other-wise, they are invisible.

The 'obedience' of Christ is the fact of his historical person in service to us; his 'love' is God's saving act in him (Rom. 5.8; 8.35, 37, 39; Gal. 2.20; II Cor. 5.14f.).

IO

THE QUESTION OF WONDER[1]

THE CONCEPT of *wonder* is understood in two ways. (1) A wonder is an act of God (of deity, of gods) as distinct from an occurrence which is the result of natural causes or of human will and effort. (2) A wonder is an amazing event contrary to nature (*contra naturam*) – 'nature' connoting the regular orderly sequence of natural events.

In either sense, the idea of wonder can be further extended. On the basis of a wrongly understood idea of omnipotence, all that happens in the world is interpreted as God's action and thus the difference between the regular sequence of world events and God's action vanishes. Or, on the other hand, a wonder is equated with a supernatural event, or an event contrary to nature which is indeed ascribed to God but in a way which represents God merely as a supernatural causal agent and which precludes any real understanding of the event itself as an act of God. What one has is simply the idea of a *miracle*. In theological discussion these concepts are often set against one another; actually when applied to the idea of wonder they are closely inter-connected.

I. *The Abolition of the Idea of Miracle*

The idea of wonder as miracle has become almost impossible for us today because we understand the processes of nature as governed by law. Wonder, as miracle, is therefore a violation of the conformity to law which governs all nature, and for us today this idea is no longer tenable. It is untenable, not because such an event would contradict all experience, but because the

[1] Unpublished. For the use of the term 'wonder' (*Wunder*) in this essay cf. Ps. 77.14; Joel 2.30; Acts 2.19; Rom. 15.19; II Cor. 12.12; *et al.* The content requires a distinction between 'miracle' and *Wunder*. TRANSLATOR.

conformity to law which is a part of our conception of nature does not require proof but is presupposed as axiomatic, and because we cannot free ourselves from that presupposition at will.

The idea of conformity to law, the idea of 'Nature', underlies explicitly or implicitly all of our ideas and actions which relate to this world. This conception is not 'an interpretation of the world', 'a judgment about the world', 'a world-view'; it is not a conclusion about the world, either subjective or based on a conscious decision. It is *given in our existence in the world*.[2] We act always in reliance on a sequence of world events conforming to law. When we are acting responsibly we do not reckon on the possibility that God may suspend the law of gravity or the like. 'The mere resolve to work includes the notion that the things on which we work will in their origin and activity obey laws which our thinking can comprehend.'[3] Our intercourse with other men, when we show them something, ask them to do something, etc., takes for granted this conception of general conformity to natural law. We recognize as real in the world only what can be set in this context of the rule of law; and we judge assertions which cannot be accommodated to this conception as fantasies.[4]

The notion of the universal validity of natural law, of nature's conformity to law, did not arise for the first time in modern science. It is a very primitive idea indeed, for it is a part of human existence. It is revealed in the fact that at the primitive stage, the concept of causality was applied also to wonder. Wonder was merely assigned to a causality different from that which produced the everyday events which man can control and which he puts to his own use for his living. Wonder depends on a causality which man – at least in the beginning – does not know. But the idea of two causalities, different in kind, working concurrently, is not really conceivable and indeed was not held.

[2] W. Herrmann, *Offenbarung und Wunder*, Giessen, 1908, pp. 39f.
[3] *ibid.* pp. 36f.
[4] Unintentionally, the defenders of miracle provide evidence of this attitude when they try to prove that a miracle has really occurred. They attach the 'miracle' directly to the sequence of world events by asserting that this or that event cannot be understood without positing a wonder, that observation of the event concerned leads to the X, called wonder. They themselves, therefore, subordinate the 'wonder' to the notion of conformity to law and thereby nullify the concept of wonder.

Rather, when divine action is believed to issue in a higher causality, God is thought of simply as a man who knows more and can do more than other men. If other men can just imitate the method (as, for example, a magician does), they can do the same.

The result of further cultural development is, of course, that more and more events which at first seemed supernatural are understood as conforming to law. The notion of universal conformity to law, which was implicitly present in the idea of everyday regularity, is developed more radically. In this way the idea of miracle becomes that of an occurrence contrary to natural law. At the same time, however, the impossibility of accepting such a miraculous event as real becomes increasingly clear.

The idea of miracle has, therefore, become untenable and *it must be abandoned*. But its abandonment is also required because, in itself, it is not a notion of faith but a purely intellectual notion. As is well known, miracles can help or harm, can be desired or feared. As there is black and white magic, so also wonders can be done either by Satan or by God, by wizards or by prophets. The 'higher' causality can be divine or demonic. And no specific miracle carries a label telling whether it proceeds from God or from the devil. One must know God beforehand, before the miracle happens, in order to be certain; one must have a criterion beforehand, in order to know whether a wonder comes from God or not. But to say that is to admit that understanding a wonder as a miracle is to abandon the idea of God's action as an inherent element in miracle.

Hence the Christian faith is apparently not concerned with miracles; rather it has cause to exclude the idea of miracle. No argument to the contrary can be based on the fact that *in the Bible* events are certainly recorded which must be called *miracles*. That fact merely makes necessary the use of critical methods which show that the biblical writers, in accordance with the presuppositions of their thinking, had not fully apprehended the idea of miracle and its implications. The authority of Scripture is not abandoned when the idea of miracle is relinquished. The real meaning of Scripture can be rightly seen only after the idea of wonder as God's action has been made clear.

II. *Abolition of the Outworn Conception of Wonder*

There is now a different problem to consider. Faith is un-questionably concerned with wonder, since 'wonder' means God's action in distinction to the sequence of events in the natural world. The question therefore arises, *whether this concept of wonder does not involve miracle* and whether if the concept of miracle is abandoned the concept of wonder is not lost also. To guard against this loss is certainly the motive for refusing to discard miracles. One thing was accomplished with the concept of miracle; it served to denote specifically an event which is not a part of the natural world-process andth us apparently fits the requirement of the concept of wonder. Can that concept be retained if the idea of miracle is abandoned?

When the idea of miracle is given up, the procedure favoured today is also to abandon the definition of wonder as an action of God consummated contrary to the natural sequence of world events and to assert, with a reference to the belief in creation, that *everything that happens in the world is a wonder.* 'Wonder' then becomes 'the religious designation for event' (Schleiermacher). 'This religious concept of wonder has noth-ing to do with contradiction of natural law. For it, the laws of nature are the forms and instruments used in the fulfilment of God's works.'[5] This idea is suspiciously close to the Roman Catholic teaching according to which God, as the First Cause (*prima causa*), can use secondary causes at his pleasure. But the conception is no longer tenable for anyone who has radically thought through the idea of nature and its conformity to law. If the specific character of the conception of wonder is that it is God's action as distinct from natural world events, and if we can think of that sequence only as governed by law, then *the idea of wonder contradicts nature absolutely* and I eliminate the idea of nature if I talk of wonder.

The *idea of creation* does not help at all, since that idea also eliminates the notion of nature, as conforming to law. For in such a conception, the world process is without spatial or tem-poral limit; but the idea of creation includes a beginning and an end. Therefore if one tries to apply the ideas of creation and wonder to the unending, law-conforming process which we call

[5] H. Schuster, *Lebenskunde*[2], 1927, p. 8.

nature, the whole idea of wonder becomes meaningless. If all that happens is wonderful, then there is nothing further; God and world are equated. God, creation and wonder are then only edifying names for the factual complex of events which I confront concretely in my actual life, and with which I deal as parts of the scientifically discoverable, unending sequence of all happening, as nature and as natural events.

In such pantheistic dissolution of the idea of wonder there is a double error:

1. *The idea of creation and omnipotence is not an axiom of science*, under which the whole world process can be subsumed. It is not an intelligible, generally valid assertion which is discovered or perhaps believed and then held as proved. As an idea of faith, it is to be distinguished from a scientific idea, not because it is attained in an astonishing or non-rational way; that is, it is not differentiated by its origin (so far as origin is understood as a cause and therefore as a fact of the past); but because it can never be held as proven and applied like a scientific idea. It must always be won afresh; it can never be separated from its origin which is always present in it. It always is true only as it arises. But that means that I cannot achieve the idea apart from my own existence; I cannot understand or 'interpret' something outside myself as creation of God or act of God. When I so speak, I am primarily saying something about myself.

But I am not saying something about myself as seen from the outside as an objective entity in the world. I am speaking only of my concrete existence here and now. I can speak of God's act of creation only if I know myself as a creature of God. And to see myself in this way involves, for example – since God's creation is good – seeing myself as good, as without sin. But that I can obviously never do at any time; and certainly that is not the way I act. Rather, I act habitually as if I were myself a creator. In my everyday work, in the use of my time, etc., I regard the world as at my own disposal. The world and my action in it are godless throughout. I can perhaps say that I *ought* to see the whole world as God's creation, that every event or act *ought* to be a wonder. But as actual fact, I do not find myself in a position to make that assertion.

2. The second error now becomes plain. The *idea of the world*

is also mistaken. For if 'wonder' means God's action in contradiction to the world-process which includes my own acts, then a specific understanding of the world is affirmed in it. World must then mean primarily not nature, not the law-governed complex of all that happens, but the specific reality in which I live and act, *my* world. The thought of God and his action is primarily related to my life, to my existence, to the knowledge that this existence is godless, since I do not find God in it and cannot see him. He declares that I can only see him if he shows himself to me through his deed and that I have no right to speak of him at my own will and to explain whatever event I like as his action.

III. *Wonder as God's Action*

1. *Its Hiddenness*

First of all, it is now clear that faith is directed to wonder as an action of God which is different from the world process; faith can be established only through wonder; in truth, *faith in God and faith in the wonder are essentially the same.*

Therefore, just as every pantheistic concept of wonder is excluded, so also is every dogmatic concept. For example, considerations like the following are inadmissible: from the belief in God's omnipotence, it follows that he can do wonders. For since I have faith in God's omnipotence only through faith in wonder, I cannot use the omnipotence as apologetic to justify the belief in wonder. I can, of course, have the *idea* of the omnipotence of God, that is, I can depict God to myself as an omnipotent being (the godless can do that also). But in so doing, I do not yet have *God*, the Omnipotent – for I cannot have him otherwise than in wonder.

One certainty in regard to the concept of wonder is now attained. In no sense whatever is wonder as wonder an observable event in the world, not in any place nor at any time. To claim an event as an observable wonder would be to separate it from God and understand it as world. God is not provable by observation. *Wonder is hidden as wonder*, hidden from him who does not see God in it. Therefore it is also clear (1) that the wonder of which faith speaks cannot be a miracle, for a miracle is an observable event; and (2) that wonder is not the

basis of faith in the sense that as an observable event it leads to
the conclusion that the invisible God exists. For then God's
hiddenness would be conceived in terms of the invisibility of a
natural force (something like electricity); God would be
thought of as world. Faith can testify only to that on which it
believes, never to something else because of which it believes.

But if the question of whether I see a wonder is identical
with the question of whether I have faith – if, that is to say, it
is the question of whether I will to have faith, will to see a wonder, and is therefore a question requiring immediate decision –
then it is clear that *the hiddenness of the wonder as wonder counter-
poises its visibility as a world event.* That is, the assertion that an
event is a wonder is an express contradiction of the affirmation
of it as a world event.[6] Faith is faith as opposed to sight; it is
faith expressly contradicting all that I see. So, too, faith in
wonder must mean the contradiction of all that I see in the
world.

Since faith has this character because I am by nature godless,
the impossibility of seeing world events as wonders must obviously have its cause in my godlessness. My inability to see
world events as wonders has been developed and formulated
in the *idea of nature* as a sequence governed by law; therefore
this idea must obviously be adjudged *godless.* But that does not
mean that I simply abandon it. I cannot do that. It merely
becomes clear to me that godlessness is not something which
man can discard by a strong act of will; on the contrary, godlessness is a mode of my being, my existence is determined by
sin.

I understand very well what wonder means: God's action. I
understand also that in the sequence of events in the world
God's wonders ought to be visible to me. But I know that I do
not see them. For the world appears to me as nature, conforming to law, and I cannot free myself from that view of it by
deciding that it ought to look otherwise. And I must beware of
inducing in myself the feeling that I could see it differently.

---

[6] Cf. Luther on Rom. 8.26 (Ficker, p. 204, lines 11ff.): 'For it is necessary
that a work of God be hidden and not understood at the time when it is
done. But it is not hidden otherwise than under the contrary aspect of our
conception or way of thinking.'

2. *The Reality of Wonder*

The *hiddenness of God* does not mean invisibility in general. It does not mean primarily that God is inaccessible to the senses, or to experiment. It means that he is hidden from *me*. No statement is being made about deity in general, about the nature of deity; no statements of a kind I could make without speaking of myself. Equally, to speak of wonder does not mean to speak of wonders in general and to discuss their possibility.[7] To speak of wonder means to speak of my own existence; it means to declare that in my life God has become visible. Therefore it is to speak not about the universal visibility of God but about his revelation. If I see that God's hiddenness means that he is hidden *from me*, then I also see that his hiddenness means my godlessness and that I am a sinner. For he *ought* not to be hidden from me.

There is therefore only *one* wonder: the wonder of the *revelation*, the revelation of the grace of God for the godless, the revelation of forgiveness. But the forgiveness is understood strictly as *event;* it is not an *idea* of forgiveness, a *notion* of the grace of God as an attribute of the nature of God. Forgiveness is God's *act*.[8] But this meaning needs to be more fully developed if it is to become clear: (1) that forgiveness is a wonder, in contradiction to the world process; and (2) what the reason is for the possibility of confusing wonder and miracle.

Why is asking for a *sign* characteristic of the Jews (I Cor. 1.22)? The reason is that in this desire the characteristic nature of their godlessness is so prominent – the seeking 'their own righteousness'. They estimate themselves by what they achieve and estimate others by what they achieve. And as they wish to certify themselves before God through their achievements, so God must certify himself to them through his achievement.

But that is basically the sin of the world in general: *to estimate itself and God by achievement and work.* Therefore, in so far as the world seeks God, miracle is an object of desire to the world; but *the* wonder, which does not have the character of a certifying achievement, is a stumbling-block. We have seen that the primitive notion of miracle fits into the understanding of the

[7] W. Herrmann, *Offenbarung und Wunder*, pp. 33f., 38.
[8] Cf. R. Bultmann, 'The Concept of Revelation in the New Testament', 1929, see p. 228, n. 10.

world as a working world in which we take for granted the
regularity and the conformity to law of all that happens.
Miracle is a violation of the law of this world, but it is thought
of entirely in the terms of this world since it is a demonstrable
achievement of God within it. But the concept of wonder
radically negates the character of the world as the manageable
world of everyday work. Wonder is not a demonstrable act of
God; everyone is free to understand the event that is asserted
to be a wonder as an occurrence which accords with natural
law in the world.

Wonder confronts man with the critical question of how far
he understands the world rightly when he understands it as the
working world amenable to his control; how far he rightly
understands himself when he estimates himself by his work and
aims at making himself secure through his work. Thus the concept of wonder radically negates the character of the world as
the controllable, working world, because it destroys man's
understanding of himself as made secure through his work.

Our action can always be understood in two ways: as the
production of something – that is, from the point of view of
something which has been done; or as action now being done.
Therefore we are also given two possible ways of understanding
ourselves: *from what is done or from the doing.*

Our action, that is to say, occurs either as the fulfilment of
the claim which confronts us, under which our *now* always
stands – in which case the action is nothing but obedience; or
it occurs so that something is produced or attained by it, and
this something gives the action its meaning. If our act occurs
as obedience, something is certainly produced or attained by
it; the meaning of the act, however, does not lie in what is
accomplished by it, but in the obedient doing of the act. In the
same way, the meaning of a gift lies, not in the gift but in the
act of giving.

When the latter understanding is really accepted, it includes
the corollary that man, after he has acted, cannot remain with
what he has done, stop at an attained goal and estimate himself
by it. He can only say that as a servant he has done 'only what
was [his] duty' (Luke 17.10). He is not to look back on what he
has done, but forward to what he still has to do. He must look
forward, not because he wants to put this or that future task

behind him and so looks in haste and anxiety; he looks forward simply in obedience.

If our action is action under the claim of God, then it is never completed. We produce no achievement after which we can stop, representing ourselves to ourselves as men who have in some sense finished their work. We must remain in the unremitting activity in which the claim of God sets us. This activity is the activity of *life*. No more than we are to look back should we keep looking forward to arrange a programme for all that must still be done. For then we should be again estimating ourselves on the basis of what is done, is finished – even though the finishing is, of course, not yet accomplished. But all the same, we should be seeing ourselves as questioned about what has been finished, we should be estimating ourselves by what is accomplished. God's claim, however, brings us, not into the unrest of anxiety and care about something lying ahead of us which must be brought to completion; but to the unrest of life. It tears us loose from ourselves as we are, that is, from our past, and directs us to the future.

But since our action always does produce some effect, it carries within it the hidden temptation to estimate ourselves from what has been done and to attach ourselves to what has been done. In fact we are continually yielding to this temptation and so lapsing into the past – what is done is always past. When we estimate ourselves really from what is accomplished, though the accomplishment may be in the future, even our future action is already past, branded by sin and death. It confronts us actually as a work, as an established, attained position.[9] It is plain to us that we are all trapped in such an estimation of ourselves, since we all fear death. For this fear arises from the desire to keep ourselves as we are and the secret knowledge that we cannot do so.

We are all trapped in such an estimation of ourselves and we cannot by any exertion of our own free ourselves from this lapse into the past, into death. The freedom we are striving for would again be thought of as our own work, as the highest and best goal which we would win by our struggles. Such action would

[9] Luther on Rom. 8.26 (Ficker, p. 205, lines 5f.): 'It always happens that we know our own work before it is done; but God's work we do not know until it has been done.'

already belong to the past even before it was undertaken. Only if we could forget our own work, should we be free; only if we were acting solely from obedience.

The question is, therefore, how we can arrive at such obedience, at such true listening to God's claim. The question is really, *can* we so listen? Obviously we cannot simply make a resolution that we will hear; nor can we wait to find out whether we are hearing, for we are always already in the middle of some action through which we want to gain something. Every *now* to which we come is already distorted by the self-understanding we bring to it. Our past from which we come to the present moment always clings to us.

There is only one possible way to become free *from the past*, free for a true hearing of the claim which comes to us in the present moment; that freedom is given to us *through forgiveness*. For as temporal beings we cannot be free from the past in the sense that the past is simply cancelled and ignored, that we receive something like a new nature – if we should receive it, we certainly could not keep ourselves in it. We always come to the present moment out of our past and bringing our past with us. For we are not plants, animals or machines; and our present is always qualified by our past. The critical question is whether our past is present in us as sinful or as forgiven. If the sin is forgiven, that means that we have freedom for the future; that we are really hearing God's claim and can yield ourselves to him as 'his instruments' (Rom. 6.12ff.).

It has now become fully clear why *forgiveness* must be understood *as wonder* – that is, as God's action in contradiction to the world process. The world to which it stands in contradiction is our working world which lies at our disposal, in which from the beginning all action is understood as getting things done, as achievement; in which all that happens – even in the future – is always thought of in terms of the past. If God's forgiveness is a wonder, that is, if God in this wonder takes away our understanding of ourselves as achievers who as such are continually relapsing into the past, then simultaneously he has abolished the character of the world as the working world under our control.

Since in action something is always done, there is always the possibility of understanding all action as what has been done and all happening as what has happened. *For the eye of unbelief, God's action is also a world event which has happened.* And since the believer also knows that it can be so seen and that the possibility always exists for himself so to see all that happens, he must when he speaks of God's action speak of it as a wonder which happens contrary to nature *(contra naturam)*. He must say that when he speaks of a wonder he is nullifying the idea of conformity to natural law. But to apply the notions of wonder and of creation to the world understood as nature is senseless; for the world seen as past is not seen as creation. It preserves its character as creation only if we, as those who are forgiven, stand open to the future and can therefore see the world open before us as the field in which we are to hear God's claim and to act under it.

To see the world in this way is *not* to have a *'world view'*; it is not a theory about the world in general. The world is so seen only when the claim of God is heard on the basis of forgiveness. Hence the error of understanding ourselves and the world as past must be continually combated. This means that our 'working ideas' in which we count on the controllability of the world, that is, on its conformity to law, must always be limited by our 'conceptions of faith'. Furthermore, in our actual living, conceptions belonging to work and those belonging to faith are interchanged in such a way that the former are always delimited by the latter.[10] For his working ideas, man needs the conception of nature. To what extent he must use it cannot be stated in general terms. He uses it in so far as he is required to use it in a specific task. If he lets it become his master, then the use becomes sin.

The *idea of miracle* is now understandable and so also is its amalgamation with the idea of wonder. Either, the idea is a despairing expression of the secret knowledge of relapse into the past; it has become impossible for man to understand the world as creation and to see God's action in it; when man speaks of God's action he can only conceive it on the analogy of the sequence of world events as a special achievement and he still remains wholly imprisoned in his old understanding of the world. Or, the conception of miracle is a primitive, unclear

[10] Cf. W. Herrmann, *Offenbarung und Wunder*, p. 37; Luther, *op. cit.*, p. 265, lines 4ff.

expression of the understanding that God's action is in contradiction to the world process, to all the activity of the world.

The *empty pantheistic concept of wonder*, too, is now understandable. The right motive is operative in it, the desire that faith
be able to see the world as creation and to speak of ever new
wonders because God's action can be seen in the world-process.
But it is necessary to be on guard against the misunderstanding
that the believer possesses a Christian world-view, which is at
his disposal like a bill of exchange, so that he can now interpret
all activity and every event as wonder. Faith must always be
won afresh in the battle against the working conceptions which
would corrupt it. Every wonder is visible only on the basis of
the one wonder, forgiveness. But the wonder of forgiveness is
not a fact of the past. I always have it only as a forgiveness just
grasped. 'It must always be believed' (*semper credendum*); the
Christian always stands in 'grace' (*gratia*).

But if that is so, then it is really possible for the Christian
continually to see new wonders. This world process, which to the
unbeliever must appear as a sequence of events governed by
law, has for the Christian become a world in which God acts.
And since he himself hears God's claim on him and acts in
obedience, his own action is no longer a part of the world process; he is doing a wonder.

The reality of all wonder, therefore, depends on the relation
of faith to the *one* wonder of forgiveness in Christ. It is then
wrong to claim, apart from this relation of faith, a difference
between the Christian and the pagan conception of wonder.
Both can be primitive; both can be understood radically. Both
can cling to miracle and in both the idea of God's action can be
consistently developed. The difference between Christianity
and paganism does not lie in a different idea of wonder – no
more than it lies in a different idea of God. The difference is
that Christianity speaks of the real God because it can speak of
the real wonder.

IV. *The Wonders of the New Testament*

In the New Testament, wonders are recorded which have the
character of miracles – particularly wonders of Jesus. In so far
as these are acts of Jesus (healing of the sick, etc.), they are acts

which were important events for those immediately concerned. Even if all of them were historically verified (or so far as they are so verified), it is still true that as deeds of a man in the past they do not directly concern us. Seen as such they are not works of the Christ, if we understand by the work of Christ the work of redemption.[11]

Therefore, in any discussion, the 'wonders of Jesus' are entirely open to critical investigation. It should be most strongly emphasized that Christian faith is not concerned with proving the possibility or the actuality of the wonders of Jesus as events of the past. On the contrary, such concern would be wrong.

If Christ is present for us as the preached Christ, then the wonders of Jesus are relevant only in so far as they are a part of that preaching, that is, as witnesses. And they are witnesses which reveal the whole *ambiguity of the Christian preaching*. They show that the wonders definitely are not to be understood as demonstrable events which provide a basis for faith, for every one is left free to explain them by a causality understandable to him. They are not secured against being explained as demonic activities (Mark 3.22) or as achievements by which Jesus guaranteed himself (Mark 8.11f.), on the basis of which the people want to make him king (John 6.14ff.), or as a means to be used in the service of individual lives (John 6.26). They therefore carry the same ambiguity as the wonder of Christ himself. For Jesus Christ is to the unbeliever a demonstrable fact of the past, historically involved in a specific situation of the past and historically comprehensible.

The question is simply whether we will to see him as a fact of the past, as an historical figure, as a personality or something of the sort; or to see him as the wonder of God, that is, to see see him as the One who is here for us now as the Word of forgiveness spoken by God. There is always the temptation to transform his presence now into an objective presence in the

[11] Luther on Gal. 4f. (Weimar ed. XL, I, p. 568, lines 9ff.): 'Christ also gives commandments, but that is not his real office; it is incidental even as are his benefits: teaching, comforting, helping. These are not works peculiar to Christ. For the prophets also taught and did wonders. But Christ is God and man, who submits to the law of Moses and foreign tyranny, conquers Moses and that tyranny, contends with the law and suffers and afterwards in his resurrection damns and destroys our enemy.' Those other acts are 'common acts'.

past. Continually, the stumbling-block of the 'was made flesh' must be overcome. Anyone who chooses to affirm God's revelation in the historical personality of Jesus lays himself open to Kierkegaard's taunt that he is smarter than God himself, who sent his Son in the *hiddenness* of the flesh. To apply the conception of revelation to the historically demonstrable personality of Jesus is as senseless as to apply the conception of creation and of wonder to the world seen as nature.

But the wonders of Jesus are also witnesses giving *evidence that the Christian faith in God is neither pantheism nor monism*; that it has no right to speak of God's act whenever it pleases, but can so speak only when it perceives God's action in the single concrete case. Christian faith in God is not a world view. It is always won in the moment, and it says, 'Lord, I believe, help my unbelief' (Mark 9.24). Therefore it is not a faith which consists in a man's spiritual attitude. It is always and only faith in God who does not stand, as does an entity in the world, available to the observation of men at their pleasure. It is faith in the God who is seen only when he wills to reveal himself.

Therefore doubt of God which asks for a criterion by which God can be demonstrated must be cast aside. Man must be led to *that* doubt in which he doubts himself. That is, he must come to doubt whether he can exercise control over himself and the world. He must despair.

II

THE CHRISTOLOGY OF THE
NEW TESTAMENT[1]

THE PROBLEM of the christology of the New Testament is the problem of the New Testament teaching about Christ. 'Teaching', however, is not a precise concept and scientific discussions of New Testament christology in general suffer from a failure to consider the *concept of teaching*. The understanding of 'teaching' which guides such discussions is for the most part determined by the understanding of science which dominated earlier dogmatics.

Now this concept of science is part of the Greek tradition. In Greek thought, the object of knowledge is the world which is present at hand, which is apprehended by *seeing*, and is understood when it is seen as a connected whole determined by law, as a 'system' (σύστημα), a 'cosmos' (κόσμος), or as a segment of that whole.[2] This conception is not fundamentally altered when, in addition to the world which is perceived by the senses and is capable of being grasped by rational thinking, a divine world on a transcendent level is admitted and the origin of the knowledge of that world is counted as supernatural revelation. There is no real change in the concept so long as the mode of being in the higher world and its phenomena are present at hand in the same way as the phenomena of this world and so long as the method of investigating them is understood as a seeing.[3]

[1] Unpublished.

[2] This developed concept of science rests, of course, on a naïve way of understanding the world and of seeing all that exists as objective entities. Obviously this naïve understanding of being can also prevail outside the Greek tradition wherever no critical ontological thinking has been developed. It can prevail even where such a concept is incongruous with a particular understanding of existence, as in the New Testament.

[3] For the concept of *Vorhandensein* (present at hand) cf. M. Heidegger,

I. *The Personality of Jesus*

When historical research investigated the teaching of the New Testament about Christ, it made the unconscious assumption that this concept of teaching was shared by the New Testament. That is to say, it understood *the statements of the New Testament about Christ as statements about a world phenomenon*, about an entity whose 'nature' can be correctly described and whose relation to other world-entities is determinable positively and negatively.[4] In Melancthon's words, 'to know Christ' was understood as 'to discern his natures, his modes of incarnation' (*'Christum cognoscere eius naturas modos incarnationis contueri'*). Since modern research naïvely measured the teaching of the New Testament by the modern scientific view of the world, the teaching appeared to be mythology. Therefore the historical investigation of New Testament christology was its destruction. Research performed the same work of destruction on the New Testament which it had performed on the history of the dogma of the early church. To that history, New Testament christology now in fact became the preamble.

Research alleged a *development of christology in early Christianity* which was clearly traceable in the New Testament. As a result of this development, the man Jesus, who knew himself to be or who was believed to be the divinely-chosen king of the last aeon, became a heavenly being. Pre-existence was ascribed to him as a cosmic power who shared in the creation of the world. The heavenly being became a man, died and rose again, ascended into heaven and there as a divine being is enthroned beside God, is honoured by the community as deity, hears prayers, bestows marvellous powers, and will come again to be the judge and to conquer those cosmic powers opposed to God – death and the devil. This development could

---

Sein und Zeit, pp. 44f., 72ff., 356ff.; ET *Being and Time*, pp. 69ff., 101ff., 407ff.
    [4] Cf. for example, J. Weiss, *Christus, die Anfänge des Dogmas*, Tübingen, 1909: 'In what category of beings did it [the oldest Christian tradition] classify him [the ascended Christ]' (p. 29)? 'To what category of beings did Paul assign this heavenly Son of God (p. 37)? I use as illustrations the statements of my honoured teacher, J. Weiss, because he felt no temptation to gloss anything over. He saw the situation so plainly, and clearly recognized the complications.

proceed so quickly because the mythological conception of a Redeemer, long present in Judaism and paganism, had been attached to Jesus.

The progress of this development, marked by the concepts of Messiah and Son of David, Son of God and Son of Man, Lord (Kyrios) and Word (Logos), by the stories of his marvellous birth, the transfiguration, the resurrection and the ascension, does not need to be recapitulated. It is sufficient to say that its culmination was that 'we must think of Jesus Christ as we think of God' (II Clem. 1.1).

None of these conceptions was *new;* they came *from old mythologies*, from ancient hopes and dreams. The *new* element was simply the fact that all these assertions were made about this specific historical man, about Jesus of Nazareth. But the conceptions were not essentially altered by this ascription to a specific person. Rather, this historical figure, because of the strong impression he made on people, became the occasion for believing the old wishes and fantastic dreams to be reality.

At first it was assumed that in *one* respect these visions had been modified, enriched and deepened. Because of the historical events, because of the earthly work, the passion, the cross of Christ, the profound conception of the self-abasement of the Godhead, of the suffering redeemer and his sacrifice of himself for sinful men was incorporated into the old myth. But this idea proved to be a delusion. Not only do the pagan mysteries know the figure of the dying redeemer God, but pagan gnostic mythology also knows the figure of the pre-existent divine being who, obedient to the will of the Father, accepts suffering and poverty, hate and persecution, in order to build for his own the road to the heavenly world – exactly as Jesus is presented in the Gospel of John – the figure of the redeemed redeemer. According to this understanding the christology of the New Testament contains *nothing specifically Christian*, but simply shows the process by which ancient mythology was transferred to a concrete historical figure so as to conceal his individual features almost completely.

A certain shock must result. Has not christology turned into mythology? However, it was precisely this research which seemed to have re-opened the road from *teaching about Christ* to *faith in Christ*. Because of its destructive work, access seemed to be open to *the historical figure, Jesus of Nazareth, to whom faith must look.*

Indeed, for the first time, the real significance of the teaching about Jesus seemed to have become clear. That significance does not lie at all in the mythological content of the presentation. Such teachings are in fact relevant and necessary only for that particular age; for us they are entirely unauthoritative as a form of expression for the religious significance of Jesus. 'We should not forget that all these assertions are basically only a multiform expression for one conviction, the conviction that in the person of Jesus was given the highest that can be thought, the ultimate fulfilment of all prophecy and hope, the final, unsurpassable self-revealing of God, the absolute *revelation*.'[5] 'Early Christianity used forms and concepts which were already at hand, in order to express the overpowering impression of the person of Jesus in a generally understandable but at the same time in an unsurpassable way.'[6] 'From all these fumbling attempts to express the nature of Christ in formulae, we can learn only how powerful his personality must have been to inspire men with such faith, to arouse their imagination thus and to dominate their thinking for centuries. The less we can understand and accept the christology, the more strongly are we forced back to the person of Jesus. To understand him, to gain an impression of him, to let ourselves be drawn by him into his life with the Father, is more important for us than to find a credal formula by the use of which we could be both dogmatically correct and true to historical fact.'[7]

This kind of research also included a further investigation which turned from the problem of the christology of the New Testament to an *inquiry into the religion, the piety of the New Testament.* Hence it is natural that J. Weiss should follow his *Christus,* 1909, with a study entitled *Jesus im Glauben des Urchristentum,* 1910. Here his purpose is to show 'the kind of position Jesus held in the religion of the first Christians; how their inner life was related to him and how their faith in him was connected with the practical duties of their life' (p. 1.) 'The teachings' about Jesus are only 'indications of their actual attitude towards him'. Instead of arguing about the teachings we ought rather 'to

[5] J. Weiss, *Christus, die Anfänge des Dogmas,* p. 6.
[6] *ibid.,* p. 87.   [7] *ibid.,* p. 88.

study the *religion* which produced them as a very simple and very incomplete expression of that which moved men's hearts' (p. 1).

Here 'religion' is understood as a faith in God which is wholly untheoretical, as a feeling of dependence on God to which man can yield himself in love and trust like a child.[8] Statements which relate to Jesus do not affirm a belief in him as does a confession of faith; they express a 'personal relation to him' 'which man can rightly call faith in him'.[9] The impress of his deep emotion and his sincerity, of his certainty, his warmth, his spiritual depth, and his love for men wins the heart, moves the conscience, and gives that feeling of the nearness of God.[10]

Therefore in the primitive community the concern is not with faith in Christ but with faith in God under the influence of Jesus' personality, which leads to the acknowledgement of him as Messiah. The belief that he is the Messiah, that a new age has begun in the world, is the result of their present felicity. In so far as they are hoping for the future, that hope is a remnant of Jewish thinking.[11] They do hope for Jesus' return, but more important to them is the fact that they 'feel his immediate nearness in the heavenly power which permeates them and in which they recognize the Holy Spirit'.[12] 'As children are unconsciously led by their parents into parental ways of feeling and acting, by a sort of hidden "contagion", so Jesus (I could perhaps say) has inoculated his followers with his life of sonship to God, his way of feeling and thinking, and to a certain degree his way of acting. It cannot be denied that since the days of Jesus there has existed among us, to the blessing of mankind, a certain type of child of God, who in essentials draws the power of his life from the original presentation of the personality of Jesus'.[13] 'Now the really definitive effect of Jesus on the souls of those who are his is this: he has given them *the courage to believe in their own salvation* – simply because he not only talked of the loving Father in heaven but also demonstrated in his own person how securely and joyfully he himself relied on that fatherly love.'[14]

---

[8] J. Weiss, *Jesus im Glauben des Urchristentums*, Tübingen, 1910, p. 3.
[9] *ibid.*, p. 2.   [10] *ibid.*, p. 3.   [11] *ibid.*, p. 8.
[12] *ibid.*, p. 10.   [13] *ibid.*, p. 14.   [14] *ibid.*, p. 16.

On this interpretation, the imitative discipleship *of Jesus* is the only legitimate relation to him. The practice of prayer to the risen Christ already represents a fundamental misunderstanding, because it depends on an idea of his heavenly nature which is only itself a projection of the experience of the Christians into the metaphysical world.[15]

On the basis of the passages cited, one aspect of the interpretation of the New Testament seems very questionable. The New Testament never speaks at all of the imitation of Christ. It knows very well the meaning of following him to the cross. Such discipleship is commanded; but it is not motivated by the impact of his personality. A discipleship which could be described as letting one's self be infected with his faith is irrelevant, since nowhere in the Gospels is there mention of the faith of Jesus.

In a conception of discipleship such as J. Weiss describes, Jesus stands as *the guarantee for belief in God*, that is for belief in God the Father, belief in the certainty of salvation, in the power of love and the duty of loving. And Jesus has this meaning by virtue of the impact of his personality in which such faith and such love were vividly alive. Even if that conception is accepted as true, Jesus could have this meaning only for those who had been personally associated with him; not for those born later. Even on the assumption that an image of his personality was preserved in the community, the most that such an image can effect would be to make faith in God and love of neighbour appear to me as beautiful and desirable. It can never give me that faith and love – only pietism and romanticism could so misjudge what is possible.

At the moment when I doubt, the perception that someone else – even Jesus – had faith and love does not help me at all. At most, the faith and love of someone now associated with me can help me. Of course, I could be mistaken about him, as he can be mistaken about me. In any case, he can be no more than a momentary stimulus to me. I can never base my faith in God upon the faith which someone else has. If the faith of the early Christian community had been faith in God in this sense, it would have been an illusion. Jesus would have been understood as a guarantee which relieved the individual

[15] Cf. esp. *ibid.*, pp. 31f.

of the necessity of a faith of his own. As a matter of fact, Jesus was never understood in the New Testament as one who relieves a man of the necessity of decision. What was required, to be sure, was a faith *in him*. How this was understood is still to be investigated.

But first it should be noted that Weiss's basic assumption is false. The community did *not* preserve an image of the personality of Jesus at all. Such an image can only be reconstructed by the imagination from his proclamation, which is preserved in the Gospels. Such a reconstructed image remains highly subjective, and always crumbles under critical scepticism. If the significance of Jesus lay in his personality, that significance would have ceased with the first generation of Christians.

It is futile to seek in all directions for proof that the historical personality of Jesus is a determining factor in the christological affirmations of Paul and John. With Paul, as J. Weiss of course recognizes, the relation to Christ is a relation to the ascended Christ. But Weiss claims that the image of the heavenly Christ is enhanced by the image of the Crucified and that Paul's relation to the ascended Christ thereby acquires the character of self-sacrificing gratitude. But is not the gratitude chimerical, if the image of the one who by self-humiliation attained to exaltation is a mythical image?

But in reality there can be no possibility that an impression made on Paul by the person of Jesus was the basis of Paul's faith. Weiss works hard to defend the probability of such an impression. Paul as persecutor must have had an impression of Jesus' personality. '[Paul] could not have been the spiritual, truth-seeking man we know him to have been, if the spirit of the first witnesses and the spirit of Jesus working in them did not make a deep impression on him. It requires a low estimate of the personality of Jesus himself to doubt that it shone luminously through the medium of his adherents and also of his traducers. In short, the only reasonable assumption is that Paul, before Damascus, had been more deeply moved by the personality of Jesus than he himself perhaps knew or admitted.'[16]

That is by no means the only reasonable assumption. On the contrary, in the light both of the Gospel tradition and of

[16] *ibid.*, p. 23.

Paul's own statements, it is fantasy. And it is most certainly fantasy to assert on the basis of II Cor. 5.16 that Paul once met Jesus on earth. 'A personality which aroused so much enthusiasm and so much hate, must have been a human being who by his outward appearance and demeanour, by his look and expression, by his words and gestures, would have riveted the attention of an earnest, serious man like Paul.'[17] Perhaps Paul had seen Jesus suffer. 'A look into the face of Jesus outweighs many words and teachings; the sight of his crucifixion would be more important than the knowledge of many stories of healings and wonders. . . . Indeed, the experience of Paul is inconceivable without such direct or indirect contact with Jesus. . . . Paul *must* have had, he really did have a luminous, living image of the ethical and religious personality of Jesus.'[18]

In this fashion J. Weiss also applies to Paul the same idea of discipleship and he thinks to free Paul's idea of the ascended Christ from its mythological wrappings so that for Paul the image of the exalted Christ bears 'not only the personal but also the spiritual traits of Jesus'.[19] Thus for Paul, too, the genuine christological teachings are explained as a 'theoretical expedient'.[20]

Such an interpretation maintains that the Pauline theology is a monstrous misunderstanding of itself. Precisely that content which Paul himself emphasized most strongly is eliminated, or else is given a meaning wholly different from that which Paul intended. Instead of faith in Jesus Christ who became man, was crucified and rose from the dead, it ascribes to Paul a religion which consists in a general belief in the Fatherhood of God and it asserts that Paul was convinced of the validity of this belief through the impression made on him by the thrilling personality of Jesus.[21]

II. *The Christ Cult*

The recognition that such an interpretation did violence to

[17] *ibid.*, p. 23.   [18] *ibid.*, p. 24.   [19] *ibid.*, p. 26.   [20] *ibid.*, p. 26.
[21] J. Weiss subjects the Johannine christology to the same interpretation (*ibid.*, pp. 27–31). 'John's portrayal of Jesus rests on a double image – the historical person and the supra-historical heavenly being.' And so J. Weiss finds in John's presentation the historical figure of Jesus with its 'human, warm and winning traits'.

the christology of Paul and John and of the New Testament as a whole (with the possible exception of the Synoptic Gospels) led to an entirely different attempt to understand New Testament christology. But the new attempt was still based on the presupposition that christology as teaching is only a secondary expression of the real religion of the New Testament.

This attempt is magnificently carried out in W. Bousset's *Kyrios Christos*. Here the true nature of this 'early Christian religion' is much more clearly presented. In the earlier research, that religion was judged to be a general belief in the Fatherhood of God, really a kind of optimistic, altruistic world view. The religion is clearly understood by Bousset as a definite and limited phenomenon of psychic life. Since the actual christology is a creation of Hellenistic Christianity, Bousset's main interest is focused there. He differentiates it sharply from Palestinian Christianity.

His characterization of the latter has chiefly the negative significance of showing that the Palestinian community did not have the conceptions characteristic of Hellenistic christology. In particular, it did not use the title of 'Lord' (κύριος) and it therefore had neither a real christology nor a real faith in Christ. Jesus was accepted by the Palestinian Christians as Messiah in the Jewish sense, and the community applied to him the conception of the Son of Man, which completely vanished in Hellenistic Christianity. Bousset does not differ from previous research in this positive characterization of the belief of the primitive community.[22] The negative element is the essential one in his judgment. It is seen as preliminary to the first stage of christology, to the history of the Kyrios cult and faith in the Lord (Kyrios).

The Kyrios cult appears as the real backbone of the Christian religion and the driving force in its development. The picture presented is basically the same as before in so far as it describes the development of doctrine. The man Jesus becomes the divine being, Jesus Christ, the pre-existent Son of God, a cosmic figure who becomes man, brings revelation, is crucified, rises from the dead, and as the ascended Lord reigns at the right hand of God. But the essential factor is that all these

[22] Cf. W. Bousset, *Kyrios Christos*, 2nd ed., Tübingen, 1921, esp. pp. 17f.

assertions are true of one who is still immediately present with the community, acting in it by wonders and signs, inspiring it with enthusiasm and heroism, bestowing his power in the sacraments and implanting the divine nature in the believers. Hellenistic Christianity is a cultic religion. Basically it is a wholly new religion, in contrast to the original Palestinian community.

The teaching of this religion did not (as A. von Harnack thought) arise from a Hellenization of Christianity; not, that is, from the speculative or philosophical interest of Greek Christians who were under the influence of Greek learning. Rather, the theology or the christology is simply the expression of the cultic piety. Bousset has eliminated the necessity of understanding the christology as an expression of a personal tie with the historical Jesus and the concomitant necessity of undertaking a violent re-interpretation of the sources. An actual phenomenon, cultic piety, has been presented, and the christology can be understood as its expression.[23]

Primitive Christianity grew into a cultic religion on the soil of Hellenistic syncretism, where under the influence of the *mystery religions* it acquired its sacramental piety, its emphasis on the Spirit, its dualistic world view, its speculation and mythology. In the picture there are variations of detail: the extent of the domination of cultic and mystic piety, of the influence of the gnostic emphasis on the Spirit and gnostic mythology, and finally of the acceptance of the ideas of the rational Hellenistic enlightenment philosophy.

But even where for the communities Jesus Christ was the teacher of true faith in God and of pure ethics (where, consequently, the synoptic tradition could play its role), this view was subordinate to the assumption that the community assembled to worship the Lord Christ who was present in it. Thus the 'quite simple and rational Christianity, the religion embraced by the Judaism of the Diaspora for which Jesus was lawgiver, teacher and judge' 'was propagated on the soil of a community practice and service of worship, the determining elements of which came to be more and more the Kyrios cult

---

[23] To this corresponds in the field of systematic theology E. Troeltsch's attempt to define the significance of Jesus for the Christian community by his place in the cult.

and the sacraments.'[24] And when the Apologists discovered the value of the Stoic concept of the Logos for christology, this also served the Christ cult. The concept was used 'to defend and justify the fact that the Christians pay divine honour to Jesus of Nazareth who once appeared here on earth and was crucified. The Apologists stand wholly on the ground of the community belief and the community cult with respect to the adoration of Jesus.'[25]

More important is another variation which does not have its origin in the external factors but arises from internal differences; for the cultic piety varies in different individuals with different religious propensities. Thus a lofty spirituality exists alongside a naïve belief in the sacraments, religious theoretical speculation beside inspired enthusiasm. The solitary religious individualist emerges from the level of community piety. But all see in Christ Jesus their Lord; for all, he embodies the presence of deity, whether in the religious experiences of the group assembled in worship or in the spiritual experiences of the individual. He is Lord equally both in the external events of life and in inner spiritual experiences.

Thus the *religion of Paul* presupposes the cult piety of the community but rises above it as spiritual, individualistic mysticism. Paul's christology centres on the assertion: 'The Lord is the Spirit' (ὁ κύριος τὸ πνεῦμα). Jesus Christ is the divine power which rules in the community, which permeates and supports Paul and changes him from glory (δόξα) into glory. This power makes Paul the spiritual man who does wonders, who has speculative insight into the secrets of the divine plan of salvation, who authoritatively commands the community. This divine power raises him above all historical limitations; he is already a wondrous being. The theology of Paul, in so far as it is anthropology and soteriology, is simply an expression of this spiritual piety; all life is interpreted from the standpoint of the ecstatic. In so far as it is belief in justification, it is an apologetic theory which he needed in his missionary work.[26]

For *John*, the historical Jesus meant as little as for Paul. Christ mysticism is equally the determining factor for John's piety. The figure of Jesus, in which history and myth are

[24] W. Bousset, *Kyrios Christos*, pp. 302f.   [25] *ibid.*, p. 317.
[26] This thesis, as is well known, has already been advanced by W. Wrede.

combined, the figure of the God-man, enkindles the vision which makes the worshipper himself divine and gives him eternal life. The Word which the God-man speaks is a wonder-working mystery word. Believing it means true vision and the possession of eternal life.

The differences between Paul and John can be ignored here. In both of them – they are the chief exemplars – appears clearly the definitive character of the early Christian religion as Bousset understands it. It is a phenomenon of the psychic life; it is piety, specifically the piety of the redeemed, against the background of a dualistic world view. It is a mystery religion, which as such is nourished by the consciousness of deliverance from the darkness and misery, from the wickedness and death, which are inherent in physical-material existence; it is nourished also by the consciousness of enjoying this liberation in inner experience in the cult worship and by the sense of union with the worshipped deity who bears in himself the forces of the world of light and who in the cult ritual bestows these forces on the mystics. And this liberation is also to be found in individual experiences of ecstasy and mystic union.

The christology is simply the theoretical explanation of this piety under the influence of the mythology of the mysteries and other traditions. Faith is not a real faith *in* Christ, but is rather the spiritual mood (διάθεσις) of the piety. Bousset then finds in Philo a prototype of the Pauline conception. Even when a specific object of faith is named, that object can really be none other than God – in which case, of course, God means only divinity in general. Thus with John, faith is identical with the vision of the divine. Christ may be named as the object of faith, but such an actual doubling of faith's object[27] is really illegitimate since Christ is simply the embodiment of the divine power, the symbol of the invasion of the darkness by the divine world of light.

III. *Faith in Jesus Christ*

It is easy to understand that Bousset, in spite of his sensitive appreciation of this cultic piety of redemption, still finds it alien and contrasts its supernaturalism with the pure ethical

---

[27] Bousset, *Kyrios Christos*, p. 149.

gospel of Jesus as he understands that gospel. However, our present purpose is not to discuss such comparative evaluations but simply to consider whether the christology of the New Testament, primarily that of Paul and John, is correctly described by Bousset. Undoubtedly his presentation is superior to the older liberal understanding. He is also right when he says that Hellenistic Christianity, if it is judged from the point of view of the history of religion, is something new in relation to Palestinian Christianity and that it belongs in the same class as mystery religions and gnosis. It centres in the worship of the Lord (the Kyrios cult), which was wholly unknown in the original Palestinian Christianity. But what is in actual fact the cultic character of *Pauline religion*?

For Paul *the church* (ἐκκλησία) is not primarily the assembly for worship but an historical-eschatological entity, the true Israel, in which all the individual communities are bound together. The saving events of the Old Testament were the preparation for it; it was founded by the final saving event, the sending of Jesus Christ, by his life and death; and it is waiting for its fulfilment. To it belong those who are called by the preaching of the gospel (II Cor. 5.19). The sacraments constitute this fellowship, not because contact with heavenly power and endowment with such power is experienced in them (for Paul, any psychological interpretation is wholly inadmissible), but because they are actions in which the saving event, the death and resurrection of Christ, becomes an event in the present as something which happens objectively to the believer.

No 'medicine of immortality' which guarantees eternal life is supplied by the sacraments, for a man can be lost in spite of the sacraments (I Cor. 10.1–13). Indeed a man can take the sacraments to his damnation (I Cor. 11.27–29). But he who partakes of the sacrament shares in the saving event if he yields himself obediently to God to be used as God's instrument (Rom. 6.3ff., 13ff.). The life which is bestowed in the sacrament stands under the imperative as much as under the indicative (Rom. 6.13; Gal. 5.25).

The Christian fellowship of which Paul speaks is not a fellowship of mystical life which takes the mystic out of the common life of men; the Christian fellowship enables the Christian to face suffering and labour *in* this life. Paul does not share the 'life of Jesus' apart from his own sufferings and work in particular experiences of immersal or ecstasy; the sharing of the life of Jesus is achieved *in* that suffering and work which as a believer he understands afresh (II Cor. 4.7–18). 'In Christ' is not the formula for a mystic communion; it means simply that the believer belongs to Christ.[28] The interpretation, as stated in II Cor. 5.17, is: 'If anyone is in Christ, he is a new creation.'

It is clear that 'in Christ' designates not a mystic but an eschatological fact. In Christ, the Christian has righteousness, justification (II Cor. 5.21; Gal. 2.17), and freedom (Gal. 2.4). He belongs to the new age, to the new race of men which has begun with the saving event.

If Christ is the Spirit ($\pi\nu\epsilon\tilde{\upsilon}\mu\alpha$), he is not Spirit in the sense of a mystic power which permeates the community and the individual, but as the One who frees the community and hence also the individual from the law and thereby also from sin. As 'flesh' described the old nature of man, his godlessness, so 'spirit' describes the new possibility of life in freedom. 'If we live by the Spirit, let us also walk by the Spirit' (Gal. 5.25). Our new life in the Spirit is a 'walking according to the Spirit' (Rom. 8.4–11; 12f.).[29] If 'flesh' is the sphere of the world of objective entities and designates behaviour 'after the flesh' ($\kappa\alpha\tau\grave{\alpha}\ \sigma\acute{\alpha}\rho\kappa\alpha$), an understanding of one's self as an object and a seeking security of one's self from objects, in that case the 'spirit' ($\pi\nu\epsilon\tilde{\upsilon}\mu\alpha$) means what is non-objective and 'walking after the Spirit' ($\kappa\alpha\tau\grave{\alpha}\ \pi\nu\epsilon\tilde{\upsilon}\mu\alpha$) means a life which loses itself – for nothing, from the standpoint of the world – in order to live from the future.

Therefore the religion of Paul could be described as a new self-understanding. It is the consciousness of standing in a new world in which he moves, free from law and sin, in obedi-

---

[28] 'To be in 'Christ' ($\grave{\epsilon}\nu\ X\rho\iota\sigma\tau\tilde{\omega}\ \epsilon\tilde{\iota}\nu\alpha\iota$) = 'to be Christ's' ($X\rho\iota\sigma\tau\upsilon\tilde{\upsilon}\ \epsilon\tilde{\iota}\nu\alpha\iota$): Gal. 3.28ff.; 5.24; II Cor. 10.7; Rom. 8.9; 14.8. Cf. I Cor. 6.19; Rom. 14.7f.

[29] The following three passages taken together show how for Paul 'to be in Christ' is at once an eschatological fact and a concrete way of living. 'For neither circumcision counts for anything nor uncircumcision, but keeping the commandments of God' (I Cor. 7.19). 'For in Christ Jesus neither circumcision nor uncircumcision is of any avail, but faith working through love' (Gal. 5.6). 'For neither is circumcision anything, nor uncircumcision, but a new creation' (Gal. 6.15).

ence under God and in love for his neighbour. He is free from the past, from death, free from himself as a self who was imprisoned in a self-understanding determined by objects, by law, and by his own achievements. This new life is not possessed at special moments, in cultic worship and in ecstasy. It determines the whole life of the believer.

The meaning of Christ for this life is absolutely clear. It is no longer possible to separate piety and teaching and then to understand the teaching as a theoretical explanation of the piety. On the contrary, the life itself is founded on faith in Christ, and that means it is founded on what is taught about Christ in the community. For the new life, dominating the historical life, is neither the mystical state of particular moments nor a power which is mysteriously instilled into the believer, guaranteeing him immortality. Nor, however, is it an idea which has been revealed, by which the nature of God, hitherto misjudged, would now be correctly known so that by it the human soul would be illuminated and freed from delusion. The new life is *a historical possibility created by the saving event and it is a reality wherever it is grasped in the resolve to act.*

Precisely this resolve is *faith*, the faith which believes in God's act of salvation as it happened in Christ and as it is taught in the proclamation of the church, and which obeys it. Through this saving act the new life is offered as possible for men. Of themselves they do not have this possibility; it is therefore not enough to have it called to their attention by some illuminating instruction. For they are sinners before God, imprisoned by their past, by what they have done as well as by what they have left undone. They gain the new life only through the forgiveness effected in Christ. They do not gain that forgiveness through an idea of the grace of God. Forgiving must be an event; it is an event which actually has occurred – as the proclamation asserts – in Christ in whom God reconciled the world to himself (II Cor. 5.18f.). Faith means acceptance of that forgiveness; and such acceptance involves obedience. Acceptance means to allow the judgment against us to be spoken, to take the cross of Christ, to live no more for ourselves but for him and therefore for our neighbours (Gal. 2.19f.; 6.14; II Cor. 5.14f.).

To *have faith in Christ*, therefore, does not mean to hold

particular opinions about his nature, although one can certainly have such opinions. Nor does it mean an imitative following of him, in the sense of allowing one's self to be drawn into his faith in God and his way of life. The faith of Jesus has no place whatever in Paul's thought. What Paul calls faith first comes into existence after the death and resurrection of Christ – not before. Faith is certainly following Christ – but by accepting his cross, not at all in the sense of imitation, but as grasping the forgiveness and the possibility of life created by the cross. Paul is concerned neither with the human personality of Jesus – that would be 'Christ after the flesh', who is dead (II Cor. 5.16) – nor with the nature of Christ as a heavenly divine being. Faith certainly depends wholly on the person of Jesus, but in such a way that his person and his work are seen as one. In other words, Paul's concern is with Jesus as *a historical event*. That event happened 'when the fulness of the time was come' (Gal. 4.4); that event brings in the new age and gives the possibility of new life which is grasped in 'the obedience of faith' (ὑπακοὴ πίστεως).

In what sense Paul can speak of faith in Christ is then clear. There is no 'doubling' of the object of faith. Faith in Christ is not an illegitimate expression either of the impact made by the personality of Jesus or of a strengthened faith in God. Nor does it mean a mystic relation to a cultic figure in which the deity is symbolically represented. Faith in Christ is complete submission under that which God has done in Christ. In this sense, not in the cultic sense, Christ for Paul is the Lord and Paul is his slave.

What then is meant by *christology*? It is not the theoretical explanation of experiential piety; it is not speculation and teaching about the divine nature of Christ. It is proclamation; it is summons. It is the 'teaching' that through Jesus our justification is achieved, that for our sakes he was crucified and is risen (Rom. 3.24f.; 4.25; 10.9; II Cor. 5.18f.). At the moment when this is proclaimed the hearer is summoned. He is asked whether he is willing, in the light of this fact of Christ, to understand himself as a sinner before God and to surrender himself and all that externally he is and has, to take the cross of Christ, and at the same time to understand himself as the justified one who shares the new life in the resurrection of Christ.

For the natural man such a proclamation is first of all the call to repentance, to the knowledge that he stands under the 'wrath' (ὀργή) of God. The proclamation is directed to the conscience of the hearer (II Cor. 2.14–16). In it the saving act becomes contemporary with the hearer; the reconciliation given by God through Christ now becomes a *present* reality for him. 'We beseech you, on behalf of Christ, be reconciled to God . . . behold now is the acceptable time: behold now is the day of salvation' (II Cor. 5.20; 6.2).

So far as the teaching is proclamation and summons, nothing further is set *beside* it as accessory, neither a theoretical explanation nor even simple historical information. The preaching is a part of *the event itself*; Christ is present in the word. Simultaneously with the cross of Christ God has instituted the 'ministry of reconciliation', that is, the 'word of reconciliation' (II Cor. 5.18ff.). As Christ can be called the 'power' (δύναμις) of God (I Cor. 1.24), so also the preaching itself, the 'gospel' is 'a power of God for salvation to every one who has faith', (Rom. 1.16). For by the preaching comes faith (ἡ πίστις ἐξ ἀκοῆς) (Rom. 10.13–17).

Pauline christology, therefore, is nothing other than *the proclamation of the saving act of God which took place in Christ.* Faith is response to the Word; the new self-understanding is the response to the proclamation. Now so far as this faith, this new self-understanding – that is, the *response* to the summons – is given expression in words, the verbal response is christology. This response in words can be formulated in various ways: as the simple confession that Jesus is the Lord (Rom. 10.9; Phil. 2.11), or in detailed statements in which man's new understanding of himself and the world is elaborated. In so far as such more fully developed ideas are not empty speculation but come out of the historical situation, out of the necessities of building the community, of polemic, and of defence, they are still christology in the sense of summons, but of course the summons is indirect.

Paul had need to develop such ideas in his struggle against both Judaism and gnosticism. And in that struggle he developed his christological thinking explicitly. Wrede and Bousset are correct in understanding the doctrine of justification as a polemical doctrine. Indeed, theology as a whole has its significance only as criticism and polemic. But they are wholly wrong in supposing it to be of secondary importance for that reason, and in failing to recognize that it presents conceptions which were for Paul central both christologically and theologically. The doctrine of justification makes explicit the way in which man's whole existence is affected by the saving event and what kind of new understanding of human existence is given in it. The conceptions made explicit in that teaching are at the very centre of Paul's understanding of his new life, as is demonstrated by the fact that he employs the same basic ideas when he opposes the gnostic spiritism in Corinth.

The basic ideas in his polemic against Judaism and gnosticism are these: the cross is a 'stumbling-block' and 'folly' because in it judgment is pronounced against all human boasting, whether boasting based on the 'works of the law' or on human 'wisdom'. Only in the cross could God's grace be revealed, because the original sin of both Jews and heathen is that they do not glorify God but set up their own 'boast'. Through the judgment, grace enters. If all human pride is broken – as it is broken in the cross by which all human ideals receive the death sentence – then man stands before God unequivocally as recipient and is justified by God's 'grace' (χάρις). By surrendering to the cross, man is freed from himself – and precisely that is his salvation. Then he is crucified with Christ; he is 'in Christ'; he is a new creation.

Paul's teaching of justification is, it could be said, his real christology, for 'to know Christ is to know the benefits he confers' (*hoc est Christum cognoscere, beneficia eius cognoscere*: Melanchthon). The teaching of justification demonstrates forcibly that christology does not consist in speculation on the nature of Christ; that christology is the proclamation of the event of Christ's coming, and that an understanding of the event requires not speculation but self-examination, radical consideration of the nature of one's own new existence.

How, then, are those mythological representations which research has verified in Paul's writings to be related to this teaching? Every theological exposition of the saving event and of the Christian's existence is constructed with the use of contemporary conceptions. There is always discussion about man and his world, and it is carried on in anthropological and cosmological concepts which become traditional. Since such conceptions change with the passage of time, neither Paul's theology and christology nor that of any other Christian thinker can be understood uncritically. For example, Paul takes over from contemporary usage the concepts of 'flesh' and 'spirit' in their accepted meaning. Both terms meant a material substance which is also a force. How are are these concepts really suited to express what Paul wants to say? Clearly not in so far as the meaning is substance, for when Paul speaks of 'flesh' and 'spirit', he means to speak of the mode of the old life and the new. Paul therefore must always be read critically.

The fault of the earlier research is not that its proponents used critical methods, but that they used those methods in dependence on a modern world view which they did not question but took, instead of the text itself, as their standard of criticism. Naturally no criterion exists for proving that the meaning of a text is rightly apprehended; every interpretation is a venture. But the risk can be taken if one is clear about what one is doing and approaches the text with questions, not with a fixed point of view.

If we have rightly understood Paul's fundamental purpose, then the standard for the criticism of his anthropological, cosmological and christological statements is the recognition that the teaching is proclamation of the Christ event as a summons and that the explanation of it is the presentation of the Christian's understanding of his existence. Concepts and presentations which are not rooted in the proclamation collapse under criticism, even though they could once have been for Paul a genuine expression of what he intended to say. The mythological picture of Christ as a pre-existent heavenly being served Paul as a way of saying that in the Christ event we are not confronted by a person of this world nor the fate of a man of this world; but in that event *God's act* confronts us. We no longer need that particular image; yet we do still hold the christological belief of Paul.

We have made a distinction between christology which is kerygma as a direct summons to men and christology which is indirect summons and is the theological explanation of the new self-understanding of the believers, a critical-polemic explanation made necessary by Paul's historical situation and elaborated with the use of contemporary conceptuality. But that distinction is not meant to imply that Paul's statements can be divided neatly into two separate groups. The two elements are closely interwoven. Actually the kerygma is made by communicating faith's understanding and it issues out of that understanding.

Therein lies the chief difficulty of interpretation, and it is a difficulty which must be kept steadily in mind. There lies the real risk which research must not seek to avoid. The task of interpretation is never simple, nor can it be completed once for all – any more than the task of dogmatic theology, which has the same relation to the proclamation of the church, can ever be finished. But it is essential to understand the kind of questioning of the text which is the only legitimate road to the interpretation of New Testament christology.

What has been said of Paul holds also for the interpretation of *Johannine christology*. John differs from Paul in his specific mythological representations; but such differences are insignificant. This is true even of the chief difference between them. Paul saw the earthly Jesus 'emptied' of his 'glory' (Phil. 2.7), while to John the 'glory' shines out in him who became flesh (John 1.14). Certainly if 'glory' (δόξα) is viewed as a heavenly material and luminosity, Christ on earth according to Paul had no 'glory'; but in that sense neither did the Johannine Christ. According to John, the vision of the 'glory' of Jesus is possible only to the eye of faith, the glory is paradoxical. The glory of Christ is not heavenly luminosity but the Passion – his work in the service of the Father. Such glory is not an 'attribute', not a kind of impersonal natural quality. It is Christ's work in deed and word as he summoned his hearers to decision. And in that sense it can be said that for Paul also the earthly Jesus and his cross reveal the divine 'glory'. And when John calls the work of Jesus on earth the work of the Son of God, he has only made use of a form of expression which was inherently possible for the christology of Paul.

But for John, as for Paul, christology is proclamation, as is manifest from the fact that John – adopting a mythological term – calls Jesus *the Logos, the Word of God*. The Christ neither is nor represents anything other than the Word. He *is* the Word:

'. . . I do not judge him . . . the word which I have spoken will
be his judge . . .' (John 12.47f.). This is presented in wholly
paradoxical fashion in the way John records the proclamation
of Jesus. What Jesus proclaims as God's revelation is Christ
himself, is christology. And the content of the christology is
not a specific conceptual or ideological content; it is the message that he himself has been sent, the message that his having
been sent is the event which is decisive for the world, is the
'crisis' (χρίσις) for condemnation and salvation.

Here, too, therefore, the event of Christ's coming, as the act
of divine judgment and of divine love, is at the same time the
content of christology. It is in John's account especially that this
proclamation, with the understanding of existence included in
it, leads automatically to a criticism of the contemporary
conceptions prevailing in the world. For John abandons the
mythological eschatology which Paul still holds.

> Truly, truly, I say to you, he who hears my word
>   and believes him who sent me
> has eternal life
>   [and] does not come into judgment,
> but has passed from death to life.
> Truly, truly, I say to you, the hour is coming and now is
> when the dead will hear the voice of the Son of God
> and those who hear will live (John 5.24f.).

Essentially Paul and John are in complete agreement on this
point. For Paul, too, the time is fulfilled and the present time is
the day of salvation. For both Paul and John the new age has
dawned in the event of Jesus Christ.

John emphasizes the unity of Jesus and God more strongly
than does Paul. And for this emphasis, John, too, uses mythological forms of presentation. It is not, however, the case that
the ideas of Jesus' divine nature are developed further and
brought to a climax. What is asserted is that in Jesus God is
acting, that in Jesus and in him only is God to be found. 'For
as the Father has life in himself, so he has granted the Son also
to have life in himself' (John 5.26). The Father is not honoured
along with the Son; whoever honours the Son is honouring
the Father (5.23), for the Father has given all into his hand
(3.35; 13.3). He who sees the Son, sees the Father (14.9), and
the Father enters the hearts of believers when the Son enters

(14.23). Therefore only in Jesus, that is, only in the event of the resurrection, only in the Word which God speaks in Jesus and which proclaims Jesus, is God accessible to men.

In that case, however, the entire development from the man Jesus to the eternal Son of God is to be seen in a new light and the difference which Bousset correctly recognized between Palestinian and Hellenistic Christianity receives new meaning. The man Jesus came, to be sure, as prophet and teacher. He gave no teaching about his own person, but he said that the fact of his work was the ultimate decisive fact for men. His teaching is not a new teaching because of its conceptual content; for in its content it does not differ from pure Judaism, from the pure prophetic teaching. The unheard of thing is that he is speaking *now*, in the final, decisive hour. What is decisive is not *what* he proclaims but *that* he is proclaiming it. *Now* is the time, and

> Blessed is he who takes no offence at me (Matt. 11.6).
> And I tell you every one who acknowledges me before men,
> the Son of man will also acknowledge before the angels of God.
> But he who denies me before men
> will be denied before the angels of God (Luke 12.8f.; cf. Mark 8.38).

Whether Jesus knew himself as Messiah or not is unimportant. Such a knowledge would only mean that he recognized the decisive character of his work and related it to a contemporary Jewish concept. But his call to decision certainly implies a christology – not as metaphysical speculation about a heavenly being nor as a characterization of his personality somehow endowed with a Messianic consciousness, but a christology which is proclamation, summons.

When the *primitive community* calls him Messiah, they are showing in their own fashion that they have understood him. The great enigma of New Testament theology, *how the proclaimer became the proclaimed*, why the community proclaimed not only the content of his preaching, but also and primarily Christ himself, why Paul and John almost wholly ignore the content of his preaching – that enigma is solved by the realization that it is the fact, '*that* he proclaimed', which is decisive.

There appeared to be an 'enigma' only because attention was focused on 'religio-ethical' concepts and on the world-view instead of on the event itself. Then the existence of a double gospel was claimed, two proclamations with different ideas were alleged, and a development which was determined by the history of ideas or by other external causal relations, was postulated. This concept of development was correct in so far as it was applied to the *forms* of presentation. But the really essential and decisive element was ignored.

The proclaimer must become the proclaimed, because it is the fact *that* he proclaimed which is decisive. The decisive thing is his person (not his personality), *here* and *now*, the event, the commission, the summons. When the primitive community called him Messiah they were confessing that he was the decisive event, the act of God, the inaugurator of the new world. The definitive element in the concept of the Messiah is not the kind of nature which may be ascribed to him. The Messiah is he who in the final hour brings salvation, God's salvation, the eschatological salvation which brings to an end all human ways and wishes and is salvation only for the obedient; for all others it is judgment.

The only task which the future could set for the community was the task of explaining the fact of salvation, of showing first of all how the decision which man must make when confronted by the person, Jesus, has acquired a particular character because of his death on the cross and so of *incorporating the cross in the proclamation*. When mythological representations and cultic concepts of Hellenistic syncretism take the place of the figure of the Messiah in the Hellenistic communities, these are only the means used to express the significance of the person, Jesus, as the decisive, eschatological saving act of God. The unity of Palestinian and Hellenistic Christianity is clear, once it is fully recognized that the *titles* of Jesus were not meant as definitions or descriptions but as a confession of faith.

On the other hand, the difference between the two groups demonstrates the right and the duty of critical investigation, for the difference discloses the secondary character of the concepts used – concepts which depend on the world-view connected with the titles. It also shows that every age and every culture must re-state the decisive act in its own terms, using the representations peculiar to it.

Thus the investigation of New Testament christology leads to a positive conclusion. This christology is proclamation, summons, the proclamation of the fact of salvation. In Jesus Christ God has reconciled the world with himself. Christ is God's Word. When this Word is preached, the hour of decision is here. Whoever hears him, hears the Father; whoever sees him, sees the Father; whoever honours him, honours the Father.

The interpretation of New Testament christology similarly shows also how in the christology of the kerygma a christology is presented which is in fact the explanation of faith's understanding of the new being. It shows how the first proclaimers solved the problem with which the church is faced afresh in every age, the problem of framing a christology which meets the requirement: *hoc est Christum cognoscere, beneficia eius cognoscere.*

12

THE CONCEPT OF THE WORD OF GOD IN THE NEW TESTAMENT[1]

THE QUESTION which underlies the following discussion does not ask how the New Testament understands the phenomenon which *we* call 'God's Word'. What is to be investigated is rather what the New Testament means when *it* speaks of the 'Word of God' (or 'words of God', the 'voice of God', 'God speaks'). This question requires the questioner to determine accurately the historical possibilities available to the New Testament writers and therefore to examine the linguistic usages of 'word' and of 'word of God' according to which the New Testament statements relating to the Word of God are made.[2]

I. *The Terminology in the Old Testament and Judaism*

For the Old Testament use of 'word of God,' two points are significant:

1. 'God's word' can be equivalent to God's action or God's acts.[3]

---

[1] Unpublished. Cf. 'Vom Worte Gottes [On the Word of God]', *DT* III (1931), pp. 14–18.

[2] Consequently the question here is different from that asked in my discussion, 'The Concept of Revelation in the New Testament', 1929 (see p. 228, n. 10). There the question asked was what the New Testament has to say about what *we* call revelation, and the investigation of the New Testament ideas necessarily started from the consideration of the preliminary understanding of revelation which prompted the question. Here, on the contrary, a historical investigation is the first requisite.

But such a historical investigation also serves indirectly to criticize and clarify our present understanding of 'word'. For the areas whose terminology must be investigated not only set the conditions for the New Testament use of the term but also demonstrate specific possibilities for understanding 'word'.

[3] God's word and God's action stand in synonymous parallelism, e.g. Pss. 33.4; 145.13.

2. 'God's word' can mean God's counsel, God's command.

Both meanings can be traced back to a primitive conception of '*word*'. *The word possesses power;* and like the word of a man who holds power, the word of God is effective[4] merely by being spoken. 'By the breath of his mouth' God brings all things to life.[5] And it is said of his word (as is said in Babylonian and Assyrian) that it has immutable force and perpetuity.[6]

It is not always clear how far the 'word of God' is thought of as audible,[7] as articulate divine speech, or how far the 'word' does not mean simply the manifestation of God's power. In the course of time the idea that God actually uttered words, of course, vanishes, as is clear from the metaphorical phrases: God 'sends' his word; the word 'falls', etc.[8]

How should this fact be understood? Why is the *manifestation of God's power* called his *word*? I do not mean this as a psychological or ethnological question about the way the idea of the word as an active power may be explained from the idea of the magic word. Rather, the question is how the phenomenon of the word in this usage is to be primarily regarded. Here the aspect which is definitive for the concept of word is that *it is spoken* – not its content. What is definitive is that the Word of God is spoken, that it is an event in time – not that it conveys eternal truth.[9] And the Word is certainly a word spoken *to*. . . . It is direct address, not a logical judgment. And as the Word of God, it is a command:

> For he spoke and it came to be;
> He commanded and it stood forth (Ps. 33.9).

Now when events in nature and in the world are attributed to the Word of God, God's Word is his contingent, voluntary act of power. It has no relation to the 'Logos' (λόγος) in the sense of the conforming of all events to law. But God's Word is not addressed only to the objects of nature which he calls

---

[4] E.g. the word of the king; Isa. 11.2–4; or of the prophet, II Kings 1.10ff.; Num. 22–24.

[5] Ps. 33.6; cf. Isa. 40.26.   [6] Isa. 40.8; 45.23; 55.10f.

[7] E.g. thunder as the voice of Yahweh, Ps. 29.3–9.

[8] Isa. 9.7; Ps. 107.20.

[9] It is, of course, obvious that the Word has a content with meaning. God *says what* is to happen; and *what* he says, then happens. The opposite conception of magic, in which only the sounds, the meaning of which may be unintelligible, constitute the 'word', was already discarded.

into being and rules through the Word. Man also receives this
Word of God who rules nature, as a word speaking to him.
God speaks to man in the events of nature. God's manifestation of power in nature is God's Word to man, since the might
which confronts man in nature 'says something' to him and
because the man 'lets something be said' to him by that Word.
He lets himself be told that he as a creature is dependent on a
power which governs the world, which is manifest to him in
violent natural events in such overwhelming force that he
must flee to God and glorify him.[10]

But God's Word is also 'word' in the ordinary sense, as a
word spoken in human speech, audible and understandable
to men, giving authoritative *direction* to men, as the word of the
prophet or priest. Man has been told what is right (Micah 6.8);
God's commands are his 'words' (II Chron. 29.15); and the
Ten Commandments are often called simply the 'ten words'.[11]

The connection between the two meanings is obvious;
God's Word is always his sovereign command. The inner
relation appears clearly in Ps. 147.15–19:

> He sends forth his command to the earth;
>   his words run swiftly.
> He gives snow like wool;
>   he scatters hoar frost like ashes.
> He casts forth his ice like morsels;
>   who can stand before his cold?
> He sends forth his word and melts them;
>   he makes his wind to blow and waters flow.
> He declares his word to Jacob,
>   his statutes and ordinances to Israel.

Such a description of God's Word requires as a basis a
specific understanding of existence. If one looks behind the
primitive conceptions of a word acting with power and the
words of inspired prophets or priests and seeks to learn what is
revealed about man's understanding of himself by such presentations, and if one then considers the meaning of this
conception of God and of his Word, it becomes clear that

---

[10] Pss. 29 or 145.

[11] Ex. 34.28; Deut. 4.13, etc. Philo and Josephus also call the Ten
Commandments 'the ten words' (οἱ δέκα λόγοι). The 'word' (*dābār*) of
Yahweh and his Torah, his 'judgments' (*mišpātīm*) and his 'commands'
(*miṣwōt*) or 'precepts' (*piqquotim*) stand in parallelism.

God's Word designates God as he is present and accessible for men. *God's Word is God* in so far as he calls man into being, limits him, and enigmatically encompasses him.

God's Word is God's act, not because the Word is reasonable but precisely because it is incomprehensible. But God's Word is God also in so far as he claims men by an understandable command under which man stands. Therefore God's Word consigns man to darkness, but at the same time in a specific way brings him into the light. The two effects are inter-related. As the Word of God in nature gives life and destroys life, so the word of the law 'is no trifle for you, but it is your life and thereby you shall live long' (Deut. 32.47).[12]

God's incomprehensible, terrifying and arbitrarily benign power in nature *says* something to men, directs him to his real place. Man, confronted by the enigmatic God, understands himself as a dependent creature. And God's word as direction for his life is in fact understandable in its content but unverifiable in its motivations. God's commands can no more be deduced from an ethical concept than his sovereign power can be deduced from natural law. In relation to both, man knows himself dependent on the power and will of God. The Word of God does not thereby acquire the significance of an epitome of theology as a teaching about God and the world. Not by observation (θεωρία), but in hearing, does a man win understanding of himself. God's Word teaches him on each occasion to understand his *now*.

In *later Judaism*, the formal sense of 'God's Word' is the same. Both in the Apocrypha and with the rabbis, God's Word is his creating Word.[13] It is often stated that God's Word has power.[14] The Targum's substitution of God's *Memra* (Word) for *God* in the Old Testament text is well known.[15]

---

[12] Cf. Deut. 30.19. With the word of the law the either-or of death and life is set before the eyes of the people. And by the word of the prophet, according to Jer. 21.8, the people are confronted with the same either-or. Therefore the promise is also bound up with the command; cf. Prov. 19.16: 'He who keeps the commandment keeps his life; he who despises the word will die.'

[13] In the Targum, the text frequently speaks of creation through the word where the Old Testament uses general terms in relation to the creative activity of God.

[14] Cf. Wisdom 12.9; 16.26; 18.15f.

[15] Jewish scholars and Billerbeck rightly deny that the 'Word of God' is

In Judaism this conception is certainly subordinated to the dominating idea that the law is the Word of God.[16] The Word of the law is also thought of as exerting power; this is evident from the way in which the written words of the law were used as amulets.[17] But primarily the written and transmitted words of the Torah were considered as God's Word in the sense of his command. God's Word is accepted unquestioningly as his summons to man; it is God's demand upon him. Man can neither exercise control over it nor ask the reason for it.

Even if at a specific time, God's Word sounds no more and no more prophets appear,[18] yet the Word, which in the written law lies before men's eyes, has not lost its character of event. The Torah does not contain eternal truths and is not the embodiment of a timeless moral law. It is spoken by God to Moses and is being spoken again in the Jewish community. It confronts the individuals of the community as a summons of God which requires obedience.[19] Consequently, even in Judaism the 'Word of God' has not become an epitome of doctrine or of a religious view of the world. God's Word is not directed to the intellect but to the will. It is not seen but heard. Not scientific investigation but obedience makes it understandable.

Jesus' conception of the Word of God remains within the frame of the Old Testament-Jewish conception. For him, it is self-evident that God's commanding Word confronts man in the Old Testament.[20] But it is also self-evident for him as a prophet sent from God, that God acts in the present through the word

---

hypostasized in the Targum. But it is equally wrong to understand the use of *Memra* as simply a convention of translation, 'an abbreviation of the designation of God as "He spoke and the world came into being" '. It is, in fact, clear that the old meaning of a word acting with power is definitive for the meaning of *Memra*. Just as in the Old Testament word (*dābār*) and spirit (*ruaḥ*) occur frequently in parallelism, so in the Targum *ruaḥ* is often replaced by mēmrā', and thus *mēmrā'* is often used in parallelism with 'might' (*g^ebūrāh*), 'will' (*r^{ec}ūtā'*) and especially with *š^ekīnāh*. That is, God's Word is the manifestation of his power, the real manifestation of God. It is God present, the *praesens numen*.

[16] Cf. Ecclus. 24.23; 36.2; Baruch 4.1.

[17] The *mezuzim*, small boxes which contained a parchment roll (cf. Deut. 6.4–9; 11.13–21), were fastened to the right door-post of the house. Cf. W. Bousset, *Die Religion des Judentums*[3], Berlin, 1926, p. 179.

[18] The *Bath Qol* may be ignored in this connection.

[19] This is the reason for the non-historical exegesis which relates the whole law to the present time.

[20] Cf. Mark 7.13, 'making void the word of God through your tradition'.

which he, Jesus, speaks. In the Synoptic tradition, Jesus is presented as preaching and teaching, as speaking the Word; and the Christian community collects and transmits his words. There is no doubt that he recognized himself as proclaimer of the Word. Admittedly, the characterization of his preaching as 'gospel' (εὐαγγέλιον) may belong to the Hellenistic community; and the verb 'preach the gospel' (εὐαγγελίζεσθαι) may first have been put in his mouth by the community.[21] The scene (Luke 4.16–30), in which Jesus presents himself as the messenger of good tidings prophesied in Isa. 61.1f., may also be a creation of the community. But even so, there is no doubt at all that he is bringing the message as commissioned by God: God's kingdom is at the door, it is even now breaking in. He comes with the Word; the Word and nothing else is the instrument of his work.[22]

Jesus brings, not rites and practices, but the Word. And he brings the Word, not as a teaching about God, a world-view, but as a call to repentance before the coming kingdom of God. He proclaims the will of God. His Word is summons, a call to decision. Nothing that he says is new; but when he speaks, the hour is the decisive hour, the *now* when the Word is spoken, the event of the Word.

Everything depends on hearing this Word. He who has ears to hear, let him hear! Take care what you hear! Hear and hold it fast![23] The hearing, therefore, is not a mere physical act; it is obedience which entails action. He who hears and does nothing, who is like the man building on sand, has really not heard at all, although he has ears.[24] For the Word of God is the will of God. Instead of Mark's 'who does the *will* of God' (3.35), Luke has (8.21) 'who hear the word of God and do it'.[25] That is true exegesis. Man encounters the will of God in God's Word, and to accept this will is the only way to understand it. Nothing else establishes a relation to the Word, nothing guarantees its authority other than the Word itself as it is spoken. Jesus rejects the demand to authenticate himself by a wonder (Mark 8.11f.). He does not appeal to his personal

[21] It occurs only once in the 'sayings source', Matt. 11.5; Luke 7.22. Also cf. J. Schniewind, *Euangelion*, Gütersloh, 1927, 1931.

[22] Cf. A. Schlatter, *Die Geschichte des Christus*, Stuttgart, 1921, p. 135.

[23] Mark 4.9, etc.; Luke 4.24; Mark. 7.14.

[24] Matt. 7.24–27; Mark 8.18; 4.12.   [25] Cf. Luke 11.28.

qualities. The Word alone, as it confronts the hearer in the summons, demands decision. This Word has the power which belongs to the will of God. For in the hearer's decision, the fate of the hearer is decided.

> For whoever is ashamed of me and of my words
> in this adulterous and sinful generation,
> of him will the Son of Man be ashamed
> when he comes in the glory of the Father with the holy angels
>
> (Mark 8.38).

The way in which Luke in 12.8f. has 'who acknowledges me before men . . . and who denies me before men' instead, shows that the person of Jesus is merged in his words. This means also that his Word is event, an event which is the power and will of God, like the prophetic word in Israel.

II. *Greek and Hellenistic Terminology*

Of course, the Greek world also knows the magic word, the potent formula, and knows also the word of the oracle, the inspired divine word. Paramount for Greek usage, however, is the meaning of *Logos* (word) as *the meaningful content of what is said*. Thus the *word* is not primarily regarded as the event of its being spoken, but as possessing comprehensible meaning. The original meaning of λέγειν (say) is not 'summon' but 'explain'.[26]

The dominant meaning of *Logos* is 'declaration' (ἀπόφανσις); the word makes its contents known. That the Logos does this in audible words, by being spoken, is therefore secondary and can be wholly disregarded. *Logos* acquires the sense of proof, of cause. It is the meaning, not the being spoken, which is constitutive. The single spoken Logos acquires its validity as

---

[26] The root meaning of λέγειν is *colligere* = gather up; but in the sense of a selective gathering, cf. Homer, *Odyssey* 24, 107f., 'it is even as though one should choose out and gather together (κρινάμενος λέξαιτο) the best warriors of the city' [Lang's translation]. In the further development of the usage, the element of judging (κρίνειν) in the gathering was emphasized, so that λέγειν acquires the sense of estimating, classifying, analysing, explaining. Cf. E. Hofmann, *Qua ratione* ἔπος, μῦθος, αἶνος, λόγος . . . *adhibita sint*, Dissertation, Göttingen, 1922. Cf. also Frag. 56 (Epicharmus), Diels, *Fragmenta der Vorsokratiker*, I, p. 129, lines 8f.: 'Life requires of men much calculation (λογισμοῦ) and number (ἀριθμοῦ); we live by number and calculation; these are the salvation of mortals.'

Logos because it is linked to the general Logos (κοινὸς λόγος), to the timeless meaning of the whole. So long as that connection is not explicitly made for the 'calculation' (λογισμῷ), even a 'true judgment' (ἀληθὴς δόξα), an interpretation true in itself, has only relative value.[27] Since the significance of the Logos lies in what is said, in its content, not in its being spoken, Logos can be used alone without an explanatory genitive. But the Word in the Old Testament, as the word of a specific speaker, requires a genitive – either expressed or implied.

In Greek, therefore, Logos does not have the character of a summons. In fact, the idea of summons is wholly absent. Anyone who listens to the discourse of a philosopher should agree with the Logos – not with the *philosopher*. Anyone who hears the Logos does not feel any claim upon him which arises out of the immediate situation confronting him. If he does become inwardly conscious of a claim, it is a claim which he understands correctly only when he knows that basically it is he himself who makes the claim in order to transcend his own limited perception (ἰδία φρόνησις). He hears no *Thou*; he hears himself, whose real existence is an existence in the Logos. Therefore Socrates can understand the oracle of the Delphic god, 'know thyself' (γνῶθι σαυτόν), as directing him to the pronouncements of reason (λόγοι).[28] Therefore an absolute claim is never presented by a single Logos, as it is by the Word in the Old Testament. The single statement must always remain open to argument; that is it must always be questioned anew. Therefore the *speaker* has no authority. Each man must listen even to the rocks and trees and decide 'whether they speak the truth' (εἰ μόνον ἀληθῆ λέγοιεν).

This conception of the Logos dominates Greek thought to the end. Man as a living entity possessing reason (ζῷον λόγον ἔχον) has his real existence in the pronouncements of reason (λόγοι), in the Logos. Man does not understand his existence as historical existence which is determined by the interaction of *I* and *Thou*. He seeks to understand his existence in the world from the standpoint of the thinking self. He does not need to 'hear'; he wants to 'see'. The Logos is not summons but declaration (ἀπόφανσις). It is assumed that the being of the cosmos is determined by the same pronouncements of reason

[27] Plato, *Meno* 97C-98A.   [28] Plato, *Phaedo* 96ff.

as is the existence of man. The thinking man finds himself again in the cosmos and finds his particular existence assured thereby. The necessity which governs his thinking is the same necessity which governs the continuance and the operation of the cosmos as a whole. To separate and unite, to measure and limit, to see all things together in a unified design, is the function of the Logos in man, just as it is in the whole which is the cosmos. 'Geometrical accuracy has great power among gods and men' (ἡ ἰσότης ἡ γεωμετρικὴ καὶ ἐν θεοῖς καὶ ἐν ἀνθρώποις μέγα δύναται) (Plato, *Gorgias* 507E–508A). The 'for what purpose' (οὗ ἕνεκα) which directs human thinking also seems to rule in the cosmos and to give it its order (τάξις). Thus the Logos is both proof and basis; it is not merely the evidence of the unified structure of all existing things, but is at the same time the structure itself. So it is understandable that Heraclitus calls the law of all becoming the Logos, and that for Parmenides being and thinking coincide.

Just as for Leucippus Logos and necessity (ἀνάγκη) belong together, so for the Stoics Logos and nature (φύσις) coincide. In this latter combination the Logos-concept acquires a new meaning – a meaning which it had originally at the beginning and which is perhaps still operative in Heraclitus. The Logos is an active force. The problem of the dualism of form and matter – arising out of the conception of the cosmos as a work of craftsmanship (τέχνη) – which occupied Greek philosophy from the beginning, is solved for the Stoics in the sense that the Logos is thought of as spirit (πνεῦμα), as an impalpable matter like air, like fire or ether (αἰθήρ), which permeates (πνεῦμα διῆκον) the whole world-structure as an energizing force (τονικὴ δύναμις), as 'seminal reason' (λόγος σπερματικός). Thus the comprehensible and calculable form and the seminal force of nature are united in concept. This Logos which is the universal law of nature (κοινὸς νόμος φύσεως) and which makes the cosmos a living organism (ζῷον ἔμψυχον) is for the individual, as right reason (λόγος ὀρθός), the law (νόμος) to which he must give explicit assent (συγκατάθεσις) in order that he may realize his own identity with the world-Logos.

In the Stoic view, the Logos is immanent world law; but on the other hand the individual encounters it as something which belongs outside the world, since he must always first establish a relation with it. It is this dual conception which provides the link with *the further development of the idea of the Logos*. On the one hand, the conception of the Logos as a divine force immanent in the world is firmly held; on the other hand, the transcendence of the Logos in relation to every particular entity, every empirical phenomenon is emphasized. This transcendence is stressed especially in relation to the human individual who ought to find his real self in the Logos, but who can fail to do so. Also under the influence of the Platonic and Aristotelian tradition, the deity came to be thought of as more and more separated from the world. When God and the world were thus torn apart, the Logos gained a unique intermediate position. For while the Logos belongs with God whom it represents and for whom it deputizes in the world, it also belongs to the world which has its actuality and order in the Logos.

The separate stages and the many variations in the development of cosmological dualism cannot be detailed here.[29] They are designated by the names of the authors who wrote on the 'cosmos': Plutarch, Numenius, Plotinus, the Corpus Hermeticum, and also Philo and the gnostics.

The most important factors are the following:

1. The approach of Greek thought in understanding deity and world as a unity from the viewpoint of matter and form is abandoned; and for the dualism of matter and form is substituted the *dualism of two substances*, the divine and the earthly. The cosmos results from the mixture of the two. The relation of the divine forces, or of the divine force, in this mixture to the transcendent deity can be thought of only in the concept of emanation.

2. Mythologies were available as a means of making intelligible the conception of the Logos as intermediary between God and man, so that the Logos becomes a half personalized and finally a wholly personalized being. The Logos is also classed with such divine figures as have *cosmic and soteriological* functions. The Logos still includes whatever man can comprehend as ordering the world, such as forces and laws, forms and patterns. And since in these forces and patterns, the otherwise

---

[29] The substitution of the term 'mind' (νοῦς) for Logos makes no real difference.

invisible and unknowable God can be discerned, the Logos is the revealer of God.

This, however, brings about a modification in the idea of the Logos. The fact that the Logos has been spoken becomes important. Hence the Logos is Hermes sent to men by the gods as herald (κῆρυξ) and messenger (ἄγγελος) to make the will of God known (Cornutus).

In fact, the ancient belief in the power of the word again comes to the fore, and the Logos is understood as the potent, effective word of the primal deity. The Logos becomes the creator of the world. And as the concept of the Logos is influenced more and more by the analogy of the holy word in the mysteries – the word which is both a magic formula and traditional teaching – the knowledge which the Logos communicates as revealer becomes less and less knowledge of the world and its laws, and acquires more and more the sense of a mysterious doctrine which presents a mixture of traditional science and mythological speculation. The more radically the knowledge imparted by the Logos is thought of as supernatural, the more the Logos must be conceived as a person, as the 'son' of the highest god, the god who rules, unknowable, beyond the world, and as the one 'sent' by that god.

Is an analogy to the 'Word of God' in the Old Testament to be found here? The mythological hypostasizing of the 'word' can be ignored. The fundamental factor is that here 'being spoken' does pertain to the word and that it is this spoken word which shows man his place in the world and his road to salvation. But in the Greek concept the decisive characteristic is lacking. *The word is not a summons in the true sense and it is not a temporal event in a specific situation, an event in a specific history.* In the Greek view everything still rests on content, on the mysterious wisdom.[30] The spoken word has its significance not as a summons but as a mysterious source of the teaching which supposedly cannot originate in human wisdom. Symptomatic of that understanding is the idea of the *silence* of the deity, which corresponds to the idea of the word.[31] The 'silence'

[30] In the Hermetic writings there are, of course, single passages in which the word of revelation, preaching repentance, has the character of direct address. But the summons puts no compulsion on the man addressed.

[31] Cf. Ignatius, *Magn.* 8.2, 'That there is one God, manifesting himself

is the depth of the deity which is unknowable to man, the
hidden deity (*deus absconditus*). The Logos is his revelation,
deity revealed (*deus revelatus*).

For the Old Testament, God is present to men specifically
in the word and only in the word. But in gnosis there is an
insistent longing to reach beyond the Logos to the silence of
God. So also for Philo, the Logos can guide only to the threshold
of the vision of God. The goal is the silence; and in cultic or
ecstatic silence, man is really with God. In the Old Testament,
on the contrary, it is precisely by the word that man is relegated to the place which belongs to him before God, the place
in which he actually exists. In the preaching of Jesus, the
Word of God is not separate from God; but God is understood
as 'united by a real and true will' with his Word, so that his
Word 'is the supreme power and the highest good'.[32]

III. *The Word of God in the New Testament*

For the New Testament, the use of 'word' which prevails in
the Old Testament, in Judaism and in Jesus' preaching is
definitive. The primitive meaning, according to which the
spoken word exerts power and acts as a magic word, appears
partly in its original form, partly in a derivative application.[33]
Thus God's Word is known as the powerful word of creation
and correspondingly as the *word of* annihilating *judgment*.[34]
God's Word is also his command which, in conjunction with the
promise, is spoken in the Old Testament.[35] That the words of
God in the Old Testament are summons and not theological
teaching nor a world-view to be accepted after observation and

---

through Jesus Christ, his Son, who is his Word (λόγος) coming from silence'
(ἀπὸ σιγῆς).

[32] A. Schlatter. *Die Geschichte des Christus*, Paderborn, 1921, p. 136.

[33] Jesus' words which healed the sick were preserved as 'unintelligible
sounds' (ῥήσεις βαρβαρικαί): Mark 5.41; 7.34. For wonder-working words cf.
further, Matt. 8.8, 16; Luke 4.36; Acts 5.5. The word has sacramental
force, Eph. 5.26; I Tim. 4.5; cf. also Rev. 6.9; 12.11. For a derivative use,
cf. John 15.3; 17.17.

[34] Word of creation, II Peter 3.5, 7; Heb. 1.3; 11.3. Word of judgment,
Rom. 9.28 (after Isa. 10.22f.); Heb. 4.12; II Peter 3.7.

[35] God's command as contained in the Old Testament, e.g. Acts 7.38;
Heb. 2.2; 4.2. God's word of promise, e.g. Rom. 3.2; 9.6, 9; I Cor. 15.54;

intellectual consideration is taken for granted; but it is also expressly stated.[36]

The concept of the 'Word of God' is understood in the same way when it refers to that for which it generally stands in the New Testament – *the Christian kerygma*.[37] It is a Word which has power,[38] which acts with power.[39] For this Word it is essential that it be spoken. It is proclaimed and it must be heard.[40] It is prophecy, it is command; and it must be performed, it must be kept.[41]

The concept of the Word of God in its normative sense is therefore not new in the New Testament. But in distinction to the Old Testament, the New Testament does not speak of the Word of God as a force acting in natural events, except for an occasional mention of creation by the Word.[42] The concept of the Word of God in the New Testament is almost exclusively described as spoken in human speech to men.

The speaking which is God's Word differentiates itself from

[36] Rom. 3.19; 15.4; I Cor. 10.11. Scripture, like the contemporary preacher, dispenses the 'word of exhortation' (Acts 13.15; Heb. 13.22). This conception gives rise to unhistorical and allegorical exegesis. The Word of God in the Old Testament is addressed to the present time.

[37] The kerygma as the 'word of God': I Cor. 14.36; II Cor. 2.17; 4.2; Acts 4.29, 31; Rev. 1.9; 3.8 etc. (The 'Word of Christ': Col. 3.16; Heb. 6.1. 'Word of the Lord': I Thess. 1.8; I Peter 1.25; Acts 8.25, etc.) 'The Word', without a genitive, is used for the Christian kerygma: Gal. 6.6; Col. 4.3; James 1.21ff.; Luke 1.2, etc. Other phrases are: 'the word of the kingdom' Matt. 13.19; 'of the cross' I Cor. 1.18; 'of truth' Eph. 1.13 (cf. Col. 1.5); II Tim. 2.15; James 1.18; 'of life' Phil. 2.16 (Acts 5.20; John 6.68); 'of salvation', Acts 13.26 (Eph. 1.13); 'of reconciliation' II Cor. 5.19; 'of his grace' Acts 14.3; 20.32; cf. 'the word (τὸ ῥῆμα) of faith' Rom. 10.8 (Gal. 3.2, 5) *et al.*

[38] It is said of the Word that it 'works effectually' I Thess. 2.13; that it 'speeds on' II Thess. 3.1; 'increases' Acts 6.7; 12.4 *et al.*; 'bears fruit' Col. 1.16. It 'abides for ever' I Peter 1.25 (after Isa. 40.8). Cf. further statements such as Acts 20.32; James 1.18, 21; I Peter 1.23.

[39] Cf. phrases like 'word of life', etc., n. 37 above.

[40] 'Preach' (κηρύσσειν) Mark 13.10; 14.9; Rom. 10.8, 14f., etc.; 'preaching' (κήρυγμα) I Cor. 1.21; 2.4, etc.; 'preacher' (κῆρυξ) I Tim. 2.7; II Tim. 1.11; 'proclaim' (καταγγέλλειν) Acts 13.5, etc.; 'preach the gospel' and 'gospel' (εὐαγγελίζεσθαι and εὐαγγέλιον) often; 'speak' (λάλειν) Acts 4.29, 31, etc.; 'speak', (ἀποφθέγγεσθαι) Acts 2.4, 14; 26.25 *et al.*; 'hear' (ἀκούειν) Rom. 10.14, 18; Gal. 4.21, etc.; 'hearing' (ἀκοή = preaching) Rom. 10.16f.; Gal. 3.2, 5, etc.

[41] 'Do' (ποιεῖν) Luke 8.21 (James 1.22f.); 'keep' (τηρεῖν) John 8.51f., 55, etc.; 'keep' (φυλάττειν) Luke 11.28; John 12.47; 'pay close attention' (to what has been heard) (προσέχειν τοῖς ἀκουσθεῖσιν) Heb. 2.1.

[42] Cf. above, pp. 297, n. 34.

other human speech by not having its origin in human considerations and human intentions; it comes from God. It has validity therefore as given by God, as inspired, as the work of the Spirit. But this does not mean that the event of the spoken Word is viewed as a psychic experience; not is it given as a criterion by which God's Word can be distinguished from other words.

The psychic experience which sometimes occurs is merely an indication that the word is divinely determined and is authoritative. The Word is not thought of as an expression of a condition of soul or of personal character. It is not manifest to the observer that it is a work of the Spirit; but for the hearer its validity as such is established. Since in the primitive outlook of the period and environment of the New Testament all phenomena which appear abnormal or supranormal are always referred directly to a superhuman cause, ecstatic speech appears to be the work of the Spirit. But since the question can be raised whether the Spirit of God or a demonic spirit produces such speech, it is clear that the psychic manifestation as such does not prove a speech to be God's Word. That question must be decided by the content of what is said or by its significance for the community (I Cor. 12).

Therefore, although God's Word can sound clearly in ecstatic speech and the supernatural origin can thus be guaranteed, this form does not prove the origin to be from God. Exactly as in the Old Testament, on the one hand the ecstasy of the prophet does not guarantee his authorization by God; and on the other hand, the Word of God is certainly not to be heard only in the prophet's ecstatic speech. It is also heard in his 'intelligent' ordinary speech and in the dry words of the law. The same holds also in the New Testament. Against the temptation to recognize God's Word, particularly in ecstatic speech, Paul contends by setting limits to the 'speaking in a tongue' and subordinating it to speaking 'with the mind' (ἐν νοΐ: I Cor. 4.19).[43]

[43] When Paul claims to give directions to the community as one who has 'the Spirit of God' (I Cor. 7.40), he is not thinking at all of ecstatic speech. Nor is that the meaning when he says 'we impart this in words not taught by human wisdom but taught by the Spirit' (I Cor. 2.13). Nor is ecstatic speech meant when it is stated (Acts 6.10) that no one could 'withstand the wisdom and the spirit' in which Stephen spoke. Nor is it meant

The primary meaning of the gift of the Spirit to men is not a man's psychic condition but a way of 'walking' (περιπατεῖν), a conditioning of the whole way of life. Every act of brotherly service and every achievement in the community is referred to the Spirit. So not only ecstatic speech but also every prayer and hymn, every prophetic and edifying discourse, is a gift of the Spirit.[44]

From the outside there is no way to discover what in human speech is God's Word. *God's Word is always summons* and is understood as God's Word only when the summons is understood and *heard* in the real sense of the word. Therefore God's Word has no authentication; it demands recognition. From a neutral standpoint it cannot be understood as God's Word; 'the unspiritual man does not receive the gifts of the Spirit of God for they are folly to him and he is not able to understand them because they are spiritually discerned' (I Cor. 2.14).

This 'spiritual discernment', however, is only possible where the man allows the judgment of 'folly' to be pronounced on *his own* wisdom, where he renounces every criterion by which he might identify God's proclamation and prove it to be God's wisdom. For that would mean that he himself would be doing the speaking and would be listening to himself. It would mean the demand that God should authenticate himself to men. Therefore it is possible to hear God's Word only where man renounces all 'boasting' (καυχᾶσθαι) and accepts the 'folly' of the 'word of the cross' as God's Word: where, therefore, a man allows God's Word to be pure summons, where it is the question before which all a man's own questioning ceases. The same idea is expressed in II Cor. 4.3f.: 'And even if our Gospel is veiled, it is veiled only to those who are perishing. In their case, the god of this world has blinded the minds of the un-

---

when, according to Mark 13.11; Matt. 10.19f., the Spirit speaks in confessors brought to trial.

[44] In I Cor. 14.14-16, 'in the spirit' means 'in ecstasy'. But this interpretation is to be made only because of the antithesis to 'in the mind'. Actually, in chs. 12 and 14, Paul ascribes all Christian speaking to the Spirit. And it is specifically in response to the intelligent speech, which convinces (ἀνακρίνειν) and convicts (ἐλέγχειν), that the 'outsider' (ἰδιώτης) and the 'unbeliever' (ἄπιστος) must confess, 'God is really among you' (14.25).

believers, to keep them from seeing the light of the gospel of the glory of Christ.' This is true because the preaching is directed to the conscience of the unbeliever.[45]

But at the same time the New Testament affirms that the Word of God, although it is subject to no human criterion and is in itself authoritative, is still an *understandable* word. It does not work by magic, nor is it a dogma which demands blind submission or the acceptance of absurdities.[46] To be true summons, a word must necessarily reveal man to himself, teach him to understand himself – but not as a theoretical instruction about the self. The event of the summons discloses to the man a situation of existential self-understanding, a possibility of self-understanding which must be grasped in action. Such a summons does not give me a free choice of this or that in case I wish to make a choice. It requires decision, it gives me the choice of myself, the choice of who I will be through the summons and my response to it.

Thus the Word of God has the same character in the New Testament as in the Old. It is not an oracle which would give me light and direction while I consider the possibilities of my activity in the world. Rather it confronts me with my 'salvation' (σωτηρία) or 'destruction' (ἀπώλεια), with 'life' or 'death', with 'justification' or 'condemnation'. But the Word is not instruction explaining these possibilities in general, either as ethical teaching, 'a way of life' and 'a way of death', or as a scientific or a mysterious world-view. In the instant of the proclamation and the hearing of it, the way to life and the way to death are opened to me.

In other words, the preaching demands *faith*. But this faith does not mean that the man accepts the Word and then afterwards so directs his living by it that it leads to 'life'. It is this faith itself which gives life and rescues from death. As men who have received life through the Word alone, Christians are termed 'called' (κλητοί), and as those who through

---

[45] II Cor. 4.2, 'we would commend ourselves to every man's conscience'; 5.11, 'and I hope it is known also to your conscience'.

[46] Paul subsumes even the incomprehensible 'tongues' under the principle of comprehensibility, not only because they are to be interpreted into intelligible speech in the community, but also because he considers them to be a sign for unbelievers – that is, they are a phenomenon which 'says' something to them (I Cor. 14.22).

the Word alone have received life they are termed 'believers' (πιστεύσαντες) or 'believing' (πιστεύοντες).

It must, therefore, be made still clearer that *this faith is really an understanding.* For if the theme and intent of the Word is intelligible to every man, then since the Word brings life, salvation, justification, it must also be understandable how these possibilities become open in this specific Word. The answer is: the Word is the Word of life because it proclaims as life *forgiveness, justification.* Throughout the New Testament it is assumed that every hearer can understand what forgiveness is and can understand that forgiveness is life. This holds true since it is assumed that every man, when he asks about his salvation, must be asking about *God.* And if he asks about God, he is asking about his *Lord* to whom he is *accountable.* And he must recognize himself to be a *sinner* before God. Therefore the Word of God has the power to show man his sins and at the same time to forgive his sins. This power is what characterizes the Word of God. But the Word can do this only as true summons, by asking the hearer whether he is willing so to understand himself, whether he is willing to see his real situation before God, and therefore whether he is willing to understand the Word, which confronts him here and now, as God's Word. This Word is pure summons and carries no authentication; it presents no proof. It is to be understood, not as a *theory* about the grace of God, but as God's *act* of grace, now being performed, whether it brings life or death. It is the Word of life as it is the Word of judgment.

The possibility of understanding the Word coincides with man's possibility of understanding himself. He is asked whether he *wills* to understand himself as he is told by the Word. He *can* understand himself in this way; and therein lies the sole criterion for the truth of the Word. Or, more accurately stated – the man who asks for a criterion is referred back to that alone, and the task of preaching, therefore, is to present the Word in such a way that the possibility of understanding does not appear as a question of theory, of world-view, but becomes an actual possibility which is disclosed by the word and which must be grasped by the will.

In the New Testament this character of the Word is made clear in various ways. Acts 2.37f., for example, shows the pattern: 'Now when they heard this they were cut to the heart, and said to Peter and the rest of the apostles, "Brethren, what shall we do?" And Peter said to them, "Repent, and be baptized every one of you in the name of Jesus Christ for the forgiveness of your sins."' In Corinth, when the Word rings out in the prophetic speech of all the community, then the outsider and the unbeliever 'is convinced of his sin by them all, he is called to account by them all, the secrets of his heart are exposed, and he will fall down on his face and worship God and declare that God is really among you' (I Cor. 14.24f.). Heb. 4.12f. sums it up: 'For the Word of God is living and active, sharper than any two-edged sword, piercing to the division of soul and spirit, of joints and marrow, and discerning the thoughts and intentions of the heart. And before him no creature is hidden, but all are open and laid bare to the eyes of him with whom we have to do.'

How the man who is confronted by the Word can and ought to understand himself is made especially clear in the theology of Paul. First, in relation to the Jews, Paul designates the law as 'the custodian to bring them to Christ'; and declares, 'the Scripture consigned all things to sin that what was promised to faith in Jesus Christ might be given to those who believe' (Gal. 3.22). 'Law came in to increase the trespass; but where sin increased, grace abounded all the more' (Rom. 5.20). In a similar way, Rom. 7.7ff. shows how under grace the situation of the man under the law is clarified, and how the word of grace is intelligible even to one who is under the law.

No difference appears *in relation to the heathen.* The missionary preaching of Paul, the substance of which we learn from Rom. 1.18f., assumes that the heathen have the possibility of understanding the wrath of God which is kindled against them. They have a knowledge that God decrees righteousness (1.32) and 'what the law requires' is 'written on their hearts'; they have a conscience (2.14f.). And since they have a conscience, they can understand the word of forgiveness.

Paul's fight against gnosticism in Corinth shows plainly that for the Christian the decisive factor is the relinquishment of the old self-understanding in which a man trusts his own wisdom and seeks his own glory. In that dispute, the foolishness of the word of the cross is set in opposition to human wisdom; the paradoxical glorification of weakness is set against human pride. The power of God and the life of Jesus are described as manifested in the fact that we are brought to share the death of Jesus.

The character of the Word is presented with the same clarity by John. The Word speaks a language strange to this world (8.43), since it challenges the world's self-understanding, its control over its own possibilities; the Word subverts the jugment of 'sensible men' and demands assent to the verdict that man lives in darkness and sin. Every authentication of the Word is rejected; it is itself 'witness', and there is no other witness beside the Word which man acting under his own control could first test and find correct, so that he could then decide to believe. The Word leaves no time for that. The Word itself constitutes the crisis and when the Word is no longer being spoken – and that time comes – then it is too late.

There is thus no difference between the Old and the New Testament in the characterization of the Word of God as it is encountered in the speech of men. All the characteristics of the Word in the New Testament as they have been given above describe equally the prophetic preaching of the Old Testament.

But if the content of the Word is examined, a difference does seem to emerge. It appears to lie in the fact that in the New Testament, the Word of God is fundamentally *one* word, and not manifold as in the Old Testament. In the New Testament it is always and only the Word of Christ. A problem also appears which has been overlooked. The content of the word as summons is forgiveness, justification, life. But is not the New Testament Word also a communication as well as a summons? And not merely communication about the grace of God which is now offered, but communication about a *historical fact*: the event of Jesus Christ? The question arises, how are summons and communication related? Or, how is the event, Jesus Christ, which occurred in the past, related to the event of the summons which occurs at the present moment? The question of the relation to the Word of the Old Testament and the question of the relation of summons and communication is given an almost schematic answer in Heb. 1.1f.: 'In many and various ways God spoke of old to our fathers by the prophets; but in these last days he has spoken to us by [the] Son.'

But the difference between the New Testament and the Old is not the kind of difference it seems to be at first. In the Old Testament, too, the Word of God is essentially *one* word, because it is God's Word. It is *one in its demand*; it tells man 'what is good; and what does the Lord require of you but to do justice and to love kindness, and to walk humbly with your God?' (Micah 6.8; cf. Amos 5.14f.; Hos. 6.6; Isa. 1.16f.). Likewise it is *one in its promises*; he who acts according to it will live (Deut. 32.47; Prov. 19.16; and cf. above, pp. 289f). In all forms of expression and in all situations one thing is always demanded: that man in complete obedience, without self-glorification, should let God show him his way – the way of right, justice, good. Then truly this Word means both judgment and salvation for men at the same time.

It is, however, more significant that in the Old Testament this command, this threat and promise, is – whether explicitly or not – *at the same time the communication, and indeed communication about historical events*, about what God has done for the nation. The summons is addressed to that nation which God has called and which he has made a nation by the call out of Egypt, the passage through the Red Sea, the giving of the law and the journey through the desert to the land of Canaan. This nation, 'the chosen people', which has this history, is summoned in the Word, and the summons is based (explicitly or not) on what God has done in history. Both command and promise are based on that:

> Yet I destroyed the Amorite before [you] . . .
> Also I brought you up out of the land of Egypt,
> And led you forty years in the wilderness,
> to possess the land of the Amorite.
>
> I raised up some of your sons for prophets
> and some of your young men for Nazirites.
> Is it not indeed so, O people of Israel? (Amos 2.9–13).
>
> But now thus says the Lord,
> he who created you, O Jacob,
> he who formed you, O Israel:
> Fear not, for I have redeemed you;
> I have called you by name, you are mine (Isa. 43.1).

In the Psalms (Pss. 105; 135; 136) God is praised as the One who has led the people throughout its history.

The relation to history is therefore a constitutive characteristic of the Word in the Old Testament. And whatever historical event may be mentioned, whether the liberation from Egypt is carried back in fantasy to the patriarchal age or whether God's acts in the most recent past are recounted, the history is regarded as a unit, as a single act of God out of which the present issues. It is this act of God which gives the present its character and therefore gives character to the Word of God spoken in the present. In this sense, *the Word as summons is also communication.* The two functions form a unity because what is communicated, *the history, is a part of the summons in the present.* Therefore obedient submission under the present encounter of the Word is at the same time fidelity to what God has done in the past for the nation and for the individual. *Faith is obedience which is at the same time fidelity and trust.* Communication of the past, therefore, is not to be considered a historical report, but is a summons in which the past becomes contemporary.

But the history becomes contemporary, not through poetic remembrance,[47] nor through reconstruction by research, but in the tradition which is summons, tradition in which the history itself 'comes to words', as it were becomes the Word. But then it follows that in spite of the 'many and various ways' (Heb. 1.1), the Word of God in the Old Testament is always one and the same Word, simply because it stands in unity with a specific history. What is proclaimed in the Word as God's will, as judgment and as grace, is not a set of general, eternal truths, not an ethical code, not a world-view, but is God's demand at the moment, a demand which stems from a specific history.

Now if *in the New Testament* the only content of the Word of God is *Christ*, his cross and resurrection, a difference from the Old Testament is not to be seen either in the fact that the content of the Word is a single theme, or in the fact that summons and information are combined in the Word. In the New Testament as in the Old the two form a unity.

For Paul, as is immediately clear, *cross* and *resurrection* are to be understood, not as mere facts of the past, but as they become contemporary for the individual in the baptism which is a dying with Christ and a rising again with him. The whole

[47] Naturally the contemporization can easily take a poetic *form*.

life of the believer is a 'being crucified with Christ' (Gal. 2.20), 'always carrying in the body the death of Jesus' (II Cor. 4.10). And since the Christian life is a life of faith, it is at the same time a sharing in Christ's resurrection. The resurrection is not an isolated event in the past; it marks the beginning of a new humanity.

And if, as a corollary, it was possible to understand the Christ event as a cosmic fact analogous to the fateful role of the deity in the mysteries and in gnosis, as a cosmic fact which affects the individual in mysterious fashion through the sacraments, it is still clear that for Paul this possibility of partaking in the saving event is given through the preaching and the faith that hears the preaching. Christ becomes contemporary in the preaching.

The reconciling act of God in the cross of Christ is at the same time the beginning of the 'ministry of reconciliation' (διακονία τῆς καταλλαγῆς) and the 'word of reconciliation' (λόγος τῆς καταλλαγῆς). Christ himself, indeed God himself, summons men in the preaching of the apostle. 'Now then we are ambassadors for Christ, as though God did beseech you by us; we pray in Christ's stead, be ye reconciled to God' (II Cor. 5.20). As the Christ event is the eschatological event which ends the old aeon and begins the new, so the same is true of the preaching of the apostle: 'Behold now is the acceptable time; behold now is the day of salvation' (II Cor. 6.2). In the gospel, as in the preaching of the Word, God's power for salvation is revealed to every one who believes (Rom. 1.16). So the preaching apostle whom God sends through the world so as to reveal through him the fragrance of the knowledge of God is 'the aroma of Christ to God among those who are being saved and among those who are perishing, to one a fragrance from death to death, to the other a fragrance from life to life' (II Cor. 2.15f.). When Paul spreads the Word abroad, he spreads life.[48]

The conception of tradition and of the *church* is based on this

[48] This is basically the theme of II Cor. 2.14 – 6.10. The same thinking prevails in the deutero-Pauline literature. According to the spurious doxology, Rom. 16.25f., the secret of God is revealed in the Christian kerygma. Similarly, according to Col. 1.25ff., the Christian preaching is the 'mystery' which is now revealed. According to II Tim. 1.9ff.; Titus 1.2f., the life which God has given to the world has been revealed through preaching.

assurance that the Christ event is further consummated in the preaching of the Word. Because the content of the Word is not a statement of universal truths, but a specific message, the transmitted tradition of the Word is a part of the saving event, of the act of salvation performed by God. The act is present in this tradition only; and for the sake of this tradition, God has appointed in the 'church' (ἐκκλησία) the proclaimers of the Word (I Cor. 12.28; Eph. 4.11). The community is built on the foundation of the apostles and prophets (Eph. 2.20). The walls of the heavenly city have twelve foundation stones which bear the names of the apostles (Rev. 21.14). The church founded in this tradition is the 'body of Christ'.[49]

If the proclamation of the Word is a continuation of the Christ event, and if Christ is present in the word of the church, then the conception as a whole leads to the affirmation that *Christ is himself the Word*. And that is the meaning of Heb. 1.1f.: God has spoken in Christ. The identification is fully explicit in John, where Jesus is presented *as the Logos, the Word*.

There is no doubt that when Jesus was called Logos, the pattern was provided by the old mythology. The Logos figure of the Prologue of John's Gospel is the figure of the Son of God and the emissary of God who as creator and revealer mediates between God and the world. That figure bears the name of Logos, Word. In that figure the Evangelist has found a way to express what Jesus means to the Christian community; he is God's Word, God's revelation. Admittedly, in the Gospel the use of the title Logos is limited to the Prologue. But the Prologue is not for that reason any less an organic part of the whole, nor is it to be judged as secondary.[50] On the contrary, the whole Gospel is the elaboration of the theme: Jesus is the Word.

All the activity of Jesus is centred in the Word; his works are his words; his words are his works. When he does his Father's will and consummates his work,[51] that work is his speaking the Word, his witnessing to what he has heard and seen with the Father:

---

[49] Cf. I Cor. 12.12ff.; Col. 1.18, 24; Eph. 1.23; 2.16; 4.4; 5.23, 30.

[50] Such a view is certainly mistaken, since the mythology of the Prologue permeates the whole Gospel.

[51] John 4.34; 5.36; 10.25, 32f., 37f.

'My Father is working still, and I am working. (5.17).

> For the Father loves the Son
> and shows him all that he himself is doing;
> and greater works than these will he show him,
> that you may marvel' (5.20).[52]

But of what sort are these works? The Father has put into his hand to 'judge' and to 'give life'. And how is that work done?

> He who hears my word and believes him who sent me
> has eternal life; he does not come into judgment
> but has passed from death to life.
> Truly, truly I say to you, the hour is coming, and now is
> when the dead will hear the voice of the Son of God,
> and those who hear will live (5.24f.).[53]

As one believes *in him*,[54] so also one believes his words, hears his words.[55] As one 'receives' him,[56] so one receives his *Word* or his 'witness'.[57] As one 'abides' in him,[58] so one abides in his *Word*.[59] As he has the *words* of eternal life and his *Word* gives life,[60] as in truth his *words are* life[61] and as his *Word is truth*, so he himself is the truth and the life.[62] As his Word judges,[63] so has the Father given him full power of judgment.[64] Furthermore, he is and becomes all this, not because he is something *of* himself, not because *his* own honour is concerned. If that were so, his witness would not be valid;[65] he would not be the judge.[66] He is judge only because he speaks the *Word*, because he *is* the Word. Therefore the person of the Logos, the Word, in John 1.1 can be identical with the Logos, the 'Word of life' (λόγος τῆς ζωῆς) in I John 1.1. As it was said of Jesus that he 'was manifested' (I John 3.5, 8), the same can be said of 'life' (ζωή) (I John 1.2).

Such an identification establishes the fact that the 'Word' does not represent a complex of ideas. It is not God's Word

---

[52] 3.11, 32; 8.26, 38, 40; 12.49f.; 15.15, etc.

[53] For examples of Jesus' word and work in parallelism cf. 8.28 (cf. v. 38); 14.10; 15.22, 24; 17.4, 6, 8, 14.

[54] πιστεύειν εἰς αὐτόν, 2.11; 3.16, 36; 4.39. πιστεύειν αὐτῷ, 5.38, 46; 8.31, 45f.; 10.37f.; 14.11.

[55] 5.47 or 5.24; 6.60; 8.43.

[56] 1.12; 5.43.

[57] 12.48; 17.8 or 3.11, 32f.

[58] 6.56; 15.4-7.

[59] 8.31; 15.7.

[60] 6.68 or 5.25f.; 8.51f.

[61] 6.63.

[62] 14.6.

[63] 12.48.

[64] 5.22, 57.

[65] 5.31.

[66] 8.15; 12.47.

because of its conceptual content. Jesus does not bring a teaching which one receives from him and which one can afterwards know so that one no longer needs *him*. Men do not go to him as to a hierophant to gain a mysterious wisdom; they *come to him*. He *is* the truth; he *is* the Word. Understanding the Word is therefore not an apprehension of content; it is *faith*. That this faith becomes a reality is not humanly explicable, but can only be called the act of God. Therefore the content of Jesus' Word cannot be separated from its character as event and summons. John in fact emphasizes this so strongly that he records almost nothing from the tradition as the words of Jesus. Almost the whole of what he lets Jesus say is this, *that* he is speaking the words of God.

Therefore the question, what is the Word of God?, cannot be answered by listing specific conceptions. The Word does not consist in timeless ideas – such as the idea of the wrath and grace of God, or the idea of judgment and forgiveness. On the contrary, God's Word comes to pass only where wrath and grace, where judgment and forgiveness become actual events. But John – and the rest of the New Testament with him – asserts that this event is brought about only in the words of men and precisely in that human word which proclaims judgment and forgiveness.

Though such a Word can be only the Word of Jesus, the Word which he himself *is*, this does not mean that the Word is a reproduction of the preserved words of the historical Jesus and that all depends on the question of their historicity and authenticity. Nor does it mean that a word can be proclaimed here and there as the words of Jesus, just as in the Old Testament one prophet stands beside another. In that case, Jesus would be thought of as the 'historical Jesus', as a prophet, not as the 'Word'. That is why John always represents Jesus as saying almost nothing except that he is speaking the Word of God. For John, from beginning to end, Jesus is not meant to be the 'historical Jesus'; he is the 'Word', the Word of the Christian proclamation. Jesus speaks this Christian proclamation, he *is* this proclamation. And this is true because this Word in which judgment and forgiveness, death and life become actual events is initiated, authorized, authenticated by the event Jesus. Therefore nothing needs to be taught about

Jesus except 'that', nothing except *that* in his historical life the event had its beginning and the event continues in the preaching of the community.

Now only at this point is the difference from the concept of the Word of God in the Old Testament to be recognized. In the Old Testament, Word and history are separate. The history is what the nation has experienced, that from which it has come to its present situation; and the word of prophecy or the word of law[67] speaks to this present situation. The unity with the past is established by the fact that the Word which now confronts the nation recalls the past and thereby makes that history contemporary and continues it. But the Word of the Christian proclamation and the history which it communicates coincide, are one. The history of Christ is not history already past, but the history is being consummated in the proclaiming Word. For remembering Jesus does not mean that he is remembered, like Moses, for what he brought to the nation, for what the nation experienced with him and to which it owes fidelity. Jesus himself confronts the hearer in the present Word; for the hearer, the history begins *now*. The recalling of what once happened is only the summons to the establishment of the Word; it is not a reminder of what once happened to me because I am a member of that national community in whose history it occurred. The preaching of the prophets had its basis in the history of the *nation*. The preaching of Jesus has its basis in the ἐκκλησία, in the church which has no history (in the sense that a nation has a history), since it is an eschatological community and stands at the end of all world history. Therefore the individual is not reminded of what God once did for his people and therefore did for him.

But that means that the event of Jesus Christ is the end of the aeon; he is the final Word which God has spoken and is speaking.[68] The history of the proclamation of the Word is not a segment of world history but is consummated outside that history or above it. Therefore for John, Jesus is not a prophet but *the* prophet, or better, the Son. He is God himself revealed

[67] Of course, the Word never loses its character (previously stressed) as a historical event.

[68] So in the New Testament we do not find the Old Testament phrasing, 'The word of the Lord came to . . . .' in relation to the Christian proclamation.

Faith and Understanding

(1.1). Through him alone is God accessible (1.18). Whoever sees him, sees the Father (14.9; 10.44f.). The relation to God becomes manifest, through the relation to him; for he who does not know him, does not know God (5.37f.; 8.19, 42, 47, 54).

Therefore John can also speak of the pre-existence of Jesus and accept the myth of the 'Word' – not only that the Word is the revealer but also that he is the creator. For God is Word; that is, God is revealed in the creation and in the Christian proclamation. The revelation is *one* revelation. He who is revealed in the creation is the same who is revealed in the preaching as light and life.

13

THE PROBLEM OF 'NATURAL THEOLOGY'[1]

IN THE *Catholic* tradition 'natural theology' means the doctrine of God so far as, without revelation, man can have such a doctrine. God is assumed to be knowable to man 'by the light of natural reason' (*lumine naturalis rationis*); that is to say, his existence as the 'originator and avenger of the natural moral law' is knowable.[2] Proof is deduced from the creation[3] and the doctrine provides the foundation for dogmatics, since the propositions of the natural knowledge of God which are reached by rational arguments function as the 'preamble for faith' (*praeambula fidei*).

For *Protestant* theology, such a natural theology is impossible. Not only, nor even primarily, because philosophical criticism has shown the impossibility of giving a proof of God, but especially because this view of natural theology ignores the truth that the only possible access to God is faith. Catholic theology must understand revelation primarily as the communication of doctrines which are superior to the natural knowledge of reason, not in kind but only in degree. God is regarded as an existent entity, of the same kind as the world, an entity which like the phenomena of the world can be an object of knowledge. So – in fidelity to the Stoic tradition – God's being can be proved from the world; and this means that for the Stoics God is fundamentally an existing entity of the same kind as the world. But faith speaks of God as other than the

---

[1] Unpublished.

[2] Joseph Pohle, *Lehrbuch der Dogmatik*, I,[4] Paderborn, 1908, p. 11.

[3] In addition, further proofs are presented from the 'supernatural': the fulfilment of prophecies, the miracles of the Old and New Testaments, Christ and his work, *et al.* (*ibid.*, p. 18.)

world. Faith knows that God becomes manifest only through his revelation and that in the light of that revelation everything which was previously called God is not God.

Equally impossible for Protestantism, however, is the revival of natural theology in *modern theological work*, which, while renouncing the possibility of any proof of God, and refusing to see in God an object of knowledge, wants none-the-less to provide a so-called basis for dogmatics through the philosophy of religion. Such an undertaking makes it necessary to regard religion with its faith in God as a universal human phenomenon, characteristic of humanity as such, whether the approach is by way of the history of religion or the psychology of religion, or whether it is by the attempt to establish a religious *a priori*.

The undertaking therefore results in the transformation of faith, which is understood as religion, into a human attitude, in the elimination of the 'wherein' (Rom. 5.2), and therefore in the elimination of God as the 'Beyond', as the Other in relation to man. Revelation and faith, which constitute the two parts of the relation between God and man, become processes of the soul or of consciousness. The dogmatics for which this kind of investigation was to have furnished the foundation is in fact nullified.

Against every open or veiled affirmation that 'there is a God within us' (*est Deus in nobis*), Protestant theology must insist that God is visible only for faith and that faith is obedient submission to God's revelation in the word of the Christian proclamation. Nevertheless, the problem of natural theology does not cease to exist for Protestant theology. It arises from three facts:

1. From the *fact of understanding*. The Christian kerygma can be understood by the man whom it confronts. The affirmations of faith can obviously be understood as conveying meaning even by the unbeliever.

2. From the *phenomenon of religion*. Even outside Christianity and faith, men speak of God and to him.

3. From the *phenomenon of philosophy*. Philosophy claims to be able to understand the existence of man, and consequently, faith as a function of existence must in some way be within philosophy's field of vision.

I

The fact that *the Christian proclamation can be understood by a man* when he is confronted by it, shows that he has a *pre-understanding* of it. For to understand something means to understand it in relation to one's self, and means to understand one's self with it or in it. Understanding presupposes a coherent life-complex in which the one who understands and what is understood belong together. When something strange and new confronts me in the relationships of my life, it is, as something strange, investigated from within this coherence and is understood by being fitted into it. It is, of course, possible that through this strange new thing, my old understanding of the coherence is made questionable, is shattered and renewed – say, by a stroke of fate, whether fortunate or destructive. But even then the new is understood from the old – even if it negates the old.

Can it now be said that through the revelation not only is the old understanding of life's coherence shattered and reconstructed anew, but also that the coherence itself is so destroyed that no pre-understanding for the new can exist in the old at all? That would be true if the coherence of life were a coherence of nature and consequently the revelation were a natural event. But the life-coherence in which man lives cannot be set up, like an object in nature, as an objective entity to investigate for the purpose of understanding it. On the contrary, the coherence itself is only constituted fully by the understanding.

If faith is an event in historical life, then it comes within life's coherence, which is conditioned by the understanding. And if an understanding in faith is given, an understanding which displaces and replaces all earlier understanding, then that earlier understanding must include a pre-understanding. Otherwise, through revelation and faith, the old man would be completely annihilated and a new man, who had no continuity with the old, would take his place. That would be the view, for example, of the Hellenistic religious revelation in the Corpus Hermeticum. But faith specifically rejects this view when it declares the event of revelation to be the forgiveness of sin. For in the acceptance of forgiveness, man claims his past. Forgiveness involves the continuity of the believer as the new man with the old man. It is he, the man, who believes – 'at once sinner and justified' (*simul peccator, simul iustus*). The sinner is the justified.

Nor does the assertion of dogma that faith is the work of the Holy Spirit who makes the believer a new man deny the continuity. For the man is new simply because he believes, not because he has been given newly existent qualities. Unless the work of the Holy Spirit is to be understood as an act of magic, recognition of that work cannot mean that the act of faith takes place without understanding. On the contrary, man does understand when he is told of sin and grace, when he is called to repentance and love. Anyone who denies that, is no longer talking about the human being who repents, who believes and loves; he is talking about a mysterious something in him or in his stead.

All this does not mean that man carries within himself a special 'organ' responsive to the divine, that a 'better self' is alive in him and serves as a point of contact for the revelation, or anything of that sort. Faith denies that absolutely. Faith knows that man without revelation is wholly a sinner. But unbelief is not an accidental phenomenon appearing in man or the manifestation of a particular organ or capacity (somehow related to religion), any more than faith is. As unbelief governs the whole of man's existence, so also faith is a way of life. Faith, therefore, does not understand the revelation as a new *thing*; faith is understood only when the man understands *himself* anew in it.

Existence in faith comes to be in a new understanding of existence. Similarly, unbelief does not consist in the rejection of single articles of faith, but in an understanding, achieved in existence, of existence itself. Existence is not something which a man possesses and which he can observe on occasion; man is himself existence. Therefore it is equally meaningless to talk of a special 'organ' for the divine in man, of a point of contact for revelation; or on the other hand, to deny that a pre-understanding of faith is given in the old existence and its self-understanding. For faith itself is a way of existing and of the self-understanding given within it. Since this is what faith is and faith as such questions the old self-understanding, it is therefore understanding and understands the revelation. The possibility for man to come to God lies in precisely the fact that he is a sinner. *The revelation can put in question only what is already question-able.* The revelation brings to actuality the questionableness in which human existence, with its natural self-understanding, always stands. That questionableness is not a dogmatic label for existence; it is an active element of existence as mystery.

The task which 'natural theology' might undertake would be to discover how far the unbelieving existence and its self-under-standing is ruled and affected by the questionableness which only becomes clear as such in the understanding of existence in faith. Conscience, for example, would be interpreted as such a phenomenon; and that interpretation corresponds to the fact that the Christian kerygma is addressed to the conscience (II Cor. 4.2). That is why it is possible for the kerygma to be a call to decision and for faith to be a decision.

Just as faith includes an understanding, so also does unbelief, for the same reason. Unbelief includes understanding not only because a man has a pre-understanding of the revelation before believ-ing. It is equally true of unbelief when, confronted by the proclamation, it re-constitutes itself afresh. There are two forms possible for the unbelieving hearing of the proclamation: apparent belief and explicit disbelief.

Consequently, no exegesis or theology which interprets or explicates the affirmations of the proclamation and of faith is assured of being itself in possession of faith. By admitting that it may itself be without faith, it also admits that to a degree the achievement of believing understanding is possible outside faith. This is true because faith as a possibility of existence can be understood even by the unbeliever as a possibility of existing and understanding.

Certainly, if unbelief is, according to the meaning given in the Gospel of John, the rejection of the Christian proclamation wherever it is encountered, then clearly such unbelief has a preunderstanding of the proclamation. The disbeliever rejects only what he understands, and he understands at least that faith is a way of existence in which his own former way of exist-ence is annuled. He understands the call to faith as the call to give up his former self-understanding. In distinction to this disbelief, which is the explicit rejection of the proclamation, existence which has not yet been confronted by the proclama-tion, or existence in itself, viewed apart from the fact of the proclamation, can be called 'pre-believing' (cf. John 9.41).

II

What does it mean *when other religions or when men in general outside the Christian faith speak of God or to God?*

Faith asserts that they are not really speaking of and to God, because they are not speaking of and to the true God. All religions, apart from faith, remain fixed in unbelief, in idol worship. Faith rejects the idea that God is revealed everywhere in religions and in religious people. In that case, it must be possible to give an answer to the question, of what and to what do such religions and such men speak?

What has been and is *missionary practice?* Was it or is it necessary for missionaries, when they proclaim God's revelation, to invent a new *word for 'God'?* Or, if they use a word already existing in a particular language, do they not admit that a a knowledge of God exists everywhere and that such knowledge inheres even in the conceptions of God which the missionaries call idols or anti-gods?

What is spoken of when men speak of God apart from faith? Must faith declare: what they have in mind are demons, is *the devil?* Apart from faith, man does not see, he is blinded, he is misled. But if Paul, for example, makes that statement (II Cor. 4.4) and if it is correct, at least what is spoken of is a power belonging to the 'Beyond', which, even if antagonistic, is still analogous to the power of God. Anyone who speaks of the devil can also speak of God! Proof of that is the peculiar fact that in the translation of the Bible into an African dialect, the word chosen for 'God' was the word which the earliest missionaries had used to translate 'devil'.[4] Certainly those religions intend to speak, not of the devil but of God. But what does that mean? What have they in mind? Is it enough to answer: *they are speaking not of God but of the world?* Whether, in primitive religions, natural objects or world phenomena and the 'elemental spirits' of the world (Gal. 4.8f.) are accounted gods; or whether – as in the Stoa and Stoic tradition – the world in its unity and conformity to law is regarded as God; or whether, as in modern 'religious experience', something divine is seen in states of consciousness and attitudes of soul, obviously it is the world which

[4] N. Söderblom, *Das Werden des Gottesglaubens*, Leipzig, 1916, p. 92.

is there spoken of. Certainly. But why then do they use the word *God* instead of *world*? And when religion is understood as a phenomenon of consciousness, why speak *to* God? Is it perhaps because what is here called God, what faith unmasks and knows to be world, is nevertheless intended to be something other than world? Is it a sufficient answer to say: *man speaks there of illusion*; of something non-existent, a nothing? Even if all such speaking can be unmasked as illusion by Christian criticism or by a Feuerbach, still what is the significance of such talk, of the illusion? What is it that has been revealed to be nothing? What is meant?

All sorts of different answers are possible! If one looks at the common element in all such presentations, one could say, 'God' is everywhere the designation of *a* or of *the 'supreme being'*. And very different things can be hidden in this speaking of the supreme being.

The egoism of man, his anxiety and his wishes, his drive for self-preservation and for good fortune can lay claim to supreme being. In that case, when God is spoken of, the meaning is simply whatever man desires joined with the knowledge that he himself has not the power to fulfil his desire. *Man speaks of God because he knows himself beset by his own desires and fears, because he knows himself helpless before the unknown, before the enigma.* He hypostasizes his dream-wishes and his fears into a being who can bring fulfilment or annihilation to his life. This supreme being is certainly not the God of whom faith speaks. But could it perhaps be said that in this representation is disclosed a knowledge which is reaching towards the God of the Christian faith? Yes and No. No, since it is precisely the purpose (*intentio*) of the natural man which is broken by faith. But just because in faith what was once the aim is now feared, and what was once fled from is now sought, the *Yes* holds. When man speaks of God, he reveals a certain understanding of himself, actually the understanding of himself as delivered over to the enigma, to overmastering power. Combined with this is an understanding of himself as providing for himself, making himself secure, recognizing that power and wanting to possess it.

For just such a man, God's revelation is given; just such a man can understand it. As he was pursued by desire and fear, so he was pursued by God. He thought of God and of himself together.

If the 'supreme being' is claimed by the intellect for the purpose of understanding the *origin and unity of the world*, the God is simply the 'first cause' (*prima causa*); the concept of unity, of conformity to law, of the unconditioned origin. Nothing else is aimed at when the question of God is raised.

But after all, what motivates the questioning itself? Is it only because of intellectual curiosity that man questions the basis and unity of the world? Or, since in the revelation the human answer, even the human question, is shattered as faith bows before the Creator of the world, is it not manifest here also that the questioning is really a seeking after God? Do not the question and the answer betray the fact that here, too, there is a basic self-understanding which is summoned to decision about itself by the word of proclamation? Does not the question arise from the knowledge of the moment's enigma? And is it not the intent of the answer to dominate the moment? Is it, then, not true that in the question and answer the knowledge of being claimed and the desire for freedom are combined? And is not faith in the Creator obedience to the moment? Is it not a hidden knowledge of the claim of the moment which forces the question? And is not the flight from before God into cosmology, into a world-view, the knowledge of the Creator hidden from itself?

Alternatively, the 'supreme being' can be claimed as the *guarantor of the moral law*, as the origin of the knowledge of good and evil, as the voice of conscience. Here what is really meant is only the *idea* of the moral law, the idea of the good. The conscience is not the voice of God, but a call issuing from a particular existence to itself. But is it not what Paul said of the Jews true of those who speak like this (Rom. 10.2): 'they have a zeal for God but it is not enlightened'? And does not Paul interpret the Jewish legalism as the road to grace? 'Law came in, to increase the trespass; but where sin increased, grace abounded all the more' (Rom. 5.20). 'Why then the law? It was added because of transgressions, till the offspring should come to whom the promise had been made' (Gal. 3.19). 'But the scripture consigned all things to sin, that what was promised to faith in Jesus Christ might be given to those who believe' (Gal. 3.22).

In the knowledge of good and evil, in the 'ought' under which man places himself, is there not hidden the knowledge of the demand of God at each specific moment? Is not the interpretation of this knowledge as an obligation which a man in freedom pronounces upon himself really the rejection of the bondage of which man is dimly conscious when he rejects it? And if in fact the conscience does develop in the historical intercourse of men, is not the phenomenon of conscience the sign that man does know that God's demand becomes audible at the moment of encounter with a *Thou*?

Or if the conception of the 'supreme being' is separated as far as possible from the conception of God which is discarded as a rationalistic mantle, if God is described as the *irrational*, as the *numinous*, and the like, then faith certainly responds that such terms designate only the enigma of human existence and that God becomes understandable to faith because he is revealed in love.

But does God's revelation mean that he is knowable? Has he through the revelation become available for observation or for investigation by the reason of men? Is not the use of the terms 'irrational' and 'numinous' a necessary protest against theological rationalism and moralism? And if here again the human formulation is shattered at the recognition of the revealed God, is not the emphasis in that formulation a sign of the unconscious knowledge that the way to God cannot be found by men; man is enclosed in the enigma and the mysterious. Is it not from this darkness, which this formulation begins to recognize, that the revelation of God rescues men? And is that knowledge not perverted, here as everywhere, because man falsely pretends that his bondage is freedom, meanwhile cunningly mastering the enigma by calling it God?[5]

Now have all these considerations re-constituted a natural theology in the old sense? Have they constructed a foundation for dogmatics in the philosophy of religion? No!

1. There is no question at all here of anything amounting to a *proof of God* – no sort of 'consensus of peoples' (*consensus gentium*). If it is true that all religions seek after God, that in all religions God is the aim, and that when the Christian proclamation speaks of God, it uses the word from the language of religions, that does not in the least mean that the God whom the religions are seeking is a reality. The reality of what is sought is

[5] Cf. F. Gogarten, *Zeitwende*, VII (1931), pp. 31f.

not proved by the search. The truth is rather that the goal of the search only becomes manifest to faith in the God of the revelation.

Therefore the truth of the Christian proclamation cannot be proved to the heathen by pointing to their search for God; it can only be made understandable to them in this way as Paul made it in his teaching on the law. Nor is the truth of the Christian faith to be certified for Christian apologetics by references to the facts of the history of religion. If the God of the Christian faith is being sought for in superstitious talk of God, that God could still be an illusion. The acknowledgment of him is always only faith's decision to acknowledge the Word which proclaims him.

2. It has not been in any way suggested that the Christian faith consists in the purer disclosure of the knowledge of God which exists in all religion. That would mean simply that Christianity had the idea of God in the purest form, that the Christian conception of God represented the most mature and the highest stage of man's thinking about God. Christianity would then be incorporated into a development of religion or a development of the history of thought. Even if this pattern could really be traced in the historical material, the justification of Christianity would still lie wholly outside the proofs of such an asssertion.

The comprehension of a conception of God does not mean the possession of God. For God is accessible only to faith responsive to revelation. In other words: the existence which understands itself without faith cannot of itself move over to or change to existence in faith. It therefore remains true that all human speaking of God, outside faith, speaks not of God but of the devil. But it also remains true that such speaking wants to speak of God, even and especially when it violently repudiates any speaking of God.

God is not unknowable (ἄγνωστος) outside Christianity, in the sense that man cannot comprehend the idea of God. Even the natural man can speak of God, because in his existence he knows about God.

How can man know about God if God is 'beyond' the world? Knowledge of God cannot be extracted from the world! But it is also true that unbelief is not extracted from the world; it is unbelief itself which constructs this world as the world of an existence which understands itself without faith. And unbelief is only faith denying itself; 'men . . . by their wickedness suppress truth' (Rom. 1.18). Unbelief is disobedience. If faith is the hearing of the demand of God at the moment which is constituted by the judging and forgiving Word of God spoken in it and by the neighbour encountered in it, then unbelief is disobedience to the demand of the moment. Even unbelief, as the self-understanding of a being with historical existence, knows the specific moment. Man's disobedience consists either in denying it or in assuming himself master of it. He denies it when in the immediate 'Now', he clings to his past self in naïve egoism or in self-justification by a world-view. He assumes mastery of it when he understands it on the fatal assumption that it is equivalent to the original moment in which his existence determines and understands itself. In so doing he repeats the original effort of his existence to establish its freedom and he understands his action as the only action of existence in which he wins his own individuality.

Neither through denial, nor through claiming mastery does man nullify the demand of the moment; that is, he cannot nullify the historical nature of his being. Precisely when he theorizes philosophically about existence, he knows its historical nature, and to this extent he also knows about God. So it is understandable that he also seeks after God and yet makes the idea of God serve his own self-established freedom. While unbelieving existence cannot of itself change to existence in faith, it still, since it is historical existence, has the possibility of understanding the Word of the proclamation which imparts a new quality to the moment. But the *question* is not the *answer*, even though the unbelieving existence always yields to the temptation to interpret it as the answer. Only faith can say that the question is the answer; and when it says this, it banishes 'natural theology'.

III

Philosophical ontology as existential analysis makes the problem of natural theology crucial because when it deals with existence and its historical character, with the moment and with under-

standing, it makes statements which are analogous to those of
the theology which characterizes faith by such concepts. Is it
not a fact that theology is taking over the philosophical analysis
of existence? Is not theology 'incorporating' that analysis and
'crowning' it with specific theological assertions, so that philosophy functions like natural theology in the old sense of providing a foundation?

Obviously philosophy and theology are rivals, since both
deal scientifically with existence. For whatever else may
be said of the content of dogmatics, existence in faith belongs in
it. Since its theme is *existence* in faith, that is, the *man* who believes, there is an area of competition with philosophy – an
area within which – regardless of what other tasks are included
– the analysis of human existence certainly belongs, whatever
may be the motivation of the inquiry.

The situation may be illustrated by two examples. In an
article on the future of Christ,[6] Eduard Thurneysen asserts that
through Jesus Christ man's concept of the future is radically
altered in a way which breaks the continuum of time. The future
of Christ, instead of being a yet unknown segment of time due
to appear, which will at some time become present and then
past, is the future which marks an absolute limit and is 'always
the opposite of every conceivable and possible present'. Clearly
the 'future of Christ' means – or at least needs to mean – nothing more than futurity *per se*, which is always the opposite of
every conceivable present. Here, therefore, we have expressed –
although admittedly less clearly – an understanding of human
temporality in contrast to the temporality of nature, such as we
find in Heidegger.

It is certainly true that the theological exposition of Christian
existence requires the concept of historical time or temporality.
But it is equally clear that this concept has already been
attained in the philosophical analysis of existence. The protest
against understanding historical temporality in terms of natural
temporality was not made first or only by theology. Furthermore, when Thurneysen says that Jesus Christ, although a
phenomenon of the past, is future as an event confronting us,
waiting for us and overtaking us, he is saying no more than that
the possibility of the moment which must be grasped on each

    [6] 'Christus und seine Zukunft', *ZZ*, 9 (1931), pp. 187–211.

occasion in decision, is concomitantly determined by the past. If clarity is not achieved at this point on the relation of the philosophical and theological assertions which concern the future or the historical nature of man, then nothing significant can be said about the 'future of Christ'. It is evident from Thurneysen's arguments that theology makes statements which philosophy also makes or that philosophy has already stated what theology also has to say. Both equally are interpreting human existence.

Paul Althaus, in the *Lutherjahrbuch* for 1931, contends that the divinity of God was the true meaning of Luther's doctrine of justification; and he wants to prove that the doctrine of justification is theocentrically conceived. Althaus intends to show that for Luther the basis for the rejection of legalistic righteousness and for the establishment of the ordinance of grace is not found in the actual situation of man as a sinner, but is founded, apart from the human situation, in the will of God or in the divinity of God.

Because God is God and man is man, God wills to deal and can deal with men not otherwise than through grace. To this extent, the doctrine of justification represents 'a simple application of the statement that God alone acts'. 'Luther's doctrine of justification is at bottom founded on his conception of God.' This idea means that the way of moralism as an alleged way of justification is a fiction, not only, nor even primarily, from the ethical point of view, but from that religion. For the way of justification can be disclosed only by God's grace.

Now it is clear that this conception of God is not dependent on revelation, but that in itself it is entirely possible for human thinking. This fact is expressed by Luther when he says of the 'nature' (*natura*) of God: 'It is God's nature to give to all, to help all' (*Gottes natura est quae omni dat et iuvat*). (*Weimarer Ausgabe*, ed. J. C. F. Knaake, *et al.*, Weimar, 1883ff., 17. 1. 233, 4), or when he speaks of God's 'office' (*officium*) (Paul Althaus, *Lutherjahrbuch* p. 21, note 29). But it is especially manifest when Luther 'makes the theocentric character of his doctrine serve as proof of its truth': 'My doctrine lets God be God; therefore it cannot lie since it gives glory to God' (*ibid.*, p. 23). The theology of the cross (*Theologia crucis*) is grounded on this conception (*ibid.*, pp. 25f.): 'for because he is God, this is his peculiar office to make all out of nothing.'[7] The doctrine of justification is therefore not specifically Christian in its theocentric form; it is understandable in itself as a doctrine in which the conceptions of God and man are developed logically.

What, then, is specifically Christian in the doctrine? The answer is twofold:

1. Justification is *forgiveness of sins*. Obviously, purely human thinking or philosophy does not speak of sin but of humanity and its finitude. If nothing is really altered *formally* for theology when it says 'sin' instead of humanity, then the concept of sin must be only a speculative theological interpretation of human existence, which radically clarifies a phenomenon which is not in itself hidden from philosophy either.

In fact, what was said earlier in relation to the concept of 'God' (cf. above, pp. 318f.), can also be said here. Sin is talked of in human speech, and when theology speaks of sin it uses a traditional word. If theology speaks of sin in a more radical way, so that sin is not reduced to an equivalent for humanity and creatureliness, then this radical meaning must be defined as distinct from the traditional meaning.

2. Theology teaches not merely the *concept* of justification, but teaches it as an actual *event*, since theology speaks of Jesus Christ. The specifically theological statement of justification is 'Christocentric'. But again: if theology wants to define the nature of the event of justification – is it a juristic act, a cosmic event, a magical-sacramental process, a symbolic act, a genuinely historical event? – it can do so only in categories which have been originated and perfected by philosophy.

The question is not whether such concepts and ideas first appeared historically in Christianity and its theology. For if it is at all proper for theology to speak philosophically, then the fact of a possible historical priority contributes nothing to the problem. What is decisive is that theological statements can obviously be understood by an unbelieving philosophy. So Feuerbach, for example, can understand Christianity more

---

[7] Another illustration is the fact that Heinrich Frick could present 'the division between Catholicism and Protestantism as a primal phenomenon of the history of religion' (*Kairos*, 1926, pp. 346–84). Note especially the discussion of God's grace as the sole agent in Indian Baakti piety (pp. 346ff.) and in Japanese Amida-Buddhism (pp. 352ff.).

truly than a certain kind of Christian theology can do.[8] And Kierkegaard's analysis of existence, which was made on the basis of faith, can be understood and can be made philosophically fruitful by Jaspers and by Heidegger.

Obviously *philosophy and theology* coincide in certain statements. Certain assertions of theology appear to be anticipated in philosophy. How is this relationship to be adjudged?

Perhaps it should be said that they treat different things. The theme of philosophy is *unbelieving* existence; that of theology is *believing* existence. In that case, the assertions of philosophy are correct but apply to a different object. But there is then a counter-question of how philosophy would re-act to this assertion. Philosophy certainly claims to understand existence as such and therefore must also claim to include an understanding of the act of faith, since this is an activity of existence.

The actual situation shows that believing and unbelieving existence are not in simple juxtaposition like two totally unrelated entities. For when theology speaks, for example, of the historical nature of existence, of the understanding of existence and of the decision-making character of existence, it obviously refers to the same phenomena as those described by philosophy. It is therefore evident that it is possible to speak of existence *per se*, and that the structural elements of existence which philosophy presents are also valid for existence in faith.

This is shown to be true not only by the actual situation, which could be the result of an aberration of philosophy but also by the assertion of faith itself that it is unbelieving existence which comes to faith. Faith does not change human nature into something else; the justified does not possess any new qualities which are demonstrable – the justified one is the sinner.

Nor, evidently, can it be said that philosophical analysis ought to be supplemented and corrected by theology. By its very nature, philosophical analysis does not allow such supplementation, but claims to cover existence as a whole. Its picture must be right or wrong as a whole. Theology can no more supplement the picture than it can correct it at single points – perhaps in preferring to substitute 'love' (ἀγάπη) for 'anxiety' as

---

[8] Cf. Karl Barth, *ZZ*, 5 (1927), pp. 11ff. [or cf. Barth, *Theology and Church*, New York and London, 1962, pp. 217–37].

the basic concept of existence.[9] By so doing, it would meet philosophy on a common level and would so itself become philosophy. Theology can only accept philosophical analysis or reject (or ignore) it.

Could perhaps a phenomenon of existence be designated which is only discovered by theology and is inaccessible to philosophy? Unbelief or faith? So far as unbelief and faith are encountered as phenomena within existence, there is no reason why philosophical analysis could not explicate them. So far as faith and unbelief are single acts of existence, philosophy can in fact point out the conditions of their possibility. But theology must answer that unbelief is in no way a contingent attitude which appears in existence, that it is not a determination in favour of a specific position which could be understood philosophically, from the point of view of the determination, as an attitude of human existence in its authenticity. Theology asserts, rather, that unbelief is the basic position of human existence, that it is the constitutive element of it as such.

Does this, however, not put an end to the rivalry? Has it not been proved impossible for theology to accept the description of the structure of existence from philosophy, while philosophy, which professes to describe the fundamental conception of existence, refuses to see at all the phenomenon which for theology constitutes the basic element of that conception? No! For philosophy does see clearly the phenomenon which theology calls unbelief. But for philosophy that phenomenon is freedom, the original freedom in which existence is constituted.

But what about faith? Does not theology assert that faith, too, is a basic condition of human existence, which can only exist as believing or unbelieving? And if this is true, must not faith, too, lie within the view of philosophy? Or if not, does not the question which was apparently settled arise again – the question whether existence in faith and existence apart from faith are not such different things that it is impossible to speak of existence as the common theme of theology and philosophy?

In fact, philosophy does know of faith, knows it just because it knows of the questionability which is an essential part of its

[9] Cf. W. Koepp, 'Merimna und Agape,' Reinhold Seeberg Festschrift, 1929, pp. 99–139.

freedom. Precisely when it knows the determination for freedom by which existence asserts control of itself, it knows of another possibility, the rejection of that determination. But what kind of knowledge of faith does philosophy possess? It knows it as a lost, meaningless possibility; lost because human existence from its beginning is constituted and persists in this freedom and can have its actuality only in it; meaningless, because everything that has meaning for philosophy is defined according to the sense given to it by existence in this freedom.

Therefore philosophy, when it hears faith spoken of as an ever-present possibility and reality, can understand by faith only a resolve being realized within existence as determined by freedom. It is an event occurring within existence and philosophy can indicate the conditions in existence which make it possible. But this corresponds exactly to the character of faith as it understands itself. Faith understands itself as a specific resolve, as a specific decision in a concrete situation which is determined by the Word of the proclamation and by the neighbour. But faith asserts that such a specific resolve reconstitutes the basic conception of existence so that henceforth there is also an existence in faith alongside the existence outside faith. That assertion is its specific claim, its offence. Not only is the assertion unprovable, because obviously existence continues and existence in faith, too, can be made ontologically intelligible; but according to the meaning of faith it may not be proved. For faith understands itself as an eschatological event.

This has a dual significance:

1. Faith in its own sense of a revolution of existence is not demonstrable. As God's act which affects man, and as *justifying faith, it is not a phenomenon of existence.* Justification by faith is not a demonstrable fact of existence. For the justification is only before God and the justified is only righteous before God and on earth is a sinner. Even the man of faith remains in existence; he does not have a new structure of existence created for him. His faith as a historical act is always the concrete resolve in the moment. And that means that faith always exists only in the overcoming of unbelief. As a human being, the man of faith always comes out of unbelief; he always remains in the paradox of 'I believe, Lord help my unbelief'.

2. As an eschatological event in which reconciliation be-

comes a reality, *faith leads back to the original creation.* This means
that the lost, meaningless possibility of faith as original obedience, of which philosophy knows, is made actual in the Christian faith.

It could therefore be said: unbelief as the resolve for freedom
which determines the character of human existence is from the
beginning superimposed on faith. If the pre-Christian existence
includes an unknowing knowledge of God, then it also includes
a pre-understanding of the Christian proclamation. And if
philosophy explicates this understanding of existence, it also
explicates this pre-understanding. When this analysis is intro-
duced into the work of theology, it becomes a new statement,
since its character as pre-understanding is now made clear. It is
just this interpretation of existence before faith and its self-
understanding, as made within faith, that is 'natural theology'.

It becomes clear that *this natural theology* does not have the
significance of a foundation for dogmatics in that it does *not*
provide *any special segment prior to or within genuine theology.* If the
character of faith is rightly described as the continual overcoming of unbelief, then faith and the development of an understanding in faith can be theologically explicated only in continual debate with the understanding of natural existence. In
other words, natural theology is a permanent accompaniment
of dogmatic work, as it clearly is for Paul and for Luther.

This answers the final question – the question of the usability
for theology of ontological work, if the ontology is ontically
rooted. It is not so rooted when an ontology is sketched from
some random world-view to correspond with it.[10] Rather, the
understanding of existence in which the ontology is rooted reveals itself in the very outline of the world-view. The existence
which is ontologically understood in philosophy is understood
thus on the basis of the original understanding of being in which
it is already constituted.

Since there is no other existence than that which constitutes
itself in its freedom, the formal structures of existence treated in
ontological analysis are 'neutral'. That is, they are valid for all
human existence. Therefore they are also valid for the existence
which is confronted by the proclamation, both for existence

---

[10] This misunderstanding of Heidegger's ontology, it seems to me, appears
in K. Löwith's presentation, *TR* N.F. II (1930), pp. 26ff., 333ff.

outside faith and for existence in faith, which believes only in the constant overcoming of unbelief.

Therefore, since the theology which utilizes the philosophical analysis of existence is itself performing the action of philosophizing, it must be deliberately performing an act of unbelief. And theology has the right so to act only if it knows what it is doing and does not imagine that it could be doing anything except an act of unbelief which can be justified only by faith. As an act of unbelief originating in faith it stands under the 'as if not' (ὡς μή) of I Cor. 7.29–31. It can be based only on the specific moment. It cannot be theoretical speculation about an idea in a system of thought; it must be only a specific act of faith in obedience to the demand of a specific situation.[11]

Since 'natural theology' is present in the work of theology from the beginning, and since it constantly permeates theological work, the question of natural theology must finally go back to the question of the meaning and the possibility of theology itself.

[11] Cf. above, pp. 213f..

INDEX OF NAMES

INDEX OF SUBJECTS

INDEX OF BIBLICAL REFERENCES

OLD TESTAMENT

APOCRYPHA

NEW TESTAMENT

APOSTOLIC FATHERS